AF383168

JESUS

OF NAZARETH

Publication of this book has been sponsored by the Biblical Research Institute, a doctrinal and theological resource center that serves the General Conference of Seventh-day Adventists through research, publication, and presentations. adventistbiblicalresearch.org

JESUS
OF NAZARETH

HIS LIFE • HIS MESSAGE • HIS PASSION

WILLIAM G. JOHNSSON

Andrews
University Press
Berrien Springs, Michigan

Andrews University Press
Sutherland House
8360 W. Campus Circle Dr.
Berrien Springs, MI 49104–1700
Telephone: 269–471–6134
Fax: 269–471–6224
Email: aupo@andrews.edu
Website: http://universitypress.andrews.edu

ISBN 978–1–940980–18–8

Printed in the United States of America
22 21 20 19 18   1 2 3 4 5

Library of Congress Cataloging-in-Publication Data

Names: Johnsson, William G., 1934- author.
Title: Jesus of Nazareth : His life, His message, His passion / William G. Johnsson.
Description: Berrien Springs : Andrews University Press, 2017. | Includes index.
Identifiers: LCCN 2017032283 | ISBN 9781940980188 (hardcover : alk. paper)
Subjects: LCSH: Jesus Christ—Biography—Textbooks. | Jesus Christ—Person and offices—Textbooks. | General Conference of Seventh-day Adventists—Doctrines.
Classification: LCC BT307 .J64 2017 | DDC 232.9/01 [B]—dc23 LC record available at https://lccn.loc.gov/2017032283

To the students and faculty

of Spicer Memorial College, India,

where I first taught the life and teachings of Jesus

CONTENTS

PART III. HIS PASSION

PREFACE

As a teenager I read through the Bible and fell in love with Jesus Christ. Several years later, as a student at Avondale College in Australia, I fell in love with His life and teachings. I felt that it would be a supreme joy if one day I might share Jesus in a classroom setting.

Within only a few years that dream came true. In a development totally unexpected, I found myself at Spicer Memorial College in India and was assigned to teach the Life and Teachings of Jesus class. I stayed twelve years at Spicer, teaching that class every year (apart from furloughs). I was blessed immeasurably.

After Spicer came the Seventh-day Adventist Theological Seminary at Andrews University and new classes focused on Jesus of Nazareth. Later still, after many years, I received an invitation to teach about Jesus in the School of Religion at Loma Linda University.

Jesus is bigger than any book about Him. This effort of mine cannot do justice to the magnificence of His life, His ministry, His teachings, and His Passion—especially His Passion. All I can do is share what I have discovered in my exploration of the Gospels. So this book, while it builds on sound scholarship, is much more than an academic's exploration: it is the expression of my heart.

The book bears the title *Jesus of Nazareth*. Not just "Jesus," because there were others called Jesus who lived during the time of the Jesus who changed the course of human history. Jesus, a Greek name, was the equivalent of the Hebrew Joshua; it was a common name.

Further, when we say Jesus of Nazareth, we designate a flesh-and-blood person in time and place. Jesus of Nazareth wasn't simply an idea or an ideal, and certainly not a fantasy. He was a living, breathing person who was born, lived, died, and was interred (but that wasn't the end of the story).

A vast number of books have been written about this Jesus. New works continue to appear; for example, Reza Aslan portrays Jesus of Nazareth as a zealot, a Muhammad-like figure who attempted to raise an army to liberate the Jews from Roman rule.[1] But Aslan's Jesus runs counter to the story of Jesus that we find in the Gospels—Matthew, Mark, Luke, and John. Aslan can only argue his thesis by de-emphasizing and discrediting much of the biblical material.

That pattern of selective use of the Gospels, or cherry-picking, holds true for most of the hundreds—perhaps thousands—of books written about Jesus. The writer commences the work with preconceived ideas—such as that babies cannot be conceived without a father, or no one can rise from the dead—and raids the Gospels for evidence that support his or her position.

In this book I attempt to adhere to a strictly biblical approach. I want to let the Gospels themselves tell the story of Jesus. And if we allow those Gospels to speak to us directly, what a story they tell! The Jesus who emerges is a dynamic person—amazing, challenging, disturbing, shocking, and altogether wonderful.

Jesus of Nazareth is intended for people around the world who are interested in knowing the Man of Galilee. I have tried to make the language accessible to all and tell the story of this remarkable Person unencumbered with scholarly footnotes and jargon.

In preparing this work, I am indebted to three people in particular. My wife, Noelene, keyed in the manuscript and provided many helpful suggestions. Dr. Ángel M. Rodríguez was the first to suggest that I write the study as a textbook; he also checked and reviewed the manuscript. Finally, Dr. Ekkhardt Mueller of the Biblical Research Institute of the General Conference of Seventh-day Adventists gave strong encouragement to the ongoing project.

The text of the Bible will be the primary source of study, so the student should first read the key passages referenced for each chapter. For further insights we have suggested readings from the works by Ellen G. White and other relevant literature.

William G. Johnsson
Loma Linda, California

THE LIFE OF JESUS FORETOLD
SEVEN HUNDRED YEARS IN ADVANCE

See, my servant will act wisely;
   he will be raised and lifted up and highly exalted.
Just as there were many who were appalled at him—
    his appearance was so disfigured beyond that of any
       human being
    and his form marred beyond human likeness—
so he will sprinkle many nations,
   and kings will shut their mouths because of him.
For what they were not told, they will see,
   and what they have not heard, they will understand.

Who has believed our message
   and to whom has the arm of the Lord been revealed?
He grew up before him like a tender shoot,
   and like a root out of dry ground.
He had no beauty or majesty to attract us to him,
   nothing in his appearance that we should desire him.
He was despised and rejected by mankind,
   a man of suffering, and familiar with pain.
Like one from whom people hide their faces
   he was despised, and we held him in low esteem.

Surely he took up our pain
   and bore our suffering,
yet we considered him punished by God,
   stricken by him, and afflicted.
But he was pierced for our transgressions,
   he was crushed for our iniquities;
the punishment that brought us peace was on him,
   and by his wounds we are healed.
We all, like sheep, have gone astray,
   each of us has turned to our own way;
and the Lord has laid on him
   the iniquity of us all.

He was oppressed and afflicted,
   yet he did not open his mouth;
he was led like a lamb to the slaughter,
   and as a sheep before its shearers is silent,
   so he did not open his mouth.
By oppression and judgment he was taken away.
   Yet who of his generation protested?
For he was cut off from the land of the living;
   for the transgression of my people he was punished.
He was assigned a grave with the wicked,
   and with the rich in his death,
though he had done no violence,
   nor was any deceit in his mouth.

Yet it was the Lord's will to crush him and cause him to
     suffer,
   and though the Lord makes his life an offering for sin,
he will see his offspring and prolong his days,
   and the will of the Lord will prosper in his hand.
After he has suffered,
   he will see the light of life and be satisfied;
by his knowledge my righteous servant will justify many,
   and he will bear their iniquities.
Therefore I will give him a portion among the great,
   and he will divide the spoils with the strong,
because he poured out his life unto death,
   and was numbered with the transgressors.
For he bore the sin of many,
   and made intercession for the transgressors.

Isaiah 52:13–53:12

"I am far within the mark when I say that all the armies that ever marched, and all the navies that were ever built, and all the parliaments that ever sat, and all the kings that ever reigned, put together have not affected the life of man upon this earth as powerfully as has that One Solitary Life."

—James Allan Francis

Prologue

OBJECTIVES
- Grasp the impact of Jesus in human history.

- Learn the historical facts about Jesus from Scripture and non-biblical ancient literature.

SCRIPTURE
- Revelation 1:12–18

Of all the names given children since the dawn of time, one stands alone and immovable. Although many men and women now take that name in oath or jest, one day every knee in heaven and earth will bow before Him who bears it and declare that He is King of Kings and Lord of Lords (Phil. 2:10–11; Rev. 19:16). That name is the sweetest sound to come from infant lips. It sustains us through life, and it will be our refuge when we embark on our final journey.

The Incomparable Christ

Jesus. All our hopes—for this world and the next—center in Him. Our best joys, highest aspirations, and cleanest motivations spring from Him. While every other name will pass away, His never will. He is incomparable.

He was named before He was born. "You are to give him the name of Jesus," the angel instructed Mary and Joseph separately (Matt. 1:21; see also Luke 1:31). It was a common name. The Greek equivalent of the Hebrew name Joshua, it meant "deliverer" or "savior."

Originally, He wasn't called Jesus Christ. "Christ," which corresponds with the Hebrew "Messiah," meant "the Anointed One." Just as in ancient Israel kings and priests were consecrated by oil poured on their heads, signifying God's blessing (e.g., Exod. 30:30; 1 Sam. 10:1; 16:13), so this Jesus would receive the abundant overflowing benediction of the Spirit. Over the centuries the people of God—struggling to cope with defeat, exile, and foreign occupation—had come to hope in the coming of the Messiah, God's Anointed One, who would bring deliverance. "Messiah" wasn't a name. It was a title of office.

During Jesus's lifetime He was simply Jesus of Nazareth, son of Joseph. Gradually, some of His followers began to recognize that He was in fact the long-awaited Messiah or Christ. He was Jesus the Christ. After His death, as the new religion grew and spread, name and office became joined. He became known as "Jesus Christ," but only for those who believed in Him. For the pagan Romans and the great majority of the Jews, He was simply Jesus. To call Him Jesus Christ was a statement of faith: it meant that you believed that He was the Messiah.

Today, many people say "Jesus Christ" or "Christ" thoughtlessly or as a profanity. They do not make any claim to believe in who He was. It's just a commonplace name to be tossed out and kicked around without thinking. Strangely, those same people don't use the names of other religious figures this way. I don't hear "Muhammad" or "Buddha" or "Krishna" being used as cuss words. Why is that? What is it about the name of Jesus of Nazareth that evokes such sharply different reactions—confession or cursing?

It was like that from the beginning. During Jesus's lifetime He aroused both adoration and hatred. Already those who opposed Him and His work thought up some strong epithets—"demon-possessed," or "Samaritan" (John 8:48), which was a racial slur. Jesus was a controversial figure. Forget about "gentle Jesus, meek and mild." He was anything but mild. He was radical in His life, His words, and His work. He offended a lot of people, particularly those who belonged to the religious establishment. He called a spade a spade. He was direct, at times blunt, and fearless.

The Jesus of the Gospels bears little resemblance to the Jesus who is preached and worshiped in many Christian churches. The Jesus of most Christians today is a comfortable person who doesn't rock the boat. He doesn't challenge the status quo—He's part of it. Even the pictures of Him often depict a pale figure not at home amid the stresses and strains of twenty-first-century society.

In this book we will attempt to discover what Jesus was *really* like. As we work through His life, ministry, and teachings, we'll look for the actual person, not the often-dehumanized figure that came to replace Him. And, upon finding Him, we can begin to figure out what the real Jesus has to tell us about how to live in our twenty-first-century world.

Jesus is so amazing, wonderful, and incomparable that the Bible contains not one account of His life but four. One of the writers, the beloved John, with understandable hyperbole, would write at the close of his Gospel: "Jesus did many other things as well. If every one of them were written down, I suppose that even the whole world would not have room for the books that would be written" (John 21:25).

The study of the life and teachings of Jesus of Nazareth is the most important and rewarding of all studies. He is incomparable. His life is amazing. His teachings are wonderful in simplicity and depth. Anyone who seeks to be educated should not bypass Jesus. He changed, and still changes, the world.

In Boris Pasternak's *Doctor Zhivago*, the Nobel Prize winner described the profound difference that Jesus of Nazareth made:

> Rome was a flea market of borrowed gods and conquered peoples, a bargain basement on two floors, earth and heaven, a mass of filth convoluted in a triple knot as in an intestinal obstruction. Dacians, Heruleans, Scythians, Sarmatians, Hyperboreans, heavy wheels without spokes, eyes sunk in fat, sodomy, double chins, illiterate emperors, fish fed on the flesh of learned slaves . . . all crammed into the passages of the Coliseum, and all wretched.
>
> And then, into this tasteless heap of gold and marble, He came, light and clothed in an aura, emphatically human, deliberately provincial, Galilean, and at that moment gods and nations ceased to be and man came into being—man the carpenter, man the plowman, man the shepherd with his flock of sheep at sunset, man who does not sound in the least proud, man thankfully celebrated in all the cradle songs of mothers and in all the picture galleries the world over.[1]

Biblical scholar Reynolds Price asserted: "It would require much exotic calculation, however, to deny that the single most powerful figure—not merely in these two millenniums but in all human history—has been Jesus of Nazareth. Not only is the prevalent system of denoting the years based on an erroneous sixth-century calculation of the date of his birth, but a serious argument can be made that no one else's life has proved remotely as powerful and enduring as that of Jesus."[2]

Even the great scientist Albert Einstein, who wasn't a Christian, attested to the impact of Jesus on him: "As a child I received instruction both in the Bible and in the Talmud. I am a Jew, but I am enthralled by the luminous figure of the Nazarene. . . . No one can read the Gospels without feeling the actual presence of Jesus. His personality pulsates in every word. No myth is filled with such life."[3]

Five Facts from History

Anyone who sets out to discover why Jesus of Nazareth profoundly changed the course of human history confronts a big question: *Who was He?* Born and raised in obscurity, this man never went to school, lived out His days in an insignificant corner of the Roman Empire, and died young. How did He change the world?

Considered from the bare facts of the matter, what happened to give birth to a new world religion based on Jesus? Christianity is surely the unlikeliest religion ever to arise. There were other rabbis in ancient Palestine who gathered a band of disciples around them, but none of them became founder of a world faith. There were other rabbis who were executed by crucifixion, but from none of them did a new religion spring forth. *What happened?* Did Jesus of Nazareth give rise to the world's most widespread religion up to our times?

Setting aside for the moment any consideration of faith in Jesus, five facts confront us. These are all unassailable matters of history. How we interpret the facts is a different issue, but the facts stand beyond reasonable doubt.

1. Jesus of Nazareth Was a Real Person

Occasionally, in the past and even in our times, someone will attempt to argue that we can't even be sure that Jesus existed. That claim is bogus. Quite apart from the four Gospels written by believers, historians contemporary with Jesus who were not believers made occasional reference to Him. These references are incidental and unstudied, dropped into a larger context. In His time Jesus did not create waves outside of Palestine: He was a minor figure overlooked by those who wrote about what was happening. But His life and death intersected with others who were considered prominent in society—such as Pontius Pilate, the procurator (governor) of Judea.

Thus the Roman historian Tacitus (AD 56–c. 120), writing about the great fire that destroyed much of the city of Rome in AD 64 and which was rumored to have been lit by the Emperor Nero, noted:

> To cut short the public outcry, Nero had to find someone guilty, and blamed a race of men despised for the perversity of their rites and commonly called Christians.
>
> The name comes from Christus [Christ], who was put to death when Pontius Pilate was pro-consul and procurator of Judea.
>
> Now, this pernicious superstition has broken out anew, not only in Judea, the place of origin of this scourge, but even in Rome, where all that is shameful and abominable comes together and is accepted.[4]

Other references to Jesus from the first century occur in the writings of the Jewish historian Flavius Josephus (AD 37–c. 100) and the Roman Suetonius (c. AD 57–c. 117).

Thus people today may decide that Jesus was not what His followers claimed about Him, but they cannot validly argue that we don't know whether He even existed.

2. Jesus Was Crucified

The irreducible, minimal account of the life of Jesus of Nazareth comes down to His crucifixion. Jewish and Roman records testify to it, as does Christian tradition from the earliest years. The cross became the badge of the new faith. Significantly and perhaps surprisingly, Christians made no effort to conceal or excuse the manner of Jesus's death.

Yet death by crucifixion was slow and agonizing. Rome reserved it for the worst offenders and employed it only against non-citizens. When occasionally Romans were crucified, reports of what had happened led to riots in the streets of the capital.

Crucifixion was carried out in public. As the victim hung impaled for hours and sometimes days in full view of passersby, its message shouted out the punishment that Rome would exact upon anyone who dared to oppose her rule.

Jesus of Nazareth died by crucifixion. So familiar is that fact to Christians that most fail to grasp its raw import, which is this: *Jesus was considered a threat.* He was no mild rabbi or champion of the status quo. The Jewish authorities wanted Him dead, plotted to kill Him, and had their way.

3. Jesus's Body Disappeared

Something happened to Jesus's body, but what? It was taken down from the cross and placed in a tomb. This was on a Friday afternoon when the Passover moon was at the full. But by early Sunday morning the body had vanished. From that day until now, people have put forth theories to explain what happened:

- His disciples came and stole the body while the guards slept.

- Jesus didn't really die on the cross; He fainted.

- Later, in the coolness of the tomb, He revived and walked out.

- The disciples wanted so badly for Him to come back to life that they imagined He had done so.

- Peter and his fellow disciples didn't want to go back to a life of fishing so they invented the story of His resurrection and began to preach it.

And so on. The fact remains, no satisfactory explanation has ever been advanced to account for the disappearance of Jesus's body.

4. Testimony of the Disciples

The disciples went everywhere proclaiming the message. The book of Acts mentions several of their sermons, and they centered on two certainties: Jesus of Nazareth rose from the dead, and He sent the Holy Spirit as evidence of His victory.

The writings of the New Testament throb with the confidence that Jesus is alive. His followers experience His presence bringing peace, joy, and hope. He is real; He can be known by anyone who is open to Him. And He is Lord of the new community, the church, where He guides, empowers, instructs, and comforts.

It would require a colossal degree of self-deception or crookedness for this certainty to spring from deluded or deceitful men. And even if one might concede the unlikely idea that Peter and his fellow disciples made it all up, a huge obstacle to the argument has to be confronted: the apostle Paul, earlier known as Saul (Acts 13:1).

Saul wasn't one of the Twelve. Raised a strict Pharisee, he initially opposed the followers of Jesus with every fiber of his being. He gave his energies to harassing and harrying believers. He ferreted them out, threw them into jail, tortured them, and compelled them to recant their belief in the Nazarene.

But something happened to Saul on the road to Damascus where he intended to seek out followers of Jesus. Suddenly struck by a blinding light, he heard a voice.

"Saul, Saul, why do you persecute me?"

"Who are you, Lord?" Saul asked.

"I am Jesus, whom you are persecuting" (Acts 9:4, 5).

This dramatic encounter led to Saul's reversal of attitude. From persecutor he changed to preacher, and from enemy to advocate. Saul of Tarsus became Paul the apostle, missionary extraordinaire to the Roman world, planting congregations in the West, writing letters to young churches, and always on the move traveling, working, speaking, and struggling to spread the new faith.

Saul, later named Paul, is an amazing figure in history. If Christianity sprang from the unlikeliest of soil, its leading advocate arose from the unlikeliest of men. Whether one chooses to admire Paul or scorn him, the fact remains: Paul believed passionately that Jesus had risen from the dead and commissioned him for a special work (Acts 26:15–20).

5. Christianity and the Resurrection of Jesus

Christianity quickly spread. We already noticed the comment of the historian Tacitus concerning its taking root in Rome. Within thirty years of the death of its founder, the new faith had won followers in Caesar's household (Phil. 4:22). It spread among soldiers, slaves, and free people. Its message of the Nazarene who had been crucified but who had broken the chains of the grave and could be personally known was unstoppable. It brought the Empire, "a flea market of borrowed gods and conquered people," to its knees.

In this book we will go back to how it all began. We will focus on its founder, working through the life, ministry, and teachings of Jesus.

Jesus will be center of all our reflections in this book. He has to be; it cannot be otherwise. Christianity stands or falls by Him. If His story is true, following Him is the most important thing we can ever decide to do. If it isn't true, the whole Christian enterprise falls flat.

No other world religion rests on one person as does Christianity. Islam, for instance, doesn't rest on Muhammad: Muslims are people who submit to Allah, not Muhammad. Nor does Buddhism rest on Gautama, who became the Buddha, and even less does Hinduism rest on mythical figures like Krishna or Rama.

Throughout this book—in all respects—what we are dealing with is *real*: real people, real places, events that actually happened, and, above all, a person. He changed the world. He still changes it.

QUESTIONS FOR DISCUSSION

1. Read through the Gospels of Matthew and John and make a note of the differences. How does this help us to understand Jesus?

2. How does the extra-biblical evidence for the existence of Jesus help us in proclaiming the gospel to the world?

PART I

HIS LIFE

"Jesus will ever be the creator of the pure spirit
of religion; the Sermon on the Mount will
never be surpassed."

—Ernest Renan, *The Life of Jesus*

1

His Land and Times

<table>
<tr><td>OBJECTIVES</td><td>• Understand the physical, social, and political climate of the time of Jesus.</td></tr>
<tr><td></td><td>• Gain a concrete, accurate image of what Jesus and His followers looked like and how they lived.</td></tr>
<tr><td>SCRIPTURE</td><td>• Isaiah 52:13–56:12</td></tr>
</table>

The story of Jesus of Nazareth found in the Gospels has released a flood of speculation on the part of both believers and non-believers. What was He really like? What were His inner thoughts? What is the secret of His being?

These topics engaged the finest European scholars for more than a century. Beginning in the eighteenth century and extending into the twentieth, German and French theologians—especially German—wrote a series of "Lives" of Jesus. Children of the Enlightenment, they sought to portray a Jesus stripped of theological speculations and freed from ecclesiastical constraints—a truly human Jesus.

The enterprise came to a crashing halt with the publication of Albert Schweitzer's *The Quest of the Historical Jesus* in 1906. With devastating analysis, Schweitzer, critiquing each "Life," demonstrated that, while claiming to set forth the "real" Jesus, it was more a portrait of the writer himself. Jesus had emerged in the form of a German professor or a French teacher.

After demolishing the previous "Lives" of Jesus, Schweitzer sketched his own portrait. It was a radical Jesus, one utterly out of step with the spirit of optimism in inevitable progress that characterized the nineteenth century. This Jesus was an apocalyptic figure who believed in the end of the world and who threw Himself on the wheel of history to try to bring about the End.

Schweitzer's reflection on Jesus had a profound influence on his own life. Already he had earned doctorates in theology and music—he had revived the music of Johann Sebastian Bach. Now he went back to school and earned yet a third doctorate in medicine. Then, forsaking the comforts and prestige of Europe, he gave himself to serving the people of equatorial Africa by constructing and running a hospital in Lambaréné.

The scholarly "Lives" of Jesus came to a full stop, but the fascination with the man of Nazareth continues unabated. Jesus is never far away for novelists, playwrights, and screen writers. He is "Jesus Christ, Superstar," as Andrew Lloyd Webber's musical declared. All this creative outpouring about Jesus, from the pens of scholars to the spotlights of Broadway, doesn't help us to figure Him out. It tells us far more about the author or playwright than about Jesus Himself.

To get to the real Jesus we must go back to the times in which He lived. His wasn't a make-believe world but one with real places and people. These people wrote about their times, and many of their writings have been preserved and can be studied. Two of them in particular provide much information: Flavius Josephus, a Jew who lived AD 37–100 and wrote extensively about his people, and Philo of Alexandria, another Jew who lived c. 20 BC to AD 50 and also wrote a lot, shedding light on the times of Jesus.

Then there is archaeology. The towns mentioned in the Gospels, plus others in Palestine that are not, have been excavated. The accumulated evidence is huge. We now know how people lived, what they ate, about their life expectancies, and much more.

The world of Jesus has come to light. We can see Him for real in His land and times.

The Land

If you ever get a chance to visit the Holy Land, you will find the experience interesting, exciting, deeply inspirational, and surprising.

The first surprise is that Israel is so *small.* You fly into Tel Aviv and head east toward Jerusalem. You go up, just as the

"View of Modern Nazareth"

"Tiberias and the Sea of Galilee"

Bible speaks about going "up" to Jerusalem (Acts 21:12), because Jerusalem, at 2,490 feet (758 m), is the high point. The journey from Tel Aviv is only 37 miles (59 km). Keep going east, and the road descends sharply toward Jericho and the Dead Sea. After only another 22 miles (35 km) you will arrive. Amazed, you have crossed the Holy Land in just a couple of hours; it's only 59 miles (95 km) west to east.

South to north it's farther but still a tiny country. From Beersheba way down south to the Galilee and the headwaters of the Jordan is about 160 miles (257 km); the total area is only 8,019 square miles (20,770 square kilometers).

So much happened in this tiny land. So much of significance is still focused here. Anciently, armies marched back and forth across its face—Egypt to Babylon and Assyria. Today it sits nestled among powerful Arab nations; it is the cockpit of the Middle East.

Another surprising aspect is how *varied* this small country is. It's a land of hills and plains, of fertile areas and desert—always changing, never constant. In its far north are the cedars in the cool mountains of Lebanon; in the south is the huge salt sea, so dense that you can't sink in it. The Mediterranean forms its western boundary; the Great Rift Valley of the Jordan defines it to the east, falling to the lowest point on Earth (1,368 feet; 416 m) below sea level.

Anciently, these different parts of the land—so different from one another although not large in themselves—were named: the Negev (the dry land to the south), the Arabah (the valley of the Jordan), and the Shephelah (the Judean foothills).

Of all the regions of the Holy Land, the Galilee most delights and fascinates me. Here the Jordan River, hardly bigger than a stream, flows into the lake with its waters glistening under the bright sun. Here on hills and in valleys people still grow olives, tend vineyards, and launch their boats to harvest fish.

The lake itself is exceedingly beautiful. Pear-shaped, it is 13 miles (21 km) long and 8 miles (13 km) wide, already 700 feet (213 m) below sea level. Although a comparatively small body of water, it is very deep: 141 feet (43 m). On its western side the cliff slopes gradually to the water; on the east, the land rises sharply to the Golan Heights. The setting of the lake spawns sudden windstorms that descend, sometimes with fury, to lash the calm waters.

In Galilee, even with modern highways and cities, much is still the same as it was when the Bible was written. You step back into history, amazed and transfixed as you walk the streets of Capernaum, Cana, and Nazareth. It was *His* land. He grew up, worked, and ministered here. For a time, He was wildly popular. But to the religious leaders in Jerusalem, His coming from Galilee marked Him for contempt. "Look into it, and you will find that a prophet does not come out of Galilee," they said (John 7:52).

What Did Jesus Look Like?

Was Jesus tall or short? What color was His hair? His eyes? Was He right- or left-handed? Did He speak in a deep voice? What sort of gestures did He use to make a point? Could you tell that it was He who was approaching from the way He walked? These are the details we expect to find in a biography. Yet, although the Bible has four accounts focused on Him, they are totally silent with regard to His person.

Ancient accounts didn't necessarily omit personal details, especially when the writer had a negative view of the subject.

Thus, a pagan description of the Apostle Paul takes pleasure in painting an unflattering portrait: It describes him as short, bald, and hook-nosed. Paul himself notes what his opponents said about him: "His letters are weighty and forceful, but in person he is unimpressive and his speaking amounts to nothing" (2 Cor. 10:10).

Jesus also had enemies, and they called Him names. They said He was a glutton (Matt. 11:19), a drunkard (Matt. 11:19), conceived out of wedlock (John 8:41). But nowhere in the Gospels do we hear them singling out any aspect of His person for attack. The conclusion seems clear: there was nothing about Jesus's physical appearance that set Him apart from others. He looked like the other Galileans of His generation.

In the Book of Isaiah we find a fascinating description of the Suffering Servant, whom Christians understand to signify Jesus:

> He grew up before him [the Lord] like
> a tender shoot,
> and like a root out of dry ground.
> He had no beauty or majesty to attract
> us to him,
> nothing in his appearance that we
> should desire him. (Isa. 53:2)

Hollywood may portray Jesus as a superstar, but He wasn't like that at all. He would become the most influential person to ever walk this planet, but the power came from within—what He was, not what He looked like.

So, if Jesus was like the people around Him, what were they—and He—like?

Thanks to archaeology, we have a good idea. The Jews placed their dead in tombs; but after a year or more, when the flesh had fallen off, they gathered the bones and placed them in large stone containers called ossuaries or in a niche in the tomb. Hundreds of these skeletal remains have been unearthed and they reveal a great deal about life in the time of Jesus.

The average man was about 5 feet, 3 inches (1.6 m) tall and weighed about 132 pounds (60 kg). The average woman was scarcely five feet (1.52 m) tall. She weighed less than 99 pounds (45 kg). How tall was the real Jesus? Much shorter than Western artists portray Him, and much shorter than most readers of this book. Probably about 5 feet, 6 inches (1.68 m).

Jesus was Jewish, so He would have had brown or black hair and dark or hazel eyes. Put aside those images of the fair-skinned, blond Jesus with blue eyes—they don't match the real person.

The tombs tell us much more, however. Many of them were burial places of the wealthy and influential, but to the trained eye the bones reveal a shocking picture. Life expectancy was desperately low, with half the population dying before they reached age thirty. The bones cry out: in the tomb of Jason, out of twenty-five skeletons, only three lived beyond twenty-five years. In Caiaphas's tomb, out of sixty-three people, only one-third reached adulthood.

The bones witness to the diseases that wracked humanity and brought people down to an early grave—parasites, such as tapeworms, for instance. In light of the wretched condition of the people of Jesus's day, we understand better why He devoted so much of His ministry to relieving suffering. The comment in the Gospel of Matthew takes on new meaning: "He took up our infirmities and bore our diseases" (Matt. 8:17).

Life in Jesus's Time

For the great majority, life was a struggle to stay one step ahead of poverty and starvation.

A ruling class, perhaps one to two percent of the population, had it easy. They lived in cities in richly ornamented homes and dined sumptuously. The high priestly family belonged to this group. Beneath them and making up most of the remainder of the population were farmers, artisans, and fishermen. They ate just twice a day, with bread and fish constituting the main items of diet. They rarely ate the meat of lambs, goats, and cattle—generally just during the three annual visits to Jerusalem for Passover, Pentecost, and Tabernacles. Jesus belonged to this group: He was lower middle class. Below this class were people on the margins: lepers, the destitute, the utterly broken, and the utterly helpless.

Jesus grew up in Nazareth. A town of about seventy thousand inhabitants today, in Jesus's time it was a hamlet of two hundred to four hundred people. The center of village life was the synagogue, where everyone gathered for worship on Sabbath and likely where school was conducted during the week.

Jesus may have known Greek, but His native language was Aramaic. The entire New Testament is written in Greek, which was the literary language of the first century, but three times in Mark's Gospel he mentions Jesus's actual Aramaic words (see Mark 5:41; 7:34; 15:34).

Contrary to what many Christians think, Nazareth was not an isolated, backwater village. A major road passed nearby, and a few miles away lay the city of Sepphoris. In His work as a carpenter, Jesus may have had business there, but the Gospel accounts do not mention that He visited Sepphoris at any time.

Like the people around Him, Jesus's dress would have consisted of two garments—a long tunic known as a *chitōn* and a cloak called a *himation*. His head covering was a hat of either straw or felt, or a type of headscarf.

In John's account of the crucifixion of Jesus, he mentions that the soldiers who kept watch at Calvary divided Jesus's clothing into four pieces and cast lots to see who would receive what. The four items presumably were Jesus's tunic, cloak, loincloth, and sandals. The tunic, John tells us, attracted particular attention because, unlike the usual *chitōn*, which consisted of two rectangular pieces of cloth sewn together, this one was seamless, woven from top to bottom in one piece and therefore more valuable (John 19:23, 24).

If the soldiers confiscated Jesus's clothing, what covered Him as He hung on the cross? Probably nothing at all. Crucifixion as practiced by the Romans was not merely an agonizing form of execution; it was—by intent—public and shameful to maximize the deterrent effect. Criminals commonly hung on the cross naked, and most likely Jesus did also. A Christian observation dating from the second century states that this was the case.

Many Jews of Jesus's time wore a tassel or fringe on their garments. This was in harmony with instruction given to Moses (Num. 15:38, 39; Deut. 22:12) that was intended to continually remind the wearer of his relationship to God. In the Gospels, we read of people pressing close to Jesus just to touch the fringe of His tunic. So it seems obvious that Jesus, like other observant Jews, wore the fringe (see Matt. 9:20).

As a carpenter, Jesus probably spent much of His time outdoors. During His public ministry He seems to have been outside most of the time. He traveled from village to village teaching and healing. He frequently crossed the Lake of Galilee in a boat. Occasionally we find Him in Jerusalem, but He seems to have avoided the large cities of Galilee—Sepphoris, Tiberius, and Caesarea Maritime. In John's Gospel we read: "Then they all went home, but Jesus went to the Mount of Olives" (John 7:53–8:1). Did He spend the night there? Perhaps. He was an outdoors person.

From the time Jesus embarked on His public ministry, He was constantly on the move. But so far as we can tell, only once did He get a ride. That came at the very end when, in a deliberate act designed to draw attention to Himself as fulfilling the ancient prophecy of Israel's king, He rode into Jerusalem on a donkey (Matt. 21:1–9; see also John 12:12–15).

The rest of the time, Jesus walked. He hiked the 160 miles (257 km) from Galilee to Jerusalem and back for the annual festivals. Of course, in doing so Jesus was just like His contemporaries: they didn't possess an automobile, not even a bicycle. They walked. Jesus was no weakling. His arms were strong from hard work, His legs powerful from hundreds of miles on the road, and His face tanned from countless hours spent in the open.

The Times of Jesus

Rome ruled the world, with Palestine an obscure province on the eastern outskirts of the empire. The governor of Judea in this Roman territory during the period of Jesus's ministry was Pontius Pilate, who ruled AD 26–36. His name has come to light on an inscription unearthed in 1961 at Caesarea Maritime; he is designated "prefect of Judea."

THE HERODS MENTIONED IN THE BIBLE

- *Herod the Great:* King of Judea and all Palestine at the time of Jesus's birth. An Edomite, but a Jew by citizenship and religious profession, he ruled 37–4 BC. Cruel and merciless, he murdered three of his sons and one of his wives. Beginning c. 20 BC, he rebuilt Zerubbabel's Temple, which was in a dilapidated condition (Matt. 2:1–19).

- *Herod Archelaus:* Ruler of Judea and Samaria during Jesus's childhood (Matt. 2:22).

- *Herod Antipas:* Ruler of Galilee and Perea during Jesus's ministry. He married Herodias, his niece and the wife of his half-brother Philip (Matt. 14:3–12).

- *Herod Philip:* Brother of Antipas and first husband of Herodias (Luke 3:1, 19).

- *Herod Agrippa I:* Son of Aristobulus (son of Herod the Great) and Bernice (daughter of Herod's sister Salome), brother of Herodia (Acts 25).

- *Herod Agrippa II:* Son of Agrippa I. He was the Herod before whom Paul stood in Caesarea (Acts 25–26).

It was a difficult region to administer. Both before and after Pilate, Palestine smoldered with tensions that periodically erupted in open conflict—Jews against Gentiles, Jews against Romans, Jews against Samaritans, rich against poor, rural populations against city dwellers. Home-grown terrorists known as *sicarii* ("dagger men") openly assassinated opponents (see Acts 21:38). The province eventually exploded in AD 66 in war against Rome.

The ensuing conflict, brutal and bloody, ended in the destruction of the temple when the Roman general (and future emperor) Titus sacked the city in AD 70.

The Jews had lost their independence in 73 BC, when Rome conquered the last Hasmonean rulers and annexed Palestine. They installed a client king, Herod the Great, who reigned from 37–4 BC. Although Jewish by religion and citizenship, Herod was Idumean by bloodline and therefore hated by the Jews. Brutal and ruthless, Herod the Great murdered Antipater, an action condemned by John the Baptist (see Matt. 14:3; Mark 6:14–20).

The Jews hated the Roman garrisons, the foreign soldiers marching through the land, and having to pay taxes to Caesar. They looked and hoped for a new king to arise from within their midst, an anointed one like King David of old who would drive out the occupying armies.

Then John the Baptist burst on the scene. Luke informs us: "The people were waiting expectantly and were all wondering in their hearts if John might possibly be the Messiah" (the Greek word *Christos* is equivalent to the Hebrew word "Messiah"; Luke 3:15).

But John answered that he was not the hoped-for Messiah: that person would very soon appear.

Among the Jews in Jesus's time were three distinct sects or groups—Sadducees, Pharisees, and Essenes. The first two of these feature prominently in the Gospel accounts as being opposed to Jesus; the Essenes are not mentioned. We know much about them from the writings of Josephus and the Dead Sea Scrolls, some nine hundred documents that survived in caves from

three of his own sons and one of his wives. He is the king mentioned in Matthew 2:16–18 who ordered the slaughter of the infants of Bethlehem.

Following Herod the Great's death, Palestine was divided between his sons Archelaus and Antipater (Antipas). Both these kings are mentioned in the Gospels, as is a third son Philip, whose wife Herodias divorced him and married his brother

"Pontius Pilate Inscription"

their community at Qumran in the desolate hills above the Dead Sea. The Essenes were sharply critical of the Jewish religious establishment, which was dominated by the priests and centered in the temple.

Jewish religion centered in the Torah, the law given to Moses. A professional class of religious teachers, the scribes, specialized in the interpretation of the Scriptures. Their subtle interpretations and applications of Torah to differing life situations came to be considered of equal value to the law itself. Later, these interpretations were gathered and codified in the Mishnah and then in the Talmud.

The teachers of the law of Jesus's times were Pharisees. In the Gospel accounts we often find Jesus strongly denouncing them for their hypocrisy and misinterpretations of Scripture that placed heavy burdens on the people.

The theology of the day taught that the rich had the best of both worlds. For the Sadducees, Pharisees, and teachers of the law, the very fact of wealth indicated God's blessing. Contrariwise, the great majority of common people, with their frequent illnesses and struggles to put bread on the table, were objects of scorn. The contemptuous attitude of the religious establishment was summed up by words of the chief priests and Pharisees: "But this mob that knows nothing of the law—there is a curse on them" (John 7:49).

This then was the world into which Jesus of Nazareth came—a troubled time with unrest, revolt, and assassinations. It was a broken world, with people wracked by disease and dying young. And a benighted world in which wealth went hand in hand with religious profession but left the common people grasping for a ray of hope. And it was a world in which expectation of the coming of the deliverer, the Messiah, burned in the hearts of men and women.

In the Fullness of Time

"But when the set time had fully come, God sent his Son, born of a woman, born under the law," wrote the Apostle Paul to the churches of Galatia (Gal. 4:4). This idea was already sounded in the Gospels. As Jesus embarked on His preaching ministry, He proclaimed: "The time has come. . . . The kingdom of God has come near. Repent and believe the good news!" (Mark 1:15).

Jesus came on time—God's time. Nothing by chance here, nothing haphazard. "But like the stars in the vast circuit of their appointed path, God's purposes know no haste and no delay."[1]

Old Testament prophets had foretold His coming in a series of specific passages. The book of Daniel had given a time frame when Messiah would appear (Dan. 9:24–27). The clock, as it were, struck the hour in heaven. After so long a time, the moment had come.

This view of time gives us the clue to understanding the genealogy of Jesus with which Matthew begins his Gospel (Matt. 1:1–17). The listing of Jesus's ancestry, going back to David and Abraham, is selective in several regards, but the key is found in verse 17: "Thus there were fourteen generations in all from Abraham to David, fourteen from David to the exile to Babylon, and fourteen from the exile to the Messiah."

In the fullness of time, right on God's time—this is when Jesus came to this earth. God—for Whom past, present, and future are contemporaneous—saw and planned it all.

Does this mean that Jesus's life, ministry, and death were cut-and-dried in advance, with the end determined before He was born? Not at all. As we study the story we will see how vulnerable He was and how He could have failed in the divine mission. But through it all Jesus had an abiding sense of God's time. "My hour has not yet come," He said frequently during the days of His ministry (John 2:4; see also 7:6, 8, 30); and then at the end, at the climax—"The hour *has* come" (John 12:23; see also 12:27).

Historians have observed how Jesus appeared at the crux of history—how the world had been prepared to facilitate the spread of the good news that He

"Scale Model of Jerusalem in the Second Temple Period," Israel Museum

preached and lived. They have pointed to the peace and stability over a large surface of the earth because of the Pax Romana, the peace that Rome brought. They have mentioned the fine system of roads, all leading to Rome, that enabled international travel, and the purging of the seas from pirates. In addition, the unification of language—Latin the official language of the Empire and Greek that of literature—facilitated communication. Thus, Paul could write letters in Greek and they would spread far and wide.

All of these factors, and others that could be mentioned, give deeper meaning to those words of Paul: "When the set time had fully come, God sent His Son" (Gal. 4:4). Jesus came right on time as the climax and fulfillment of thousands of years of human expectation and divine

"Herod's Temple Model"

preparation. He came, just as the prophet Daniel had predicted in the prophecy of the seventy weeks (see Dan. 9:24–27).

QUESTIONS FOR DISCUSSION

1. Why does the author say that of all the regions in Israel he likes Galilee best?

2. Put yourself into the sandals of a first-century Jew. What would it be like to live under Roman rule? Make a list of pros and cons.

3. Does Jesus fit into any of the Jewish parties? If yes, which? If not, why not? Explain your answer.

2

Can We Trust the Gospels?

OBJECTIVES

- Identify the challenges and criticism of the New Testament Gospels.

- Explain the nature of the four New Testament Gospels: Matthew, Mark, Luke, and John.

- Establish the reliability of these Gospels as sources for the life and teachings of Jesus.

SCRIPTURE

- Mark 1:1; Luke 1:1–4; John 19:35; 20:30, 31; 21:24, 25

Long before Christians came on the scene, the Greeks had a word for news—*euangelion*. They associated this word with a messenger who brought a good report. *Euangelion*, in fact, was a technical term for news of victory. The messenger would appear, lift his right arm in greeting, and call out in a loud voice: "Rejoice, we won!" The messenger's very appearance signaled that he brought good news: his face shone, he wore a crown on his head, he swung a branch of palms, and his spear was decked with laurel. At this message the city would go wild. The people would garland the temples and offer sacrifices of thanksgiving. And they would honor the messenger with a wreath.

Then Jesus of Nazareth appeared. Profoundly impacted by His life, teachings, and death—especially His death, because of what His followers believed happened that Sunday morning—Christians looked for a word that said it best. They plucked out the centuries-old term *euangelion*, but filled it with new content. That is the word we translate "gospel."

Gospels and Jesus

At first "gospel" meant a message—*the* message about Jesus. This is how Paul, who often referred to it in his letters, used it, as in Romans 1:16—"For I am not ashamed of the gospel, because it is the power of God that brings salvation to everyone who believes: first to the Jew, then to the Gentile."

Then, a little later in the first century AD, the sayings of Jesus began to be gathered together and His story written down. Luke, who probably wrote in the AD 60s, tells us that by his time "many" had undertaken to draw up an account of what happened (Luke 1:1). We don't know how many accounts were produced—they continued for another

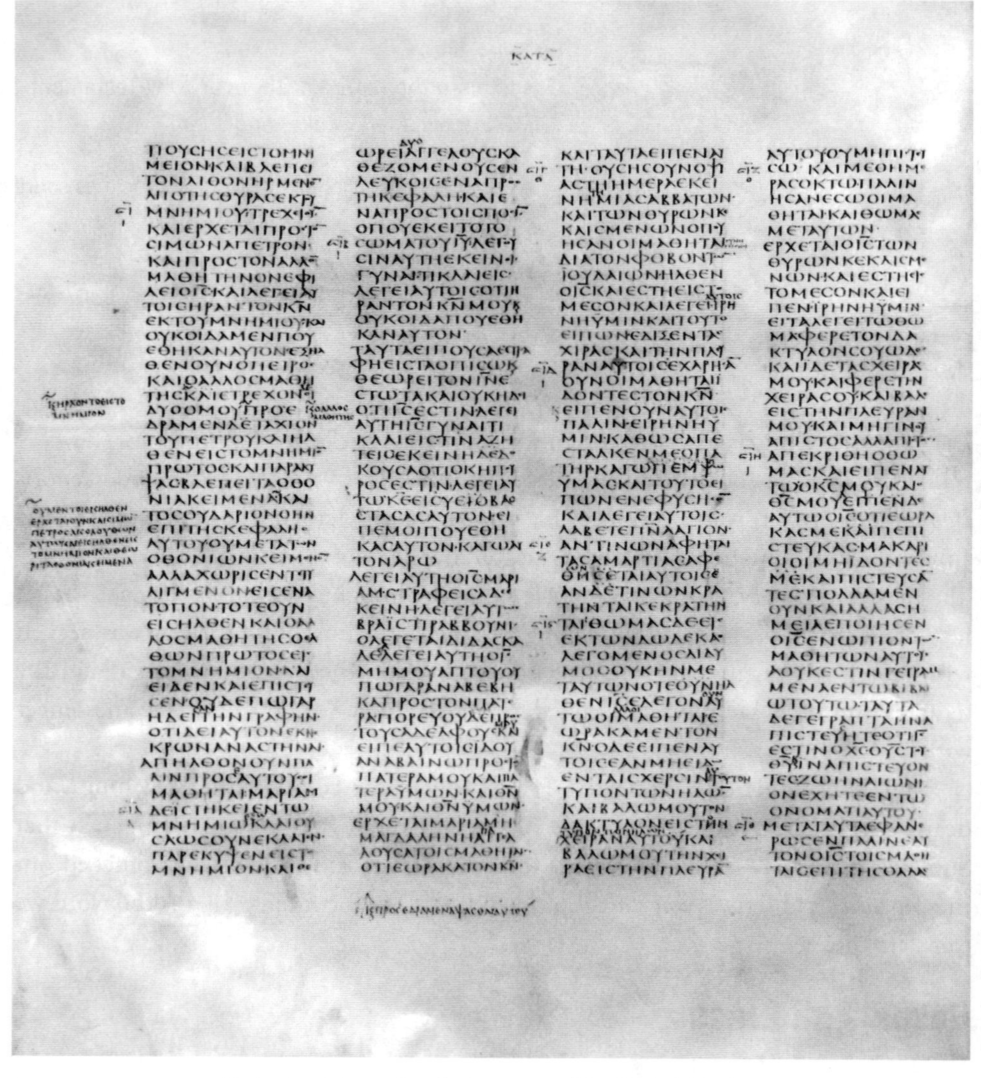

Codex Sinaiticus, a handwritten copy of the Greek Bible from the Gospel of John 20:1—21:1

century after Luke wrote—but we do know that eventually Christians recognized four of them as authentic: those of Matthew, Mark, Luke, and John.

These accounts, although biographical in form, differ significantly from usual biographies. They center on Jesus of Nazareth—He dominates the story—but they omit many facts about Him that we expect to find in a biography. For example, they tell us little or nothing about His birth and early years. We learn that at age twelve He stayed behind in the temple (Luke 2:41–52), and that He was about thirty years old (Luke 3:23) when He began His public ministry, but they pass over in silence His years as a teenager and a twenty-something.

Each of these "biographies" focuses on the three-plus years of His ministry, but in the telling devote disproportionate attention to the final week of His life. Thus, Matthew's account contains twenty-eight chapters, but of these the final eight take up the last week. For Mark, the proportion is even greater: sixteen chapters altogether, six on the final week. For Luke, the numbers are twenty-four and six; and for John, twenty-one and nine—nearly half the "biography" deals with Jesus's final week.

Later in this chapter we shall reflect more deeply on these most unusual "biographies" and their exceptional form. Suffice to notice that these writings, dominated by the person of Jesus and His teachings, also become known as "Gospels." The story that each attempted to tell was itself *euangelion*, good news.

These four Gospels are the primary source for studying about Jesus. Without them we would be cast upon scattered references to Jesus in the Book of Acts and from contemporary, non-Christian sources and writings of believers in later centuries. So flimsy are these other sources that we would have only a vague outline of the life, ministry, and message of Jesus of Nazareth.

If the Gospels are thus so critical for our study of Jesus, can we be confident in their reliability in aiding our search for the real Jesus? Yes. I am convinced of their trustworthiness. This is my settled conclusion after a lifetime of study and reflection, and I will tell you why.

But first, let me sound a note of warning. The study of Jesus with its focus on the four Gospels has become a source of fierce controversy. Earlier, we noticed how the "Lives" of Jesus produced by scholars in the eighteenth and nineteenth centuries dried up in the sands of unbelief and skepticism, brought to a full stop by Albert Schweitzer's *The Quest of the Historical Jesus*. Since then, much of the scholarly effort has focused on the Gospels themselves rather than on the person of Jesus. Sadly, the end result for many people has been loss of trust in the reliability of the Gospels and loss of faith in the Jesus Whom the Gospels set forth.

What do I mean? Read many—maybe most—of the scholarly studies in the Gospels and you find the following assertions stated as established fact:

- Only a small percentage of the Gospels reflect what Jesus actually said and did.

- The Gospels weren't written by people in a position to know what Jesus was like.

- Primitive cultures believed in miracles like the virgin birth and resurrection; we know that they are impossible.

- Many, perhaps most, of what Jesus is supposed to have said was invented years later by His followers.

- Other so-called Gospels like the Gospel of Thomas should be given equal weight with, or preferred over, the accounts of Matthew, Mark, Luke, and John.

- Because the four Gospel writers had a theological interest in what they wrote, their history cannot be trusted.

Large numbers of students studying in universities and even in seminaries have accepted these ideas from teachers who present them as proven beyond reasonable doubt. These ideas have gone beyond the classroom into the public arena, as some scholars with sensational-sounding theories about Jesus have courted the media, rather than subjecting their ideas to the scrutiny of their peers in academia.

All of the positions mentioned above have either been disproved or are weakly supported by the evidence. The common Christian, however, trying to sift truth from error, would never know this from what some theologians tell them.

Obviously, this whole area could engage our attention in the rest of this book. That is not our object: we want to learn about the real Jesus, who is Himself the *euangelion*, the good news, and the Jesus of the Gospels of Matthew, Mark, Luke, and John. However, because these Gospels, so essential to our endeavor, have come under such fierce attack as to their reliability, we need to at least give a response to the main criticisms.

Presuppositions

How is it possible that many scholars today, studying the Gospels, have concluded that Jesus wasn't born of a virgin, that His miracles never happened, and that He did not rise from the dead?

The answer lies in the presuppositions on which these same scholars based their work. In any line of inquiry no one starts from scratch: we all assume from the outset fundamental propositions that we consider so basic that they don't need to be proven. This is true in scientific inquiry also: the scientist assumes that the universe is governed by fixed laws such that if he or she combines three parts of hydrogen with one part of nitrogen, the result will always be ammonia. Anyone can repeat the experiment and the result will always be the same.

As scientists go about their investigations, they do not look for any factor outside the operation of natural law. On a personal level they may believe in God and that He intervenes in human affairs and in history, but they do not consider that He will play a part in the lab. God won't act, for instance, to bring about a different chemical—say, sodium chloride—when one mixes hydrogen and nitrogen together.

The scientific approach to studying the world, known as the "scientific method," is comparatively recent in human history. For most of the era since Jesus, the Church—that is, the Roman Catholic Church—controlled all inquiry and was considered to be the repository of all knowledge. But the Protestant Reformation of the sixteenth century broke away from the Church and sparked independent inquiry into the cosmos. Then came the Enlightenment in the eighteenth century with the exaltation of reason over dogma, and the scientific method emerged.

Science and its accompanying technology have largely supplanted the role once occupied by the Church of the Middle Ages. Today if we become sick, we go to a physician, not to a priest. When we study science, we conduct experiments rather than consult the writings of the church fathers.

Scholars of the Bible have been impressed by the scientific method. They seek to place their inquiries into the life and teachings of Jesus on a solid foundation so that the results of investigation won't be simply one person's opinion against someone else's views. This has led most of them today to base their work on three presuppositions.

Only What Is Part of the Natural World Is Valid

Since the supernatural cannot be investigated, it cannot be accounted for. These scholars contrast the thinking of "primitive," prescientific men and women with that of modern people. For the primitives, miracles seem to happen because they don't have knowledge of the natural causes behind them. It is a world in which sick people are suddenly healed and dead people come back to life.

But that is not the world of modern people, with doctors and nurses, advanced medicine, chaplains, and undertakers. In this world babies are born every day, but always and only through the fertilization of a female ovum with sperm from a male. In this world everyone dies and is buried or cremated in a one-way procession. No one reverses the direction: dead people don't come back to life.

Thus, these scholars of the Gospels, following what they consider to be a scientific approach in their studies, totally reject all that is outside the normal course of events. They give no place to possibilities of the supernatural. For them, Jesus wasn't born of the Virgin Mary; He had a natural conception. His miracles all had a natural explanation and can be explained without introducing any factor outside our normal experience. For instance, when the disciples in a boat thought that they saw Jesus walking on water, He was really walking along the shore. Finally,

Jesus's own resurrection didn't actually happen: His disciples either made up the story or were deluded.

The other presuppositions follow logically and can be summarized quickly.

History as a Continuum of Cause and Effect

According to this view, everything that has happened is to be explained and

understood by what now happens. The supernatural cannot be entertained as a possibility to account for events in human history; everything has a natural explanation that will come to light with sufficient investigation. Just as the world around us operates by unchanging natural law, so does human history. There is no divine intervention, no angels, no devil, and no God. If God exists, He does not interrupt the flow of human events. God isn't necessary to understanding the past or the present.

The Gospels Are a Wholly Human Product

The Bible is not considered the word of God. Like other ancient writings, it has valuable ideas but also bad ones. It contains errors and is flawed. Because the writers lived in a pre-scientific age, they reflect primitive modes of understanding.

Thus, the four accounts of Matthew, Mark, Luke, and John contradict each other and are full of errors. They were written long after Jesus's time and cannot be trusted. Jesus was only a man. He did not consider Himself to be the Messiah, let alone God. Gradually, during the years following His death, His followers attributed divine status to Him and made up sayings about His divinity that eventually were inserted into the four Gospels. When the writers of the Gospels—whoever they really were—wrote up the story of Jesus, their theological agenda distorted the true history.

Perhaps the most glaring example of the impact of these presuppositions on the study of the Gospels is found in the work of the Jesus Seminar. This is a group of some 150 scholars and lay people who, since the 1990s, have met periodically to try to decide which sayings and acts of Jesus are genuine. After discussing each saying, they cast ballots for or against! So far they have concluded that 18 percent of Jesus's sayings and 16 percent of His deeds as recorded in the four Gospels are authentic. They included the Gospel of Thomas in their discussions.

The Jesus Seminar has been roundly criticized by the majority of New Testament scholars. But its participants don't seem to care—they court the media instead, releasing from time to time sensational statements that have high shock value. The public reads these press releases, which are printed without a scholarly critique giving the other side, and falls into agreement with the misleading picture of Jesus and the Gospels.

The critical approach to Jesus and the Gospels that is so widespread in current study at first glance seems formidable. Proclaimed confidently by scholars with impressive credentials, the arguments can destroy trust in the Gospels as reliable history and faith in Jesus Christ. But we need not feel overwhelmed. There is another side based on sound scholarship that leads to exactly the opposite conclusions.

Why We Can Trust the Gospels

Five lines of evidence lead us to have confidence in the Gospels as a reliable source of information about Jesus.

They Match with Reality

Over and over, what the Gospels describe matches the way things really were in early first-century Jewish Palestine. The Gospels speak of real *people* like Pontius Pilate, Herod the Great, Herod Antipas, Annas, and Caiaphas. We know about these people from non-biblical writings of the time and archaeological discoveries, and the information agrees with what we find in the Gospels. For example, Herod the Great was infamous in history as an unusually cruel and ruthless king. Apart from the Gospel of Matthew, we have no record of his ordering the slaughter of the infants of Bethlehem, but the horrendous act is altogether congruent with his actions.

Likewise, the Gospels speak about *events* like the death of John the Baptist, who was beheaded at the order of Herod Antipas (Mark 6:14–29). The Jewish writer Josephus confirms that this actually took place.

The Gospels tell of real *places*—villages, cities, roads, lakes, and mountains. Other historical sources and archaeology confirm that they existed and clarify our understanding of them.

Again, the Gospels record real *customs*, like the Passover purity concerns, the Sabbath, and divorce law. All of these are corroborated by contemporary writings and archaeology.

The Gospels tell about real *institutions*, such as the synagogue and the temple, and what they record matches the way things really were.

Finally, the Gospels mention *beliefs* of Pharisees and Sadducees with their interpretation of Scriptures (e.g., Mark 7:1–3; 12:18). Once again, what we read corresponds with information from other sources.

This matching of the Gospel accounts with reality of life in first-century Palestine is referred to as verisimilitude. The amount of factual evidence is very large and imparts credibility to the data of the Gospels. So great is the verisimilitude that archaeologists often compare their findings with what they see already in the Gospels.

The Gospels, centering on Jesus, tell about His life, ministry, and teachings. Archaeology cannot provide confirmation in these areas; contemporary Greek and Roman writers had no interest in writing about a Jewish rabbi. However, if in all those areas where the Gospels can be checked against external evidence—people, events, places, customs, institutions, offices and officers, and beliefs—they match the way things really were, should we not also be confident in their reliability where no external sources offer comparison?

Eyewitnesses

Luke tells us that the early accounts of the life and teachings of Jesus were based on information "handed down to us by those who from the first were eyewitnesses and servants of the word" (Luke 1:2). Luke himself carefully investigated everything and set out to write an orderly account (v. 3). Luke wasn't an eyewitness, but he relied on eyewitnesses for his work.

The writer of the Gospel of John claims to have been an eyewitness. Concerning Jesus's crucifixion, he writes: "The man who saw it has given testimony, and his testimony is true. He knows that he tells the truth, and he testifies so that you also may believe" (John 19:35). At the close of his Gospel he confirms: "This is the disciple who testifies to these things and who wrote them down. We know that his testimony is true" (John 21:24).

According to early Christian tradition, the Gospel of Mark was written by John Mark, who is mentioned in the Book of Acts (12:12, 25; 15:37) and who wrote on the basis of recollections of the apostle Peter. Mark's Gospel mentions in three places the actual Aramaic words used by Jesus (Mark 5:41; 7:34; 15:34). It also includes a curious personal detail about a young man who fled naked when seized by the soldiers who arrested Jesus in the Garden of Gethsemane (Mark 14:51, 52). It is the sort of recollection that only an eyewitness could supply.

The Gospels mention a tax collector named Matthew (also known as Levi) who became one of the disciples (Mark 2:14). Tradition attributes to him the Gospel that bears his name.

Thus, the Gospels, which exhibit a high degree of verisimilitude, claim to be based on eyewitness testimony.

We should note a final point concerning the eyewitnesses. They were willing to die for their account and many actually did. People hardly die for a lie!

Unbroken Chain of Transmission

Matthew, Mark, and Luke were probably written in the AD 60s or 70s, perhaps earlier. This puts them at the end of the first generation of people who were alive when Jesus was on earth. If, as the skeptics allege, these Gospels were legends rather than fact, they would have been refuted and not taken seriously.

The Gospel of John bears evidence of having been written last. Christian tradition places it in the AD 90s when John was an old man; its perspective is that of someone looking back on the events he describes.

A small fragment of John's Gospel, John Rylands Papyrus P52, dating from early in the second century, has been discovered in Egypt. It must be very close to the "autograph," the original manuscript. Furthermore, a larger number of ancient manuscripts of the Gospels have survived. Even though they are copies of copies of copies, they show only minor variations in the text.

Even the skeptics acknowledge that the apostle Paul wrote some of his letters very early, within twenty to twenty-five years of Jesus's death. In Galatians and 1 Corinthians, he mentions his encounters with some of the original twelve disciples. He tells us that he went up to Jerusalem to inquire of or get information from Peter; the verb he uses is *historesai*, from which we get "history." In 1 Corinthians, Paul mentions the words spoken by Jesus at the Last Supper (11:23–25), and passes on the tradition about Jesus that he had "received" (15:3–7).

We also have the testimony of others who were born in the first century and who were acquainted either with the original disciples or with those who knew one of them. Papias, born about AD 60 and later bishop of Hierapolis, describes his eagerness to seek information from "elders" who had been acquainted with the apostles. He names Andrew, Peter, Philip, Thomas, James, John, and Matthew.

Finally, we have the testimony of Quadratus (c. AD 70–130). He claims that eyewitnesses of the ministry of Jesus were still living at the end of the first century, and so were some people whom Jesus had healed.

Other witnesses to the story of Jesus might be mentioned, such as Polycarp (c. AD 69–156) and Clement of Rome, who wrote a letter to Corinth about AD 96. It is clear, therefore, that our understanding of the Gospels rests on an unbroken chain of transmission from the time of Jesus Himself on through the first century and beyond.

Early Hymns to Jesus

In some of the earliest writings of the New Testament we find embedded hymns exalting Jesus as truly God and Lord of all. So we find the apostle Paul, writing to the church in Philippi about AD 63, suddenly breaking into song:

> Who, being in very nature God,
>   did not consider equality with God
>   something to be used to his own
>   advantage;
>   rather, he made himself nothing

by taking the very nature of a servant,
    being made in human likeness.
And being found in appearance as a man,
    he humbled himself
    by becoming obedient to death—
    even death on a cross!

Therefore God exalted him to the
    highest place
    and gave him the name that is above
    every name,
    that at the name of Jesus every knee
    should bow,
    in heaven and on earth and under
    the earth,
    and every tongue acknowledge that
    Jesus Christ is Lord,
    to the glory of God the Father.
    (Phil. 2:6–11)

We find other hymn portions in Colossians 1:15–20, 1 Timothy 3:16, and Revelation 5:12, 13; 7:10. All these passages focus on Jesus. They are important because they show us that Christians very early sang hymns to Jesus as God in their worship. That fact refutes the arguments of scholars who assert Jesus did not Himself claim divine origin and that His followers only gradually began to regard Him as an object of worship.

Alternative Presuppositions

We saw above that the radical criticism of Jesus and the Gospels rests on a series of presuppositions, not on evidence. In fact, the evidence from archaeology and contemporary writers subjects these presuppositions to serious question.

Let us be quite clear: what we are dealing with has nothing to do with science per se. Science deals with the natural world; it neither denies nor affirms the supernatural. To suggest that in order to have a "scientific" approach to the Gospels we must from the outset rule out the supernatural shows a confusion in understanding.

Rather, the opposite holds true for inquiry into the Gospels. They are not merely history; they are faith history written by believers with the purpose of leading others to faith. John makes this point explicitly: "Jesus performed many other signs in the presence of his disciples, which are not recorded in this book. But these are

<table>
<tr><td colspan="2">FOUR GOSPELS</td></tr>
<tr><td>Matthew, Mark, Luke</td><td>John</td></tr>
<tr><td>"Synoptic" = common viewpoint</td><td>Different viewpoint</td></tr>
<tr><td>Focus on Galilee</td><td>Wider focus, including Judea</td></tr>
<tr><td>Short period of ministry</td><td>Longer period of ministry</td></tr>
<tr><td>Much material in common</td><td>Largely different material</td></tr>
<tr><td>Matthew: Jesus as King</td><td>Jesus as "Word made flesh"</td></tr>
<tr><td>Mark: Jesus as Son of God</td><td></td></tr>
<tr><td>Luke: Jesus as Savior of the world</td><td></td></tr>
</table>

written that you may believe that Jesus is the Messiah, the Son of God, and that by believing you may have life in his name" (John 20:30, 31).

In any field of investigation, the method employed must conform to the nature of the subject matter. That holds true for the Gospels also: only as the *faith* factor is given full sway can the student hope to arrive at valid conclusions.

But this type of open inquiry is more than a dispassionate academic exercise. Anyone who accepts the message of the four Gospels—the message of Jesus—cannot remain the same. That message will call them to decision with changes that may be upsetting. Thus, toward the close of his careful study of the historical reliability of the Gospels, Dr. Craig L. Blomberg observes: "The critical scholarship that has already abandoned these beliefs virtually never considers where its investigations might lead if it questioned its starting point and took seriously the possibility of the divine origin of Scripture and of Jesus."[1]

A Fascinating Study

Study of the Gospels is fascinating and richly rewarding. Just think:

- So wonderful was and is Jesus that it took not just one but four accounts to tell the story.

- The Gospels introduced a different literary genre, a biography unlike regular biographies, and focused on the final week of Jesus's life.

- So powerful was the impact of the Gospels that the pagans attempted an imitation. Philostratus in the second century wrote a counter-Gospel based on Apollonius of Tyana, a miracle worker. But it didn't succeed, because Apollonius wasn't Jesus.

- Matthew, Mark, and Luke write from a common perspective; hence they are called synoptic (literally, "one view, seeing together"). They have much in common, in places word for word, but in other places they show surprising differences.

- John's Gospel, written last, provides profound theological insights into the life and teachings of Jesus. Part of John's purpose in writing was to fill in gaps in the Synoptic Gospels rather than merely repeating their accounts.

- All four Gospels are based on eyewitness testimony and therefore one should not be surprised to find different emphases and even apparent disagreements.

Ellen G. White said it well:

There is variety in a tree, there are scarcely two leaves just alike. Yet this variety adds to the perfection of the tree as a whole.

In our Bible, we might ask, Why need Matthew, Mark, Luke, and John in the Gospels, why need the Acts of the Apostles, and the variety of writers in the Epistles, go over the same thing?

The Lord gave His word in just the way He wanted it to come. He gave it through different writers, each having his own individuality, though going over the same history. Their testimonies are brought together in one Book, and are like the testimonies in a social meeting. They do not represent things in just the same style. Each has an experience of his own, and this diversity broadens and deepens the knowledge that is brought out to meet the necessities of varied minds. The thoughts expressed have not a set uniformity, as if cast in an iron mold, making the very hearing monotonous. In such uniformity there would be a loss of grace and distinctive beauty.[2]

QUESTIONS FOR DISCUSSION

1. What part does faith play in studying the Gospels?

2. What presuppositions do critical scholars have concerning the Gospels? How do they affect the interpretation of the Gospels?

3. What is meant by "verisimilitude"? Why is it important for consideration of the reliability of the Gospels?

The Eternal Word

OBJECTIVES

- Gain a comprehensive perspective of the eternal story of Jesus.

- Examine the key passage, John 1:1–18, noting its themes and development of thought.

SCRIPTURE

- John 1:1–18

The story of Jesus begins long before He was born. In this respect His "biography" differs radically from all other accounts of great men and women. Writers customarily seek to identify the influences that helped shape the life of their subject, sifting through the family tree for clues of what was to come. But not so with Jesus's story. It begins further back than our minds can stretch—back before Adam, before the world began.

We call Him Jesus, but that was only His name during the period of His earthly sojourn. Meaning "savior" or "deliverer," that name was given before birth to both Joseph in a dream (Matt. 1:21) and to Mary by the angel Gabriel (Luke 1:31). What was His name before—and after? The Bible suggests two designations rather than a name. One is "the Word" and the other "the Son." The words are simple but the meanings profound. We shall explore what each implies later in this chapter and throughout the entire book.

Descent and Ascent of Christ

All four Gospels make clear that the story of Jesus takes the form of a U-shaped curve (see diagram on next page). The curve starts with a line that stretches back into a past eternity. Then it abruptly dips to a short line indicating the period of His earthly life when, as the apostle Paul tells us, Jesus "did not consider equality with God something to be used to his own advantage; rather, he made himself nothing by taking the very nature of a servant, being made in human likeness" (Phil. 2:6, 7). And even this phase

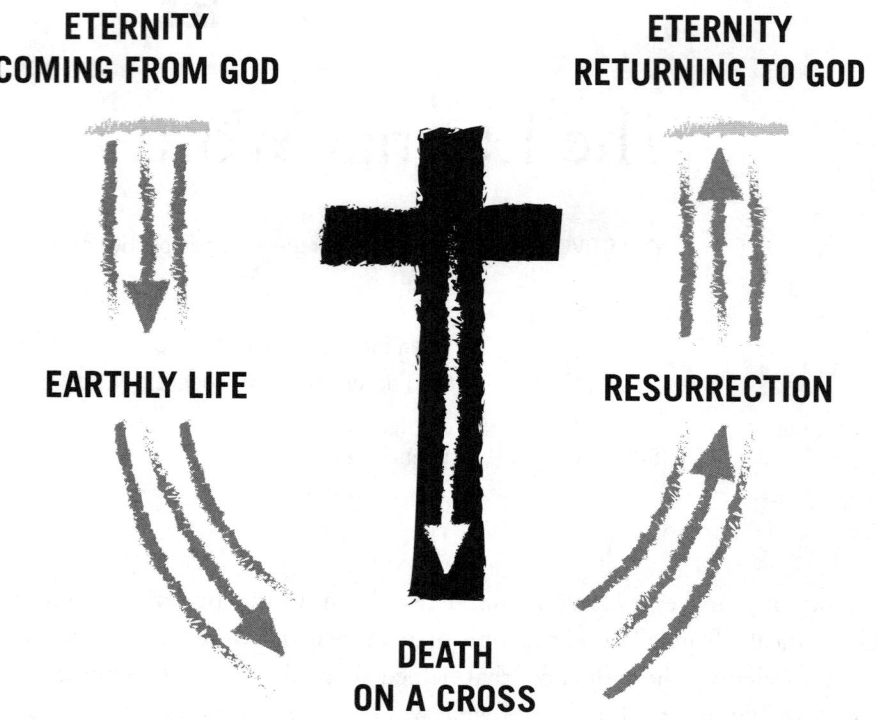

was marked by a low point—indeed, the lowest point in human experience—when Jesus "humbled himself by becoming obedient to death—even death on a cross" (v. 8).

The cross, however, was not the last word in the story of Jesus. "God exalted him to the highest place and gave him the name that is above every name, that at the name of Jesus every knee should bow . . . and every tongue acknowledge that Jesus Christ is Lord" (vv. 9–11).

Throughout the Gospel of John we find frequent references by Jesus to His coming from God and returning to God. For example: "I am the bread that came down from heaven" (John 6:41, see also 6:51, 58); "What if you see the Son of Man ascend to where he was before!" (v. 62); "I am with you for only a short time, and then I am going to the one who sent me" (7:33); "You are from below; I am from above" (8:23); "I have come here from God. I have not come on my own; God sent me" (8:42); "And now, Father, glorify me in your presence with the glory I had with you before the world began" (17:5).

Beyond the many individual references to God's "sending" Jesus and His coming and returning, one long passage of John's Gospel sets forth the U-shaped trajectory of the story of Jesus in magnificent language. It is one of the greatest passages in the whole Bible and in the literature of the human race. It warrants our prayerful, careful study.

John 1:1–18

The words of John 1:1–18 are simple in both English and the original language. Students of New Testament Greek customarily begin translation exercises right here. The vocabulary is basic and the grammar straightforward. The concepts expressed through this beguilingly simple language, however, are profound. They are majestic, sweeping us beyond and outside ourselves and stretching our minds. Ultimately, they bring us squarely before a Man—Jesus, the Word made flesh.

For centuries Christian scholars have analyzed and reanalyzed these simple words. They have debated their relation to the rest of John's Gospel: Is the passage an introduction, an introit to what follows? Is it a prelude? A summary? The passage stands apart, self-contained. If you read it through and move to the verses that follow, the contrast is striking. After the lofty concepts of the first eighteen verses, John changes to a narrative about the role of John the Baptist. Language and grammar stay the same, but the ideas are on a different plane.

John 1:1–18 cannot be seen as merely a précis or summary of what is to follow. Some of its leading ideas do not appear in the rest of the Gospel—the key words "Word" (found four times in the passage) and "grace" (four times also) in particular. On the other hand, "sign" and "glory," terms that play a major role in the Gospel, are absent from John 1:1–18.

Music, to me, is the best category in which to place the passage and its relation to the rest of the Gospel. It is an overture that sounds themes—some, not all—that will follow in the Gospel. Most of all, John 1:1–18 is an overture in the *tone* it sets. That tone is worship, sweeping us off our feet and drawing us into eternity—presenting us with Jesus, Who is the Word made flesh and grace embodied.

In this hymn-like overture we first hear strains of the mystery of eternity—intriguing, captivating, calling us home. Then we hear, as it were, the trumpet sound in the clear, sure voice of the herald of Jesus. A plaintive theme follows, infinitely sad, as the God-man is despised and rejected—"a Man of sorrows and acquainted with grief" (Isa. 53:3, NKJV). The final theme is pure adoration—the full-throated organ of rejoicing like the "Joyful, Joyful, We Adore Thee" set to the music of Beethoven's Ninth Symphony.

I see four stanzas or movements in this hymn of adoration of Jesus, the Word made flesh. Each stanza or movement stands distinct, yet each is part of a unity—an overall plan that is being developed. Where did the beloved John find these words? Did they arise out of a long life of contemplation on the story of Jesus as the Holy Spirit moved on his heart and mind? Were the words perhaps already a hymn of adoration sung by John's fellow Christians that John adopted to begin his Gospel? It really doesn't matter. The passage is all about Jesus, not John or anyone else.

Stanza #1: The Song from Eternity (John 1:1–5)

> In the beginning was the Word, and the Word was with God, and the Word was God. He was with God in the beginning. Through him all things were made; without him nothing was made that has been made. In him was life, and that life was the light of all mankind. The light shines in the darkness, and the darkness has not overcome it.

Note the word repetitions that carry the thought along from verse to verse in chain-like fashion:

Verses 1–2: Beginning . . . Word . . . Word . . . God . . . Word . . . God . . . God . . . beginning

Verse 3: made . . . made . . . made

Verses 4–5: life . . . life . . . light . . . light . . . darkness . . . darkness

This rhythmic pattern imparts a stately, hymn-like quality to the description.

The words with which the passage opens—"In the beginning"—remind us of the way in which the Old Testament commences: "In the beginning God created the heavens and the earth" (Gen. 1:1). That "beginning" marked the Creation, but John's "beginning" stretches back beyond it.

When all things began, the Word already was. As far back as we can stretch our minds, the Word was there. Before any beginning of anything, the Word existed. The Word has no beginning.

We are creatures of time. Our little lives are specks against the canvas of eternity. We count the seconds, the minutes, the hours, the days. How fast they run through our fingers until our span of seventy or eighty years has run its course.

Everything we see around us comes to an end. The grass sprouts, grows, browns, and dies. Flowers blossom and flourish, fade and die. Leaves of trees turn yellow, brown, and red, and then fall to the earth. Last of all, the tree itself dies.

The majestic words of the prologue to John's Gospel assure us that there is much more than human lifespans. We are finite but the Word is infinite; we are temporal but the Word is eternal.

This opening stanza of the prologue rings the changes on three terms—"Word," "life," and "light."

"In the beginning was the Word"— what a way to start a Gospel! The words, so simple taken individually, form a mysterious, intriguing package. What is this Word?

Scholars have suggested a variety of sources for John's thought. They have pointed to the speculations of Greek philosophy, where the *logos* (Greek for "word") was diffused throughout the cosmos. Some have suggested roots in Jewish teachings on the divine wisdom (as in Prov. 8). Still others have argued from the mythology of Gnosticism, a hybrid Christian-pagan teaching that arose in the first century and posited a series of eons or supernatural powers that came between God and the world.

As interesting as these speculations may be, we need look no further than the Old Testament to understand the meaning of the Word (*logos*) in John 1:1–3. The early Christians were familiar with the account of the Creation in Genesis, with its repeated refrain: "And God said. . . . And God said. . . . And God said" (Gen. 1:3, 6, 9). They knew that "by the word of the Lord the heavens were made, their starry host by the breath of his mouth. . . . For he spoke, and it came to be; he commanded, and it stood firm" (Ps. 33:6, 9). This was the "word of the Lord" that had come upon the Old Testament prophets (such as in Jer. 1:4; Ezek. 1:3; Hosea 1:1). It was more than an audible voice. Just as human words express the thoughts and character of the speaker, this Word expresses the mind and character of God.

Further, John describes the Word in language that Greek or Gnostic teaching could never entertain: "The Word became flesh and made his dwelling among us" (John 1:14). Greek and Gnostic thought held to a dualism of matter and spirit, with spirit being good and matter bad. They could not have assented to the Word becoming "flesh."

In John 1:1–4 we learn five things about the Word:

1. The Word is eternal.

2. The Word was with God.

3. The Word was God.

4. The Word is the Agent of all creation.

5. The Word is the Source of light.

"The Word was with God . . . the Word was God." Here we gain a glimpse into the mystery of God. The great affirmation of the Old Testament, known as the Shema, sets out the only-ness of God; "Hear, O Israel: The Lord our God, the Lord is one" (Deut. 6:4). But John's Gospel takes us a step further: within the one God there are eternal, personal distinctions. The Holy Spirit is not mentioned here, but with His inclusion the concept of God as one yet three will be complete (as in Matt. 28:19).

Verse 3 of John 1, dealing with the Word in relation to the Creation, may be understood in two different ways in the original. We may see the entire verse as expressing the thought that no single thing came about without the Word, or by linking the final words of verse 3—"that has been made"—to the first part of verse 4, changing the meaning of "in him was life." We find these different understandings reflected in various Bible translations.

"Life," introduced in verse 4, is a key word of John's Gospel. We find it in notable passages like "I have come that they may have life, and have it to the full" (10:10) and "whoever hears my word and believes him who sent me has eternal life and will not be judged but has crossed over from death to life" (5:24).

The Greek has two words for life— *bios* and *zōē*. The first connotes biological, natural life, as in our word "biology." The other word, from which we get "zoology," points to life on a higher plane—life to the full with a capital *L*. This is the life referred to in John 1:4 and the teachings of Jesus.

"Light" is another leading idea of the prologue and the Gospel of John. We find it referred to seven times in John 1:4–9 and connected to *zōē* life in a fascinating combination: "that life was the light of all mankind" (v. 4). This means that the new life we find in Jesus illumines our entire being. We have left the realm of darkness and now live as children of light—followers of Jesus, Who is the Light.

In verse 5 we find another translation possibility. When John tells us "the light shines in the darkness, and the darkness has not *katelaben* it," he could mean either "understood" or "overcome." Both options make good sense; however, in view of the theme of conflict between light and darkness that we find elsewhere in the Gospel, I favor "overcome."

Understood in this way, John 1:5 is wonderfully encouraging. Our world is a mixture of good and evil, of the beautiful and the ugly. All around we see corruption, hatred, rape, murder, cruelty, and death. The darkness seems so powerful, but the light overcomes the darkness. It always has and always will. No matter how deep the darkness, light will triumph at the close of the struggle between good and evil.

Stanza #2: The Herald of the Light (John 1:6–8)

There was a man sent from God whose name was John. He came as a witness to testify concerning that light, so that through him all might believe. He himself was not the light; he came only as a witness to the light.

Once again we see the rhythmic pattern: witness . . . witness . . . light . . . light . . . witness . . . light. There is a sharp contrast with the opening stanza, however. The song of eternity, mysterious and intriguing, gives way to the trumpet blast of the herald.

The short passage emphasizes just two characteristics of John the Baptist—he was sent from God and he came as a witness to the light (better "Light," because Jesus is the Light of the world). In a later chapter we shall take up John's ministry in greater depth, comparing and contrasting it with that of Jesus's. We shall note John's boldness and fearless devotion to God in life and preaching. Here, however, we find no mention of these things but only that John was God's man sent on a mission to testify to the Light that was to come.

The passage explicitly denies that John himself was the Light. Why was it necessary to make such a statement? Could it be that some of the people for whom the beloved John wrote his Gospel were in danger of confusing the work of the Baptist with that of Jesus? Yes, some evidence suggests this possibility. During John the Baptist's ministry, which apparently lasted only a short time, he enjoyed a large following. Mark tells us "the whole Judean countryside and all the people of Jerusalem went out to him" (Mark 1:5). Luke informs us that among the crowds were tax collectors and soldiers (Luke 3:12–14). Matthew says that it included many Pharisees and Sadducees (Matt. 3:7).

The Baptist's message, "Repent, for the kingdom of heaven has come near" (Matt. 3:2), electrified the nation. Not surprisingly, many wondered if John might be the long-awaited Messiah (Luke 3:15). The religious leaders in Jerusalem sent a delegation of priests and Levites to ask him who he was. They put the question point-blank to him: "Are you the Messiah?" He replied, "I am not," and pointed to the One who came after him, the straps of whose sandals he was unworthy to untie (John 1:19–27).

John's ministry was cut short by the murderous act of King Herod Antipas, but apparently his influence lingered on. In the Book of Acts we read of Apollos and other Christians who had been baptized in John's baptism of repentance rather than in the name of Jesus (Acts 18:24, 25; 19:1–7).

We do not know how widespread John the Baptist's movement was after his death. Scattered hints from church history suggest that it may have been more significant than we customarily understand. We do know of at least one sect, the Mandaeans, that exalted the Baptist over Jesus. Remnants of the sect survive to this day in Mesopotamia.

This background helps us understand the reference to John the Baptist in John 1:6–8 with its affirmation and denial. John was a good man—a great man—but he wasn't the Light. God raised him up and sent him on a mission—to testify to the Light that was about to come.

Stanza #3: The Light Comes Into the World (John 1:9–13)

> The true light that gives light to everyone was coming into the world. He was in the world, and though the world was made through him, the world did not recognize him. He came to that which was his own, but his own did not receive him. Yet to all who did receive him, to those who believed in his name, he gave the right to become children of God—children born not of natural descent, nor of human decision or a husband's will, but born of God.

The rhythmic pattern again occurs: His own . . . His own . . . receive. . . . receive. And once again the tone changes. We hear the minor key of sadness as the Light comes into the world—the world that He had made—but instead of welcome He faces rejection. The world did not recognize Him, although He was and is the Source of all that is. The world did not receive Him. People turned their backs on Him and finally murdered Him.

The original Greek makes a subtle distinction in John 1:11 in the two places translated "his own." In biblical Greek, all nouns and pronouns are distinguished by being masculine, feminine, or neuter. "That which was his own" (literally, "his own things") is neuter, whereas "his own" who did not receive Him is masculine. That is to say, the Light came to His own things—the world that He had made—but its *people* did not receive Him. Nature obeyed His voice: the storm became calm and the sun covered its face as Jesus hung on Calvary. Nature didn't reject Him but people did: they turned away from Him, refusing to hear, despising Him, and ultimately nailing Him to a cross.

How could it be that the Creator of all—the Word, the Life, the Light—could be unrecognized and rejected? The answer lies in the great conflict between good and evil, between the light and the darkness. Jesus Himself, in His conversation with Nicodemus, explained why He would be rejected: "This is the verdict: Light has come into the world, but people loved darkness instead of light because their deeds were evil. Everyone who does evil hates the light, and will not come into the light for fear that their deeds will be exposed" (John 3:19, 20).

Again, after Jesus had healed the man born blind, the religious leaders opposed Him, calling Him a Sabbath breaker and a bad man. He replied, "For judgment I have come into this world, so that the blind will see and those who see will become blind" (John 9:39). The story of Jesus is a story of rejection. When the Light came into the world, its people rose up in protest. "Put out the light!" they shouted.

But not everyone turned their backs on Him. To those who received Him and believed in His name, He opened up new life and new possibilities. They became new creatures—children of God born not by the usual human processes but by God Himself.

How will we respond when the Light shines on us? This passage shows that we become children of God simply by receiving Him. By welcoming the light, we discover that Jesus is the best Friend of all.

Stanza #4: The Glory of the Word-Made-Flesh (John 1:14–18)

The Word became flesh and made his dwelling among us. We have seen his glory, the glory of the one and only Son, who came from the Father, full of grace and truth. (John testified concerning him. He cried out, saying, "This is the one I spoke about when I said, 'He who comes after me has surpassed me because he was before me.'") Out of his fullness we have all received grace in place of grace already given. For the law was given through Moses; grace and truth came through Jesus Christ. No one has ever seen God, but the one and only Son, who is himself God and is in closest relationship with the Father, has made him known.

In this final stanza the hymn rises to a glorious climax. The beloved John finds himself overwhelmed with wonder as he contemplates the life of Jesus, the eternal Word, pitching His tent among us, full of grace and truth. From eternity He was the Word—the agent of God to the universe. He was the Angel who wrestled with Jacob (Gen. 32:22–32), accompanied the twelve tribes in their desert wanderings (Exod. 32:34), and appeared to Joshua (Josh. 5:13–15) and Gideon (Judg. 6:11–24) and others.

Throughout the course of human history God spoke. He did not leave humanity to grope in silence, alone in an alien cosmos. "In the past God spoke to our ancestors through the prophets at many times and in various ways, but in these last days he has spoken to us by his Son, whom he appointed heir of all things, and through whom also he made the universe" (Heb. 1:1, 2). Now God spoke in supreme fashion. "The Word became flesh" (John 1:14). Humans not only heard—they saw, touched, and experienced the Word. The Word became flesh and His name was Jesus.

What was He like? Glorious, with the glory that comes from God alone. Not glorious because of thunder and lightning as at Sinai. Not glorious in pomp and pageantry, but glorious in *life*. The life of Jesus, with its unceasing deeds of kindness and love, of gentleness and purity, was glorious as no life before or after has been. Now we know what humanity may be in its fullness.

In attempting to describe Jesus, John in this passage turns to an old Greek word and gives it new meaning—"grace." Originally the word *charis*, from which English words like "charisma" and "charismatic" derive, meant either "gratitude" or "attractiveness." We find *charis* used occasionally with these meanings in the New Testament, as we do in everyday speech: we call the blessing over a meal "the grace," and we may name a beautiful baby girl Grace.

The early Christians developed *charis* far beyond these ancient uses, however. Seeking to express the impact of Jesus, they took a familiar word in the Greek language and poured into it new meaning. *Charis* became a distinctly Christian word, as it is today—not a new word, but an old one filled with new content.

Grace expresses God's incredible goodness and kindness to us who do not deserve it. Grace is God seeking the lost and winning us to Himself—forgiving, transforming, and restoring us. Grace was in the world before the Word became flesh, but only when Jesus came did we understand what it really meant. He was full of grace. His entire life, ministry, and teachings demonstrated grace.

In John 1:14–18, we find the word *charis* (grace) four times. Two of these occurrences are in verse 16, where the text literally reads: "Out of his fullness we have all received grace in place of grace already given." Interestingly, we do not find the word again in John's Gospel. But we see Jesus. He *is* grace! Everything that follows the prologue shows Jesus, full of grace and truth.

We have devoted most of this chapter to studying John 1:1–18. Obviously, it won't be possible to deal with the rest of the material of the four Gospels in such detail. This examination of the prologue to John's Gospel, however, has not only demonstrated how rich is the biblical text and how rewarding its careful study but has also given us a magnificent entry into the story of Jesus that has no beginning and no end.

QUESTIONS FOR DISCUSSION

1. In the past and even today, some people have held that Jesus was created at a point in time. How does John 1:1–18 refute this idea?

2. How does Jesus's "biography" in the Gospels differ from other kinds of biographies? What does this tell us?

3. Why was Jesus rejected by His own people? What about today?

4. What sort of life does Jesus offer us?

4

God with Us

OBJECTIVES
- Separate the biblical record of Jesus's birth from popular traditions.

- Compare and contrast Matthew's and Luke's accounts of Jesus's birth.

SCRIPTURE
- Matthew 1, 2; Luke 1:5–2:52

Christians usually celebrate the birth of Jesus on December 25. In many countries that event is observed as part of a festive season that includes pageantry and special services. Reenactments are common, with portrayals of Mary and Joseph, the babe in the manger, shepherds, and wise men, who are given the names Melchior, Caspar, and Balthazar.

As deeply rooted as the observance of Christmas is, much of what is commonly practiced is based primarily on tradition, not on the Gospels. Two Gospels, Matthew and Luke, open with birth stories of Jesus, but they differ in major ways from what Christians believe and practice.

First, the date of December 25 is almost certainly wrong. Luke informs us that when Jesus was born, "there were shepherds living out in the fields nearby, keeping watch over their flocks at night" (Luke 2:8). But not in late December: the weather is too cold in Palestine, and flocks are kept inside for the night.

How then did December 25 come to be observed? It was already in use in the Roman Empire in connection with a pagan festival, the Saturnalia, that celebrated the commencement of the gradual lengthening of daylight hours after the encroachment of the dark during the autumn months. As Christianity spread throughout the Roman Empire, eventually supplanting the old paganism, various festivals from the old religion became attached to Christian practices. The most notable was the observance of Sunday, the long-standing day of worship of the sun, in place of the biblically based Sabbath, the seventh day of the week.

Christian pageants often feature the wise men, the Magi, as kings. Matthew's Gospel, which records their visit to the infant Jesus, gives no such designation to them.

They came to worship the One who had been born King of the Jews (Matt. 2:2) and they brought gifts fit for a king (v. 11), but they themselves were not kings.

Further, some time elapsed between the birth of Jesus and the visit of the Magi. Again Matthew corrects the common misunderstanding, telling us that when the wise men arrived in Bethlehem, the baby Jesus was no longer in a manger at the inn but in a house (v. 11). The passage of time, presumably several months at a minimum, is also indicated by the orders issued by Herod the Great. Rather than commanding that all the newborn children in Bethlehem be slaughtered, Herod directed that all boys two years old and under be killed. This, Matthew notes, was "in accordance with the time he had learned from the Magi" (v. 16).

Finally, the names attributed to the Magi—Melchior, Caspar, and Balthazar—come wholly from tradition, not the Bible. We do not even know that the Magi were three in number; this tradition arose from the fact that they brought three types of gifts—gold, frankincense, and myrrh.

To gain a true picture of the birth of Jesus, we must rely on the Gospel accounts. What we find is a scene much humbler than that of the Christmas celebrations. It is a picture of lowliness that shocks us but that, as we contemplate it, causes us to bow in adoration with the shepherds and Magi before the King who is Immanuel, God with us.

In the beginning of the Christian church, the Gospels circulated separately as individual documents. Only in the second century were Matthew, Mark, Luke, and John brought together for followers of Jesus to study. This means that for several generations Christians learned about Jesus's birth from either the Gospel of Matthew or from Luke's writings. These accounts, read separately, present significantly different perspectives, which nevertheless are complementary.

According to Matthew

Matthew opens his Gospel with "the genealogy of Jesus the Messiah the son of David, the son of Abraham" (Matt. 1:1). The wording immediately underscores the purpose of this Gospel: it will portray Jesus as son of *David* and of *Abraham*.

The long list of ancestors clearly establishes that Jesus comes from royal blood: He is in the line of the kings of Judah. He is a king, as the Magi's question emphasizes: "Where is the one who has been born king of the Jews?" (Matt. 2:2). His birth in Bethlehem fulfills the prophecy of Micah 5:2. Matthew quotes the ancient words but with a significant variation. Whereas the Hebrew text reads, "Bethlehem . . . small among the *clans* of Judah," Matthew interprets it as "Bethlehem . . . are by no means least among the *rulers* of Judah" (Matt. 2:6).

Matthew sets the birth story in the context of a clash of royal claims. Jesus is born in the days of Herod the king, but He, Jesus, is King of the Jews. His royal dignity is corroborated by genealogy and birthplace, by the fulfillment of Scripture, by Magi, and by the star.

The theme of kingship appears many times in Matthew's Gospel. Jesus begins His preaching with the pronouncement, "Repent, for the kingdom of heaven has come near" (4:17), and throughout His ministry He makes frequent references to it—we find about fifty references to the kingdom in this Gospel. At last, at the conclusion of His ministry, Jesus enters Jerusalem in triumph, riding a colt down the Mount of Olives, following the path traced by Israel's rulers of old (Matt. 21:1–9; see also Zech. 9:9). And finally, He hangs on a Roman cross that, according to Matthew, bears the inscription, "THIS IS JESUS, THE KING OF THE JEWS" (Matt. 27:37).

Matthew stresses that Jesus, Son of David, was also son of Abraham. That is, Jesus was a Jew, and Matthew writes his Gospel especially for a Jewish audience. Although Matthew does not quote the Lord's words to Abraham that all nations will be blessed by his offspring (Gen. 12:3; 18:18; 22:18), the promise echoes in the opening assertion that Jesus is the son of Abraham.

Matthew does, however, frequently refer to sayings of the Old Testament that Jesus fulfilled. Often Matthew uses formulaic expression to capture the idea: "All this took place to fulfill what the Lord had said through the prophet" (Matt. 1:22. See also 2:5, 17, 23; 4:14; 8:17; 12:17–21; 13:35; 21:4; 27:9). These references presuppose an acquaintance with the Scriptures such as Jewish readers would have.

Women in Christ's Genealogy

At first reading, the long list of names in the first chapter of Matthew seems uninteresting. But look closely and a fascinating feature emerges: four women are mentioned.

That is unusual. Genealogies customarily dealt with males, as do most of Matthew's (and all of Luke's). But Matthew singles out four women in Jesus's ancestry: Tamar, mother of Perez and Zerah (Matt. 1:3); Rahab, mother of Boaz (v. 5); Ruth, mother of Obed (v. 5); and Solomon's mother Bathsheba, who had been the wife of Uriah the Hittite (v. 6, see also 2 Sam. 12:9).

Each of these women had an unusual, even notorious, background: Tamar disguised herself as a prostitute and became pregnant with Perez through her father-in-law, Judah. Her sad story is told in Genesis 38. The Canaanite Rahab was a prostitute in Jericho who hid the Israelite spies sent out by Joshua to reconnoiter the city (see Josh. 2:1–21). Ruth was another person outside the Israelite circle. A Moabite, she displayed an unusual level of devotion to Naomi, her Jewish mother-in-law. The book of Ruth tells the story. Bathsheba, the lawful spouse of one of King David's chief soldiers, Uriah the Hittite, was seduced by the king in a fit of passion. David then contrived to have Uriah killed in battle so that he could have Bathsheba (2 Sam. 11, 12).

Why does Matthew insert these four women into his genealogy of Jesus, the King of the Jews? He doesn't tell us, so we can only speculate. I think these women are intended to show the brokenness of the human condition—how messed up people were and still are. These women weren't particularly bad people. On the contrary, at least one—Ruth—possessed an exemplary character. Two of them were victims of the customs that prevailed in their times: Tamar should have been given to Judah's youngest son, Shela, after the older brothers died in turn; denied justice, she resorted to desperate measures. Bathsheba fell prey to David's lust, as he played the part of a despot who seized anyone and anything he desired. We do not know Rahab's background, but she showed faith in the God of the Israelites and is even listed among the heroes of faith (Heb. 11:31).

By including these women, Matthew shows us that the Messiah is for all people—regardless of race, circumstances of life, and brokenness. His name is Jesus, Savior, "because he will save his people from their sins" (1:21) and especially, perhaps, women, who since the Fall of humankind have so often—up to this day—been exploited, denied justice, and treated as objects of men's sexual pleasure.

Joseph: A Righteous Man

In this connection we should notice how Joseph, the husband of Mary but not the father of Jesus (Matt. 1:18), appears in the story. Joseph was a righteous and faithful man (v. 19), apparently much older than Mary. Joseph and Mary were pledged to marry when a startling fact came to light—Mary was already pregnant! They had not had intimate relations, so the news must have come as a devastating blow to Joseph. By law he could have exposed Mary to public shame and disgrace; but good man that he was, he resolved to handle the matter discreetly. He would quietly divorce her. But he did not follow through with the plan. The Lord intervened, sending an angel to assure Joseph in a dream that Mary had not been unfaithful to him: the child growing in her womb had been conceived through the Holy Spirit, not by a man.

Immanuel: "God with Us"

Before moving on to Luke's account of Jesus's birth, we must notice Matthew's comment: "All this took place to fulfill what the Lord had said through the prophet: 'The virgin will conceive and give birth to a son, and they will call him Immanuel' (which means 'God with us')" (Matt. 1:22, 23). This is the only place in the four Gospels where Jesus is called Immanuel. How well it describes the life of Jesus of Nazareth!

According to Luke

Matthew positions the story of the birth of Jesus in a Jewish context. In his Gospel, it is to Joseph rather than Mary that the Lord appears in a series of dreams (Matt. 1:20; 2:13, 19, 22). The reverse is the case in Luke's account. Mary dominates while Joseph remains in the background. God sends the angel Gabriel to the young woman and informs her that she is to bear a child through a miraculous conception Who "will be great and will be called the Son of the Most High" (Luke 1:32). He is to receive the throne of David and reign forever (1:32, 33).

Luke further informs us about Mary's visit to her relative Elizabeth, with whom she stays for about three months (Luke 1:39–45, 56). Here, while with Elizabeth, Mary bursts into a song of praise (vv. 46–55), known as the Magnificat by many Christians for whom it is a regular part of worship.

We find no mention of the Magi or the star in Luke's account, nor of Herod the Great's slaughter of the children of Bethlehem. Instead, we read that shepherds, keeping watch over their flocks by night, are privileged to be told of the birth of a Savior, Christ the Lord. The shepherds respond eagerly to the angelic visit and hurry off to find the babe wrapped in cloths and lying in a manger (Luke 2:8–20).

If one reads the two accounts separately, the contrast is stark. For Matthew it is a royal setting and for Luke it is a wider setting—the Gentile world. With the opening words of his Gospel, Luke dedicates his account to a Gentile, Theophilus, apparently someone of note of whom we have no record. The approach followed by Luke was a common practice to commend one's writing to a wider audience. Luke, who also wrote the book of Acts, has a keen interest in history. He locates the story of Jesus in time, spelling out contemporaries: tetrarchs, emperors, governors, kings, and high priests (Luke 3:1, 2). Matthew, however, simply mentions that Jesus was born during the reign of Herod the Great (Matt. 2:1).

Luke also includes a genealogy of Jesus (3:23–38). His list of ancestors differs from Matthew's in several respects, the most notable being that whereas Matthew traces Jesus's lineage through David to Abraham, Luke goes all the way back to Adam. This makes the point that Jesus is not just a Jew: He belongs to the whole human race, Gentile as well as Jewish.

We shall study Jesus's ministry in subsequent chapters of this book, noting the differing selection of materials and emphases of each of the Gospel writers. Luke's account, we will find, is notable for its portrayal of Jesus as the Man for all sorts of people: for Gentiles and Jews, as well as those on the margins of society like tax collectors, lepers, Romans, and women. All this is part of an intentional presentation designed to attract Gentile readers to Jesus.

In Matthew's account of the birth of Jesus, the accent falls on Joseph, not Mary. Joseph is mentioned by name seven times, but Mary only four. Also mentioned are two kings—Herod and Jesus—costly gifts, Magi who come from afar to worship, and the flight to Egypt to escape the evil designs of a jealous king. This account includes no manger or shepherds, only royalty.

In Luke, there is no room in the inn. The newborn babe is wrapped in cloths and placed in a manger! Is this the way to greet royalty? No wise men show up carrying treasures; instead there are only shepherds, who were considered so low on the social scale that their testimony was routinely discounted in courts of law.

The accounts don't contradict one another; rather, they are complementary. Matthew is framing his Gospel to portray Jesus as King of the Jews, Israel's long-awaited Messiah. Luke, on the other hand, writing for a Gentile audience, presents the lowliness of Jesus, the Man for others. Because He, the King of heaven, left the glory that was rightfully His and took the form of a servant, every son and daughter of Adam, no matter how lowly, may find in Him a Savior and Friend.

Born of a Virgin

While the two birth accounts highlight different details, they agree in essentials. They both affirm that Jesus was born of a virgin—He was conceived without a human father. Luke in his Gospel devotes some space to the birth of John the Baptist, which also involved a miraculous element. Jesus's birth differs radically from John's, however. John was born of parents who had passed the age of childbearing; nevertheless, Elizabeth was enabled to conceive (Luke 1:5–25). John's birth was highly unusual but not unique in sacred history: nearly two thousand years earlier, Sarah had conceived in old age and borne Isaac to Abraham.

Jesus, however, was born of a virgin by the Holy Spirit. There had never before been such a birth in human history, nor can there ever be another. "What is conceived in her is from the Holy Spirit," the angel told Joseph (Matt. 1:20). "The Holy Spirit will come on you, and the power of the Most High will overshadow you," Gabriel told Mary (Luke 1:35). No human father was involved, but conception by divine intervention.

In their respective genealogies, Matthew and Luke carefully avoid leaving the impression that Joseph was the biological father of Jesus. Matthew traces Jesus's lineage from Abraham (Abraham begot Isaac, Isaac begot Jacob, etc.), but when he comes to Joseph he changes the pattern to "Joseph, the husband of Mary, and Mary was the mother of Jesus, who is called the Messiah" (Matt. 1:16). Luke commences his genealogy with: "He [Jesus] was the son, so it was thought, of Joseph, the son of Heli" (Luke 3:23).

Not surprisingly, from the earliest years of Christianity, critics and skeptics have cast scorn on the idea of a virgin birth. In Jesus's lifetime He faced mocking about who His father really was. In a debate about His origin, the Jewish leaders taunted Him, "We are not illegitimate children" (John 8:41), implying that Jesus was born out of wedlock. Later, a story circulated that a Roman soldier impregnated Mary, a naïve girl who didn't yet know the facts of life.

Today, the virgin birth is still widely rejected. Not only unbelievers, but many theologians and pastors, have abandoned the teaching because it flies in the face of human experience. But so do all the miracles associated with Jesus, including the crowning one—His resurrection from the dead.

The virgin birth and the Resurrection are like bookends on the story of Jesus. At both ends of His life the divine intervened in ways utterly outside the usual course of human events. From a natural viewpoint, both are impossible to accept. But if Jesus of Nazareth was in fact Who the Bible says He was—the Word made flesh, Immanuel, God with us—then the impossible becomes reality.

Mary

We should pause to think more about Mary, the virgin chosen by God to bear the Messiah. By any reckoning she must be considered a remarkable person. Women married young in the society of her times; since she wasn't yet married, she was probably quite young, as a girl's betrothal was often at about twelve years of age. What a mind-boggling declaration for any young woman to receive!

But Mary's response to the bewildering words was simply: "I am the Lord's servant. . . . May your word to me be fulfilled" (Luke 1:38). Here is a young person of faith and courage who knows the Lord personally and is accustomed to submitting to His will. Mary is an example for all followers of Jesus, whether they be eighteen or eighty-one.

Unfortunately, after the time of the New Testament writings, ideas from the Greco-Roman world began to be attached to Mary: that she herself was conceived in such a way as to be without flaw (the immaculate conception); that she forever remained a virgin; and that raised to a status almost equal to that of Jesus, she became the mediatrix between God and humanity. All such teachings are utterly without biblical support. Mary, who was a wonderful example of trust and submission to God's will, was another human being like us. She wasn't faultless; like us she needed the salvation that her Son came to bring to all humankind.

Jesus and Moses

Matthew alone records the flight to Egypt to escape the murderous plot of King Herod. The gifts of the Magi supplied the means necessary for this journey. But Matthew adds a prophetic insight: "And so was fulfilled what the Lord had said through the prophet: 'Out of Egypt I called my son'" (Matt. 2:15, quoting Hosea 11:1).

Especially in the Gospel of Matthew we see Jesus set forth as the new Moses. Not only does Jesus, like Moses, come out of Egypt, but He is teacher par excellence, proclaiming God's will in five great sermons, just as Moses's teaching comprised five books:

Matthew 5–7	The Sermon on the Mount
Matthew 10	The Sermon on Discipleship
Matthew 13	The Sermon on the Kingdom
Matthew 18	The Sermon on the Church
Matthew 24, 25	The Sermon on the End

Thus, we see that Jesus is not only King—He is the new Moses.

Matthew tells us that, after a short stay in Egypt, Joseph was instructed to return to Israel. Herod the Great had died, but his son Archaelus, also ruthless, reigned in Judea. So Joseph decided to go north to Galilee, where another of Herod's sons, Antipas, had been made king (Matt. 2:19–22). Thus, Jesus, born in Bethlehem, grew up in Nazareth. Matthew's Gospel passes over the intervening years and moves straight to Jesus's ministry. Luke's, however, supplies additional information that helps us flesh out the story.

Circumcision and Dedication of Jesus

Jesus grew up within the orbit of Judaism, like any other Jewish child. On the eighth day, He was circumcised and named (Luke 2:21); thirty-three days later, following the Levitical law, He was presented to the Lord in consecration (see Lev. 12:1–8). The Law stipulated that after giving birth to a son, the mother was to offer in a ceremony of purification a lamb and a pigeon or dove. However, if she could not afford a lamb, two doves or two pigeons might be substituted. Joseph and Mary could not afford a lamb (Luke 2:22–24).

This visit to the temple in fulfillment of the Law of Moses took on a deeper significance, however. Two godly people, Simeon and Anna, received prophetic insight concerning the baby and made dramatic pronouncements concerning who He was and the mission that He would accomplish.

Simeon, taking Jesus in his arms, praised God that he had been spared to see in person the One who would be a light to the nations and the glory of Israel. Then, in a chilling prediction of Jesus's rejection, he told Mary: "A sword will pierce your own soul too" (Luke 2:35).

Anna, an eighty-four-year-old prophetess, came up to Joseph and Mary. She gave thanks to God for the redemption that God would bring about through the child (vv. 36–38). We can only imagine the emotions that must have swirled through the minds of Jesus's parents. How were they to raise such a child of divine purpose? What would the future bring? What did Simeon mean by the sword that would pierce the soul of Mary?

Luke does not reveal Joseph's thinking to us, but twice in his account he shares Mary's heart: "Mary treasured up all these things and pondered them in her heart" (2:19, after the visit by the shepherds), and "his mother treasured all these things in her heart" (2:51, after the visit to the temple when Jesus was twelve).

Jesus grew up in Nazareth. Like any other child, His body developed and His mind expanded. He was an intelligent child, "filled with wisdom" (Luke 2:40), and "in favor with God and man" (v. 52). In later centuries, some Christians invented all sorts of stories about the child Jesus. They imagined Him performing miracles—shaping birds out of clay and causing them to fly, reciting the alphabet in infancy, and so on. No. This boy of miraculous birth—this God-man, Immanuel—grew up with developing body and brain like any other child.

When did the boy Jesus begin to realize Who He was? When in that developing consciousness did He begin to grasp that He had come with a divine mission to fulfill? We do not know, but Luke's Gospel makes clear that by age twelve Jesus already had insights into both His identity and mission. When His parents, following their custom, took Jesus with them to Jerusalem for the Passover festival, their son slipped away from the group that was returning to Nazareth. After three days of stressful searching, Joseph and Mary found Jesus among the rabbis in the temple courts, engaged in earnest discussion. "'Why were you searching for me?' he asked. 'Didn't you know I had to be in my Father's house?'" (Luke 2:49). "My Father's house" was not the home in Nazareth, but the temple; it was not Joseph as His father, but God.

During those days in Jerusalem, as the twelve-year-old Jesus witnessed the slaying of the Passover lamb and later as He sat among the rabbis, did the mystery of His mission begin to dawn? Could it be that He would in due time be God's Passover Lamb?

But for now, back to Nazareth. Humbly, obediently, He returned with Joseph and Mary to Galilee. There He would work quietly, helping Joseph at the carpenter's bench. There He would continue to think, pray, and grow. And at last the moment in heaven's timetable would arrive. The call would come to Him—clear and insistent—and He would leave the carpenter's shop forever.

QUESTIONS FOR DISCUSSION

1. What are some misconceptions surrounding Jesus's birth? Where did these come from?

2. Note some of the differences between Luke's and Matthew's portrayals of Jesus's birth. How do these differences fill out the story?

3. Why does the virgin birth matter?

5

Man with a Mission

OBJECTIVES   • Describe Jesus's family background.

• Understand why Jesus was baptized.

• Learn the significance of Jesus's temptation.

SCRIPTURE   • Matthew 3:1—4:11; Mark 1:1–13; Luke 3:1–23; John 1:19–34

Jesus was about thirty years old when He embarked upon His public ministry (see Luke 3:23). His life had been spent in Nazareth, a small town in Galilee, where He worked as a carpenter (Mark 6:3). But one day He left the carpenter's bench and Nazareth forever. He left in obedience to a divine summons. The Call had come and was resounding in His being. It was time to go.

Except perhaps for His mother, Jesus's family did not encourage Him in the decision that would uproot Him from home and friends. He had four brothers—James, Joseph, Judas, and Simeon—as well as sisters whose names we do not know (Mark 6:3). These family members no doubt were stepbrothers and stepsisters rather than siblings. They show up several times in the Gospel accounts, and always in a manner that indicates a lack of understanding of Jesus's mission.

During His ministry in Galilee, Jesus became hugely popular with crowds who followed Him everywhere He went. So busy did He become that at times He and the disciples could not find opportunity even to eat. That was too much for the family: "When his family heard about this, they went to take charge of him, for they said, 'He is out of his mind'" (Mark 3:20, 21). Jesus's mother and brothers arrived at the house where He was teaching. Standing outside, they sent a message to call Him out to them. But when Jesus received the information, He didn't move. "'Who are my mother and brothers?'" He asked. Then he looked at those seated in a circle around Him and said, 'Here are my mother and my brothers! Whoever does God's will is my brother and sister and mother'" (vv. 33–35).

On another occasion Jesus's brothers offered unsolicited advice concerning the conduct of His mission. The Feast of Tabernacles was approaching, and they told Him that, if He wanted to be a public figure, He should go down to Judea to attend the festival. The beloved John, who relates the incident, adds, "For even his own brothers did not believe in him" (John 7:5).

The manner in which Jesus's family relates to Him in these instances is that of older siblings attempting to correct a younger family member whose behavior they cannot understand and who needs to be put on the right course. We cannot envisage younger siblings setting out like this to correct an older brother.

Gathering together the clues from the Gospel accounts, we can therefore reconstruct an outline of Jesus's family. Mary was Joseph's second wife and much younger than he. Joseph already had at least six living children—four sons and at least two daughters—when Mary gave birth to Jesus. So the family dynamic included the tensions that often come with blended families.

Joseph disappears from the narrative along the way. We last read of him in the account of the visit to Jerusalem when Jesus was twelve. Presumably Joseph had died before Jesus embarked upon His mission. Interestingly, Ellen G. White notes that the report of John the Baptist's activities "was told in the carpenter's shop that *had been* Joseph's."[1]

Would Joseph have been supportive of the son of Mary when Jesus began to dream about a mission that would take Him far away? Perhaps; we cannot know. The decision was Jesus's alone. The Call had come; He would answer the Call.

Jesus was the first to respond to that Call. Over the centuries, thousands of young people, and some older ones, would follow in His footsteps. They would leave home and family, work and friends—their comfort zone—to go near or far, to the ends of the earth, and wherever that Call directed.

The Call still comes. It came to me not at a carpenter's bench but in a laboratory, where as a young man I worked in research and development. It led me far from the town where I grew up—far from family, friends, and my native land.

It was—and is—the Call to join Jesus's mission. We can never be just like Him; His mission was infinitely greater than any task in which we can be engaged. But we can walk in His footsteps: when the Call comes to us and we feel it in every fiber of our being, we can say, "Yes!"

Jesus's Baptism

All four Gospel accounts link the commencement of Jesus's ministry to the preaching of John the Baptist. They quote the Book of Isaiah as foretelling John's message and work:

A voice of one calling:
"In the wilderness prepare
   the way for the Lord;
Make straight in the desert
A highway for our God." (Isa. 40:3;
      see also Matt. 3:3; Mark 1:2, 3;
   Luke 3:4–6; John 1:23)

Mark also includes a prediction from the Old Testament: "See, I will send my messenger ahead of you, who will prepare your way" (Mark 1:2; see Mal. 3:1).

In the next chapter of this book, we shall devote more attention to this forerunner of Jesus. John is a major figure of the New Testament; his life and work hold valuable lessons for us who, late in earth's history, await the coming of Jesus a second time. Here we shall limit discussion to the circumstances surrounding Jesus's baptism.

Jesus and John

John had never met Jesus. He was born in the south, in the hill country of Judea, and grew up in the desert. Jesus of Nazareth lived many miles away in Galilee.

While Jesus was still working in obscurity at the carpenter's bench, John burst like a meteor on the Judean scene. He came seemingly out of nowhere, proclaiming a startling message: "Repent, for the kingdom of heaven has come near" (Matt. 3:2). In dress and lifestyle he stood apart: his clothes were made of camel's hair, he wore a leather belt around the waist, and he lived on locusts—most likely the pods of the carob tree—and wild honey (v. 4).

John's unusual dress would have reminded the Jews of Elijah, the Old Testament prophet, who also wore garments made from camel's hair (see 2 Kings 1:7, 8). He too had burst on the scene proclaiming a message of divine judgment (1 Kings 17:1). Bold and fearless, he stood before kings and did not shrink from delivering God's word. Finally, at the close of a long ministry, Elijah had been spared from death: he was translated—taken directly to heaven in a chariot of fire (2 Kings 2:11, 12).

But there was more about the Baptist to arouse deep interest and speculation. The very last words of the Old Testament foretold the return of Elijah to this earth: "See, I will send the prophet Elijah to you before that great and dreadful day of the Lord comes" (Mal. 4:5).

Message of John

The people of Israel, seeing and hearing John the Baptist, could not escape the parallels with the Old Testament prophet. Could this be the fulfillment of Malachi's prophecy?

The Baptist's message contained seven distinct features:

1. It was about *time*: "The kingdom of heaven has come *near*" (or "at hand"; see Matt. 3:2). Life would not go on as it had been; a new age was dawning. We call such a message "eschatological," a word derived from the Greek *eschatōn*, which means "the end."

2. It was about *God's rule breaking in*: "The kingdom of heaven has come near." For long years, kings and rulers had held sway over humanity, but now God was about to intervene. The Old Testament had told of this time: "In the time of those kings, the God of heaven will set up a kingdom

that will never be destroyed" (Dan. 2:44; see also 7:14, 27).

3. It was about *the imminent appearing of the Promised One*, the Messiah: "But after me comes one who is more powerful than I, whose sandals I am not worthy to carry," declared John the Baptist (Matt. 3:11).

4. It was about *decision*: "Who warned you to flee from the coming wrath?. . . . The ax is already at the root of the trees, and every tree that does not produce good fruit will be cut down and thrown into the fire," John challenged his hearers (Matt. 3:7, 10).

5. It was about *repentance*: "Repent, for the kingdom of heaven has come near" (Matt. 3:2). "Repentance," *metanoia* in the original language, signifies a break with the past. It denotes a sorrow for sin and a turning away from it to God. Repentance is a change of heart and life that is ongoing, not just a temporary or emotional experience.

6. It is about *new conduct*: "Produce fruit in keeping with repentance" (Matt. 3:8). What sort of fruit would this be? The crowd wanted to know. John answered: "Anyone who has two shirts should share with the one who has none, and anyone who has food should do the same." To tax collectors, "Don't collect any more than you are required to"; and to some soldiers, "Don't extort money and don't accuse people falsely—be content with your pay" (see Luke 3:11–14).

7. It was about *baptism*: "And so John the Baptist appeared in the wilderness, preaching a baptism of repentance for the forgiveness of sins" (Mark 1:4). This was something altogether new for the Jews. They were accustomed to converts from the Greco-Roman world undergoing baptism as a public sign that they were embracing Judaism, but not for Jews themselves. Furthermore, this baptism was to be in light of the One coming after John, who would "baptize you with the Holy Spirit and fire" (Matt. 3:11). We should note that the word "baptism" and the corresponding verb *baptizō* (to baptize) signify immersion—not sprinkling, for which a different Greek word was available.

Why Was Jesus Baptized?

When Jesus came from Galilee and requested baptism, John tried to deter Him. "I need to be baptized by you," he said, "and do you come to me?" But Jesus replied, "Let it be so now; it is proper for us to do this to fulfill all righteousness" (Matt. 3:13–15).

The other people whom John baptized confessed their sins, seeking forgiveness. Not Jesus, however. He simply asked to be baptized. He did not confess His sins because there were no sins to confess. He was the One who would solve the age-old sin problem of human guilt and brokenness. He was, as John the Baptist recognized, "the Lamb of God who takes away the sin of the world" (John 1:29).

Over the course of the centuries and still today, many followers of Jesus have placed undue emphases on the water of baptism, calling it "holy water." They have attributed magical powers to the rite of baptism as though this act in itself washes away one's sins. It does not: forgiveness of our sins is an act of our gracious God, Who delights to receive us. No water, whether set aside in a church or in a river—even the River Jordan— can of itself make us clean. No; baptism carries significance far beyond that of cleansing by water.

Jesus's baptism makes manifest this idea. If the rite of baptism is for the purpose of washing away sin, why would Jesus have asked John to baptize Him? Baptism is indeed connected to the forgiveness of sin, but in quite a different way from the cleansing by water. Repentance, confession, and baptism—these three elements combine in order to effect the transition from the old life to the new. The first two, repentance and confession, signify a heart that humbly turns away from the former life—one that forsakes reliance upon self and seeks divine mercy and forgiveness. The third element, baptism, publicly declares that this change from the old to the new has taken place (see Rom. 6:4–6) and that the person has chosen to become a follower of the Lord.

For Jesus, baptism involved no turning from a life of sin to God, but it signified a turning point—an act of public consecration to the mission for which He had come to earth. It was a turning from the structured, unhurried life of an obscure Galilean carpenter to that of an itinerant preacher Who had no place to rest His head at night (Luke 9:58).

Jesus overcame John the Baptist's objections: "It is proper to do this to fulfill all righteousness" (Matt. 3:15). That is, *obedience* to the divine will mandated this action. Jesus would set us an example; He would be our Head, going on before us, blazing the trail for us to follow. We, His followers, would be baptized just as He was baptized.

Jesus was the new Israel. God's people, despite so many admonitions, continually fell short of the divine will. Now, in Himself, Jesus would embody God's perfect plan and will, fulfilling all righteousness.

The Heavenly Affirmation

Immediately upon coming up out of the water, Jesus prayed (Luke 3:21). This is the first time in the Gospels that we find mention of His prayer life, although we may be sure that His years in Nazareth's seclusion had been bathed in communion with the Father.

Throughout Jesus's ministry, we find repeated references to His praying. He rose early in the morning while it was still dark and went away to a quiet place to start the day with God (Mark 1:35). Sometimes He spent the entire night in prayer, seeking divine wisdom and strength for fulfillment of the mission. And the final words to come from His lips as He hung upon the cross were a prayer: "Father, into your hands I commit my spirit" (Luke 23:46).

Sometimes we may think that because Jesus was the God-man, He could not have failed in His mission—that its success was assured from the outset. As it were, His story had been scripted in the courts of heaven long before He came to earth, and He knew that it would have a happy ending. This idea of predestination—that everything was predetermined by God—is still held by some people today.

If we ever begin to reason along these lines, we need to look again at Jesus's prayer life. For Him, communion with the Father wasn't merely a privilege—it was a necessity. Eternally one with God though He was, in becoming human like us, He emptied Himself and became a servant (Phil. 2:6, 7). He met temptation as we must meet temptation—by calling on divine help.

The plan of our redemption involved risk and eternal loss. Jesus could have failed in His mission. What that would have meant for Him we can scarcely contemplate, but we can be certain what the outcome would have been for us: we would be forever in our sins, without hope, lost eternally.

So, as Jesus comes out of the baptismal water, He kneels to pray. Throughout His ministry He will pray. As the mission hurries to a fearful climax, He prays agonizingly in the Garden of Gethsemane, sweating drops of blood. And on the cross we hear His moan of dereliction: "My God, my God, why have you forsaken me?" (Matt. 27:46). No make-believe here. No scripted endings. Only struggle, conflict with the forces of evil, and ultimate triumph through utter dependence on divine power.

There, on the banks of the Jordan, Jesus's prayer received a dramatic, three-fold answer. The heavens were split open, the Holy Spirit descended in bodily form like a dove upon His head, and a voice proclaimed: "This is my Son, whom I love; with him I am well pleased" (Matt. 3:17).

This heavenly affirmation as Jesus embarked on His public ministry contains several Old Testament allusions. In Mark's Gospel, the verb used for the opening heavens literally means "torn open" (Mark 1:10) and recalls the longing of God's people for Him to manifest Himself through a dramatic parting of the heavens (see Ps. 144:5; Isa. 64:1). This divine intervention was associated with renewed activity of the Holy Spirit (Isa. 63:11). And the divine words of affirmation echo two Old Testament passages: "You are my Son" (Ps. 2:7) and the Servant Songs of Isaiah (as in Isa. 42:1). The first part expresses the dignity that belongs to the Messiah, whereas the allusion to Isaiah makes clear that Jesus's mission will be that of a servant. His work would not be stamped with pomp and power, but with suffering and rejection, as Isaiah 53 foretold.

Before leaving Jesus's baptism, there is a personal, individual dimension we should notice. At that scene by the Jordan, all three members of the divine Trinity were manifested—Father, Son, and Holy Spirit. And when we decide to follow Jesus and, like Him, enter the waters of baptism, the divine Trinity is present again. Although the heavens aren't torn open, we can be confident that the Father affirms us just as He affirmed Jesus: "This is my son [or daughter], whom I love; with him [or her] I am well pleased" (Matt. 3:17). And although no dove descends visible to the human eye, the Holy Spirit just as surely rests upon us as we embark on our walk with the Lord.

In the Desert

"Then Jesus was led by the Spirit into the wilderness to be tempted by the devil" (Matt. 4:1; see also Mark 1:12; Luke 4:1, 2).

It was the Holy Spirit who led Jesus into the desert, repeating the experience of Israel of old. Jesus didn't invite temptation: He was led into the desert and there the devil came to Him. In Matthew 4:1, the original of "to be tempted by the devil" may be translated to express either *purpose*—"for the purpose of being tempted," or *result*—"and the result was that he was tempted." The latter understanding is surely the correct one.

Jesus Was Tempted

Mark briefly mentions the temptations (Mark 1:13); John does not. The accounts in Matthew and Luke are very similar except for one notable difference. Whereas Matthew mentions the devil's testing Jesus concerning making stones into bread, casting Himself down from a pinnacle of the temple, and then offering to give Jesus all the kingdoms of this world, Luke reverses the order of the last two temptations.

The reason for this difference in order is not clear. It is not a matter of great significance, however. We shall follow Matthew's order in this book. It suggests a series of tests that rise in diabolical intensity to the ultimate level of Satanic pride when the devil at last suggests a shortcut to the fulfillment of Jesus's mission.

Throughout Jesus's ministry, the devil stalked Him. Jesus faced myriad tests with the final one climaxing as He hung upon the cross and was tempted to exercise His divine power and save Himself (Matt. 27:42, 43). These tests at the commencement of His ministry in many respects embody Jesus's ongoing struggle with the forces of evil.

The Three Temptations

Each of the three temptations seeks to attack the mission of the Master and to corrupt and subvert it before He even embarks upon it. Each warrants our contemplation, for, while our experience can never rise to the level of Jesus's, the manner in which He met and bested the devil still speaks to us in our tests today.

The Reality of Evil

Jesus was in a conflict with the powers of darkness, and so are we. The apostle Paul informs us: "Our struggle is not against flesh and blood, but against the rulers, against the authorities, against the powers of this dark world and against the spiritual forces of evil in the heavenly realms" (Eph. 6:12). These evil forces are much stronger than we are. If we think we can overcome them in our own strength, we will utterly fail. We need power from beyond ourselves—from God.

How to Overcome

With each test, Jesus replied, "It is written . . ."

Test: "Tell these stones to become bread." Reply: "It is written, 'Man does not live on bread alone, but on every word that comes from the mouth of God'" (Matt. 4:4; Deut. 8:3).

Test: "Throw yourself down." Reply: "It is also written, 'Do not put the Lord your God to the test'" (Matt. 4:7; Deut. 6:16; notice how Satan misuses Scripture).

Test: "All this I will give you." Reply: "It is written, 'Worship the Lord your God, and serve him only'" (Matt. 4:10; Deut. 6:13). Satan again misuses Scripture. Jesus had armed Himself with the Word of God, and so must we if we would stand in the furnace of temptation.

The Second Adam

Jesus was the second Adam, passing over the same ground as the father of the race, but overcoming where the first Adam failed. All that was lost in Adam is restored in Jesus. "For as in Adam all die, so in Christ all will be made alive" (1 Cor. 15:22; see also Rom. 5:12–21).

The Three Tests

Jesus's three temptations had their counterparts in Adam's experience. Note the parallels between the accounts in Matthew and Luke and the Genesis story of the Fall: "Did God really say, 'You must not eat from any tree in the garden? . . . You will not certainly die. . . . For God knows that when you eat from it your eyes will be opened, and you will be like God, knowing good and evil'" (Gen. 3:1, 4, 5).

The first test, for Adam and for Jesus, was over *appetite*. Jesus was in a much more weakened state: He hadn't eaten for forty days. Our first parents weren't hungry; they were surrounded by an abundance of good food. But they saw that the forbidden fruit was "good for food and pleasing to the eye" (Gen. 3:6). They yielded to the lust of the eyes (see 1 John 2:16).

The second test involved the *word of God*. The devil quoted Scripture, trying to entice Jesus to put God to the test. It was the same in Eden: the serpent cast doubt on God's word, saying, "Did God really say . . . ?" (Gen. 3:1).

The third test centered on a devilish plan to substitute the creature for the Creator. Satan was now focusing on the mission before Jesus. The Master had spent days in prayer reflecting on the path that lay ahead. He foresaw its pain, sorrow, rejection, and struggle. Now the devil comes and whispers, "No need to go through that. You can have it all now. I'll give it to you." A crown without a cross—how subtle and inviting! But here was the catch: "If you will bow down and worship me" (Matt. 4:9). What arrogance and incredible boldness!

Yet that was the same attitude displayed in the Garden of Eden. "You will be like God" (Gen. 3:4). The creature dares to take the place that only God can occupy. Jesus's reply is that of sanity rather than such madness: "Worship the Lord your God, and serve him only" (Matt. 4:10).

The Root of Temptation

Behind the tests in the desert and the Garden was lack of trust. "Everything that does not come from faith is sin" (Rom. 14:23). Conversely, we defeat the devil by relying wholly upon God, never doubting: "This is the victory that has overcome the world, even our faith" (1 John 5:4). The Bible alone cannot give victory in the hour of temptation. As the devil did with Jesus, he can quote Scripture, wresting it out of context. But when we are rooted and grounded in the Word and wholly lean upon Jesus, the devil always meets defeat.

The temptations of Jesus, coming as they did immediately after the spiritual "high" by the Jordan, warn us to be on our guard. No place or occasion provides a haven that the devil cannot penetrate. Only by constant reliance on Jesus will we be safe. We will overcome as He overcame.

QUESTIONS FOR DISCUSSION

1. In what way was John the Baptist like Elijah?

2. Since Jesus was without sin, why did He ask to be baptized?

3. How did each of the temptations challenge Jesus?

4. What lessons can we learn from Jesus's overcoming that may assist in our daily spiritual struggles?

6

The Cousins

OBJECTIVES	• Trace key moments in the life of John the Baptist.
	• Gain an understanding of why Jesus spoke so highly of John the Baptist.
	• Compare and contrast the life and work of John the Baptist with Jesus's life and work.
SCRIPTURE	• Matthew 3:1–12; 11:1–14; 17:10–13; Mark 6:14–29; Luke 1:5–24, 57–80; John 1:19–34

Of John the Baptist, Jesus observed, "I tell you, among those born of women, there is no one greater than John" (Luke 7:28). High praise indeed! On another occasion, speaking to the Jewish leaders, He described John as "a lamp that burned and gave light, and you chose for a time to enjoy his light" (John 5:35). Yet, immediately after raising John to such a high plane, Jesus noted, "the one who is least in the kingdom of God is greater than he" (Luke 7:28). The greatest but the least—how can this be?

And that is not all. John met a terrible end, which the Gospels describe in detail. After a brief but powerful ministry in which he shone like a lamp with thousands of people flocking to hear his message, he was arrested and thrown into jail. Here he languished alone, seemingly forsaken. Jesus never paid him a visit and John began to have doubts as to whether Jesus was really the Messiah. Then his life came to an abrupt end: a drunken monarch, lured into a foolish oath by a young temptress, ordered John to be beheaded.

Why did Jesus, who spoke so highly of the Baptist, not intervene to save his life? Why did Jesus not even take the time to visit him in the dungeon and cheer John's spirits? John's story fascinates and intrigues us, even as it raises some questions. We shall trace the life and work of John, seeking to comprehend why Jesus praised him so highly. We shall also compare and contrast John's life and ministry with Jesus's as we reflect on the role of each and the interaction between them.

John and Jesus

John and Jesus were cousins, John being six months older (see Luke 1:36). They had never met before Jesus came to John at the Jordan and asked to be baptized. John did not recognize Jesus, but God gave him a sign. "'And I myself did not know him,'" said John, "but the one who sent me to baptize with water told me, 'The man on whom you see the Spirit come down and remain is the one who will baptize with the Holy Spirit'" (John 1:33).

In several respects John and Jesus were similar. Both lived in obscurity until about age thirty when, heeding a divine call, they embarked on a public ministry. John's message was, "Repent for the kingdom of heaven has come near" (Matt. 3:2), and that was the identical proclamation of Jesus when He began His ministry (Matt. 4:17). Both never married. Both died young—Jesus around age thirty-three and John probably a little younger. Both for a time attracted thousands of people who were drawn to their message. Both stayed loyal to the mission that the Lord had given to them.

The differences between them were major, however. John was a man of the desert: he grew up in the wilds and conducted his ministry there. The people came to him; he didn't go to them. But Jesus grew up in a town and worked as a carpenter. When He began to preach, He went wherever the people were—in villages and hamlets, cities, and the countryside. John lived a solitary life; Jesus was a sociable person. In Jerusalem Jesus was a popular dinner guest, invited by leading people and even Pharisees. Many of Jesus's teachings were given in the setting of a meal as He reclined with others who had also been invited to the homes of wealthy people.

While Jesus's initial message was identical with the Baptist's, the scope and thrust of His teaching differed greatly from John's. John had a single focus: the Messiah is about to appear, so repent and be baptized. The Messiah will come with judgment, gathering the wheat into His barn and burning the chaff with unquenchable fire (see Matt. 3:11, 12). But Jesus announced that the kingdom of heaven had already broken in: "The kingdom of God is in your midst" (Luke 17:21). He Himself was the Coming One that John foretold. And that coming meant far more than the revealing of Israel's deliverer: Jesus in His own person made clear the very character of God.

"No one knows the Son except the Father, and no one knows the Father except the Son and those to whom the Son chooses to reveal him," said Jesus (Matt. 11:27). When Philip asked Jesus to show the Father, Jesus replied, "Don't you know me, Philip, even after I have been among you such a long time? Anyone who has seen me has seen the Father" (John 14:9).

Furthermore, John's message did not highlight the teaching that sets Christianity apart from all other religions: grace. It was Jesus, who was "full of grace and truth" (John 1:14), who by life as well as teachings shone the spotlight on this liberating idea.

The differences between the Baptist and Jesus extend far beyond their respective teachings. Above all else, their deaths stand in sharp contrast. Both met tragic ends and were murdered by wicked men. But Jesus's death was far more than an execution with a grave miscarriage of justice. "God made him who had no sin to be sin for us, so that in him we might become the righteousness of God" (2 Cor. 5:21). As Isaiah had prophesied,

> But he was pierced for our transgressions,
> he was crushed for our iniquities;
> the punishment that brought us peace was on him,
> and by his wounds we are healed.
> (Isa. 53:5)

Jesus's death is utterly unique in human history. Through it He became the Savior of the world, taking all our brokenness, rebellion, and woes upon Himself so that we might go free to new hope and new life.

The Two Ages

Jesus and John stand between two ages. John was the last representative of the era of expectation and anticipation of the Messiah. John preached that the new age, "the kingdom of heaven," was imminent. John announced it; Jesus inaugurated it. In the person of Jesus of Nazareth the new age dawned: the kingdom of heaven was at last with humans.

For some students of the life and teachings of Jesus, the term "kingdom of heaven" (or its equivalent, "kingdom of God," which occurs with equal frequency in the Gospels) may seem strange. Most of us, no matter where we live in the world, no longer are subject to kings and queens. Further, as we study the story of Jesus in the Gospels, the Messiah rejects all the trappings of royalty with which we are familiar—all the pomp, pageantry, and power. Jesus does not look like a king or act like a king.

It may help our understanding to realize that the Greek word for "kingdom," *basileia*, also means "reign" or "rule." That is, instead of "kingdom of heaven" or "kingdom of God," we can translate the expression as "rule of heaven" or "rule of God." In this sense, the kingdom of heaven began with Jesus's life and ministry. He ruled over sickness and disease; He cast out demonic powers; He commanded nature and it obeyed Him. And wherever men or women received Him, He reigned as Savior and Lord.

Jesus *was* and *is* the King. His kingdom is a real one. Across the face of the earth, when children, young people, or older ones accept Him into their lives, the kingdom (rule) of God is present. Here's a question for you. I put it to myself also: Am I already part of God's rule on earth? Do I permit Jesus to reign as Lord of my life?

The new age, the age of the kingdom of heaven, is marked by another distinctive feature: it is the age of the Holy

Spirit. John the Baptist had predicted this also. "I baptize you with water for repentance," he said. "But after me will come one who is more powerful than I. He will baptize you with the Holy Spirit and fire" (Matt. 3:11).

When Jesus came to Jerusalem for the Feast of Tabernacles, He publicly declared that the age of the Spirit was about to begin: "On the last and greatest day of the festival, Jesus stood and said in a loud voice, 'Let anyone who is thirsty come to me and drink. Whoever believes in me, as Scripture has said, rivers of living water will flow from within them'" (John 7:37, 38). John, writing his Gospel, explains that Jesus "meant the Spirit, whom those who believed in him were later to receive. Up to that time the Spirit had not been given, since Jesus had not yet been glorified" (v. 39).

Only when Jesus had completed His work on earth and ascended to the Father could the age of the Spirit be inaugurated. The outpouring of the Holy Spirit at Pentecost was a heavenly indication that Jesus's saving mission had been successfully completed. Speaking to the crowd in Jerusalem, who stood amazed at the miracle of hearing the apostles in their various mother tongues, Peter declared, "God has raised this Jesus to life, and we are all witnesses of it. Exalted to the right hand of God, he has received from the Father the promised Holy Spirit and has poured out what you now see and hear" (Acts 2:32, 33).

Wasn't the Holy Spirit already at work before Jesus came to earth? Most certainly. The Holy Spirit moved across the face of the deep at the Creation (Gen. 1:2) and moved on the hearts of men and women throughout the times of the Old Testament. But the Spirit came in a new, powerful manifestation as a result of Jesus's triumph over evil. Jesus told His followers that it would happen: "But very truly I tell you, it is for your good that I am going away. Unless I go away, the Advocate will not come to you; but if I go, I will send him to you" (John 16:7).

The Greatest … the Least

With this background we can better understand one of the most puzzling passages in the Gospels: "I tell you, among those born of women there is no one greater than John, yet the one who is least in the kingdom of God is greater than he" (Luke 7:28). Great as John was, he belonged to the old age that was passing away with the breaking in of the kingdom of heaven. The old was like a candle compared to the sun. In the dark of night we're glad for a flashlight or even a candle, but when the sun rises we turn off the light and blow out the candle.

In Matthew's Gospel, we find Jesus elaborating the idea in words that seem strange: "From the days of John the Baptist until now, the kingdom of heaven has been subjected to violence, and violent people have been raiding it. For all the Prophets and the Law prophesied until John. And if you are willing to accept it, he is the Elijah who was to come" (Matt.

11:12–14). The key to Jesus's teaching here lies in the idea of the two ages—the age leading up to John the Baptist, which is that of the Law and the Prophets, superseded by the age of the kingdom of heaven.

The language of the kingdom of heaven—"forcefully advancing" and "forceful men lay hold on it"—isn't clear, nor have I found a satisfactory explanation for it. Jesus's overall meaning in this difficult passage seems obvious, however: by His coming to earth—His life, death, and ministry in heaven—Jesus has thrown open the gates of heaven to everyone. Under the system of the old era, good as it was, only the priests could enter the Holy Place of the sanctuary and the high priest alone once a year could enter the Most Holy Place. It was a system of limited access, but now the greater sanctuary—the heavenly one—is open to all.

The Greatness of John the Baptist

Let us pause a little longer on John the Baptist, probing why Jesus commended him so highly. In John we see the true greatness that heaven calls great. John's disciples, sent by their teacher, had come to Jesus to ask whether He was truly the Messiah or if they should look for someone else to come. "As John's disciples were leaving, Jesus began to speak to the crowd about John: 'What did you go out into the wilderness to see? A reed swayed by the wind? If not, what did you go out to see? A man dressed in fine clothes? No, those who wear fine clothes are in kings' palaces. Then what did you go out to see? A prophet? Yes, I tell you, and more than a prophet" (Matt. 11:7–9).

Greatness Isn't Based on Appearances

Throughout human history and especially in our time, people tend to judge others by how they look. The all-pervasive media, especially television and movies, place a premium on outward appearances: what matters most is "looking good" and staying "cool" with the clever riposte or funny remark. Not *what* you say but *how* you say it is all-important.

A huge industry supports and feeds on this culture of appearance. Clothes, fashion, fragrances, hairdos—every aspect of the body from crown to finger to toe—are all scrutinized. With all this vast expenditure and attention on externals, how much thought focuses on the inner person where true greatness is found? John the Baptist didn't attract because of his fine clothes. He wore a rough camel's hair garment with a leather belt around the waist; it was the garb of the old-time prophet Elijah. John's greatness lay elsewhere than in appearances.

Greatness as Adherence to Principle

John wasn't a reed blown every which way by the wind. He fit the description penned by Ellen G. White: "The greatest want of the world is the want of men—men who will not be bought or sold, men who in their inmost souls are true and honest, men who do not fear to call sin by its right name, men whose conscience

as a natural gift that enabled them to look danger in the eye and not blink. They were strong in the strength that God supplies. He enabled them to be bold, even facing the prospect of their death.

Among these biblical heroes, none shines brighter than John the Baptist. He was equally fearless in rebuking the sins of the people and the wickedness of Herod Antipas, tetrarch of Galilee, because he had taken as spouse Herodias, wife of his brother Philip. John could stand before kings

is as true to duty as the needle to the pole, men who will stand for the right though the heavens fall."[1]

because he had bowed low before the King of heaven.

Greatness and Courage

Courage is the primary virtue because it makes possible every other virtue. The Bible records stories of men and women who displayed this virtue. Ordinary people, they performed extraordinary feats of bravery. Like Daniel, they "shut the mouths of lions"; others "quenched the fury of the flames, and escaped the edge of the sword" (Heb. 11:32–34). These brave individuals did not possess courage

Greatness Lays Itself Aside

John the Baptist was wildly popular for a time as he preached the imminent appearing of the Messiah. But then, after Jesus was baptized and began His public ministry, John saw his following begin to fall away. That must have been a blow to John's ego. A lesser person might have resented Jesus's "stealing" John's followers, but the Baptist was free from the jealousies that frequently plague human relationships. Instead of voicing complaint like some of John's disciples did—"everyone is going to him," they told John (John 3:26)—the Baptist unselfishly commented, "The bride belongs to the bridegroom. The friend who attends the bridegroom waits and listens for him, and is full of joy when he hears the bridegroom's voice. That joy is mine, and it is now complete. He must become greater; I must become less" (vv. 29, 30).

What a contrast to the way most people relate to a similar situation. Too often we seek to "increase" in influence, power, and reputation. We compare ourselves with others, concerned to advance what we (mistakenly) think is important to us. But the greatness of John the Baptist shines in glorious contrast. He found his joy and satisfaction in seeing Jesus's following grow larger and larger at the expense of his own movement. "He must increase, but I must decrease," this true servant of God declared (John 3:30, KJV).

The Death of John the Baptist

Over the course of the centuries, two accounts of two different executions have attracted widespread and continuing interest. The audiences for each are vastly different, as are the underlying motivations.

The death of Jesus of Nazareth, executed by crucifixion and labeled the "King of the Jews" by the Romans, has drawn the larger number of inquiries. Millions have pondered the mystery of His cross. All four Gospels rise to a climax at the story of His closing scenes, and the other writings of the New Testament repeatedly make reference to Jesus's death. Although the execution of Jesus engages the attention of both Christians and non-Christians, by far the larger number are believers. For them, Calvary is much more than an event in history: it is God's saving act to deliver the world from sin and death. We shall consider the meaning of Jesus's death in detail later in this book (see chap. 29).

In contrast to Jesus's execution, that of John the Baptist has been of keen interest to nonbelievers. Christians have not overlooked it, but they haven't dwelled on it to the same extent, and certainly not out of the same motivations, as the others. Why has the story of John's execution occupied the creative imagination of unbelievers? Because they peruse it for the ingredients that drive Hollywood: sex and violence.

From a Christian perspective, the story is ghastly. A great man sacrificed to the oath of a drunken, lustful monarch—how can it be? The story offends our moral sensibilities. But from a carnal perspective, the account drips with tidbits that appeal to the baser instincts: a party overflowing with booze, a scheming mother, a sensuous teenage girl, a drunken monarch burning with desire, a reckless oath, and then a murder with the head served up on a platter!

What more could Hollywood need to turn the story into a box-office hit? Long before Hollywood, however, the story's carnal elements attracted attention. Music and songs were written for it, as were operas and plays. Imagination especially focused on Salome and her dance, which in time became stylized into the Dance of the Seven Veils, with the girl successively discarding each of the coverings that concealed her naked form.

What a sad development! The death of the one whom Jesus described as without peer is reduced to a spectacle for leering eyes. How shall we read this story? Not through the eyes of movie-makers and songwriters, but through heaven's eyes. Then we are enabled to see the leading players as they truly are.

Four characters dominate the story: Herodias, Salome, Herod, and John the Baptist.

Herodias, the lawful wife of Philip, Herod's brother, hates John the Baptist. He won't keep his mouth shut: he denounces Herod for taking Herodias, and he denounces her for leaving her husband to marry Herod (Mark 6:17, 18).

Herodias wants John the Baptist removed. She wants to see him dead and silenced forever. Her new partner, Herod Antipas, is king, but he is a weak man. He vacillates between the Baptist and his wife, at times angry with John and at other times listening to him. Frustrated at Herod's lack of initiative in removing John from the scene, Herodias waits for an opportunity to strike against the Baptist. Herod's birthday provides the occasion for revenge against her infuriating accuser.

We don't know the age of Salome, Herodias's daughter, but the Greek word translated "girl" suggests that she was quite young—possibly only about fourteen. That she would agree to her mother's suggestion to enter the banquet hall and dance speaks volumes about her loose morality, even as it exposes Herodias's disgusting values. No self-respecting woman would consent to perform before a debauched crowd, and even less would she even permit—forget suggest—that her own daughter do so.

The third player in this sick story is Herod Antipas. King in name he may be, but he is a moral pygmy. Slave to passion, he takes and marries his brother's wife. Yielding to Herodias's anger against the Baptist, he has him arrested and thrown into prison. But he will not go the whole distance and execute John. He is afraid of John, and sends for him from time to time to talk about his message (Mark 6:20).

The final moments in the Baptist's life are difficult to contemplate. Herod Antipas finds himself tricked into a decision by his hate-filled wife. He is flattered by Herodias's act of sending her own daughter, instead of a courtesan, to perform a sensuous dance. Befuddled by alcohol and burning with lust, the king rashly makes a promise before the dinner guests: "And he promised her with an oath, 'Whatever you ask I will give you, up to half my kingdom'" (Mark 6:23). Almost immediately Salome comes back with an answer: "I want you to give me right now the head of John the Baptist on a platter" (v. 25).

Now the king is sorry, but he is trapped. He has made a promise and confirmed it with an oath. The eyes of all the dinner guests—leading men of Galilee—are on him. He sees no way out: he issues the order for John to be executed. Soon a grisly new dish is brought into the banquet hall—the head of John the Baptist on a platter!

Herod ever afterward was haunted by his despicable act. Later, when people speculated concerning Jesus, who had become a household name throughout Galilee, Herod would only say, "John, whom I beheaded, has been raised from the dead" (Mark 6:14–16).

Why Didn't Jesus Save John's Life?

John died alone. He had languished in the king's prison alone. Jesus not once visited him, nor did He intervene at the end to deliver him.

Down through the ages, wise men seeking to define the good life have highlighted length of days and a contented end as the essence of human success. Even the book of Ecclesiastes, which for most of its reflection adopts the stance of a secular person, echoes this ideal (see Eccles. 8:15). By such human measures, John's life must be reckoned to be a failure. But then, so was Jesus's!

No, the biblical perspective is altogether different. "Success," if we adopt that term, does not depend on living a long life, just as it isn't a matter of gaining wealth or achieving fame. Success—true success—is found in a character that reflects God's and in a life lived to bless others and glorify the Lord.

Jesus left John alone in prison—unvisited, undelivered—and to be murdered under the vilest of circumstances. Jesus also died, and under the vilest of circumstances. The cousins were alike in their experiences, even up to their parting breath. But behind both executions God was working out a grand design. The nature of evil and its diabolical mastermind were being exposed to the universe. Wrong seemed to triumph, but the end of the story—both stories—was yet to be written.

QUESTIONS FOR DISCUSSION

1. King Herod reasoned that he couldn't spare John's life because of the oath he had made before the dinner guests. Was Herod's thinking correct? Give reasons for your answer.

2. Seventh-day Adventists sometimes understand themselves as proclaiming the "Elijah message" to the world. On what basis do they make this assertion? (Consider the elements of *time* and *content* of the message.)

3. John the Baptist's preaching centered on repentance and the in-breaking of the kingdom of God. How can we experience Jesus reigning as Lord of our lives?

7

Lord of the Temple

<table>
<tr><td>**OBJECTIVES**</td><td>• Discover the key role that the Gospel of John plays in the study of the life and teachings of Jesus.</td></tr>
<tr><td></td><td>• Identify the first events of Jesus's ministry according to John.</td></tr>
<tr><td></td><td>• Understand the significance of Jesus's cleansing of the temple.</td></tr>
<tr><td>**SCRIPTURE**</td><td>• John 1:19—2:25</td></tr>
</table>

Each of the Gospels is complete in itself, but when one attempts to combine all four into a single account, major difficulties come to light:

- Each Gospel relates incidents that are not mentioned in the other Gospels.

- Where the same incidents occur in different Gospels, they often do not follow the same order.

- Matthew, Mark, and Luke—the Synoptic Gospels—have much material in common, but John stands apart from them. Only about 10 percent of the Gospel of John has parallel passages in the Synoptics.

- The Synoptic Gospels all place Jesus's ministry in Galilee and surrounding areas, whereas John includes a significant portion in Jerusalem and Judea.

- Reading Matthew, Mark, and Luke, we get the impression that Jesus's ministry, which was entirely in the Galilee area, lasted only a short time—perhaps about one year or eighteen months. John's account, however, suggests a significantly longer period of three to three and a half years.

- Luke alone narrates a long, wandering journey in Perea after the close of Jesus's ministry in Galilee.

The attempt to thread together the four Gospels into a single account in chronological order is called a "harmony" of the Gospels. Around the year AD 170, Tatian produced the first such work; it was known as the Diatessaron ("made of four"). Since then many other harmonies have been set forth, but none has achieved general acceptance. The data are complex: for the most part, with the possible exception of the fourth Gospel, the writers weren't primarily concerned about writing a chronological account of Jesus's life and ministry. Under the guidance of the Spirit, they wrote selectively, drawing upon the store of material available to them, and shaping the narrative in the interests of their distinctive portrait of this incredible Man.

The Importance of John's Gospel

In form and content the Gospel of John differs sharply from the Synoptic Gospels. Whereas the latter build the story of Jesus's ministry around a series of miracles and teachings, John focuses the ministry on a comparatively small number of personal encounters. In them Jesus interacts with people from various backgrounds—high and low, rich and poor. These encounters frequently result in Jesus's giving extended blocks of teaching.

Thus, we find Jesus meeting the good Nathanael and conversing with him (John 1:45–51). Later He talks with Nicodemus, a Pharisee and member of the Sanhedrin (John 3:1). Yet He also takes time to talk to the nameless woman by the well in Samaria, a person excluded from polite company (John 4:7–42). He meets a royal official in Galilee (John 4:46–53) but also an invalid by the pool of Bethesda in Jerusalem (John 5:2–15). Later in the same city Jesus comes to the rescue of a woman who is about to be stoned for adultery (John 8:3–11) and

heals a beggar who was born blind (John 9:1–41). The crowning miracle of His ministry follows: Jesus calls back to life His friend Lazarus, who has been dead and buried for four days (John 11:1–44).

These four miracles—the nobleman's son, the man by the pool, the man born blind, and Lazarus—are found only in John's Gospel. The Synoptic Gospels record a total of twenty-nine miracles, but with one exception none of them finds a place in the fourth Gospel. The exception is the feeding of the five thousand, found in John 6:1–13. This is the only miracle recorded by all four Gospel writers. But even here John's account takes the reader far beyond what we find in Matthew, Mark, and Luke. John alone informs us that this miracle had a dramatic effect on the crowd: the people, convinced that Jesus was the long-awaited Messiah, tried forcibly to crown Him as king. Jesus, however, refused their overtures and sent the crowd away (vv. 14, 15).

It was a turning point in Jesus's ministry in Galilee. Within days the bubble of popular support began to deflate; many turned away from Him in disappointment. Thus, John's recounting of the miracle of feeding the five thousand was not so much for the event itself but for what transpired because of it.

The Christian historian Eusebius, writing in the fourth century, passes on an early tradition: John, writing his Gospel as an old man, sought to complement the accounts of Matthew, Mark, and Luke. Rather than repeating events that they had recorded, John intentionally supplied new information about Jesus's life and ministry. This tradition comports with what we find in John's Gospel. The story of Jesus here stands apart from that of the Synoptic writers, yet it does not contradict the other accounts. We meet the same Jesus and Lord, but we see Him in new dimensions.

The second feature of John's Gospel mentioned in the early tradition—that it was written by the aged John looking back on the life of Jesus—also resonates with the feel or mood of this writing. The fourth Gospel is by far the most theological of the four: John wants to tell the reader not only what Jesus did but the meaning of His life and ministry.

The Gospel of John is indispensable in gaining a comprehensive view of Jesus's ministry—that is, in reconstructing from the four Gospels the events in chronological order. John shows an interest in specifics of time and sequence that we should take seriously. Although many critical scholars reject the idea that the fourth Gospel was written by John the apostle and discount it as a historical source, I do not. To me, its frequent references to being an eyewitness account (13:23, 24; 19:26, 27, 35; 21:20–24) make it an essential resource for study.

We learn that the temple that Jesus cleansed at the beginning of His ministry had been under construction for forty-six years (John 2:20). Since we know from secular sources that Herod the Great commenced the work in 20–19 BC, Jesus's

act in cleansing it must have occurred in AD 28 (see later in this chapter for more information pertaining to this event).

John mentions three Passover festivals during Jesus's ministry:

- John 2:13, 23: Jesus attended this Passover.

- John 6:4: Jesus stayed in Galilee for this Passover; presumably He stayed away from Judea "because the Jewish leaders there were looking for a way to kill him" (John 7:1).

- John 11:55–57; 12:1; 13:1: Jesus's final Passover, when He was arrested and crucified.

In addition to these three festivals that are specifically designated as Passovers, John tells us that Jesus "went up to Jerusalem for one of the Jewish festivals" (John 5:1). Although John doesn't identify this festival as the Passover, the evidence points in that direction (see John 6:4).

We may therefore arrive at the following outline of Jesus's ministry:

- AD 28—First Passover visit (John 2:13–25)

- AD 29—Second Passover visit (John 5)

- AD 30—Third Passover; Jesus remains in Galilee (John 6:4)

- AD 31—Fourth Passover; Jesus arrested and crucified (John 13–20)

John supplies three additional items related to the time and sequence of Jesus's ministry. He tells us that Jesus, after avoiding Judea because of plots against His life there, made a visit to Jerusalem during the Festival of Tabernacles (John 7:1–3, 10). He also was in Jerusalem for Hanukkah, the Festival of Dedication (John 10:22, 23), which came about four months before the Passover. Third, on Jesus's final visit to Jerusalem, He arrived at Bethany (located just outside Jerusalem) "six days before the Passover" (John 12:1). "The next day" He made the triumphal entry, riding on a colt into the city from the Mount of Olives (vv. 12–15).

An Outline of Jesus's Ministry

We cannot determine the precise order of many of the events in Jesus's ministry. However, on the basis of the Gospel of John, we can reasonably conclude that it lasted more than three years. Furthermore, placing the Synoptic Gospels side by side with John's account, it becomes evident that the ministry took place both in Judea and Galilee.

Mark tells us that "after John was put in prison, Jesus went into Galilee, proclaiming the good news of God" (Mark 1:14). Matthew adds a significant detail: "When Jesus heard that John had been put in prison, he withdrew to Galilee" (Matt. 4:12). Jesus had up to that time been in Judea, where John had baptized Him at the southern end of the Jordan River, before it enters the Dead Sea. Following the baptism, Jesus went into the desert—presumably the barren hills above Jericho or on the other side of the Jordan—where He was tempted by the devil.

But John makes clear that Jesus also ministered in the Judean countryside with His disciples. For some time—just how long, we do not know—Jesus's and John's ministries overlapped. Both were located in the same general area; both of them baptized and gained disciples. Gradually, however, the disciples of Jesus began to outnumber those of John (see John 3:22–26; 4:1, 2).

Thus, we deduce the following sequence for the early ministry of Jesus:

- *Baptized by John the Baptist.* This was the inauguration of Jesus's ministry. Jesus came from Galilee to John, who was baptizing at Bethany on the other side of the Jordan (John 1:28; Matt. 3:1, 13).

- *The temptation.* Immediately following Jesus's baptism, it took place in the Judean wilderness.

- *Jesus's first disciples.* Andrew, Peter, Philip, and Nathanael became acquainted with Jesus in Judea (John 1:35–51).

- *Jesus returns to Galilee* (John 1:43).

- *The wedding at Cana in Galilee* (John 2:1–11). This took place "on the third day" after Jesus returned from Judea. After the wedding, Jesus with His mother, brothers, and disciples went to Capernaum, where they stayed for "a few days" (John 2:12).

- *Cleansing the temple.* Passover, spring AD 28 (John 2:13–25).

- *Visit with Nicodemus* in Jerusalem (John 3:1–21).

- *Jesus's ministry in the Judean countryside* (John 3:22; 4:1).

- *Jesus returns to Galilee* (John 4:1–3).

- *The Samaritan woman* (John 4:4–30).

- *Ministry to the Samaritans.* This lasted only two days (John 4:39–42).

- *Healing the royal official's son.* This miracle also took place in Cana (John 4:46–54).

- *Jesus goes to Jerusalem.* If we assume that the festival Jesus attended was the Passover, this visit occurred in the spring of AD 29 (John 5:1).

- *Healing the invalid by the pool.* This miracle resulted in controversy with the Jewish leaders because Jesus performed the miracle on the Sabbath (John 5:2–17). The leaders charged Him with breaking the Sabbath and became even angrier when Jesus defended His actions by claiming that in healing the crippled man He was merely following God's activities on the Sabbath (v. 17). The Jews now tried to kill Jesus.

After this visit to Jerusalem, Jesus had to be on guard for His life. He did not go to Jerusalem the following year; He remained in Galilee (John 6:4).

He purposely stayed away from Judea "because the Jewish leaders there were looking for a way to kill him" (John 7:1). When, later, the time for the Festival of Tabernacles arrived, Jesus did not join His brothers making the journey to Jerusalem, but went alone in secret after the festival had commenced (John 7:10–13).

Where should John's imprisonment be located in this sequence of events that occupied fewer than two years? We cannot be certain, only that it probably occurred in the period AD 28–29, between Jesus's first and second Passover visits because after this He avoided Judea (John 7:1).

In this book we follow the basic outline adopted in the *Seventh-day Adventist Bible Commentary*, which locates the first full year of Jesus's ministry largely in Judea and the following two years chiefly in Galilee and areas in proximity, with only brief visits to Judea to attend some of the Jewish festivals.[1]

In the remainder of this chapter and throughout the one that follows, we shall follow John's account of Jesus's early ministry, located primarily in Judea and running from just before Passover AD 28 and during the following year.

The First Disciples

The writers of the Synoptic Gospels all describe Jesus calling Peter and his fellow fishermen as they worked by the Sea of Galilee. In response to His direct "Follow me," they left everything to cast in their lot with Jesus (see Matt. 4:18–22; Mark 1:16–20; Luke 5:1–11).

John's Gospel considerably enlarges our understanding. The first contact between Peter, his brother Andrew, and Jesus occurred not in Galilee but Judea, and much earlier—perhaps as long as a year. And the fishermen were led to follow Jesus by the testimony of John the Baptist, not Jesus's direct call (see John 1:35–42).

We should distinguish between two calls—the call to discipleship and the call to full-time ministry. The first call comes to everyone in all walks of life as the Holy Spirit touches the heart and the heart answers, "Yes." This is the call to accept Jesus as Savior and Lord because we acknowledge Him as "the Lamb of God, who takes away the sin of the world" (John 1:29)—and our sin in particular. Responding to the call to discipleship, we too choose to follow Jesus. (We shall discuss the meaning of discipleship more extensively in chapter 20.)

Although Jesus calls everyone to discipleship, He calls only a small number from among them to full-time ministry. These He takes from the office, the farm, the classroom, the factory—wherever they are working—and commissions them for service. Why Jesus chooses this person and not that one resides with Him alone; a person cannot take the matter into their own hands. If Jesus calls someone, he or she may refuse; but they do not initiate the call.

Sometimes people fail to differentiate between the call to discipleship and the call to full-time ministry. With hearts glowing from their "first love" of Jesus as Savior and Lord, they feel as though they should drop whatever work they are doing and study to become a minister of the gospel. However, they should not rush into such a radical change of profession. The Lord will guide them, in His own way and at His own pace, to what He plans for their lives. He may see that they will best serve by staying right where they are—on the farm or in the office—and working as a Christian.

Occasionally, for some individuals, the two calls coincide. Saul of Tarsus, struck by blinding light on the road to Damascus, was informed not only that he should be baptized but that the Lord had selected him to be a "chosen instrument" to take the good news about Jesus to the Gentile world (Acts 9:1–22). This wasn't the case with some of those men who became the Twelve—the fellow servants of Jesus whom He commissioned to carry on His work after He was gone. They first accepted Jesus, deciding to become His followers; months later they forsook their work to be with Him on a permanent basis.

John's account of the initial call, the call to discipleship, is instructive. First, the Baptist pointed his hearers to Jesus as "the Lamb of God, who takes away the sin of the world" (John 1:29; see also v. 36). This profound insight, found only here in the four Gospels, echoes Isaiah's prophecy of the Suffering Servant, Who would take upon Himself our guilt and shame and be "led like a lamb to the slaughter" (Isa. 53:7). This is where following Jesus begins for every person, everywhere. The Holy Spirit opens our eyes and we see Him as the Lamb of God who takes away *our* sin.

Next, John 1 shows simply but powerfully how the good news about Jesus is spread by word of mouth:

- John proclaimed Jesus as the Lamb of God.
- Two of John's disciples, Andrew and another, heard John and followed Jesus (John 1:37–39).
- Andrew told Peter, his brother, about Jesus (vv. 40–42).
- Philip told Nathanael about Jesus (v. 45).

Christianity is infectious. It spreads today like it did from the very beginning. Jesus is so wonderful that, after finding Him, we want to tell others about Him.

John's account of Nathanael's encounter with Jesus supplies the only information we have about this early disciple who became one of the Twelve. Nathanael is customarily understood to be the Bartholomew in the lists of the Twelve that we find in the Synoptic Gospels (Matt. 10:2–4; Mark 3:14–19; Luke 6:12–16). We shall come back to him later when we look at the Twelve in more detail (chap. 9).

The Wedding at Cana

The first miracle Jesus performed did not come in the context of a situation of crisis or emergency, such as a person at the point of death or facing grave danger. It was a wedding feast, and the wine had run out. Surely this was a cause of embarrassment to the host and hostess. A wedding was the biggest social event, and to run out of wine exposed them to ridicule, perhaps for years following the disaster, but it was not a dangerous situation.

Jesus intervened and did something extraordinary: He changed the water in the large stone jars into wine. The merriment could continue without a hitch, with only a few people being aware how close the celebration had come to a fiasco.

Jesus's action reveals much about His values. For a start, He had shown His respect for marriage by accepting the invitation to attend. Jesus was no ascetic, humorless and long-faced. He rejoiced with those who rejoiced, even as He wept with those who wept. As Creator, He had instituted marriage in the Garden of Eden; now, by showing up in Cana for the wedding, He reiterated the value He placed on the sacred union of a man and a woman.

Jesus wanted the wedding feast to be all that the newly married couple and their parents had hoped for. From one point of view, it may seem a trivial occasion for the Lord of the universe to manifest His divine power, but for the wedding guests (and especially for the bridal couple and their parents), it was a major event. Nothing is trivial to Jesus. No occasion or situation that troubles us is too trivial to bring to His attention. He cares about us; we cannot annoy or trouble Him by our seemingly minor requests.

Mary apparently understood this. Although Jesus hadn't yet manifested His power, she knew that He was different from His siblings. In a situation of social crisis, when there was nowhere else to turn, she came to Him and simply said, "They have no more wine" (John 2:3).

Jesus's reply seems abrupt to us, especially if we read from the King James Version: "Woman, what have I to do with thee?" In the English Standard Version we read, "Woman, what does this have to do with me?" (2:4). Jesus's use of "woman" in direct address was normal and polite (see John 19:26). In essence, "My hour has not yet come" (2:4) simply assures Mary that Jesus will act at the right moment. "Leave it to Me; I have the matter under control."

Mary understood and left the situation with her Son. She didn't know how He would solve the problem, but she was confident that He would. She said to the servants, "Do whatever He tells you" (John 2:5). And they did. Imagine their trepidation when they drew out the first liquid from the stone jar they had just filled with water and took it to the master of the banquet. What confusion is about to break out over the happy occasion. But surprise! Instead they hear, "you have saved the best till now" (v. 10).

John notes that this miracle at Cana "was the first of the signs through which he revealed his glory; and his disciples believed in him" (v. 11). The word translated "signs" is the Greek *semeia* (singular: *semeion*) and is a key term in John's Gospel. It occurs sixteen times in John chapters 1–12 and then no more, except for John 20:30, 31.

Thus, the miracles of Jesus are more than spectacular acts; they are signs that reveal who He really is. They awaken faith in those who have eyes open to behold His glory—just as they engender opposition among those who refuse to see. (The word "glory" [Greek *doxa*] is a key term in John's Gospel, especially in the closing chapters, 12–21. It points in a hidden way to the cross, when Jesus is glorified.)

Cleansing the Temple

In this chapter we see Jesus in three contrasting dimensions. First, in His encounters with the first disciples, He looks into a person and sums up the heart—what it is and what it may be. To Simon He says, "You will be called Cephas [rock]," and to Nathanael, "Here truly is an Israelite, in whom there is no deceit" (John 1:42, 47). Next, at Cana we meet the sociable Jesus, mingling with guests at a wedding celebration, saving the day when the wine runs out. Now, in John 2:13–23, we see Jesus as Lord of the temple. With blazing eyes and flailing arms He drives the cattle and sheep from the area. He overturns the tables of the money changers and scatters the coins everywhere. "Get out of here!" He commands. "Stop turning my Father's house into a market" (v. 16). It is a scene of confusion—animals struggling to get away, greedy money changers scrambling to pick up coins, and tables and chairs upended. Jesus is angry, and both men and beasts flee from His presence.

The prophet Malachi had seen it all four hundred years before. "Suddenly the Lord you are seeking will come to his temple," Malachi predicted. "But who can endure the day of his coming? Who can stand when he appears? For he will be like a refiner's fire or a launderer's soap. He will sit as a refiner and purifier of silver" (Mal. 3:1–3).

THE SECOND TEMPLE

The temple that Jesus cleansed is usually referred to as the second temple. A huge, magnificent structure, it was a wonder of the ancient world. If you visit Jerusalem, you will be surprised at the extent of the site of this temple.

Solomon built the first temple. Located on Mount Moriah, it was completed about 960 BC. Babylonian armies of Nebuchadnezzar destroyed this temple in 586 BC. The site lay desolate for about seventy years. Then Jews returned from exile in Babylon and began to construct a new temple. After many setbacks, they completed it in 515 BC.

After five hundred years, this second temple badly needed repairs. In an effort to gain favor with the Jews, who hated him because he was an Idumean, Herod the Great undertook a massive rebuilding program in 20–19 BC. The work continued after Herod's death in 4 BC, only being completed in AD 63. But seven years later, in AD 70, this temple was burned by Roman armies under Titus.

The temple has never been rebuilt. Orthodox Jews look to its restoration when the Messiah comes. They gather at the Western Wall (the Wailing Wall), which is part of the retaining wall supporting the temple mount built by Herod the Great. Today the site is sacred to Muslims also: the Dome of the Rock, a shrine, occupies the site.

With this act Jesus announced to the religious establishment in Jerusalem that He was more than a rabbi from Galilee. He was a prophet who, in the spirit and power of the line of God's messengers from Isaiah and Jeremiah to Malachi, did not hesitate to denounce sin, no matter where it was found. Yes, a prophet—but more. For by cleansing the temple, Jesus did not merely denounce the commercialization in its courts; He *acted* to correct the evil. By this He demonstrated that He was the Lord of Malachi's prophecy.

We can imagine the impact of Jesus's dramatic act. The people who had come to Jerusalem to offer sacrifice in worship must have been amazed. The priests who presided over the temple—and who profited from its business—must have been momentarily stunned. Their position challenged, their livelihood threatened, they at last found breath to demand, "What sign can you show us to prove your authority to do all this?" (John 2:18).

Jesus's reply shows that He knew full well where the course He pursued would eventually take Him. Ahead lay the cross: throughout His short ministry its shadow hung over Him. But beyond Calvary would come the resurrection from the dead after He had lain for three days in the tomb.

The picture of Jesus that confronts us in His cleansing of the temple—that is, the angry Christ—is one that may surprise some Christians. Yet it isn't the only time we find Jesus associated with anger: Mark tells us of an occasion when, provoked by the hypocrisy of the religious leaders, He "looked around at them in anger" (Mark 3:5). There is both bad and good anger. Most anger arises out of our pride and selfish ambition. But good anger, sometimes called righteous indignation, comes from a passion for justice or a burning desire to see God's name honored. Good anger is rare but real. The man or woman who has never been moved by such emotion is not a full person. They are deficient in moral and spiritual sensitivity.

QUESTIONS FOR DISCUSSION

1. What are the similarities and differences in the accounts of Jesus's cleansing the temple in all four Gospels (Matt. 21:12–17; Mark 11:15–18; Luke 19:45–48; John 2:13–23)? Note also events that precede and follow each account. Did Jesus cleanse the temple twice?

2. How is a view of a gentle and meek Jesus complicated by His anger at the cleansing of the temple?

3. How can we distinguish between the two calls: the one for discipleship and the one for full-time ministry?

8

A Man for All People

OBJECTIVES
- Discover how Jesus met the needs of four different people in four different circumstances.

- Examine how Jesus adapted His approach to each person.

- Understand that just as Jesus transformed people's lives by encountering them in the past, He still can transform whoever comes to Him today.

SCRIPTURE
- John 3:1–21; 4:4–54; 5:1–47

Jesus of Nazareth was a man for all people. No one was too important or humble, poor or rich, blessed or broken, powerful or powerless, and despised or famous to be passed by. The range of Jesus's interest in humanity is extraordinary, running the gamut of society.

In this chapter we will study four encounters in which Jesus was involved. Two of the people were rich and powerful; two were considered zeros and banished to the margins of society. Two sought out Jesus, as they felt a need that only He could supply. Two did not seek Him—He came to them—although they also were in desperate need of His life-giving attention.

These four encounters, found only in the Gospel of John, occurred early in Jesus's ministry, probably between Passover AD 28 and Passover AD 29. They provide unmatched insights into the mind and values of Jesus, the matchless Man for all people.

The Night Caller

On two counts Nicodemus was one of the most powerful men in Jerusalem: he was a Pharisee and a member of the ruling council, the Sanhedrin.

The Pharisees, scrupulous in their observance of both written and oral regulations, were the religious purists. Although the Sadducees controlled the high priesthood, the

Pharisees dominated in spiritual affairs. Proud in their religiosity, they looked down on the common people who, unlike them, had neither the time nor the means to devote to rigid adherence of the law.

Throughout the Gospels, we find Jesus frequently clashing with the Pharisees. His strongest denunciations were directed at them: "Woe to you, teachers of the law and Pharisees, you hypocrites!" (Matt. 23:13, 15, 23, 25, 27, 29). To the crowds surrounding Him and to the disciples Jesus advised, "The teachers of the law and the Pharisees sit in Moses' seat. So you must be careful to do everything they tell you. But do not do what they do, for they do not practice what they preach" (vv. 2, 3).

One of Jesus's most pointed parables described two men who went up to the temple to pray: a Pharisee and a tax collector. The Pharisee's prayer went like this: "God, I thank you that I am not like other people—robbers, evildoers, adulterers—or even like this tax collector. I fast twice a week and give a tenth of all I get" (Luke 18:11, 12). But the tax collector simply said, "God, have mercy on me, a sinner" (v. 13). And it was his prayer and not the Pharisee's that God heard.

When the temple guards, dispatched to arrest Jesus, returned empty-handed because of what they heard of Jesus's preaching, the Pharisees retorted, "Have any of the rulers or of the Pharisees believed in him? No! But this mob that knows nothing of the law—there is a curse on them" (John 7:48, 49).

Over the centuries, the very word "Pharisee" has taken on negative connotations. It represents people who make a big show of religion but who in reality are hypocrites. We should be careful not to write off all Pharisees under this blanket condemnation, however. Among their number were earnest seekers of God whose meticulous attempts to keep the law sprung from hearts that wanted to please God.

Nicodemus belonged among such a group. He had heard about Jesus and his heart was moved. He wanted to know more about Him. Who was He? Why did He possess the power to perform such miracles—which Nicodemus recognized as *semeia*, signs of the presence of God? Nicodemus decided to find out for himself.

The second feature that made Nicodemus one of Jerusalem's elite was his membership in the Sanhedrin. This, the highest governing body of the Jewish people, was a group of seventy-one drawn from the priests (Sadducees), teachers of the law (Pharisees), and lay elders of the aristocracy. The high priest presided over the Sanhedrin. Nicodemus came to Jesus under cover of darkness. He was drawn to the Master, but he was protective of his reputation. In terms of Jerusalem's power structure, the wandering Teacher-Healer from Galilee—uneducated, poor, commoner—was a nobody. No one could foretell what would come of Him and His small band of followers. In a short time the Jesus movement might fizzle out.

Curious to know more about Jesus but apprehensive concerning the step he was taking, Nicodemus prepared what he would say to Jesus. His words are recorded in John 3: "Rabbi, we know that you are a teacher who has come from God. For no one could perform the signs you are doing if God were not with him" (vv. 1, 2).

"Rabbi . . . teacher . . . from God"—Nicodemus's greeting is polite and complimentary. Or so he thinks. Jesus's response, abrupt and pointed, startles the Pharisee. At a stroke, the scenario for the night meeting that Nicodemus had played out in his mind is swept away.

"Very truly I tell you, no one can see the kingdom of God unless they are born again," Jesus declares (v. 3).

While Nicodemus had come to talk about Jesus, Jesus makes the conversation about Nicodemus! The learned Pharisee finds himself in an uncomfortable position, one that he isn't accustomed to. He is used to dictating the flow of conversation, not being put on the defensive. So he resorts to ridicule. "How can someone be born when they are old?" he blusters. "Surely they cannot enter a second time into their mother's womb to be born" (v. 4).

Nicodemus knew better. The word translated "again" in Jesus's declaration, *anōthen*, has dual meanings: "a second time" or "again," and "from above." Nicodemus selected the former meaning in order to try to gain the advantage over Jesus. And he was familiar with the idea of rebirth itself. The Jews already had

such a teaching; however, they applied it not to Jews but to Gentiles who wished to convert to Judaism.

Jesus's response takes Nicodemus to the heart of his spiritual problem: *he*, not just Gentiles, needs to be born from above. "Flesh gives birth to flesh, but the Spirit gives birth to spirit," Jesus tells him. "You should not be surprised at my saying, 'You must be born again'" (vv. 6, 7). Now Jesus brings in an illustration from the wind. To catch its force, we need to realize that the Greek word for "wind" (*pneuma*) can also mean "spirit." "The wind blows wherever it pleases. You hear its sound, but you cannot tell where it comes from or where it is going. So it is with everyone born of the Spirit," says Jesus (v. 8).

Nicodemus, now utterly deflated, can only offer up a weak "How can this be?" (v. 9).

And Jesus tells it straight: "You are Israel's teacher and do you not understand these things?" What a rebuke! One may be considered learned and yet be ignorant of what matters the most. Unless one knows God, all one's teaching about God is empty. Unless one knows that Jesus is far more than "a teacher who has come from God" (v. 2) and acknowledges that Jesus is "the one who came from heaven" (v. 13), he or she speaks only on an earthly plane.

Look and Live!

The conversation between Jesus and Nicodemus follows a three-stage development, as Jesus leads the Pharisee into his own need of salvation. Again, in John 3, we find an interesting dialogue: three times Nicodemus speaks and three times Jesus begins His answer with the solemn words, "Very truly I tell you" (vv. 3, 5, 11).

Just where the conversation ends is not clear. After his feeble "How can this be?" (v. 9), we hear no more from Nicodemus, nor does John inform us of his departure. Indeed, there is even a question as to where Jesus's words stop: some interpreters end them after verse 15, making John the source of verses 16–21. Some versions of the Bible reflect this ambiguity concerning the passage. I find no compelling reason to accept the view that verses 13–21 are a commentary added by John rather than the words of Jesus. On the contrary, the ideas of this passage are so lofty, among the grandest in the entire Bible, that they rightfully belong with Jesus Himself. We will briefly summarize the material:

"Just as Moses lifted up the snake in the wilderness, so the Son of Man must be lifted up, that everyone who believes may have eternal life in him," said Jesus (vv. 14, 15). He referenced the incident recorded in Numbers 21:6–9, when, because of their rebellion against God, the children of Israel fell among venomous snakes but were saved by looking at the bronze snake on a pole that Moses made at God's direction.

Look and live—this was the message that came from the desert. And it would be the message to flow from Calvary, when the Son of Man would be offered up for the sins of the world.

For unbelievers, the crucifixion of Jesus is no more than an accident of history. Jesus was a good man who, trapped by circumstances, was put to death in a gross miscarriage of justice. But His death also had a "must be" quality about it. That is, *God* was in it, working out His plan to save the world through it and by it. And its message to humanity then and now is this: look and live!

The verse that follows, John 3:16, is the best-loved and most frequently quoted passage of the New Testament, and rightly so: "For God so loved the world that he gave his one and only Son, that whoever believes in him shall not perish but have eternal life." Notice its great ideas:

- *Our salvation begins with God, not ourselves.* He took the initiative, devising a plan to rescue us from the pit into which we had fallen.

- *Salvation springs from God's love alone.* Nothing else—no satisfaction of divine ego or selfish purpose, but only love for the world and each of us.

- *God loved us first.* Before we ever turned back to Him, and before Jesus died, God loved us. He doesn't love us *because* of Jesus; He sent Jesus because He loves us. The love of the Father cannot be separated from the love of the Son.

- *God gave His Son to the world.* A gift is free, unlimited, and eternal. The Son is forever heaven's choicest and most precious gift to the world.

- *The gift must be received.* Eternal life in exchange for eternal death: Who would not gladly seize it? Yet, strangely, many do not. The gift seems too good to be true, but it isn't. Only as we take God at His word and accept the gift can we have its eternal benefits.

Strong contrasts mark this verse and those that follow: life and death, salvation and condemnation, light and darkness. Jesus is the Divider of humanity, calling men and women to decide in favor of life.

How did Jesus's words affect Nicodemus? The conversation began with Nicodemus coming to Jesus at night; it ends on the theme that men and women must leave the darkness and come to the light. Nicodemus came to the light, not immediately but eventually. Later, when the Sanhedrin was planning to have Jesus arrested, Nicodemus spoke up in His defense (John 7:50–52). And at the cross, Nicodemus, no longer following Jesus in secret, came forward openly together with Joseph of Arimathea, who asked Pilate to release His body for burial (John 19:38–42).

"The Brazen Serpent" by Gustave Doré

Of Water and Men

A lonely woman came to the well in the middle of the day to draw water. Her life revolved around water and men. Anciently and still today in many parts of the world, it falls to women to supply water for the home. It can be hard work, especially if the water source isn't easily accessible and is located at a distance. Morning and evening find women at the spring or well; they avoid the heat of the day. When they gather together in fulfillment of their daily chore, they find relief in sharing gossip and news from their simple lives.

We know where the story recorded in John 4 took place. It was near the town of Sychar, the modern 'Askar. The well nearby at the foot of Mount Gerizim is ancient. And it is very deep, about 100 feet (30 meters). Hauling up water in a bucket from that depth took strength.

Yet here she was, approaching the well at noon with her water pot. She doesn't expect to find anyone; she doesn't want to find anyone. She is a person whose reputation has become known to all the people in the town. When she passes by in public, heads turn and tongues wag. So she avoids meeting people, choosing to perform the menial task of drawing water in the heat of the day. Water she knows; men she knows. She has lived with five different men. When Jesus tells her that, it is to her as though He knows everything about her. When she goes back into town and tells the people about Jesus, she says, "He told me everything I ever did" (John 4:39).

The contrast between this story with that of John 3—the encounter with Nicodemus—could not be drawn more sharply: a ruler of the Jews versus a nameless person. A man learned in the Torah and scrupulous in observing its finest details is compared to a woman whose life revolves around water and men, a tainted woman polite society avoids. And beyond all these differences are a Jew and a Samaritan, mutually antagonistic (see the sidebar on page 84).

To Jesus of Nazareth, however, the woman who came to the well in the middle of the day was just as important as Nicodemus. She was as much a child of God as was he. And both were equally in need of the new life that Jesus had come to make possible.

As Jesus did with everyone He encountered, He met the woman where she was. Her life was water and men; He talked with her about water and men rather than being born from above, a snake on the pole, or the incredible love of God that sent His Son into the world. Water and men were so simple and basic. Yet through these two items around which the woman's life revolved, Jesus led her, step by step, to God and the new eternal life made available to all through the gift of the Son.

It was shocking that Jesus would spend time talking to a woman and speak to a Samaritan. His disciples, who had gone away to buy food, were shocked upon returning (John 4:27). By analyzing the conversation (John 4:4–26), we gain insights into its main ideas and their development. We see that the encounter consists of two short dialogues, each with three exchanges:[1]

Scene 1a: The Living Water (John 4:5–15)

Dialogue 1 (vv. 7–10)

- *Jesus* asks for water, violating the social customs of the time.

- The *woman* mocks Jesus for not observing the proprieties.

- *Jesus* shows that the real reason for His action is not His inferiority or need, but His superior status.

- *Jesus* issues a two-part challenge: (1) if she recognizes who He is, (2) she will ask Him for living water.

Dialogue 2 (vv. 11–15)

- The *woman* misunderstands on a material, earthly level.

- *Jesus* clarifies that He is speaking of the heavenly water of eternal life.

- The *woman*, intrigued, asks for water. She thus fulfills one part of Jesus's challenge in verse 10.

Scene 1b: True Worship of the Father (vv. 16–26)

Dialogue 1 (vv. 16–18)

- *Jesus* leads the woman to recognize who He is by referring to her personal life.

- The *woman* gives an ambiguous reply.

- *Jesus* uses her answer to uncover her past.

Dialogue 2 (vv. 19–26)

- The *woman* attempts to change the subject. But by broaching the topic of worship, she is beginning to think on a spiritual level.

- *Jesus* explains that true worshipers are those born of the Spirit.

- The *woman* at last recognizes who Jesus is.

- *Jesus* affirms that He is the Messiah.

Thus, this simple but powerful conversation shows the way in which Jesus leads a person to eternal life—from absorption in material things to everlasting values. We detect four main stages in the process:

1. The awakening of a *desire* for something better (vv. 7–15)

2. The awakening of a *conviction* of personal need (vv. 16–20)

3. The call for *decision* to acknowledge Jesus as the Messiah (vv. 16–25)

4. The *action* that appropriately follows the decision (vv. 28–30, 39–42)

The woman came to draw water. At the close of the story her water pot lies abandoned, left by the side of the well. She has found something infinitely more precious than water from the well: she has found Jesus, the Living Water.

The Second Miracle at Cana

In this third encounter, found in John 4:46–54, Jesus meets another powerful person. This man isn't a religious leader but a royal official. But like Nicodemus he seeks out Jesus, traveling from his home in Capernaum to Cana. He comes with an urgent request: his son is dying,

conversation by the well, because there is no need of it. The official already believes in God, and having already heard about Jesus comes seeking His help.

But there is a problem in his attitude toward the Master. He has made up his mind that he will decide for or against Jesus on the basis of how Jesus acts. If Jesus heals his son, he will accept Him. If not, he will not believe in Him.

It is a dangerous thing to lay conditions on God. The Lord isn't subject to our reasoning. Sometimes we hear people say, "I could never believe in a God who does such and such." But these declarations tell us nothing about G o d — o n l y about the person who makes them. Ellen G. White, commenting on the royal official's attitude, observes:

> THE SAMARITANS
>
> The Samaritans were a people of mixed race and mixed religion. They date from the eighth century BC, when Assyrian kings carried away captive people from the northern kingdom and replaced them with others from Babylonia and northern Mesopotamia. These people combined the religion they brought with them with the worship of Yahweh, which the Levitical priests taught them (see 2 Kings 17:24–34).
>
> When the Jews returned from Babylonian exile, the Samaritans offered to join them in rebuilding the temple, but the leaders of the Jews rejected their overture. Thereafter the Samaritans worked against the rebuilding efforts of the Jews. They built their own temple on Mount Gerizim, where they offered animal sacrifices.
>
> Relations between the Jews and the Samaritans were marked by deep animosity. When the Jews were attacked by the Seleucid king Antiochus IV in the second century BC, the Samaritans aided the Syrians. In the time of Jesus the term "Samaritan" was used to insult others (John 8:48). A small remnant of a few hundred Samaritans survives to this time, still worshipping on Mount Gerizim.

and he begs Jesus to come heal him. Jesus's response, however, is abrupt, just as it was to Nicodemus's greeting. "Unless you people see signs and wonders," Jesus tells him, "you will never believe" (v. 48).

Jesus's words seem surprisingly sharp. We find no careful build-up as with the

Not because we see or feel that God hears us are we to believe. We are to trust in His promises. When we come to Him in faith, every petition enters the heart of God. When we have asked for His blessing, we should believe that we receive it, and thank Him that we *have* received it. Then we are to go about our duties, assured that the blessing will be realized when we need it most. When we have learned to do this, we shall know that our prayers are answered. God will do for us "exceeding abundantly," "according to the riches of His glory," and "the working of His mighty power." Eph. 3:20, 16; 1:19.[2]

When the official heard Jesus's gentle rebuke, at once he realized how false his reasoning had been. In desperation he cried out, "Sir, come down before my child dies" (John 4:49).

And Jesus's words came back, calm and comforting: "Your son will live" (v. 50).

The official left, making his way back at a leisurely pace to Capernaum. He took his time because he *knew* that all was well. He believed without seeing. And when hours later he received the news that his son had recovered, his faith in Jesus was affirmed.

Waiting by the Water

Of the four cases of need we studied in this chapter, the one in John 5:1–15 seems the most hopeless. This unfortunate person had been an invalid for thirty-eight years. With the passing of the years, hope of recovery had faded away. He'd become resigned to his fate. So low were his spirits that when Jesus came by and asked, "Do you want to get well?" he didn't cry out, "Yes!" (John 5:6). Instead, he said, in effect, "My case is hopeless." He could only think of being first into the pool of Bethesda as the source of healing, and he had no one to assist in his dash for the water.

This story strikes us as unusual. In its suggestion that the moving of the water could be a means of healing, and especially the idea that the first one in the pool gets the prize—pure competition!—it does not comport with what the Bible elsewhere teaches us about God and His ways.

If your version of the Bible includes John 5:4, look carefully at the passage in a different version. You will observe something strange: more recent translations omit verse 4, which in the King James Version reads: "For an angel went down at a certain season into the pool, and troubled the water: whosoever then first after the troubling of the water stepped in and was made whole of whatever disease he had." The oldest manuscripts of the Gospel of John do not contain verse 4. Apparently, some scribe copying the New Testament inserted the statement about an angel stirring up the water. That the people by the pool *believed* an angel came down from time to time was no doubt so. That was why they were there. And that the water of the pool periodically bubbled up is likewise true, but the cause was probably an underground spring—not an angel.

People struggling with cancer or who have loved ones whom they see slipping away are often desperate to get a miracle. They will travel to any site where healing is supposed to occur; they will exhaust life savings on potions and so-called wonder cures. The multitude by the pool of Bethesda—the blind, the lame, the paralyzed—hoped for a miracle.

The God of the Scriptures always acts out of love and fairness. He isn't capricious; God is absolutely trustworthy. He is the God whom we know through His revelation in Jesus, His Son. This Jesus didn't offer the invalid help in getting into the pool. He cut through all the superstition that had grown around the stirring of the waters. He simply said to the invalid, "Get up! Pick up your mat and walk" (John 5:8). And at once the man was cured. He picked up his mat and walked.

Nicodemus came at night asking questions of Jesus. The woman by the well asked Jesus to give her the "living water" that He said He could provide. The royal official asked Jesus to come to Capernaum to heal his son. But the invalid by the pool didn't ask Jesus for anything—neither to be made well nor for assistance to get into the pool ahead of the others. He was a broken person in body and hope. Jesus, however, acted without being asked. His compassion flowed out in healing, restoring, life-giving power. The miracle took place on the Sabbath (John 5:9), and that fact led to further developments. When the Jews saw the healed man carrying his mat, they could only think of the Sabbath being broken. That in turn led to a confrontation with Jesus, recorded in the discourse that occupies the remainder of John 5.

Later in this book we shall study the teachings of Jesus. Among those topics will be Jesus's relation to the Sabbath; in that context we shall look more closely at Jesus's discourse in John 5.

The encounter of Jesus and the invalid by the pool marked a turning point in Jesus's ministry. John informs us that as a result of the miracle and Jesus's responses to the objections raised by the Jewish leaders, they determined that He should be killed (v. 18). For about one year Jesus had ministered in Judea. Now it was no longer safe there. He left Judea for Galilee, only returning to Jerusalem for brief visits.

QUESTIONS FOR DISCUSSION

1. "Jesus met people where they were." Illustrate the truth of this statement by referring to each of the four encounters we studied in this chapter.

2. How did Jesus's disregard of conventional social rules with the woman at the well illustrate the divine initiative to meet people where they are? How might this divine initiative inform (and challenge) some of society's unwritten rules and accepted behaviors?

3. What did Jesus mean by "living water" in John 4?

4. What does it mean to "look and live" (Num. 21:6–9; John 3:14–16)?

9

Galilee and the Galileans

OBJECTIVES
- Acquire a basic knowledge of the region of Galilee.
- Analyze the qualities of the Twelve whom Jesus chose.
- Relate to the experiences of the disciples of Jesus.

SCRIPTURE
- Matthew 4:12–25; 10:1–8; Mark 3:7–10, 13–19; Luke 6:12–19, Acts 2:7

If you ever have opportunity to visit the Holy Land, be sure to visit the Galilee and see if you fall in love with it like I did.

I had taught courses in religion for many years before I saw Israel. That was a dream still unfulfilled until one day, out of the blue, I received an invitation from the government of Israel. The Ministry of Tourism was arranging a trip for a select group of Christian writers and editors—nonpolitical, no strings attached, all expenses paid. Would I be interested?

So I found myself with six others in a boat on the Lake of Galilee, Yam Kinneret in modern Israel. The land rose sharply from the water's edge. Up the sloping hill we saw a modern church built, they say, on the site of the Sermon on the Mount. Perhaps that was where Jesus uttered the famous words, "Blessed are the poor in spirit, for theirs is the kingdom of heaven" (Matt. 5:3). Perhaps not. At any rate, it was certainly not far away.

Galilee: His Land

The Lake of Galilee isn't large by most standards. Just 13 miles (21 km) long and 8 miles (13 km) wide, you see across it easily. It is much smaller than I had imagined. But hills surround the lake, which is part of the great rift that cuts from Syria to Mozambique and forms the basin for the Jordan River and the Dead Sea. As winds sweep down, suddenly the lake's waters become roiled and dangerous. Even today, as when Peter, Andrew, James, and John went fishing, sailors keep an eye on the sky.

Our boat was the *Peter*, patterned after the boats of Jesus's day. In 1986, after several years of drought, the waters of the lake fell to record-low levels. Someone spotted a piece of wood sticking out of the mud. On investigation it proved to be the remains of an ancient boat. Israeli archaeologists carefully removed the fragile remains and set about to restore it—an actual boat from the first century BC or first century AD. Jesus sailed in a boat just like that—perhaps in that very one!

Growing up in the north, in Nazareth, Jesus was a provincial, a rustic, by the norms of the Jerusalem establishment. Of this land the prophet Isaiah had cried, "Land of Zebulun and land of Naphtali, the Way to the Sea, beyond the Jordan, Galilee of the Gentiles—the people living in darkness have seen a great light; on those living in the land of the shadow of death a light has dawned" (Matt. 4:15, 16; see also Isa. 9:1, 2).

In Galilee, Jesus called disciples to His full-time service. Here He performed most of His miracles, spent most of His ministry, attracted large crowds, and became, for a time, wildly popular. "This is Jesus, the prophet from Nazareth in Galilee" (Matt. 21:11), shouted the crowds as He rode a donkey into Jerusalem on His last visit to the city. But for the religious hierarchy, His Galilean origins imposed a barrier. "How can the Messiah come from Galilee?" they asked (John 7:41; see also v. 52).

Galilee is a land of beauty and charm where the ancient abuts the modern—a land of conquests and battles and bloodshed, of heroism and religious devotion. Shepherds still watch over their flocks by night, but you also see miles of mangoes and avocados, date palms and bananas, as well as ostrich farms. I found much to surprise me, to correct preconceived ideas, and to reorder my understanding of the story of Jesus.

Jesus made the town of Capernaum His headquarters in Galilee. Receiving a cold reception in Nazareth and remarking that "no prophet is accepted in his hometown" (Luke 4:24), He went to Capernaum, which became "his own town" (Matt. 9:1). There's no town now, only remains and a garish new basilica built, supposedly, over the house where Jesus healed Peter's mother-in-law (Mark 1:29–31). By contrast, Nazareth today isn't the obscure town I imagined. It sprawls over several hills, and making one's way today from one side of town to the other can take long because of constant traffic jams.

Cana, known as Kanna today, is an ancient town that still survives. A Roman Catholic church vies with a Greek Orthodox structure for the site of Jesus's first miracle of turning water into wine at the wedding feast.

Magdala, called Migdol today, is a town lying close to the lake. Mary Magdalene (Mary of Magdala, Luke 8:2) came from here.

Bethsaida, located at the north end of the lake near the place where the Jordan flows in, was the town of Philip,

Andrew, and Peter (John 1:44) but lies in ruins today.

Gadara, know as Kursi today, is a site across the lake from Capernaum that marks the place where Jesus healed the demon-possessed man and where the herd of swine plunged into the lake and drowned (Mark 5:1–13).

Many more places exist from the days when Jesus walked in Galilee—Nain (Ne'in today), where He brought the widow's son back to life (Luke 7:11–15); Chorazin, which He upbraided because of its failure to repent and to heed His teachings (Matt. 11:21); Mount Tabor, the traditional place of the Transfiguration; and so on.

And, of course, the Jordan River. The gospel song says, "I walked today where Jesus walked, in days of long ago," but I very much doubt that the writer had ever visited Israel. He wrote, "I saw the mighty Jordan roll as in the days of yore," but the Jordan you find is only a small river, about 100 feet (30 m) across.

Of course, on the trip to Israel our hosts also took us to Jerusalem. I much preferred the open space of Galilee. Perhaps Jesus did too. Although He died in Jerusalem and, forty days later, ascended from Jerusalem, He went back to Galilee for a final visit after the Resurrection. Jesus went back north to His land, the mountains (Matt. 28:16), and the lake (John 21:1).

Galilee is where the story of Jesus's earthly life and work found focus. It started so small, but it spread to the ends of the earth.

The Galilean called other Galileans to carry on His work after He returned to the Father. Like Moses with the twelve tribes, He chose twelve men who would forever be associated with the rise of the new movement. What were they like? Why did He select these and not others?

The Twelve

Matthew, Mark, and Luke make clear that Jesus's proclamation of the kingdom of heaven and His miracles quickly attracted a large response in Galilee (Matt. 4:23–25). Word about Him spread far and wide; people came from distant places to hear Him. At times, crowds pressed upon Him so much that He had to get into a boat near the lake's shore (Mark 4:1). Sometimes He scarcely found opportunity to even eat. The sheer weight of the numbers hampered His activities (Mark 3:20).

Many came seeking healing. Others brought with them sick relatives and friends, hoping to get help from Jesus. The crowds surrounding Him numbered in the thousands and at times tens of thousands (Luke 12:1). In some instances the people trailed Him for several days from place to place (e.g., Mark 8:2).

Among the people coming to Jesus in Galilee, we may discern, as it were, several concentric circles. At the far edge stood those that the Gospel writers simply call the "crowds" (e.g., Matt. 4:25; Mark 2:13; 4:1). They came to hear and to be healed, or simply out of curiosity.

Others, however, became adherents of Jesus's message. They formed the second concentric circle. Heeding Jesus's call to follow Him, they became disciples.

The Greek word translated "disciple," *mathētēs*, simply means "student" or "pupil." In the Judaism of Jesus's time the idea was quite common. Among the Pharisees, for example, disciples apprenticed themselves to a rabbi to be instructed in the law, and then they in turn became rabbis.

The discipleship that Jesus called for demanded a new type of involvement. Based on the Master's proclamation that the kingdom of heaven was even now breaking in upon earth, it set out a radical lifestyle and mission. Jesus devoted much time training His followers in discipleship by both word and life. The concept is highly important for everyone today who seeks to take seriously His life and teachings. We shall study it carefully later in this textbook (see chap. 20).

The Synoptic Gospels nowhere indicate a number for Jesus's disciples in Galilee, but it is obvious that there were many. Luke refers to them as a "large crowd" and "whole crowd" (Luke 6:17; 19:37). Among them were a group of seventy-two whom Jesus sent out on a special mission (Luke 10:1–6). Many women also followed Jesus devotedly (Mark 15:40, 41; Luke 8:2, 3).

From among the large group of disciples, Jesus, after spending a whole night in prayer, selected twelve men.

They would be His constant companions and would carry on His mission after He returned to the Father. Mark records, "He appointed twelve that they might be with him and that he might send them out to preach" (Mark 3:14). The word "apostle" means "sent one." They would be Jesus's envoys. Under His authority they went ahead of Him throughout Galilee, healing the sick, casting out demons, and announcing the kingdom of God (Matt. 10:1, 5–8).

The Twelve played a particular role governed by time and place. They had been with Jesus and had witnessed what He had said and done. In addition, they were living witnesses to His resurrection: Jesus "appeared to them over a period of forty days and spoke about the kingdom of God" (Acts 1:3). So long as they were alive, they formed a living link to the story of Jesus.

The Twelve's role was unique and ceased with them. They did not function as an institution, nor was the apostolate self-perpetuating. Furthermore, we read of others in the New Testament who are designated "apostles"—that is, sent out (Acts 14:14; Rom. 16:7; 1 Cor. 12:28; 15:9).

In later centuries the teaching of "apostolic succession" gradually developed in Christianity. This taught—and still teaches—that there is an unbroken line of authority, based on ordination of clergy, from the time of the Twelve to today's church. The Twelve ordained clergy who in turn ordained other clergy, who in turn ordained other clergy and so on ad infinitum.

By this understanding the Church (that is, the Roman Catholic Church) claims authority to be the genuine apostolic church. The claim, however, totally lacks biblical support. Nowhere in the New Testament do we read of the Twelve ordaining other ministers. We do read, on the other hand, of people other than the Twelve who are designated "apostles": Paul, notably (e.g., Rom. 1:1; 1 Cor. 9:1, 2; Gal. 2:8, 9); Barnabas (Acts 14:14); Apollos (1 Cor. 4:6, 9); and Silas and Timothy (1 Thess. 1:1; 2:6). In fact, apostleship is listed as one of the gifts of the Holy Spirit (1 Cor. 12:27–30).

Going beyond the Twelve, we also find a fourth concentric circle of those associated with Jesus in Galilee. On several occasions Jesus singled out Peter, James, and John for special privileges: at the raising of Jairus's daughter (Mark 5:37–42), at the Transfiguration (Matt. 17:1, 2), and in the Garden of Gethsemane (Mark 14:32, 33).

The Men Chosen by Jesus

We find three complete listings of the twelve apostles in the Synoptic Gospels (Matt. 10:2–4; Mark 3:14–19; and Luke 6:13–16). In addition, in Acts 1:13 we find a fourth listing; this one, however, omits the name of Judas Iscariot.

The names in these lists bear close resemblance; there are, however, a few differences, probably to be accounted for by individuals having more than one name. The Twelve are:

Simon, later known as Simon Peter
Andrew, brother of Simon Peter
James and John, sons of Zebedee
Philip
Nathanael, also named Bartholomew
Matthew, also called Levi
Thomas
James the son of Alphaeus
Simon the Zealot or Canaanean
Judas, son of James
Judas Iscariot

The Gospel of Matthew lists the Twelve in pairs: Simon and Andrew; James and John; Philip and Bartholomew; Thomas and Matthew; James son of Alpaeus and Thaddaeus (also known as Judas the brother of James in Acts 1:13); and Simon the Zealot and Judas Iscariot. This is because they went out in pairs.

The Gospels give us little information about some of these men. Others, however, play prominent roles in the story of Jesus and later in the Book of Acts. Putting all the data together gives us a fascinating and even surprising picture of the twelve men Jesus selected to represent Him.

Unlearned Men

With the possible exception of one or two, the Twelve were unlearned. They were fishers, peasants, and rustics. The Jewish authorities looked down on them with the same contempt they had shown to Jesus (Acts 4:13). Matthew the tax collector and Judas Iscariot possibly had received an education.

Diversity

The Twelve were diverse in age, temperament, and affiliation. Peter, already married, owned a small fishing enterprise. John, son of Zebedee, probably the youngest, lived on for another seventy years or so after Jesus called him by the Lake of Galilee. He and his brother James were quick-tempered, given to outbursts of passion. Jesus humorously gave them the nickname Boanerges— "sons of tumult" or "sons of thunder" (Mark 3:17). Thomas, on the other hand, was a doubter, slow to accept a proposition on faith.

Most startling by contrast were Levi Matthew and Simon the Zealot. The former, a tax collector, cooperated with the hated Roman rulers, serving as their lackey for financial concerns. Simon was a member of the Zealots, a band of radical Jewish nationalists given to violence and uprisings. That the band of close followers of Jesus could include Matthew and Simon is extraordinary.

Flawed

The Twelve were flawed, as we all are. Slow to learn, they constantly misunderstood both the teachings and actions of Jesus.

Among them, Peter was the natural leader; he is mentioned first in all the lists. Peter was quick to sum up a situation, quick to speak, and quick to act. Often too quick! Peter drew his sword and cut off the ear of the high priest's servant in the Garden of Gethsemane (John 18:10). Peter once attempted to walk on water (Matt. 14:25–31) and another time plunged into the lake when he recognized Jesus standing on the shore (John 21:7). Peter responded, "Lord, to whom shall we go?" when many disciples turned away from Jesus (John 6:68). Peter affirmed, "You are the Messiah, the Son of the living God" at Caesarea Philippi (Matt. 16:16). He vehemently proclaimed his intention to stay with Jesus, even unto death itself. But Peter failed miserably when the test came, denying that he even knew Jesus.

We know little about Nathanael, but what we have suggests that he was a spiritual person, although flawed. Jesus spoke highly of him: "Here truly is an Israelite in whom there is no deceit," He said as He saw Nathanael approaching (John 1:47). Nathanael harbored prejudice against the people of Nazareth. All of us likewise are prejudiced against some people. We simply grow up in the midst of a society that, before we were born, classified some people as inferior because of their ethnicity, color, gender, occupation, or some other trait. The gospel calls upon us to confront these acquired dislikes and go beyond them to accept every person—regardless of how different they may seem—as a child of God.

Nathanael quickly took this step when he met Jesus. Although initially his reaction to Philip's claim to have found the one foretold by Moses was a brusque, "Can anything good come from there [Nazareth]?" (John 1:46), he soon changed his mind. All it took was a simple statement from Jesus that He had seen Nathanael under the fig tree before Philip called him (v. 48).

The fig tree was special in Nathanael's experience. Rabbis frequently studied and taught under a fig tree; for Nathanael, the fig tree was a place of private prayer. Jesus's words about seeing him there immediately revealed to this true Israelite that here was someone whose powers extended beyond normal human abilities—even if He did come from Nazareth.

Learners

The Twelve whom Jesus called may have been unlearned peasants, but the Master, who saw Nathanael under the fig tree, saw in them qualities that others did not. They were diamonds in the rough. By associating with Him—seeing His life and ministry, absorbing His teachings, and sharing in that ministry—they would gradually be shaped, molded, and perfected.

The fiery John would become the loving "disciple whom Jesus loved" (John 20:2), whose letters overflow with deep devotion to the Lord and call us to love our brothers and sisters.

Peter, impulsive and headstrong, would learn to put his trust in divine power rather than in his own abilities. He would become a strong leader in the early church. His letters would encourage Christians facing persecution and suffering to stand firm no matter what difficulties would befall them.

Of the other members of that select, privileged group of twelve, we have scant record of their subsequent history. Luke in the Book of Acts informs us that James the brother of John met an early death. Slain by order of King Herod Agrippa I, James was the first of the Twelve to suffer martyrdom (Acts 12:1, 2). Thomas, according to ancient traditions, took the gospel to India. The site of his grave is marked, and a large group of Christians in South India—"Thomas Christians"—bear his name today.

Very different is the trajectory of Judas Iscariot. Seemingly the most gifted of the Twelve—they chose him to be treasurer for the group (John 12:4–6)—his life ended in disgrace. He betrayed Jesus and later took his own life. Over the course of the centuries Christians have named sons after all the Twelve except one. The name of Judas, the apostle who became traitor, lives in infamy.

Later in this book we shall look more closely at Judas and his role in the closing events of Jesus's life. We shall probe the betrayer's motivation, trying to understand why he embarked on the course so tragic for both himself and Jesus. Here we shall confine ourselves to one issue: How did Judas ever find a place among the Twelve? The Gospel of John tells us that Jesus could read people's hearts. Why then did He not exclude Judas from the outset?

The same Gospel makes clear that Jesus foresaw Judas's betrayal: "Then Jesus replied, 'Have I not chosen you, the Twelve? Yet one of you is a devil!' (He meant Judas, the son of Simon Iscariot, who, though one of the Twelve, was later to betray him)" (John 6:70, 71).

Does this mean that Judas was predestined to be the traitor? Not at all. He was no more predestined to betray Jesus than any followers of the Master are predestined to turn their backs on Him. God has made us all creatures with the power of choice. He sets before us life and death, the good way and the bad. He does not coerce or compel. Although He loves us and longs for us to choose the good—and keep on choosing it—ultimately our destiny lies in our own hands.

Eleven apostles, starting out with much to learn and with characters greatly in need of polishing, yielded to the sweet influence of the Master. Gradually, more and more, they became shaped into His character. One, however, resisted. Although he began the journey with the others seemingly with good possibilities, he made a shipwreck of his life. What a tragedy!

The Twelve were indeed an unlikely group of people on which to build a world movement. But God was working in them and through them. That made all the difference. It still does.

The Twelve accompanied Jesus on two circuitous tours of the towns and villages of Galilee (see Matt. 4:23; 9:35; the wording is almost identical). Almost from the beginning Jesus came into conflict with various groups of people. The theme of conflict will be the focus of our study in the next chapter.

QUESTIONS FOR DISCUSSION

1. Study Ellen White's comments on the selection of Judas as one of the Twelve (Ellen G. White, "Judas" (chapter 76), *The Desire of Ages*, https://egwwritings.org/?ref=en_ DA.716¶=130.3509). What additional insights does she furnish beyond the biblical record?

2. Most of the disciples were unlearned—what does this say about Jesus's preferential option? Is this a rule (e.g., the learned Paul)?

3. What does the order of the list containing the names of the Twelve say about them? Who is named always the first and the last? What can you deduce from this order? See Matthew 10:2–4; Mark 3:14–19; Luke 6:13–16.

Jesus and Conflict

OBJECTIVES

- Identify the various sources of conflict that Jesus encountered during His ministry in Galilee.

- Understand why Jesus became a controversial figure.

SCRIPTURE

- Matthew 12:22–32; Mark 3:20–22, 31–35; 5:1–8; 6:52–56; Luke 4:16–30

For some time Jesus enjoyed widespread popularity in Galilee. People flocked to Him to hear His message or receive healing from disease and release from demon possession. News about Him traveled far beyond Galilee itself.

Mark paints a vivid picture of the effect of His ministry at this stage: "Jesus withdrew with his disciples to the lake, and a large crowd from Galilee followed. When they heard about all he was doing, many people came to him from Judea, Jerusalem, Idumea, and the regions across the Jordan and around Tyre and Sidon. Because of the crowd he told his disciples to have a small boat ready for him, to keep the people from crowding him" (Mark 3:7–9).

But not everyone joined in the general enthusiasm. Almost from the beginning some people raised doubts about Him and His work. They questioned His legitimacy and His authority to teach in the name of God. They cast doubts on His work, especially on the genuineness of the miracles He was performing. Thus, Jesus, the Prince of Peace (Isa. 9:6), found Himself in conflict. Opposition arose from four main sources. Sadly, and perhaps most distressingly to Him, it started with the members of His own family.

Conflict with the Family

The words are terse but speak volumes: "Then Jesus entered a house, and again a crowd gathered, so that he and his disciples were not even able to eat. When his family heard about this, they went to take charge of him, for they said, 'He is out of his mind'" (Mark 3:20, 21).

The family dynamic is extraordinary. His own siblings displayed a colossal lack of understanding of both Jesus's mission and how they should relate to Him. They didn't comprehend that He came to this earth by divine appointment and that every moment of His sojourn among humanity was governed by the will of the Father (John 8:29). For the family, the fact that Jesus and the disciples were too busy to pause and eat indicated that He had lost His balance. He had gone to extremes and for His own good needed to be reined in. They couldn't grasp that eating, although it is important, is not the ultimate good in life.

The disciples had witnessed similar behavior from the Master during the encounter with the Samaritan woman by the well. When they returned from the town with food they urged Him, "Rabbi, eat something" (John 4:31).

He replied, "I have food to eat that you know nothing about" (v. 32). Then He elaborated, "My food . . . is to do the will of him who sent me and to finish his work" (v. 34).

Jesus's mother and brothers did not understand the burning motivation of His life. Their thinking arose from this world but His from heaven. So they went to the house where Jesus was absorbed in ministry and, standing outside, sent in a message that they wanted to talk with Him. But Jesus didn't move; He stayed right where He was.

"Your mother and brothers are outside looking for you," they told Him.

"Who are my mother and my brothers?" He asked. Then, he looked at those seated in a circle around Him and said, "Here are my mother and my brothers! Whoever does God's will is my brother and sister and mother" (Mark 3:31–35).

Did Jesus not value family? Of course He did. We can be sure of this from His tender care for Mary. As He hung dying on the cross, He made provision for her future well-being by entrusting her into the hands of John the Beloved (John 19:25–27). Mary was the only family member who stayed by Jesus until the end. Other women, disciples who had followed Him in Galilee, were there, but none of His sisters. And certainly none of His brothers. Jesus trod a lonely path in fulfillment of His mission. As much as He would have desired encouragement and affirmation from those tied to Him by flesh and blood, He did not find it. The trail of salvation that He blazed left siblings, home, trade, and Nazareth far behind.

For many people today, as in the past, blood ties are very important. In some cultures they are all important: the family determines one's identity and must be honored whatever the cost. Slights against the family call for revenge; ancient quarrels simmer and come to the boil. Wrongs perpetuated in the distant past—Serbs against Croats, Croats against Serbs; Arabs against Jews, Jews against Arabs—live on, poisoning relationships.

Jesus's view of family differed radically from this conception: "Whoever does God's will is my brother and sister and mother" (Mark 3:35). On another occasion He said, "For I have come to turn 'a man against his father, a daughter against her mother, a daughter-in-law against her mother-in-law—a man's enemies will be the members of his own household'" (Matt. 10:35, 36). The Prince of Peace is the divider of humanity. That was true then and still true today, even among the members of His earthly family.

The Gospel accounts make clear that of all those closest to Jesus in terms of natural ties, only His mother showed some comprehension as to who He was and why He had come to earth. Mary "pondered" in her heart what she saw and heard of her unique son (Luke 2:19, 51). But, blessed though she was to be chosen as the vessel for the birth of Jesus, Mary did not in herself acquire a grace that would make her—as some claim—the mediator between God and humanity. Once during Jesus's ministry in Galilee a woman cried out from the crowd: "Blessed is the mother who gave you birth and nursed you" (Luke 11:27).

But Jesus responded, "Blessed rather are those who hear the word of God and obey it" (v. 28).

If Jesus's mother entertained at least an inkling of belief in her son, his brothers did not. "For even his own brothers did not believe in him" (John 7:5), states John regarding a later incident when Jesus's siblings attempted to direct the course of His ministry.

Yet even allowing for the strained relations between Jesus and family members, the incident recounted in Mark 3:20, 21, 31–35 is extraordinary. His brothers did not exhibit a trace of respect, let alone deference. Crowds thronged around Jesus, with many people traveling long distances to see and hear Him, but His own family decided that they had to put a stop to this nonsense.

Thereby we gain additional insights into the family dynamics. Obviously, during Jesus's growing-up years He had exhibited no miraculous powers to impress His siblings. He had seemed just like them; they failed to see beyond appearances. His loving, unselfish nature might have led them to appreciate Him—if only they had opened their eyes. Later, however, some members of Jesus's family had a change of heart. At least two of them, James and Jude, became followers and wrote New Testament books.

Conflict with the People of Nazareth

None of the Twelve came from Nazareth, nor did Jesus make Nazareth the base for His mission in Galilee. Abandoning Nazareth, He chose Capernaum to be the center from which He carried on His work.

We can imagine a very different scenario, one in which Jesus, growing up in Nazareth, early on attracted a band of followers who became the nucleus of His efforts. It did not happen. The people of Nazareth, blind to the evidence of their eyes, turned their backs on Him.

Among the inhabitants of Galilee, Nazareth was a byword. "Can anything good come from there?" Nathanael had exclaimed to Philip (John 1:46). Although the Gospels do not elaborate on the particular failings that made the people of Nazareth notorious, we gain insights into their depravity from a startling incident recorded in Luke 4:16–30.

Jesus had been away for some time from the town where He grew up. He had traveled around Galilee; He had become famous, as "everyone praised him" (Luke 4:15). Now He returns to Nazareth and on the Sabbath, following His custom, He goes to the synagogue. His presence creates a stir: the local boy who made good has come back. Maybe He will put on a show for them, performing one or two spectacular miracles that will amaze and delight.

They hand Him the Scriptures to give the public reading. Turning to Isaiah 61:1, 2, He reads, "The Spirit of the Sovereign Lord is on me, because the Lord has anointed me to proclaim good news to the poor. He has sent me to bind up the brokenhearted, to proclaim freedom for the captives and release from darkness for the prisoners, to proclaim the year of the Lord's favor" (see Luke 4:18, 19).

The passage sums up His mission. He will not be a conquering king who will spearhead a national movement to drive out the hated Roman armies. Rather, the good news He proclaims is for the poor, the broken, the captive, and the oppressed. He returns the Isaiah scroll to the attendant and sits down. Everyone is looking at Him, trying to figure Him out, wondering what will come next, and waiting for the "show" to commence.

Jesus begins to speak: "Today this scripture is fulfilled in your hearing" (Luke 4:21). He speaks well; the people of Nazareth are impressed. But they begin to wonder at the change in this man Whom they thought they knew well. "'Where did this man get these things?' they asked. 'What's this wisdom that has been given him? What are these remarkable miracles he is performing? Isn't this the carpenter? Isn't this Mary's son and the brother of James, Joseph, Judas and Simon? Aren't his sisters here with us?'" (Mark 6:2, 3).

Jesus continues speaking, and His words become uncomfortably pointed. Echoing their thoughts, He says, "Do here in your hometown what we have heard that you did in Capernaum" (Luke 4:23). But no miracle will be forthcoming. He tells them that no prophet is accepted in his hometown and gives two examples from the Old Testament—Elijah, who was sent to Zarephath near Sidon, and Elisha, who became the agent of cleansing from leprosy for Naaman the Syrian. His words cut home; the people of Nazareth are like the Israelites of old whom the Lord bypassed, working miracles among the despised Gentiles instead (vv. 25–27).

It is too much for the people of Nazareth. The words of praise for His gracious speech fall silent; they become furious.

They came to worship, but now they can only think of killing. They drive Jesus out of the synagogue and attempt to throw Him over the cliff at the edge of town. But God intervenes, and Jesus's life is spared. The synagogue in Nazareth became a dangerous place for the Preacher who felt impelled to give a straight message. Was this Jesus's last visit to His hometown? Possibly. We have no record of His ever returning in a public role. Perhaps He briefly visited His mother, but if so He kept a low profile. How stubborn and blind the people in Nazareth were. Among them were likely many sick and suffering people broken and in desperate need of the healing for body and soul that Jesus was ready to bring. But "He could not do any miracles there, except lay his hands on a few sick people and heal them" (Mark 6:5).

Mark concludes his account of the rejection at Nazareth with an arresting statement. "He [Jesus] was amazed at their lack of faith" (v. 6). Even Jesus, who read the human heart, could only shake His head at these people.

It's not so different in our times. Jesus must still be shaking His head in wonder at the stubborn refusal to believe. The big questions of the day all come back to faith: *Can* we believe? *Will* we believe? God never asks us to believe without supplying all the evidence we need. But He does not compel. Faith is an individual matter that neither family, friend, nor fellowship can bring to us. Faith is not a matter of emotion but of decision.

Nobody can claim that they cannot believe. Belief is a gift offered to us all.

Conflict with the Religious Authorities

It was inevitable that Jesus would clash with the religious authorities. He hadn't trained in the rabbinical schools; He wasn't part of the fraternity of the Pharisees and teachers of the law. Yet He taught with an authority born of immersion in the Scriptures and power of the Holy Spirit.

In the early stages of Jesus's ministry in Galilee, the religious authorities waited skeptically to see where the movement centered on the country carpenter might lead. But before long the Pharisees and teachers of the law were forced to take Jesus seriously. His miracles, exorcisms, and, above all, power to attract huge crowds could not be brushed off. They engaged Him in dialogue that grew increasingly sharp and critical.

We find three areas of conflict: Jesus's claim to forgive sins, the authorities' attempt to ascribe His miracles to Beelzebul, and Jesus's relation to the Sabbath.

The issue of forgiveness of sins arose from a miracle in Capernaum that had unusual features, as portrayed in Mark 2:1–12. Jesus was teaching in a home to a packed house—standing room only, without an inch to squeeze in another person. Along comes a paralyzed man seeking healing, borne on a mat by four men. With no possibility of getting into the room, what do they do? Climb up on the roof, remove some of the covering, and lower the paralytic down into the room. Here is faith with ingenuity indeed!

Jesus, acknowledging their faith, now speaks. But instead of saying, "Get up and walk," He says to the paralytic, "Son, your sins are forgiven" (v. 5). He recog-

nizes that the man before Him has a two-fold problem, spiritual as well as physical, and He first addresses the greater need.

His words create a buzz among the teachers of the law: "Why does this fellow talk like this? He's blaspheming! Who can forgive sins but God alone?" (v. 7).

Jesus knows what is going through their minds. They are thinking, "A fine claim. Easy to say, but the man still lies there paralyzed!" So Jesus says to them, "I want you to know that the Son of Man has authority on earth to forgive sins" (v. 10). Then He turns to the paralytic and says, "I tell you, get up, take your mat and go home" (v. 11). And the man does, amazing everyone.

In this interesting incident, Jesus links spiritual healing with physical healing.

One is not easier to do than the other; both come by the power of God. Jesus's healing of the paralytic demonstrated that He also had authority to heal the soul.

Jesus is the Healer. The Greek word for healing, *sozō*, can mean both "to heal" and "to save." Thus, in another incident when Jairus sent an urgent request for help to Jesus because his daughter was dying, he said, "Please come and put your hands on her so that she will be healed [*sozō*] and live" (Mark 5:23). This linking of healing and forgiveness already occurs in the Old Testament:

> Praise the Lord, my soul,
>   and forget not all his benefits—
> who forgives all your sins
>   and heals all your diseases. (Ps. 103:2, 3)

By His words and deeds in connection with the paralyzed man in Capernaum, Jesus pointed to Himself as the One who alone has power and authority over both sin and sickness. The teachers of the law, recognizing the import of the event, were furious: "The carpenter from Nazareth is taking to himself the prerogatives of divinity!"

But they could not deny what was evident to all—Jesus's miracles. They refused to entertain the idea that God was the source of His power, so they tried to turn His very miracles against Him. "He is possessed by Beelzebul!" they argued. "By the prince of demons he is driving out demons" (Mark 3:22).

Invoking the name of Beelzebul was a lame attempt to denigrate Jesus. But He cut to the quick in exposing their flawed logic. "Every kingdom divided against itself will be ruined, and every city or household divided against itself will not stand," He argued. "If Satan drives out Satan, he is divided against himself. How then can his kingdom stand?" (Matt. 12:25, 26).

Then came a solemn warning. In seeking to discredit Jesus by attributing His miracles to the power of Satan, His adversaries were treading on extremely dangerous ground. They were slighting the work of the Holy Spirit, whose work is to draw all men and women to God. Thus, they were cutting themselves off from the only means they—and we—have of coming to God.

Jesus's words that followed are the most serious of everything He ever uttered: "I tell you, every kind of sin and slander can be forgiven, but the blasphemy against the Spirit will not be forgiven. Anyone who speaks against the Holy Spirit will not be forgiven, either in this age or in the age to come" (Matt. 12:31, 32). The conflict between Jesus and the religious authorities here reaches a point of sharpest dissension. They allege that He is empowered by Satan, not God, when working miracles; He solemnly warns them that by this allegation they run the risk of committing the unpardonable sin.

The third area of conflict involved Jesus's relations to the Sabbath. From the viewpoint of the religious teachers, He broke the Sabbath by "working"—that is, healing people on that day (Luke 13:14). When they accused Him and His disciples of Sabbath-breaking, He defended Himself by claiming to be the "Lord even of the Sabbath"—that is, the One who alone had authority to define what is true Sabbath observance (Mark 2:28).

Later we shall take up more thoroughly Jesus's relation to the Sabbath. Suffice to note here that both in Jerusalem and in Galilee the religious leaders first resolved to kill Jesus because of His relation to the Sabbath (John 5:9, 18).

Conflict with the Powers of Darkness

Behind Jesus's conflict with family, the people of Nazareth, and the religious teachers lay a hidden but more deadly battle—with demonic forces. The battle had begun in heaven itself; now it moved to earth.

Most people go through life with their thoughts centered on this world. They rarely, if at all, give time to the supernatural. The words of the apostle Paul seem incomprehensible to them: "Our struggle is not against flesh and blood, but against the rulers, against the authorities, against the powers of this dark world and against the spiritual forces of evil in the heavenly realms" (Eph. 6:12).

Jesus, throughout His life on earth, remained keenly aware of this struggle. At the very commencement of His ministry He met Satan head-on and bested the tempter; but that wasn't the end of the conflict. At every step of the journey the powers of darkness waited, ready to pounce and derail the saving mission for which He had come to earth.

Although the religious leaders didn't recognize who He was, the demons did. They saw behind the humble appearance of the Man from Nazareth; they knew that if He succeeded in His mission their doom would be sealed.

Jesus came to a world in darkness, when the powers of evil exercised control over the minds and bodies of men and women. But He came to set men and women free from sin, disease, and demonic captivity: "Land of Zebulun and land of Naphtali, the Way to the Sea, beyond the Jordan, Galilee of the Gentiles—the people living in darkness have seen a great light; on those living in the land of the shadow of death a light has dawned" (Matt. 4:15, 16; see also Isa. 9:1, 2).

Often in Galilee, people's sicknesses were connected to demonic possession, so Jesus's saving ministry to them involved a two-fold healing—exorcising the demons and restoring people to mental and physical health (e.g., Mark 1:34; 3:10–12; 6:12, 13).

We find Jesus in conflict with the powers of darkness from the outset of His ministry in Galilee. During His first sermon on Sabbath in the synagogue in Capernaum, the worship service was interrupted by a demon-possessed man who shouted out, "What do you want with us, Jesus of Nazareth? Have you come to destroy us? I know who you are—the Holy One of God" (Mark 1:24). But Jesus ordered the demon to be quiet and come out of the man.

Two incidents in particular highlight Jesus's conflict with the powers of darkness. The first of these took place in non-Jewish territory and the second among the chosen people.

On one of Jesus's frequent crossings of the lake of Galilee, the boat landed in the region of the Gadarenes (or Gerasenes). Immediately on disembarking, Jesus was met by a wild, dangerous man who lived among the tombs. Unkempt and crazy, he shouted out night and day and gashed himself with stones. No one could restrain him; he simply tore apart the chains that bound him and broke the irons on his feet. Was ever a son of Adam reduced to a lower state? Who could glimpse a ray of hope for this unfortunate, crazy, demon-possessed individual?

Jesus could. When the wild man ran to Him shouting (and the disciples took to their heels), Jesus didn't flinch. He simply commanded, "Come out of this man, you impure spirit" (Mark 5:8). Clearly, Jesus was in charge, and the spirit had to obey. In fact, the man was possessed not by one demon but a host of them. And the demons, expelled from the man, begged Jesus to let them enter a large herd of pigs that was grazing nearby. He gave them permission; the pigs, driven by the demons, rushed down the steep bank bordering the lake and drowned in the water (vv. 9–17), which upset the local people. They pled with Jesus to go away. Score one for the demons, who apparently circumvented Jesus's ministry in that place? Only in the short term! When some time later Jesus returned, the Gadarenes flocked to hear Him (see Mark 6:53–56).

The second dramatic encounter with demons occurred after Jesus's heavenly experience on the Mount of Transfiguration. As He descended with Peter, James, and John, He came upon a large crowd that included His other disciples and teachers of the law. It was a confused scene, with a lot of arguing. A man had brought his demon-possessed son for healing, but the disciples had tried and failed (Mark 9:14–28).

They brought the boy to Jesus. The demon immediately convulsed the child: he fell to the ground and rolled around, foaming at the mouth. When the distraught father pled for Jesus to help, the Master rebuked the evil spirit: "You deaf and mute spirit . . . I command you come out of him and never enter him again" (v. 25). And after a violent convulsion that left the boy seemingly dead, the demon was gone forever.

It had been a life-and-death struggle. The whole ministry of Jesus in Galilee was one of life and death. But life won out, because Jesus was—and is—the Prince of Life.

QUESTIONS FOR DISCUSSION

1. A friend says, "I feel that I have committed the unpardonable sin; God does not hear my prayers anymore." What answers would you give?

2. What do you think was at the root of Jesus's problems with His family and hometown? What is it about familiarity that breeds contempt?

3. What were some of the key points over which Jesus clashed with religious authorities?

Jesus and the Weak

OBJECTIVES
- Grasp the extent of Jesus's ministry to those on the margins of society.

- Understand why Jesus focused on the weak.

SCRIPTURE
- Matthew 8:1–4; 18:1–4; 19:13–15; Luke 7:36–50; 8:1–3; John 9:1–7

Although Jesus ministered to all classes of people, the powerful as well as the weak, the Gospel accounts emphasize His concern for the less fortunate. The despised, outcasts, and broken were the objects of His loving concern. He singled them out and paid special attention to their cry of need.

Thus, as we read through the Gospels, we meet people in positions of power, like Nicodemus, Joseph of Arimathea, and Pharisees who invite Jesus to be their dinner guest. In His teachings He tells stories about kings and noblemen. He is anointed by Mary from a very expensive alabaster box of myrrh: it cost about three hundred days' wages (see Matt. 20:2), something like $30,000 or more in today's money.

But all these examples are the exception rather than the rule. Jesus, a poor man, befriends the poor and devotes most of His time among them. He continually looks out for anyone who is relegated to the edges, downcast, lonely, or rejected. Among the fascinating parade of the weak whom Jesus meets, we notice several groups that stand out: the common people, the sick, women, and children.

The Common People

Jesus was a man of the people. "The common people heard him gladly" (Mark 12:37, KJV). His following mainly came from farmers, fishermen, artisans, and housewives. He welcomed them; they flocked to Him. Sometimes they stayed with Him all day, through the night, and into the next day. They were intrigued by Him and His teachings.

The common people sensed that Jesus valued them. He lifted their thoughts beyond the mundane tasks that filled their days. He taught them about a heavenly Father who cared for the birds and the flowers of the field, and even more for them (Matt. 6:26, 28). Many of the common people felt broken. Their lives were short and filled with toil. They struggled just to find provisions for two meals each day. Most children did not live to adulthood; many babies died at birth or in their early years. Many women did not survive childbirth.

To these masses of poor, burdened, broken men and women, Jesus's ministry fell like refreshing dew. "Come to me, all you who are weary and burdened, and I will give you rest," He invited. "Take my yoke upon you and learn from me, for I am gentle and humble in heart, and you will find rest for your souls. For my yoke is easy and my burden is light" (Matt. 11:28–30).

Jesus's attitude toward the common people contrasted greatly with what the people were accustomed to receiving from the religious leaders. Religion had become the province of the specialists—the priestly elite, Pharisees, and the teachers of the law. They all looked down on the common people.

For the priests, the chief among whom belonged to the Sadducees, religion was big business. They profited handsomely from the temple transactions involving money changing (from Roman money to the temple shekel) and the sale of animals and birds to be offered as sacrifice in the temple. The homes of the high priests unearthed by archaeologists show that they lived in luxury.

The Pharisees and religious teachers specialized in the observance of the law, debating over variant interpretations. At the time of Jesus there were two main schools of thought: the followers of Rabbi Hillel, who was more liberal, and those of Rabbi Shammai, who tended to be more conservative.

The common people had neither the time nor the means to engage in the debates, often involving comparatively minor concerns that preoccupied the time of the Pharisees and teachers of the law. Nor could they observe all the rules of ritual purity that the religious leaders prescribed—their lives were taken up with the daily struggle for basic existence.

Accordingly, the Pharisees and teachers of the law viewed the common people with contempt. Two statements found in the Gospels capture the attitude of the religious elite: "This mob that knows nothing of the law—there is a curse on them" (John 7:49), made by the Pharisees during a session of the Sanhedrin; and the Pharisee's pious boasting in Jesus's parable of the two people who went to pray in the temple: "I thank you that I am not like other people—robbers, evildoers, adulterers—or even like this tax collector" (Luke 18:11).

In sharp contrast, Jesus welcomed the common people. Even when He took the Twelve away for what was meant to be a quiet retreat and found that the people had heard about the plan and arrived ahead of them, He didn't get impatient or angry. Instead, He greeted them and began to minister to them (Matt. 14:13, 14).

How we feel about others cannot be kept hidden for long. The loving interest that beat within Jesus's heart flowed out to the common people and they sensed that this Man was someone who cared deeply for them.

Unlike those of the religious teachers, His teachings were simple and down-to-earth. The religious leaders and Pharisees taught law; He taught life. They juxtaposed one interpretation of the law against another; He spoke of a farmer sowing seed, a woman sweeping the house to find a lost coin, and a wayward son who comes home. No wonder the common people heard Him gladly. He was one of them—poor and plain. His teachings came from their world, which was His world.

In the Jewish world into which Jesus came, a sharp divide yawned between the privileged and the rest. The privileged class of priests, Pharisees, and teachers of the law were doubly fortunate: they enjoyed wealth and status in this life as well as the favor of God who would reward their scrupulous observance of the Law with an eternal reward.

On the other side of the divide, the masses—the common people—struggled with poverty and sickness. Life was hard for them and, because they couldn't follow the rabbinical regulations as rigidly as demanded, they faced an uncertain future at the hands of a demanding Lord. The common people were weak, having no power with either God or wealthy people. Supposedly, God's curse was upon them, shown by their very status. If the Lord had blessed them, they wouldn't be as they were. He would grant them prosperity and a happier lot in life.

The Sick

Jesus came at a time of great darkness. People's minds and bodies were wracked by fear, superstition, and disease. Demonic activity had reached an intensity as the powers anticipating His coming had marshaled to thwart His work.

While the Master's ministry covered every area that affected the lives of the Galileans, healing occupied more time than any other of His activities. The Gospel accounts portray His going to every city and hamlet, with the people hearing about Him, hurrying to touch the hem of His garments, and bringing their sick in the hope that He will heal them (Matt. 4:23, 24). They came to Jesus a parade of misery—blind, deaf, mute, bent over, and crippled. But they left seeing, hearing, speaking, standing up straight, running, and praising. No wonder Jesus attracted crowds.

Lowest of the low, most pitiable of all in the parade of misery, were the lepers. Because of their disease they were shunned and had to live separately. The Mosaic law had decreed that the leper be banished from society: he must "wear torn clothes, let their hair be unkempt, cover the lower part of their face and cry out, 'Unclean! Unclean!' As long as they have the disease they remain unclean. They must live alone; they must live outside the camp" (Lev. 13:45, 46).

The Hebrew word translated "leprosy" was used for various diseases affecting the skin. It included what we usually understand by the term. Modern medicine has developed drugs that can arrest the ravages of the terrible disease, but in some parts of the world even today lepers are banished to colonies, often wretched in nature.

How would Jesus of Nazareth relate to lepers, the lowest of the low? Would He keep them at a distance, knowing that their touch conveyed risk of infection and rendered Him ceremonially unclean? "A man with leprosy came and knelt before him and said, 'Lord, if you are willing, you can make me clean.' Jesus reached out his hand and touched the man. 'I am willing,' he said. 'Be clean!' Immediately he was cleansed of his leprosy" (Matt. 8:2, 3).

Jesus's word would have sufficed, but He went further. To this poor wretch, who was shunned by society and feared to get close, Jesus extended the warmth of touch. That touch not only conveyed power to heal; it signified love and acceptance.

I find Jesus's action extraordinary and wonderful. Would I have been willing to reach out my hand? In the course of my travels I have visited leper colonies. I have seen the wretched plight of these people who, born and raised in isolation, live and die in it, knowing no other association than that of fellow lepers. Observing the lepers, I gained a new appreciation for the work of Father Damien, the Roman Catholic priest who gave his life to ministry among the lepers of Molokai in the Hawaii Islands and eventually contracted and died of the disease. I likewise applaud those Adventist ministries today that reach out to people afflicted with this terrible disease.

The sick people of Jesus's time, and they numbered many, were indeed weak. To the religion of the teachers of the law and Pharisees their affliction indicated God's displeasure. We see this common attitude reflected in the question that Jesus's own disciples asked Him when they encountered a man blind from birth: "Rabbi, who sinned, this man or his parents, that he was born blind?" (John 9:1, 2).

The rabbis drew a straight line of cause and effect between sin and disease. If a baby was born blind, then someone had sinned. Perhaps it was the parents and God was punishing them, or perhaps it was the blind person, who sinned in his mother's womb and now had to live with the consequences.

For the rabbis, the answer to the disciples' question was self-evident: *Someone sinned*.

But Jesus posited a different explanation: "'Neither this man nor his parents sinned,' said Jesus, 'but this happened so that the works of God might be displayed in him'" (v. 3). And Jesus then worked a miracle: the man received his sight (vv. 6, 7). Here we see the profound difference between Jesus and the teachers of religion. They focused on who the sinner was while Jesus focused on helping the sinner.

We live in a broken world far from God's ideal. Our actions have consequences: bad practices affect our bodies. But much that happens to us and to others is not directly or indirectly of our own doing. Bad things happen to all—even to good people.

Jesus calls us to follow in His footsteps in ministering to broken men and women. That means neither judging nor condemning others less fortunate than we are; certainly it does not invite an attitude of smug self-righteousness. Instead, we are to carry on the healing ministry of the Master, who said, "As long as it is day, we must do the works of him who sent me. Night is coming, when no one can work. While I am in the world, I am the light of the world" (John 9:4, 5).

Most Christian denominations build their activities with the church as their focus. They do not attempt to minister to the sick, leaving that work to healthcare professionals.

Seventh-day Adventists, however, take seriously the model of Jesus's ministry. He spent most of His time in relieving suffering; thus, Adventists, seeking to follow Him and continue His work, devote much effort and expense to the healing of the body as well as of the soul. They embrace the biblical view of humans that does not draw a sharp divide between the physical and the spiritual; they see people in a holistic sense.

For Adventists, the Greek word used in the Gospels for Jesus's ministry, *sōzō*, which translates as both "to save" and "to heal," sums up their mission. Like Christ, they seek to make humans *whole*. Whereas almost all other churches leave care of the body to health-care professionals, and whereas many of the latter do not view their work in spiritual terms, Adventists view the approaches of clergy and medicine as two sides of one coin. For Adventists, healing of the body without attention to the needs of the soul is deficient and one-sided, just as healing of the soul without concern for the needs of the physical, mental, and emotional dimensions represents a distortion of ministry.

Out of the Adventist understanding of people and their needs has developed a worldwide network of hospitals and clinics. An army of Adventist doctors, nurses, and other professionals devote themselves to relieving suffering, providing emergency aid, and educating people in principles of healthy living. The Seventh-day Adventist health-care network is big. Its financial accompaniments are huge. But at its heart and as its foundation and motivation is the ministry of Jesus of Nazareth, who "went about doing good, and healing all that were oppressed of the devil" (Acts 10:38, KJV).

Women

A daily prayer of men common in Jewish circles during Jesus's time expressed thanks to God for not being born an animal, a woman, a Gentile, or a barbarian. Similar prayers were also found in Greek circles. By His attitude and actions, Jesus shattered this view of women. In His dealings with women Jesus was a revolutionary. For the rabbis, women were regarded as dangerous on two scores—they were a source of defilement and a source of temptation.

The Levitical code singled out blood as an agent of impurity. Therefore, the monthly emissions associated with female menstruation rendered women ritually unclean for much of the time. Childbirth likewise made women impure for many days (Lev. 12:1–5). Thus, the pious Jew scrupulously attempting to maintain strict ritual purity should avoid contact with women.

Further, women were considered a trap that would lead men to compromise their practice of religion. Women aroused sensuous desires; they were a stumbling block to careful observance of the Law. The rabbis taught that if the pious man saw a woman approaching, he should lower his gaze to avoid eye contact. If he should stumble and fall in the effort, that was far preferable to permitting lustful thoughts to spring up within.

How vastly different the way the Rabbi from Nazareth related to women! Jesus not only had male followers who accompanied Him on His itinerant ministry, but His traveling party also included women disciples: "After this, Jesus traveled about from one town and village to another, proclaiming the good news of the kingdom of God. The Twelve were with him, and also some women who had been cured of evil spirits and diseases: Mary (called Magdalene) from whom seven demons had come out; Joanna the wife of Chuza, the manager of Herod's household; Susanna; and many others. These women were helping to support them out of their own means" (Luke 8:1–3).

We see in these verses that women played an important role in Jesus's ministry. Several in the group were people of wealth, married to prominent individuals, and they helped finance the expenses of the entire group that accompanied Jesus. Such behavior would have appalled the teachers of religion. To them, Jesus's conduct must have appeared unseemly, rash, and abhorrent. But Jesus, ever with an eye upon the weak, deliberately flouted their conventions. By His extraordinary actions He elevated women to a role parallel with that of His male disciples.

And women responded to the affirming, life-giving attitude they sensed in the Master. At the close of His life when the Twelve fled (with the exception of the beloved John [John 19:26, 27]), leaving Jesus hanging on the cross alone, women stayed. They stayed to the end, until His final, despairing cry of woe. They watched as Joseph and Nicodemus took the broken body down and laid it in the new tomb cut from the rock. They went home as the Sabbath sun sank in the west, but when the new week dawned they came back to the tomb bearing spices with which they intended to anoint Jesus's body (Luke 23:50–24:1).

Where were the men? Hiding. And Jesus, the risen Lord, appeared first of all—not to the Twelve, not even to Peter, James, and John—but to women (Matt. 28:9, 10; John 20:14–18).

Some of the female disciples of Jesus had experienced dramatic manifestations of His saving and healing power. Mary of Magdala—commonly known as Mary Magdalene—had been delivered from seven demons by the Master (Luke 8:2). Jesus had found her fallen, broken, and devil-possessed; He raised her to new hope and new life. She became a devoted follower, eternally grateful.

Was Mary of Magdala the same Mary, sister of Martha and Lazarus, who sat in rapt attention at the feet of Jesus when he visited the home in Bethany? Was she therefore the same Mary who bought the very expensive alabaster box and poured the myrrh on Jesus's feet, wiping them with her hair (John 12:2, 3)? The evidence suggests that it was one and the same person.

Even more elusive is the identity of the unnamed woman mentioned by Luke in 7:36–50. It is a striking scene: a Pharisee invites Jesus to dinner and while they are eating a woman slips in, opens an alabaster jar, and begins to pour perfume on His feet. Weeping copiously, she wets His feet with her tears, kisses them, and wipes them with her hair.

The host is offended at the intrusion. He recognizes the woman: she is a person of ill repute well known in the town. And the Pharisee is further offended by the actions of Jesus, who does nothing to stop the woman or send her away. "If this man were a prophet," he thought to himself, "he would know who is touching him and what kind of woman she is—that she is a sinner" (v. 39).

Jesus takes charge. He relates a simple story about two men whose debt is canceled—one is a large debt and the other a small one. He commends the woman for her loving expression of gratitude and says, "I tell you, her many sins have been forgiven—as her great love has shown. But [and here He exposes the smallness of the Pharisee's own heart] whoever has been forgiven little loves little." Then to the woman He says, "Your sins are forgiven. Your faith has saved you; go in peace" (vv. 47–50).

This story recorded by Luke closely parallels the accounts of the anointing at Bethany that we find in Matthew, Mark, and John (Matt. 26:6–13; Mark 14:3–9; John 12:1–8). Yet there are differences, most notably in the placement of the event in the ministry of Jesus. Matthew, Mark, and Luke put the anointing just before the Passion week, but in Luke's Gospel we find this story much earlier in Jesus's ministry (interestingly, Luke has no mention of the anointing at Bethany).

Over the course of the centuries Christian students of the Word have puzzled, speculated, and argued over the relation of the story in Luke to the accounts in the other three Gospels—is it the same event or different? If the same event, why did Luke put it so far out of the chronological order?

A categorical answer cannot be arrived at on the basis of the data. In my judgment, however, the total evidence tilts toward understanding the four accounts as describing the same event, with Luke showing extreme sensitivity to reminding his readers about the shameful past of Mary of Magdala.

Many women keep coming to light as we read through the Gospels: the woman with the bleeding for twelve years; the daughter of Jairus, twelve years old (Mark 5:21–43); the widow at Nain with her dead son (Luke 7:11–17); the widow in the temple casting all she had into the treasury (Luke 21:1–4); the woman bent over, with body distorted (Luke 13:10–17); the women of Jerusalem along the Via Dolorosa or "The Way of Sorrows" (Luke 23:27–31); and, of course, Elizabeth and Mary, mothers of the forerunner and of the Savior (Luke 1, 2).

In Jesus's day, as they are in many societies today, women were among the weak. But Jesus, friend of the weak, sought them out, affirmed them, and lifted them up to new hope and new life.

Children

In all ages children have been among the least powerful groups in society. They have neither possessions nor prestige; they are subject to the wishes and whims of adults. Often they have been bullied and beaten, counted of no value, and cast aside.

The lot of children is not much better today. We live in a time of great selfishness, in which many adults, preoccupied with their own pleasure and careers, view children as an unwelcome encumbrance. Boys and girls find themselves in a hostile environment.

Against such a background the attitude of Jesus toward children stands out in sharp contrast. He took notice of them, loved them, and welcomed them. He didn't regard them as a nuisance or as something to be ignored or treated as invisible.

The way in which a person relates to children reveals much about what they are really like. So-called important people who are too full of themselves to show acceptance and respect manifest their distorted scale of values. The truly great individuals behave like Abraham Lincoln, whose son Todd felt free to even enter unannounced the room in the White House where the cabinet was meeting.

The attitude of the Twelve toward children was very different from Jesus's. For them, children were a distraction from whom they sought to shield their Master. So when little children were brought to Jesus for Him to place His hands on them and pray for them, the disciples rebuked the people who brought them. But Jesus intervened. "Let the little children come to me, and do not hinder them," He said. "The kingdom of heaven belongs to such as these." And He placed His hands of blessing on them (Matt. 19:14, 15). Jesus went further, however. Not only did He welcome the children, but He also held them up as examples for the Twelve to emulate. While the disciples were constantly eyeing one another to figure out who was, would be, or wanted to be number one, Jesus called a little child and had him stand among them. "Truly I tell you," He said (words that indicated that the following should be taken very seriously), "unless you change and become like little children, you will never enter the kingdom of heaven. Therefore, whoever takes the lowly position of this child is the greatest in the kingdom of heaven" (Matt. 18:3, 4).

Jesus's words, so simple, are profound. In the innocent, loving, trusting face of a child we look upon the face of God. As we grow older and become entangled in the cares and conflicts of life, we gradually lose these qualities that are closest to heaven. We become devious and calculating, conscious of agendas—ours and others'. We wander further and further from the kingdom of heaven.

But Jesus went even further. The Savior uttered the strongest condemnation against anyone who causes a child to sin: "It would be better for them to have a large millstone hung around their neck and to be drowned in the depths of the sea" (Matt. 18:6). Jesus's words usually glowed with love and hope. Occasionally, however, He pointed out sin in stark terms with dire warnings. This was one of these occasions. The Protector of children left no room for misunderstanding or equivocation, condemning all who, anciently or today, exploit children by abusing them physically, emotionally, or sexually; by forcing them into armed conflict; or by otherwise destroying their innocence.

If we claim to be followers of the Nazarene, we too must do all in our power to defend and protect the weak and the vulnerable. We must become advocates for children in an age that showers hostility upon them.

QUESTIONS FOR DISCUSSION

1. Is Jesus's concern for the weak and powerless also found in the Old Testament? See Deuteronomy 24:19–21; Psalm 34:6; Amos 2:6–7; 5:11, 12; 8:4–6; Micah 6:8.

2. How did Jesus's relationship to the weak demonstrate the truth of His words: "So the last will be first, and the first will be the last" (Matt. 20:16)?

3. Contrast the attitude of Jesus with that of the Pharisees and teachers of the law toward the people. What does this tell us about the Rabbi of Nazareth?

4. The Greek verb *sōzō* means both "to heal" and "to save." Since the Gospels recorded Jesus healing the multitudes so many times, what does this suggest about how we minister to people's needs?

12

The Shadow of the Cross

OBJECTIVES

- Understand the significance of Jesus's ministry in the miracle of feeding the five thousand.

- Grasp the importance of Peter's great confession.

- Trace the development of Jesus's teaching about His rejection.

SCRIPTURE

- Matthew 16:13–20; 17:1–8; Luke 9:28–36; John 6:1–21

Jesus's ministry in Galilee expanded at a rapid pace. People came to Him from near and far—the areas surrounding Galilee, the Decapolis (ten cities east of the Jordan), Jerusalem, and Judea. They pressed in around Him, pushing to hear His words and to touch Him. They came to see and to hear, to be healed of their diseases, to be made whole.

Where would this people movement, now impossible to overlook, end?

In this chapter, we will study how Jesus's ministry in Galilee reached a climax. As rapidly as it had built up, it began to wane as the crowds came to realize that the carpenter from Nazareth was not, after all, the sort of Messiah that they were expecting. Jesus continued His ministry, but from this point on there was a difference. A shadow fell over everything.

Time was running out for the Master. He was still young, in His mid-thirties, and His work had been in progress for just a few years, but the night was coming, and He knew it. Increasingly, He tried to prepare the Twelve for what lay ahead, warning them that not far down the road lurked rejection, betrayal, suffering, and death. More and more the shadow that fell over His ministry bore the outline of a cross.

The Crisis in Galilee

In an earlier chapter we noticed that the Gospel of John does not mention Jesus's miracles recorded by Matthew, Mark, and Luke. Rather, John details, often at considerable length, several miracles that the Synoptic writers do not even notice.

There is one exception to this pattern, however. In the long sixth chapter, John describes the miracle of feeding the five thousand and Jesus's discussion with the Jews that resulted from the miracle. As we indicated, this miracle is the only one of Jesus's mighty acts recorded in all four Gospels.

Why did John depart from his usual pattern by recounting this miracle? Because of its significance. Looking back on the events of Jesus's life and ministry long after Matthew, Mark, and Luke had written their accounts, and led in his reflection by the Holy Spirit, John came to realize the nature of the events of those two days in Galilee—the day on the mountainside when Jesus provided food for the multitude, and then what followed, the day after, in the synagogue in Capernaum.

Those two days marked a turning point. On the first day Jesus's popularity reached unprecedented heights; but by the close of the second, the movement was torn by uncertainty and doubt. His followers, disillusioned, began to drift away. It was a crisis point not only for Jesus. The Twelve also would find their confidence in Jesus severely tested and would be tempted to join the deserters.

We need to look closely at the events of these two days as we seek to understand the dynamic of Jesus, the crowd, and the disciples that unfolded. Here we will treat only briefly Jesus's teaching on the second day, leaving a more extended discussion for later (see chap. 16).

John relates the story of that day with details unmatched by the other Gospel writers. John was there; Mark and Luke were not; Matthew probably was since he belonged to the Twelve. Looking back on the events of that day of jubilation and crisis, the words of Jesus and the part played by individual disciples came back to John in vivid detail that only an eyewitness could supply.

The meal had grown from a lad's simple lunch of barley bread and fish packed by a loving mother or family member (John 6:9). Though a seemingly insignificant item, John puts it in the record. This, the most powerful miracle of Jesus in impact, began with food supplied by a boy. In the hands of Jesus the offering of the least of His people—in age or status—multiplies into a boundless blessing.

John tells us that Jesus first posed a question to Philip: "Where shall we buy bread for these people to eat?" (John 6:5). The place where the crowd had gathered was near Bethsaida, Philip's hometown (John 1:44). Was He asking, "This is your territory, Philip. What do you have to suggest for feeding this crowd?"

Philip, having been with Jesus for a couple years by now, might have replied, "I don't know how we can feed this crowd, but You are able to, Lord." Instead Philip looks only at the superficial as he tells Jesus, "Two hundred denarii [that is, two hundred days' wages, about $20,000 in modern terms] would not buy enough bread for each one to have a bite!" In other words, "Forget about trying to feed them. It's a hopeless idea. We don't have money to buy food for this multitude."

But never count out Jesus. Never discount what simple means He is able to use to work wonders. Within a short time—probably one hour or so—everyone had eaten and was satisfied. In fact, there twelve baskets of food left over. A feast indeed! Counting women and children along with the five thousand men, the crowd would have been at least ten thousand. The effect of the miracle on the crowd was electric. Other miracles of the Master left them amazed; this one moved them to action.

Luke's telling of the story (Luke 9:10–17) gives no hint of what happened after everyone had eaten, but Matthew and Mark provide terse statements that suggest that there was far more to the story than in Luke's account.

Matthew: "Immediately Jesus made the disciples get into the boat and go on ahead of him to the other side, while he dismissed the crowd" (Matt. 14:22). He *made* them. What was going on?

Mark: "Immediately Jesus made his disciples get into the boat and go on ahead of him to Bethsaida, while he dismissed the crowd" (Mark 6:45).

The language in both Matthew and Mark points to strong reluctance on the part of the disciples. When we turn to John, the situation becomes clear: "After the people saw the sign Jesus performed, they began to say, 'Surely this is the Prophet who is to come into the world.'

Jesus, knowing that they intended to come and *make him king by force*, withdrew again to a mountain by himself" (John 6:14, 15; emphasis added). Now we catch the dynamic. For many weeks the Jesus movement had been gaining momentum. Jesus, following the brutal death of John the Baptist, attempts to get away for a break with the Twelve. The crowds, however, do not permit Him to elude them. They figure out where He and the disciples are headed and track them down (Matt. 14:13, 14).

For these ardent followers, the feeding is the final evidence they have been looking for. In Jesus they foresee a king who can assure them victory over the hated Romans who occupy the land. Here is a leader who can heal the wounded and feed the army. Here is the fulfillment of the second Moses spoken of in Deuteronomy 18:15. Jesus seems diffident. He doesn't thrust Himself forward, so they take matters into their own hands. They will crown this reluctant Messiah as their king, forcing Him to assume leadership of a mass movement that will liberate the Jews.

In the wilderness, after Jesus's baptism, the devil had approached Him, offering to give Him all the kingdoms of this world (Matt. 4:8, 9). Now he comes again, working through the crowd. He dangles the hook loaded with fame, earthly glory, and power before the Savior. But as Jesus did in the desert, again He refuses to accept the bait. Forthrightly, He turns the crowd away with authority, commanding them to go

"The Ancient Galilee Boat" at the Yigal Allon Museum

home. They go, but they aren't pleased. As they make their way home, praise of Jesus turns to grumbling. They feel disillusioned and angry with Him.

The Twelve also are disappointed. They don't understand their Master, Who refuses the earthly crown that they badly desire Him to have. They too begin to grumble; doubts enter their minds. Jesus acts again with authority. He orders them to get in the boat and cross over to Capernaum. He will join them later. The Twelve are slow to respond. They linger by the lake's edge, hoping that Jesus will change His mind, but eventually they weigh anchors and set sail.

Jesus, now all alone, prays. What a day it has been—one of incredibly high expectations, only to be dashed at the close. How much the Twelve have still to learn about Him and His mission.

In the middle of the night He comes to His friends. They are in deep water and in deep trouble. Caught up in a sudden squall, they fear for their lives. Then they see Jesus coming toward them, walking on the water. Terrified, they cry out; but He says, "It is I; don't be afraid" (John 6:20). He gets into the boat and they are soon safe on shore. With Jesus in the boat, they were secure. With Jesus in the boat of our lives, we too are secure.

Jesus walked on the water (Matt. 14:25). His followers who love and trust Him also walk on water in these days. They do the impossible—by faith. They do it, and yet they do not. It is His power and presence that undergird all their efforts.

The next day, many from the crowd who ate the loaves and fish come to Capernaum seeking Jesus. They hope against hope that He will reconsider and consent to be crowned as their king. It is not to be. In pointed words Jesus tells them, "Very truly I tell you, you are looking for me, not because you saw signs I performed but because you ate the loaves and had your fill" (John 6:26). Their minds are focused on earthly materials; He points them to the true Bread of life, which comes down from heaven.

The people don't like what they hear. Many turn away, saying, "This is a hard teaching. Who can accept it?" (v. 60).

Jesus feels keenly the rejection and turns to the Twelve. "You do not want to leave too, do you?" He asks (v. 67).

Peter, ever first to speak, this time replies with a gem: "Lord, to whom shall we go? You have the words of eternal life. We have come to believe and to know that you are the Holy One of God" (v. 69).

At Caesarea Philippi

During Jesus's time on earth, it was never doubted that He was truly human. No one ever came up to Him and pinched His flesh to determine whether He was real.

In later centuries some people, influenced by Greek philosophy that held that the material was bad and the spirit good, propagated ideas that Jesus wasn't really human—He only appeared to be human. But during His lifetime the evidence of His humanity was so clear that such theories did not have a chance of acceptance. Jesus was born as a baby like every child of Adam. He grew up as a child, with the powers of body and mind steadily advancing to maturity. He ate, drank, and slept as we all do. He became tired after hard work or a long walk on the road.

The issue for Jesus in His time was: *Is He in some sense more than human?* This Person whose conception in Mary's womb was shrouded in mystery—this itinerant preacher-healer-exorcist who attracted large crowds and performed amazing feats—who was He? He talked about His Father being in heaven and about Himself coming to this earth and returning. He preferred the term "Son of Man" for Himself, an expression that echoed the books of Ezekiel and Daniel. What did He mean by it? (See Ezek. 2:1, 3, 6, 8; 3:1; Dan. 7:13, 14.)

These speculations crystallized in the question: Is He the long-awaited Messiah? Has God at last, after centuries of prayers, sent the new King in the line of David to deliver His people?

The Twelve shared the general sense of wonderment about Jesus. For them, belief and doubt intermingled: they saw firsthand His incredible acts and words that liberated people from guilt, disease, and demons. But they also saw Him acting in ways that puzzled and confused them—most notably by refusing the mass movement to crown Him Israel's king.

As the days of His ministry shortened, Jesus spent more and more time in private with the Twelve. He attempted to prepare their hearts and minds for the shocking developments—ones seemingly impossible in their view—that lay just ahead. Here, in Matthew 16:13–20 we find Him taking them some 30 miles (48 km) to the north of Capernaum and the Lake of Galilee to the region of Caesarea Philippi.

Here He poses the question everyone in Galilee is asking: "Who do people say the Son of Man is?" The disciples give the usual answers: John the Baptist (risen from the dead), Elijah, Jeremiah, or one of the prophets.

Now Jesus puts the question to them: "But what about you? Who do you say I am?"

Without hesitation Peter speaks up. "You are the Messiah, the Son of the living God," he replies.

And Jesus says: "Blessed are you, Simon son of Jonah, for this was not revealed to you by flesh and blood, but by my Father in heaven" (Matt. 16:13–20).

Jesus's searching question, "Who do you say I am?" is the ultimate question. This Man of Galilee divides the ages into before and after. Where shall I place Him?—it is a question even more basic than those we usually consider to be ultimate: Who am I? Where did I come from? Where am I headed? Is there a God? Can I know God? All these other ultimate questions find their answer in the response to which Peter, moved by the Holy Spirit, gave voice.

Peter's reply is often called the great confession, and indeed it is. But Peter deserves no acclamation for it: God gave it to him. It's an answer that doesn't derive from human insights or cleverness; it comes from God alone. Human rationality will continually interpose doubts, evasions, and excuses when confronted with Jesus's question; of itself it will never articulate the great confession. The apostle Paul made the same point when he stated that "no one can say, 'Jesus is Lord,' except by the Holy Spirit" (1 Cor. 12:3).

Jesus went on to speak about the church that would be founded on the great confession. So powerful is the name of Jesus Christ that even the gates of Hades would yield before it. It would be unstoppable. The church would be the door to the kingdom of heaven; it would be God's appointed agency for the salvation of people.

Jesus's words about "rock" and "the keys of the kingdom" (see the sidebar on the next page) have been misconstrued over the centuries. They've been taken to bolster a human religious institution and justify abuses—sometimes gross—in the name of Christ. Millions have been persecuted—even to death—because of their obedience to the Man of Galilee. Haughtiness, pride, arrogance, and dissolute conduct have at times characterized those priding themselves as being the keepers of the keys to the kingdom.

Peter wasn't the first pope. The New Testament indicates that the leader of the early church was James (Acts 15:12–21). Peter played an important part in it, but he at times erred badly. On one occasion the apostle Paul had to confront him publicly over his hypocritical behavior (see Gal. 2:11–14).

In Peter we see our best qualities and our worst. Our brother Peter, just after giving voice to the great confession, blundered badly. When Jesus began to predict His sufferings and death in Jerusalem, "Peter took him aside and began to rebuke him. 'Never, Lord!' he said, 'This shall never happen to you'" (Matt. 16:22). Peter was thinking on a human plane. He had made the great confession that Jesus was the Messiah, but what sort of Messiah would He be? Certainly not a suffering, rejected, executed one. Jesus cut Peter short. "Get behind me, Satan! You are a stumbling block to me; you do not have in mind the concerns of God, but merely human concerns" (v. 23).

He Was Transfigured

Six days after Peter made the great confession, he received another divine revelation concerning Jesus. This time, however, two other apostles—James and John—shared in the experience.

Jesus took His three close friends and led them up a high mountain. The mountain isn't named in the Gospels; possibly it was Mount Tabor (elevation 1,829 feet [557 m]) or Mount Hermon (9,000 feet [2.7 km]). But we simply cannot be certain.

There, all alone on the mountain, Jesus prayed. Peter, James, and John, however, tired from the long climb, fell asleep. They awoke to a glorious scene: Jesus's face was shining like the sun, and

THE "ROCK" AND THE "KEYS"

Over the centuries it has been asserted that the apostle Peter is the "rock" on which Christ established His church, and that the Lord's statement in Matthew 16:18 so indicated. However, Peter clearly disclaims such an association. He indicates that the "rock" refers to Jesus (Acts 4:8–12; 1 Pet. 2:4–8). Jesus elsewhere identified Himself with the term "stone" (see Matt. 21:42; Luke 20:17, 18). Paul identifies Jesus as the "rock" (1 Cor. 10:4). Christ, not Peter or anyone or anything else, is the Rock on which His church is built.

The name Peter comes from the Greek *petros*, a stone. The word for "rock" used in Mathew 16:18 is not *petros* but *petra*, meaning a large, fixed immovable stone. Clearly, Jesus made a distinction between the two.

The "keys" to the kingdom are not, as the rulers of the church of the Middle Ages claimed, the power and authority to admit or refuse access to the kingdom of heaven. Scripture indicates that the "keys" are the words of Jesus (see John 1:12; 6:63, 68; 17:3; 1 Pet. 1:23). In Matthew 23:13, Jesus told the scribes and Pharisees that through their teachings they "shut up the kingdom of heaven against men."

His clothes became as bright as a lightning flash. Two men appeared with Him in splendor—Moses and Elijah. They were talking with the Master about the final events of Jesus's life that He would fulfill at Jerusalem.

Peter, startled by the glorious sight and struggling to be sure that it wasn't a dream, said the first thing that came to mind: "Lord, it is good for us to be here. If you wish, I will put up three shelters—one for you, one for Moses and one for Elijah." That is—let's plan to stay up here on the mountain for a while (Matt. 17:4).

It was a stupid remark. If Peter had kept his mouth closed, he would not have given voice to the wild idea that came into his head, for while he was still speaking the scene suddenly changed. A bright cloud enveloped them all and out of the cloud came a voice: "This is my Son, whom I love, with him I am well pleased. Listen to him!" (Matt. 17:5).

The disciples, terrified, fell to the ground. But Jesus came and touched them. "Get up," He said. "Don't be afraid" (v. 7). And when they looked up, Moses and Elijah had gone; only Jesus remained on the mountain.

Many years later Peter recalled that amazing encounter on the mountain when he and his two fellow disciples were given a glimpse of the Savior in glory. "We did not follow cleverly devised stories when we told you about the coming of our Lord Jesus Christ in power, but we were eyewitnesses of his majesty. He received honor and glory from God the Father when the voice came to him from the Majestic Glory, saying, 'This is my Son, whom I love; with him I am well pleased.' We ourselves heard this voice that came from heaven when we were with him on the sacred mountain" (2 Pet. 1:16–18).

For Jesus, the Transfiguration was a gift from a loving Father to strengthen Him for the ordeal that lay just ahead. For the three disciples, it was an experience of high privilege that might have erased all doubt from their minds. They had been given a glimpse of the glorious future when Jesus will reign as King of Kings and Lord of Lords.

For them, however, the blessing fell short of all that it might have been. Jesus prayed; they slept. They slept through most of Jesus's conversation with Moses and Elijah. It was a troubling hint of their actions only months later. In the Garden of Gethsemane the Master, in agony of soul as He faced the cross with its weight of the world's sin, would pour out His heart to the Father. His sweat would be like drops of blood falling to the ground. Again He would choose the same three closest followers—Peter, James, and John—to supplicate heaven along with Him. But once again they would be weary and fall asleep during the Master's severest trial. And when immediately following the mob would come out with lights, clubs, and spears to take Jesus, the privileged three would take to their heels and run away (Matt. 26:36–46, 56).

Very soon three crosses would be planted on Calvary's hill. Around it, at its foot, a small band of women gathered to watch and weep until the Savior's last cry, "It is finished" (John 19:30). But where were the privileged three? Jesus had selected them from among the Twelve to accompany Him into the bedroom of the daughter of Jairus and be eyewitnesses of His power to raise the dead to life. They had accompanied Him up the mountain to view His glorious, momentary transformation. When in the Garden, He reached out for support from fellow humans. They had been the only ones He asked to stay close and pray for Him. Where were they now?

Peter was hiding. Ashamed and humiliated, he had utterly failed his Lord. Filled with remorse, he felt cut off from hope. Concerning James we know nothing, except that he was not keeping watch with the women who are mentioned by name. The only one of the three who is mentioned is John. He apparently was present at the cross for at least part of the time, because Jesus, solicitous of the welfare of His mother after His demise, appointed John to take care of her (John 19:26, 27).

The Voice from heaven came three times during the ministry of Jesus. Each time it expressed divine approval; each time, explicitly or implicitly, it called on those who heard to listen to Him.

1. At the baptism: "A voice from heaven said, 'This is my Son, whom I love; with him I am well pleased'" (Matt. 3:17).

2. On the mountain: "This is my Son, whom I love; with him I am well pleased. Listen to him!" (Matt. 17:5).

3. In the temple: "Then a voice came from heaven, 'I have glorified it [the Father's name], and will glorify it again'" (John 12:28).

Thus, at the very outset of His public ministry and at its close, Jesus received affirmation and encouragement from the Father. Although that Voice does not come to each of us in audible fashion, we too may be assured of His love and support as we faithfully seek to walk in the path of His will.

The scene on the mountain, one of the most dramatic in Jesus's entire ministry, was filled with marvelous moments and forever remained cemented in the minds of the three privileged disciples. It was a foretaste and a guarantee of the day when Jesus will come again in power and great glory. On that day the redeemed of all ages will be gathered. Some, like Moses, will have died and been raised again; others, like Elijah, will never have died.

QUESTIONS FOR DISCUSSION

1. How does the feeding of the five thousand mark the watershed moment in Jesus's ministry?

2. Everyone dies, but the death of Jesus was different. In what sense is it true that He was born to die?

3. When and how was Jesus tempted to receive the "crown" without the "cross"?

4. Jesus's question to His disciples—"Who do you say I am" (Matt. 16:15)—is a question that each of us ought to respond to in our own terms. Christian discipleship depends on this particular answer about "who" is this Man to me. Who is Jesus to you?

13

Darkness and Light

<table>
<tr><td>OBJECTIVES</td><td>

• Trace the interplay of darkness with light and blindness with sight as Jesus's ministry draws to a close.

• Discern the irony in the narrative of Jesus healing the physically blind in regard to the problem of spiritual blindness.

• Study carefully the puzzling miracle of the blind man who was only partially healed.

</td></tr>
<tr><td>SCRIPTURE</td><td>

• Mark 7:1–23; 9:17–52; John 8:12; 9:1–41

</td></tr>
</table>

In the Gospel of Mark, we encounter one of the strangest incidents in the whole Bible. A blind man is brought to Jesus for healing, but at first the hoped-for miracle seems to fail. Only after a second action of the Master is the man's sight completely restored.

This story occurs only in Mark: "They came to Bethsaida, and some people brought a blind man and begged Jesus to touch him. He took the blind man by the hand and led him outside the village. When he had spit on the man's eyes and put his hands on him, Jesus asked, 'Do you see anything?' He looked up and said, 'I see people; they look like trees walking around.' Once more Jesus put his hands on the man's eyes. Then his eyes were opened, his sight was restored, and he saw everything clearly" (Mark 8:22–25).

How do we account for this puzzling incident? Did Jesus's healing power fail at the first attempt? I think the explanation lies in a consideration of the context in which Mark places the incident. The two-stage miracle, I believe, plays a critical role in Mark's telling of the Jesus story. As Jesus's ministry approaches its conclusion, the contrasts between darkness and light, and blindness and sight, emerge in sharp profile. The conflict between good and evil—between Jesus's followers and His enemies—comes down to this: Who really sees, and who is blind? Blindness afflicts people on two levels, as it still does: physical and spiritual. Light and darkness also function on those two levels.

While Matthew and Luke also record Jesus's healing of blind people, only in Mark do we find the interplay of sight and blindness so intricately woven. In the Gospel of John, however, we find parallels with Mark's treatment. Here the emphasis falls on the conflict between light and darkness in the closing months of Jesus's ministry.

We shall take up these respective treatments—Mark's and John's—in turn in this chapter. The material warrants our close study; it is marvelous as we meet Jesus, the Light of the world. And, if we listen to the Word and allow the Holy Spirit to speak to our hearts, we will face personally the question raised by the Pharisees: "What? Are we blind too?" (John 9:40).

Blindness and Sight

Mark tells us that as Jesus neared the close of His ministry, He spent much of the time attempting to prepare the Twelve for what lay ahead in Jerusalem (Mark 9:30–32). On three separate occasions He sketched the future—which was grim. With each occasion the events ahead emerged more clearly, with ever-increasing specificity:

Mark 8:31	Suffering, rejection, death, resurrection after three days
Mark 9:31	Betrayal, death, resurrection after three days
Mark 10:33, 34	Betrayal, condemnation, handed over to Gentiles, mocked, spat on, flogged, killed, resurrected after three days

The Twelve, however, could not grasp what Jesus was saying. Peter refused to accept the possibility of his Lord's death (Mark 8:32). After the second occasion, the disciples did not understand what Jesus meant and were afraid to ask Him about it (9:32). And immediately after the third, James and John came to Jesus requesting that they be given the leading places in Jesus's kingdom—a request that caused indignation among the rest (10:35–45). Instead of the disciples growing in understanding, they seemed to be increasing in blindness.

In spite of the clarity of Jesus's teaching about what lay just ahead, the Twelve remained blind in their understanding. They were still preoccupied with dreams of power and grandeur in an earthly kingdom that Jesus would set up.

The Twelve weren't the only ones who were blind: the religious leaders were, if anything, worse in their response to what they saw and heard of Jesus. Intent on safeguarding their ceremonial purity, they sharply criticized Jesus's disciples for failing to perform the cleansing ritual before they ate (Mark 7:1–5); they also faulted Jesus for a similar practice (Luke 11:38).

But with unerring insight Jesus pointed out their twisted scale of religious values. He called them "hypocrites" (Greek *hypocrites*), which means "actors." They pretended to be pious, but their religion was a sham. They were only actors playing at religion. They had devised rules that enabled them to bypass the responsibility to care for their parents as commanded in the Decalogue; and while they focused on the supposed flaws in the conduct of Jesus and the Twelve, in their hearts they were full of wickedness.

"Listen to me, everyone, and understand this," Jesus said, calling the crowd to Himself. "Nothing outside a person can defile them by going into them. Rather, it is what comes out of a person that defiles them" (Mark 7:14, 15).

How blind were the Pharisees and teachers of the law! Focused on minutiae, they broke the very same Decalogue. Preoccupied with outward purity, their inner life and thoughts were filled with "sexual immorality, theft, murder, adultery, greed, malice, deceit, lewdness, envy, slander, arrogance and folly" (vv. 21, 22).

The Twelve didn't get it either. "Are you so dull?" Jesus asked them. "Don't you see that nothing that enters a person from the outside can defile them? For it doesn't go into their heart but into their stomach, and then out of the body" (vv. 18, 19).

After this, Jesus and the Twelve were again crossing the Sea of Galilee. As they were sailing, Jesus warned them, "Be careful. Watch out for the yeast of the Pharisees and that of Herod." The disciples began to discuss His words with one another and concluded that Jesus had issued the warning because they had forgotten to bring bread along with them in the boat. Jesus, aware of the discussion, set them straight: "Why are you talking about having no bread? Do you still not see or understand? Are your hearts hardened? Do you have eyes but fail to see, and ears but fail to hear?" (Mark 8:14–18).

This section of Mark, chapters 7–10, closes with Jesus's triumphal entry into Jerusalem. Intertwined with His teachings and warnings about blindness and seeing, we find two actual miracles of blind men receiving their sight under the ministry of Jesus. These miracles, one occurring near the beginning of the passage and the other at its close, function like bookends for the section.

The first of these miracles, the two-stage recovery of sight recorded in Mark 8:22–25, follows immediately upon Jesus's sharp rebuke of the Twelve that we just noticed—that is, spiritually they were blind. Immediately following the two-stage miracle we read the account of the incident near Caesarea Philippi, when Peter made "the great confession." After so many months of being with Jesus, now at last one of them had a divine insight into Who He was.

The two-stage miracle with the blind man at Bethsaida thus had a teaching purpose: Jesus, after many attempts to point out the blindness of the Twelve through words, performed a miracle that would cause them to think. They, like the man, needed healing. They too failed to see clearly. Their ideas about Jesus were distorted, like seeing men as trees walking.

On at least one other occasion Jesus sought to impart divine truth by performing a strange act (Mark 11:12–14, 20, 21). During the final week of His life, on the road from Bethany to Jerusalem,

He saw a fig tree in the distance. It was in full leaf, which normally meant that it already had figs (young figs appear before the leaves). Hungry, Jesus expected to find some figs to eat; however, when He came to the tree He found that it had only leaves. Jesus pronounced a curse on the barren fig tree, and shortly after the tree withered from the roots.

Critics of Christianity often point to Jesus's action as an example of a display of temper. In doing so they overlook the fact that in the Jewish tradition the fig tree was a well-known symbol of the nation. Like the barren fig tree, Israel, under corrupted leaders, had not borne fruit, in spite of Yahweh's abundant blessings. The leaders of the nation displayed "leaves"—a show of outward religion—but without the deeds of justice, mercy, and humility that Yahweh required (Mic. 6:8). In pronouncing the curse on the fig tree, Jesus proclaimed in dramatic fashion the forthcoming doom of the nation. He had foretold this judgment in words; by His act He powerfully illustrated it.

The second miracle of restoration of sight in Mark 7–10 comes at the close of the passage (Mark 10:46–52). A blind beggar, Bartimaeus, sits by the side of the road as Jesus is leaving Jericho. Hearing the sounds of a crowd approaching, and learning that it is Jesus of Nazareth, Bartimaeus begins to shout, "Jesus, Son of David, have mercy on me!" The people around him tell him to be quiet, but Bartimaeus shouts all the more: "Son of David, have mercy on me!"

Above the noise of the crowd, Jesus hears the cry for help and stops. He calls for the blind beggar who, throwing aside his cloak, leaps to his feet and comes to Jesus.

"What do you want me to do for you?" Jesus asks.

"Rabbi, I want to see."

"Go, your faith has healed you." And at once Bartimaeus sees! He joins the crowd, following Jesus along the road.

Such a simple, beautiful story shows the compassion of the Master who is ever ready to respond to the humblest soul who cries out to Him for help. Of the many miracles Jesus performed, most involved healing. And of all the healing miracles in the Synoptic Gospels, with only one do we know the name of the person healed—Bartimaeus. His name is mentioned twice (note that *bar* means "son of" in Aramaic).

We know nothing about Bartimaeus beyond what we learn from this account of the miracle. Presumably he became a disciple of Jesus and was well known among the early Christians. That day when he joined Jesus on the Jericho road was the beginning of a committed relationship.

And there is even more in this account. When Bartimaeus shouted out to Jesus, he called Him "Son of David." That was a term for the Messiah, Israel's King who would come from David's line. It was a designation used by both rulers and people (Matt. 12:23; 22:42). By these words this poor blind beggar publicly expressed faith that the Carpenter of Nazareth was indeed the One long hoped for.

So here is the irony: the blind beggar sees what the sighted—the Twelve, the Pharisees, the teachers of the law—do not. He sees more clearly than those who have two good eyes.

The faith of Bartimaeus shines even more brightly when we understand it against the background of the story that comes just before. In Mark 10:17–22 we learn of a rich young man who comes running to Jesus (Luke in his telling mentions that he was a "ruler" [Luke 18:18]). The young man falls on his knees before Jesus and asks, "Good teacher, what must I do to inherit eternal life?" He seems like such an attractive prospect for the kingdom of heaven—young, earnest, energetic, responsible, seeking, talented. He perhaps could become a leader of the early church, or even write the story of the Master—a Gospel.

But it is not to be. The young man, who has great wealth, loves it too much to cast in his lot with the Savior, Who doesn't even have a place to lay His head when night falls. Jesus tells him to sell everything he has and give the money to the poor. The young man's face falls. Jesus's price is too high for him. Downcast, he walks away, never to return. He was rich and influential, seemingly having everything. But he lacked one thing more important than money or power: he lacked Jesus.

Interesting, isn't it? We don't know his name, but we do know the name of the blind beggar by the side of the Jericho road—he whom people called blind but who saw clearly what is most important.

Light and Darkness: John's Gospel

John informs us that Jesus went back to Jerusalem during the Festival of Tabernacles. This was an autumn feast that fell around October; thus, since Jesus died at Passover, a spring festival, He made this visit about six months before His death.

To go to Jerusalem put Him at great risk. The Jewish leaders "were looking for a way to kill him" (John 7:1). Therefore Jesus kept His plans secret. He didn't make the journey so as to arrive for the start of the festival, but went up only after it was halfway through.

The people had been in expectation as to whether He would appear at the feast. They were sharply divided: some considered Him to be a good man, while others said He was a deceiver. Because of the religious authorities, conversations about Him were conducted in whispers. Jesus was on everybody's minds, but no one dared to speak publicly about Him.

Then suddenly there He was, teaching in the temple courts. In a discourse over two days that covers the seventh and eighth chapters of John's Gospel, Jesus spoke more directly about Who He was and where He had come from than ever before. He openly referred to God as His Father, infuriating the Jewish leaders.

The Pharisees tried to silence Him. They sent temple guards to arrest Him, but the guards returned after a while, empty-handed. "Why didn't you bring him in?" the Pharisees wanted to know.

"No one ever spoke the way this man does," the guards replied (John 7:45, 46). Jesus had won them over by the power and truth of His words. The guards could not arrest this Man Who bore the credentials of someone from God, speaking a message from God.

"Let anyone who is thirsty come to me and drink," they heard Him say. "Whoever believes in me, as Scripture has said, rivers of living water will flow from within them" (John 7:37, 38). Here was an invitation to a life beyond anything they had ever known—a life full and abundant, overflowing with water from above.

After the guards had left, Jesus continued to teach. Now His words reached a pitch with a stupendous claim: "I am the light of the world. Whoever follows me will never walk in darkness, but will have the light of life" (John 8:12). Here is the Carpenter from Nazareth, unschooled and unsung, not only taking upon Himself the authority to teach others the way to eternal life and light but claiming to be Himself that Light. And not only for the nation of Israel but for the entire world.

But Jesus went even further. After a back-and-forth exchange about the nature of freedom, the discussion moved to the subject of Abraham. When His opponents claimed Abraham as their father, Jesus said, "If you were Abraham's children, then you would do what Abraham did. As it is, you are looking for a way to kill me, a man who has told you the truth that I heard from God. Abraham did not do such things" (John 8:39, 40). He went on to state that Abraham had foreseen Jesus's coming and rejoiced (v. 56).

"You are not yet fifty years old, and you have seen Abraham!" they retorted in disbelief.

Then Jesus uttered a statement that, if not true, would have been the height of blasphemy. "Very truly I tell you [a solemn declaration], before Abraham was born, I am" (v. 57, 58). Not "I *was*," but "I *am*." Only the eternal God is always I AM.

God revealed His special name to Moses at the burning bush. When Moses asked about His name, he was told: "I AM WHO I AM. This is what you are to say to the Israelites: 'I AM has sent me to you'" (Exod. 3:14).

The Jews treated this name with the deepest reverence. They avoided pronouncing it when they read the Scriptures (they replaced God's name with *Adonai*—Lord). Thus, when Jesus said to the people during the Feast of Tabernacles, "Before Abraham was born, I am." He was making the ultimate claim for Himself—that He was none other than Yahweh, the great I AM. No wonder that the Jews picked up stones to stone Him. But Jesus slipped away from the temple grounds and hid himself (John 8:59).

The Tabernacles visit to Jerusalem closed with Jesus healing another blind beggar. The story, found in John

9:1–41, relates how a man who sits in darkness is brought to see the light, not only physically but spiritually. At the same time, while the man, blind from birth, is moving from darkness to light, the Pharisees are going in the opposite direction. They think they see, but they are blinding themselves to the light and plunging into darkness. The story begins with a blind man who will gain his sight; it ends with the Pharisees who have become spiritually blind.

At the Festival of Tabernacles Jesus had declared that He was the Light of the world (John 8:12). Now, as a sign that He is the Light, He will give sight to a man born blind.

John 9 develops as follows:

1. Verses 1–5: The Setting

Jesus and His disciples see a man blind from birth. The disciples want to know who sinned—the man or his parents. They accepted the prevailing idea that a direct causal relationship existed between sin and sickness. If an adult became sick, his or her own behavior was blamed. In the case of a baby born with an affliction, the rabbis held that not only could the sin of the parents leave its mark on the infant (see Exod. 20:5), but the infant could also sin in the mother's womb.

Jesus does not answer the disciples' question. Instead of dealing with the *cause* of the man's blindness, He replies in terms of its *purpose*: "Neither this man nor his parents sinned, but this happened that the works of God might be displayed in him. . . . While I am in the world, I am the light of the world" (John 9:5).

2. Verses 6–7: The Miraculous Healing

Mark also mentions that Jesus used spittle with some of His miracles (Mark 7:33; 8:23). Jesus makes mud from His own spittle, puts it on the blind man's eyes, and tells him to go and wash in the pool of Siloam. This pool is situated at the southern extremity of the eastern hill of Jerusalem. Jesus heals some people immediately; others, like this blind man, He heals from a distance (compare the lepers [Luke 17:12–15] and the royal official's son [John 4:46–54]). By going to the pool of Siloam and washing, the blind man demonstrates his faith in Jesus's word. Notice the similarities with the story of Elisha and Naaman in 2 Kings 5:10–14.

3. Verses 8–34: Interrogations of the Formerly Blind Man

8–12:	Questioning by neighbors and acquaintances
13–17:	Preliminary interrogation by Pharisees
18–23:	Man's parents questioned by the Jewish leaders
24–34:	Second interrogation of the man by the Jewish leaders

4. Verses 35–41: Jesus Leads the Healed Man to Spiritual Sight

The Pharisees, however, are hardened in sin. The account is the most lively and interesting in the entire New Testament. As we summarize verses 13–41 below, notice how the Pharisees badger the man and how he answers them with equal vigor:

Pharisees: [They ask him how he received his sight.]

Healed man: "He put mud on my eyes, and I washed, and now I see."

Pharisees [divided in their opinions about Jesus]: "What have you to say about him? It was your eyes he opened."

Healed man: "He is a prophet."

Pharisees to healed man's parents: "Is this your son? Is this the one you say was born blind? How is it that now he can see?"

Parents: "We know he is our son, and we know he was born blind. But [afraid of the Jewish leaders] how he can see now, or who opened his eyes, we don't know. Ask him. He is of age; he will speak for himself."

Pharisees to healed man: "Give glory to God by telling the truth. We know this man is a sinner."

Healed man: "Whether he is a sinner or not, I don't know. One thing I do know. I was blind but now I see!"

Pharisees: "What did he do to you? How did he open your eyes?"

Healed man: "I have told you already and you did not listen. Why do you want to hear it again? Do you want to become his disciples too?"

Pharisees: "You are this fellow's disciple! We are disciples of Moses! We know that God spoke to Moses, but as for this fellow, we don't even know where he comes from."

Healed man: "Now that is remarkable! You don't know where he comes from, yet he opened my eyes. . . . If this man were not from God, he could do nothing."

Pharisees: "You were steeped in sin at birth; how dare you lecture us!" [They throw him out.]

Jesus [finding him]: "For judgment I have come into this world, so that the blind will see and those who see will become blind."

Some Pharisees [overhearing Jesus's remark and pricked in their hearts]: "What? Are we blind too?"

Jesus: "If you were blind, you would not be guilty of sin; but now that you claim you can see, your guilt remains."

5. Insights from This Story

- We see how the formerly blind man is *gaining knowledge*.

- Verse 11: To his neighbors he states that "the *man* they call Jesus" led to recovery of his sight.

- Verses 35–38: He comes to see Jesus as the *Son of Man* (see chapter 16 for a discussion of the title "Son of Man." Note especially the connection with Daniel 7:11–14, 26–28 and a judgment setting).

- While the formerly blind man grows into the light, the Pharisees fall more *deeply into darkness*.

- Verse 15: At first, they seem to accept the fact of the healing. Some are offended by Jesus's act of healing, but others seem willing to be convinced (vv. 16, 17).

- Verse 24: Abandoning all effort to learn the truth, they hurl insults at the man: "You were steeped in sin at birth; how dare you lecture us!" (v. 34). Then they throw him out.

- Verse 39: At the end of the story the Pharisees, who sit in judgment on the formerly blind man, are themselves judged guilty by Jesus.
- The Sabbath: The Jewish leaders argue, "This man [Jesus] is not from God, for he does not keep the Sabbath" (v. 16). Since the blind man's life wasn't in danger, Jesus could have waited to heal him another day. Further, by kneading the clay with His spittle to make mud, Jesus broke one of the thirty-nine Sabbath prohibitions that the teachers of the law had developed (for more about Jesus and the Sabbath, see chap. 21).

QUESTIONS FOR DISCUSSION

1. We do not know of any Jewish interpretations or extra-biblical sources from before the first century A.D. which suggest that the Messiah would suffer and die. How does this fact explain the "blindness" of the Twelve?

2. Study the replies of the man born blind to the cross-examination by the Pharisees. Which of his statements impresses you most, and why?

3. What is the meaning of the Greek term *hypocrites*? What did Jesus mean in calling the religious leaders of His time by this name? Connect your answer with the experience of the fig tree (Mark 11:12–14, 20, 21).

4. Jesus disclosed His plan progressively to His disciples (see Mark 8:31; 9:31; 10:33, 34). How can Jesus's strategy for disclosing truth inform our approaches to share the Good News with others?

14

A Spectacular Miracle

OBJECTIVES
- Trace the final journey of Jesus as He made His way from Galilee to Jerusalem.

- Understand why Jesus was so resolute on this journey.

- Grasp why the raising of Lazarus had such a huge impact.

SCRIPTURE
- Mark 7:24–30; 10:37–42; Luke 19:1–10; John 11:1–44

As Jesus approached the final six months or so of His earthly life, Jerusalem was constantly on His mind. Events that would transpire there would not only bring His ministry to a climactic close, but they would see the age-long struggle between Him and the powers of darkness reach its decisive point.

In his telling of the Jesus story, Luke devotes nearly ten chapters to the final journey of the Master. The account begins in Luke 9:51: "As the time approached for him to be taken up to heaven, Jesus resolutely set out for Jerusalem." During the course of the travels Luke frequently reminds us that Jesus is on the way to Jerusalem:

- Luke 9:53—"But the people [Samaritans] there did not welcome him, because he was heading for Jerusalem."

- Luke 10:1—"After this the Lord appointed seventy-two others and sent them two by two ahead of him to every town and place where he was about to go."

- Luke 10:38—"As Jesus and his disciples were on their way. . . ."

- Luke 13:22—"Then Jesus went through the towns and villages, teaching as he made his way to Jerusalem."

- Luke 17:11—"Now on his way to Jerusalem, Jesus traveled along the border between Samaria and Galilee."

If we possessed only the Synoptic Gospels, we might conclude that this final journey to Jerusalem proceeded without deviation. John's Gospel, however, tells us that the Master made two visits to Judea and Jerusalem during this period. The first of these was at the time of the Feast of Tabernacles, which Jesus joined when it was about half-way through (John 7:1–5, 14). Tabernacles was an autumn festival falling in October. A couple months later we find Him again in Jerusalem during Hanukkah, the Festival of Dedication (see John 10:22). After attending this feast, Jesus stayed in Judea for some time across the Jordan at the place where John had been baptizing in the early days (John 10:40–42).

Why does Luke omit these events in Jerusalem from his account (as do Matthew and Mark)? It is presumably because his focus throughout has been on Galilee, where Jesus performed so many miracles and where His movement attained heights of popular acclaim. Luke's recording of the story tends to heighten the factor of *choice* in Jesus's experience. Jesus intentionally, resolutely turned from the area where He was most popular and set out for Jerusalem where only pain, suffering, and rejection awaited Him.

During the long, circuitous journey from Galilee to Jerusalem, Jesus spent much time teaching the Twelve. He sought to prepare them for the tragic events in Jerusalem—events that would shock and dismay them—and also for the future of His movement after He was gone. The Twelve had much to learn and unlearn about true leadership and the kingdom of God.

The Resolute Christ

Mark has left us a striking image of Jesus on this final journey: "They were on their way up to Jerusalem, with Jesus leading the way, and the disciples were astonished, while those who followed were afraid" (Mark 10:32).

The way to Jerusalem was always up. Jerusalem stood at the high point in the Judean hills. Especially if one came from Galilee and followed the valley of the Jordan down to Jericho, as Jesus and the Twelve did on the final journey, the way to Jerusalem was up. The Jericho road rises sharply more than 3,200 feet (975 m) as it winds through desolate hill country inhabited today by Bedouins.

Pilgrims followed this road as they made their way to the three great annual festivals—Passover, Pentecost, and Tabernacles. Expectant with the joy of worship, celebration, and fellowship, devout Jews sang and rejoiced as they drew ever closer to the beloved city.

But there was no rejoicing among those in Jesus's band. The very atmosphere was heavy with tension. No one sang, as no one looked forward to what lay just ahead.

Jesus

Normally He walked in the midst of the disciples. On this final journey He walked alone, out in front, leading the way. The set of His countenance conveyed determination to complete His mission whatever the cost to Him personally.

Centuries before, the prophet Isaiah had sketched the scene in his prophecy of the Suffering Servant who would be "pierced for our transgressions . . . crushed for our iniquities" (Isa. 53:5).

The Disciples

The disciples were astonished, their hearts heavy with foreboding. Never before had they seen their Master look like this. *Something* was going to happen—and it would be at Jerusalem.

There was a widespread conviction in Israel that the time of the Messiah's appearing would be the Passover feast and the place would be Jerusalem, "the city of the Great King" (Matt. 5:35). The disciples shared in these expectations. Luke tells us that as the band drew near to Jerusalem "the people thought that the kingdom of God was going to appear at once" (Luke 19:11).

The Crowd

Here we get a picture of the form of Jesus's ministry. He was an itinerant preacher, healer, and exorcist. As He traveled from city to city and from village to village, His immediate circle consisted of the Twelve. Behind and beyond them, however, was a larger group of followers.

This group apparently was, at least at times, of considerable number. Luke records that on the journey to Jerusalem at one point Jesus selected seventy-two disciples (some manuscripts read seventy) and sent them two by two ahead of Him to every town and place where He was about to go (Luke 10:1). It would have been exciting to accompany the Master on His traveling ministry, hearing simple yet profound teachings and seeing mighty acts of healing and deliverance.

On His final journey, though, Jesus seemed much different and sad, having retreated within Himself and thinking His own thoughts. The crowd sensed that things were about to change. Jesus's ministry, so blessed and so welcomed in Galilee, was ending. Ahead lay Jerusalem, and the Master's face, set like flint, told them without a word that He expected something terrible to happen there. The crowd followed in silence, fearful of what lay ahead.

In chapters 25–29 of Luke we shall give close study to what happened after Jesus came to Jerusalem. He was there only about a week, but each day was packed with events and teachings of deep significance. From this careful study we hope to gain a clearer understanding of Jesus's resolve as He embarked on the final journey from Galilee.

Of this we may be sure from the outset: the sufferings and death of Jesus were no ordinary sufferings and death. From time to time we learn of people who, in times of war or other crises, go forward boldly to face the prospect of certain death. They display courage and even humor as their final moments approach. Like Socrates, who, just before drinking the hemlock, conversed calmly with his friends, their behavior contrasts sharply with that of Jesus on this journey.

In the death of Jesus we confront deep mystery—not just the mystery of our own mortality, but the mystery of good and evil, and of sin and righteousness. That is why all four Gospel accounts devote disproportionate space to the final week of Jesus's life—the Passion Week—and especially to His final moments.

If we would understand Jesus, Who He is and why He came, we must dwell on the closing scenes until the light breaks through.

The Woman Who Wouldn't Go Away

Jesus's final journey to Jerusalem did not take the shortest route from Galilee. Instead it followed a large circle that brought the disciples into areas not inhabited by Jews—Samaria (Luke 9:52; 17:11), Tyre and Sidon (Mark 7:24, 31), Caesarea Philippi (Mark 8:27), and the Decapolis (Mark 7:31).

Up to this point Jesus had largely confined His ministry to "the lost sheep of Israel" (Matt. 15:24). While He did not turn away Gentiles who, like the centurion, sought His help (Matt. 8:5–13), His focus was on those of His own people. When He sent out the Twelve on a training mission, He likewise instructed them not to work among the Gentiles or enter towns of the Samaritans (Matt. 10:5, 6).

But Jesus's mission, which the Twelve were to carry forward after His death, would embrace more people than Jews. It was to be worldwide. During these last months with the apostles, the Lord intentionally led them into Gentile territory as He continued their education. That education would go forward in two ways: by hearing the words of the Master and by observing Him in action.

A notable teaching moment for the Twelve occurred when the traveling band reached the area around Tyre. Matthew and Mark recount the incident with minor differences in detail. It's a fascinating story, puzzling at first, but ultimately deeply instructive for the Twelve—and for us. We will follow Mark's account in 7:24–30:

> Jesus left that place and went to the vicinity of Tyre. He entered a house and did not want anyone to know it; yet he could not keep his presence secret. In fact, as soon as she heard about him, a woman whose little daughter was possessed by an impure spirit came and fell at his feet. The woman was a Greek, born in Syrian Phoenicia. She begged Jesus to drive the demon out of her daughter.
>
> "First let the children eat all they want," he told her, "for it is not right to take the children's bread and toss it to the dogs."
>
> "Lord," she replied, "even the dogs under the table eat the children's crumbs."
>
> Then he told her, "For such a reply, you may go; the demon has left your daughter."
>
> She went home and found her child lying on the bed, and the demon gone.

She was a remarkable person, the Syrophoenician woman who wouldn't go away. Jesus had tried to keep secret His presence in the Tyre region, but she found out and immediately went to Him. Falling at His feet, she begged Him to drive the demon out of her daughter.

Jesus didn't answer a word (see Matt. 15:23). But she wouldn't go away.

The disciples discouraged her, wanted to send her off, even urged Jesus to get rid of her (v. 23). But she wouldn't leave.

Then Jesus spoke—and the words fell like ice on her ears. "First let the children eat all they want," He said, "for it is not right to take the children's bread and toss it to the dogs" (Mark 7:27).

Dogs! How harsh Jesus's reply sounded, especially when we remember that most people in His time considered dogs as nothing more than scavengers and carrion eaters. The words breathe the spirit of racial and religious prejudice manifested in a thousand situations across human history. On one side, the favored ones, the elite, "the children"; on the other, the lesser breed, inferior, benighted, "the dogs." This spirit spawned, and still spawns, hatred, bigotry, persecution, slavery, and murder. If you look on someone as less than fully human, you feel free to treat them like an animal—only worse than any animal you own.

Could Jesus have partaken of this spirit? Anciently and today, to call a person a dog is to heap scorn and derision on them. "Watch out for those dogs," Paul warned the Philippians (Phil. 3:2). And in the closing verses of the Bible we read, "Outside [the Holy City] are the dogs" (Rev. 22:15).

Jesus classified the Syrophoenician woman with the dogs, but even then she didn't give up. Such a seemingly heartless rejection should have crushed her, but still she stayed.

The woman's persistence provides us with a clue to Jesus's strange behavior toward her. If we could have been there to observe the expression on His face and catch the tone of His voice, I think we should immediately grasp what He was up to. His words on the surface sounded harsh and uncompromising, but His face must have shone as He spoke in love. The woman caught on: Jesus, despite what He seemed to be saying, wasn't rejecting her—He was welcoming her.

This story involves more than Jesus and the woman who wouldn't go away. Matthew's account tells us that the disciples also had a part. They wanted to send her off, urging Jesus to do so. And He said nothing—until the strange saying came from His lips: "I was not sent except to the lost sheep of the house of Israel" (Matt. 15:24, NKJV). What was He up to? He was playacting, treating the woman as the disciples would have, in an endeavor to reveal to them their prejudiced hearts—to break through the hateful, prideful spirit that they had imbibed simply by being born and growing up as part of "the chosen."

Jesus's ministry would soon conclude, and He would be gone. The Twelve would form the nucleus of a movement that He intended to go far and wide. It would begin in Jerusalem with the chosen people, but would at length burst the confines of Israel and spread to earth's farthest bounds.

True Greatness

The Twelve had an ongoing character flaw: everyone wanted to be number one. They continually argued among themselves as to who was the greatest.

Even on Jesus's final journey to Jerusalem the passion for supremacy continued. Luke indicates that right after the Last Supper "a dispute also arose among them as to which of them was considered to be greatest" (Luke 22:24). The disciples certainly did not accept Peter as their leader, even though the Master had commended him after he made the great confession at Caesarea Philippi. And Peter himself continued to be overly conscious of the others in case the Lord bestowed on one of them special favors. When, after the Resurrection, Jesus gave Peter a glimpse of what lay ahead for him, that didn't satisfy him. He wanted to know what would become of John. "Lord, what about him?" he asked the risen Lord (John 21:21).

The most blatant example of the disciples' self-seeking came in a request from the brothers James and John (Matthew informs us that their mother Salome also was involved [20:20]). They came to Jesus and asked, "Let one of us sit at your right and the other at your left in your glory" (Mark 10:37). That is, promise us that we'll be given the chief places in Your kingdom!

Their request came to the notice of the other ten apostles. How did they feel? Angry—they didn't want James and John pulling off a stunt like that! But they were all—James, John, and the rest—wrong in their attitudes and values. They were thinking as the world thinks, trying to rise higher and higher above their fellows—struggling, sweating, trampling on those below them, clawing their way to the top.

Jesus tried to set them all straight. First to the brothers He said, "You don't know what you are asking. . . . Can you drink the cup I drink or be baptized with the baptism I am baptized with?"(Mark 10:38)—that is, go through the experience that awaited Him.

Recklessly, unthinking, they replied, "We can."

Oh, the folly of human pride and self-sufficiency! Hard times indeed lay ahead, such as they could not imagine at that moment. James would be the first of the Twelve to give his life for the gospel—he would fall by the sword of King Herod (Acts 12:1, 2). John would outlast all the others, but he would suffer exile to the lonely island of Patmos (Rev. 1:9) and, according to tradition, be plunged into boiling oil.

As for greatness, Jesus made clear that the values that prevail here on earth are reversed in heaven. Here the "great" lord it over others, seeking titles of authority and others' subservience. "Not so with you," the Master said. "Instead, whoever wants to become great among you must be your servant, and whoever wants to be first must be slave of all" (Mark 10:42–44).

Jesus upends the pyramid of life. In this world people strive to arrive at the apex: the higher they rise, the more people are below. But in the upside-down pyramid of Jesus's kingdom, the leaders carry others on their shoulders. They don't rule others; they lift them up.

At the apex stands one Man who bears the weight of the whole world. "For even the Son of Man did not come to be served, but to serve, and to give his life as a ransom for many" (Mark 10:45). This is a key verse to understanding why Jesus came to this earth. We shall examine it closely when we meditate on Jesus's death.

Those brothers—James and John, the "sons of thunder"—had much to learn and change in attitudes and values. We find them again in focus during another incident on the road to Jerusalem. One day during the journey Jesus sent messengers ahead to find a place for the night. The village was Samaritan and its inhabitants, learning that the traveling band was headed for Jerusalem, didn't welcome them (Luke 9:51–56).

James and John became incensed. "Lord, do you want us to call fire down from heaven to destroy them?" (v. 54). "Sons of thunder" indeed!

Jesus turned and rebuked the fiery brothers. He didn't make a fuss; He simply instructed everyone to walk on to another village.

The Samaritans received their punishment. They didn't suffer incineration via fire from heaven; they deprived themselves of the blessing of entertaining Jesus the last time He would pass that way.

Little Man Up a Tree

From the north, down the Rift Valley of the Jordan, the traveling band at length came to Jericho, where they would take the road up to Jerusalem. Here, on Jesus's final visit to Jericho, He would be the center of an incident both amazing and beautiful.

The story involves a man named Zacchaeus. He was a "big" man—wealthy and powerful. And hated, because he was chief tax collector. This "big" man, however, was little in stature. He learned that Jesus was coming by and, having heard much about Him, badly wanted to see what He looked like. But there was a problem. Because of the crowd around Jesus, Zacchaeus couldn't catch a glimpse of the Master. So he ran on ahead and climbed up a sycamore fig tree.

Jesus came closer and eventually was right under the spot where Zacchaeus was perched. Then Jesus stopped, looked up, and called him by name: "Zacchaeus,

Fruit from a Sycamore Tree

come down immediately. I must stay at your house today" (Luke 19:5).

The people saw and heard it all. They were amazed. Jesus was going to the home of this man whom they despised and feared? Who was this Jesus, anyway? For the little man, however, it was a redemptive moment. His heart overflowed with gratitude, and he promised publicly to give half of what he owned to the poor and to pay back fourfold anyone he had cheated.

And Jesus welcomed the little man into His family. "Today salvation has come to this house," He said, "because this man, too, is a son of Abraham. For the Son of Man came to seek and to save the lost" (vv. 9, 10). That was Jesus: always open to the cry of an open heart. Always seeking and saving along the road.

And His most amazing miracle was about to happen in Jerusalem.

Lazarus

Raising the dead was one of the hallmarks of Jesus's ministry. When John the Baptist sent messengers to Him asking if He was truly the Coming One, Jesus told them to go back and report to John what they had seen and heard: the blind receiving sight, lame walking, lepers cured, and so on. Included in Jesus's list of the evidences of the in-breaking of the kingdom of God was "the dead are raised" (Matt. 11:5).

Therefore, bringing people back to life happened frequently in Jesus's ministry. We learn of only two instances during His work in Galilee—Jairus's daughter (Mark 5:35–43) and the widow's son at Nain (Luke 7:11–17). When Jesus raised His friend Lazarus from the dead, however, the case was entirely different. Lazarus had been dead and buried for four days!

A Sycamore Fig Tree

It was a spectacular miracle and caused a sensation, just as it would if it happened today. There was no way to deny it or to explain it away. With the other raising-to-life miracles, the doubters could question whether the boy or the girl had really died. Had not Jesus Himself said of Jairus's daughter, "The child is not dead but asleep" (Mark 5:39)?

From the moment a person dies, the process of decay begins. After a short while the evidence of decomposition is unmistakable. Within four days the stench of death, horrible and distinctive, pervades the corpse (John 11:17).

No wonder Lazarus's sister Martha tried to stop Jesus when He went to Lazarus's tomb and wanted to bring him out. Even though Martha upon meeting Jesus had affirmed that if Jesus had been present Lazarus wouldn't have died, and that even now God would give Jesus whatever He wanted, her faith did not encompass bringing the four-day-old corpse back to life (John 11:21).

John in his Gospel tells the story in a long, detailed account that takes up most of the eleventh chapter (vv. 1–44). As we trace what happened, we see that this spectacular miracle was timed by Jesus for maximum impact. Time was very short for the Master now—the cross cast a deep shadow—and He would perform a miracle that would bring to a head the conflict between light and darkness, and belief and unbelief.

When Jesus raised Jairus's daughter, He ordered the parents to keep the miracle to themselves (Mark 5:43). But His behavior in the case of Lazarus was just the opposite. It was designed to publicize what had happened, as we find in John 11:

- After receiving the message that Lazarus was sick, He stayed in the same place for two more days (v. 6).

- By delaying to come earlier, Jesus ensured that by the time He arrived in Bethany His friend had already been in the tomb for four days (v. 17).

- Bethany was less than two miles from Jerusalem, and many Jews came from the city to condole with the grieving sisters (vv. 19, 31, 45).

News of the amazing miracle quickly spread to the capital. The result was just what the Master planned—the hearers were confronted with a personal decision concerning Him. Many, especially from among those who had witnessed what Jesus did at the tomb, put their faith in Him (v. 45). Others, however, doubted. Instead of believing in Jesus, they turned to the religious leaders. They, in turn, called a meeting of the Sanhedrin (vv. 46, 47).

The proceedings of the Sanhedrin were thoroughly political. Instead of yielding to the evidence that Jesus was the Messiah, made incontrovertible by the spectacular miracle, the discussion focused on how they might stop His work and preserve their own authority. Caiaphas, the high priest, argued, "You know nothing at all! You do not realize that it is better for you that one man die for the people than that the whole nation perish" (vv. 49–50). So now they plotted to take Jesus's life. This caused Him to withdraw from public view and stay near the desert in the village of Ephraim (v. 54).

Another result concerned Lazarus. A walking example of Jesus's power, he became the center of attention. People wanted to see this person who, dead and entombed for four days, was now alive. The Jewish leaders, infuriated, now added Lazarus's name to Jesus's as marked for removal (John 12:9–11).

One more point should be added to the story of Jesus's spectacular miracle. In a curious manner, the reaction to the raising of Lazarus was sketched in advance in a story that Jesus told several months earlier. The parable of the rich man and Lazarus in Luke 16:19–31 involved two men. One was rich and lived in luxury, but after he died he went to "hell." The other, a beggar named Lazarus, had a miserable life, but when he died the angels carried him

"Jesus Raising Lazarus from the Dead" by William Brassey Hole

to Abraham's side. The rich man, who had five brothers, requested Abraham to send Lazarus to warn them in order that they might avoid his fate.

"If someone from the dead goes to them, they will repent," the formerly rich man argues (v. 30).

But Abraham replies, "If they do not listen to Moses and the Prophets, they will not be convinced even if someone rises from the dead" (v. 31).

So it came to pass. Someone did rise from the dead, someone named Lazarus. But they still did not believe.

QUESTIONS FOR DISCUSSION

1. Why were the Jewish leaders, in spite of all the evidence, so unwilling to accept Jesus?

2. Why was Jesus so seemingly harsh with the Syrophoenician woman?

3. What is the significance of the raising of Lazarus? What does it teach about the state of the dead?

PART II

HIS MESSAGE

When you pass through the waters,
    I will be with you;
and when you pass through the rivers,
    they will not sweep over you.
When you walk through the fire,
    you will not be burned;
    the flames will not set you ablaze.

—Isaiah 43:2

15

What Jesus Taught about God

OBJECTIVES

- Discover what makes Jesus's teachings unique.

- Define the character of God as revealed in Jesus's teachings.

- Grasp the relationship of the Father to the Son as taught by Jesus Christ.

SCRIPTURE

- Matthew 6:1–15, 25–34; Luke 15:1–32

In the Gospel accounts, Jesus is addressed as "Teacher" twenty-nine times. A large part of His ministry was devoted to teaching, either the crowds publicly or the Twelve privately.

Jesus had not attended the rabbinical schools. He had not sat at the feet of a famous rabbi, as had Saul of Tarsus with Gamaliel (Acts 22:3). He did not quote the opinions of great scholars such as Rabbi Shammai or Rabbi Hillel. Yet even Jesus's enemies called Him "Teacher" (Matt. 22:16, 24)—though perhaps sarcastically.

Jesus's words had profound import on all those who heard them. "What is this?" they said. "A new teaching—and with authority" (Mark 1:27). After almost two thousand years, His teachings still speak with a clarity and directness unmatched by those of the world's great religious leaders. Thus, even the skeptical philosopher Ernest Renan (1823–1892) declared, "Jesus will ever be the creator of the pure spirit of religion; the Sermon on the Mount will never be surpassed."[1]

When Nicodemus, a Pharisee and member of the Sanhedrin, came to Jesus by night, he began by acknowledging Jesus as a master teacher. "Rabbi," he said, showing great respect. "We know that you are a teacher who has come from God. For no one could perform the signs you are doing if God were not with him" (John 3:2). That is, Jesus's authenticity was demonstrated not only by His words but also by the divine power that accompanied the words.

His words were simple but conveyed profound truths. They did not deal with philosophical questions or formal theology; rather, they were about *life*—life here and now, and life beyond this world.

Jesus's teachings, practical and down-to-earth, employed copious illustrations. He drew upon nature and events from everyday life: the sower spreading his seed, the fisherman dragging nets from the water of the Lake of Galilee, the housewife kneading bread dough, and so on.

Following the long-standing Jewish tradition of teaching by means of *meshalim* (plural of *meshal*, a short parable with a moral lesson), Jesus's teaching included proverbs, riddles, aphorisms, and allegory. His most common and distinctive type of *meshal*, however, was the parable, a short narrative told in the third person that functions as extended metaphor.

Although we find parables in Buddhism, Hinduism, Judaism, and other religions, those of Jesus stand apart. Beginning with the familiar and the concrete, they invite rich, multiple insights with a forcefulness unmatched in the teachings of others. They beguile the reader, as they beguiled those who heard them. They catch our interest and address us personally as they call for decision and transformation of character. *We* are confronted and see ourselves in the story.

The parables teach deep morality, but they are almost totally devoid of moral direction—that is, lists of dos and don'ts. They cut beneath the surface of action to the heart, from which spring our motivations.

The parables of Jesus both illuminated and obscured truth. Matthew writes, "Jesus spoke all these things to the crowd in parables; he did not say anything to them without using a parable" (Matt. 13:34). Often, after addressing the people, He explained the meaning of the parable privately to the Twelve (see Matt. 13:36–43; Mark 4:10–20). To His enemies, however, who dogged His footsteps with ears open—not to receive divine truth but to find material to use against Him—the words of Jesus in parables were veiled. Enemies sensed that He had in some way included them in the parable, but they had nothing explicit with which to accuse Him (see Matt. 21:45, 46).

As we work through the four Gospel accounts of Jesus the Master Teacher, we observe a progression in the way He presented instruction. In the early stages of His ministry, before plans to kill Him had gelled, His teaching was direct and pointed (although illustrated). We see examples in the discourse with Nicodemus (John 3) and the Sermon on the Mount (Matt. 5–7). Then, as opposition grew, He switched to parables when speaking in public. Finally, in the last hours, alone with the Twelve, He reverted to direct instruction. "Then Jesus' disciples said, 'Now you are speaking clearly and without figures of speech'" (John 16:29).

The words of Jesus are wonderfully rewarding. We will spend the remainder of this chapter and the following nine chapters studying the leading themes of the Master Teacher, moving from direct instruction to parable and back again as the material dictates.

These teachings in most places sound simple, but don't be fooled by the straightforward language. Take time and think prayerfully.

And remember that what Jesus taught, He also lived. He told us about joy and peace and He Himself lived joy and peace. He tied these teachings directly to Himself. He calls us to change, but He also says, "I am the way and the truth and the life" (John 14:6).

We begin the study of the teachings of Jesus with what He taught us about God.

When an expert in the law tested Jesus by asking Him which is the greatest commandment, Jesus replied by quoting the famous declaration known as the *Shema* found in Deuteronomy 6:4, 5: "Hear, O Israel: The Lord our God, the Lord is one. Love the Lord your God with all your heart and with all your soul and with all your mind and with all your strength" (Mark 12:29, 30). Jesus's deeper disclosure of the nature of God was steeped into the oneness of God.

The Father

Although Jesus referred to the one God simply as "God" (one time as "Most High," in Luke 6:35), His favorite designation was "Father." We find Jesus using this term 66 times in Matthew, Mark, and Luke, and 118 times in John—a total of 184 uses.

This title used by Jesus is perhaps the most distinctive feature of His teachings. Other religions had introduced the concept of God as Father in the context of humans being divine offspring, but Jesus's meaning was altogether different.

His teaching proceeded from the creation account of Genesis 1, where humanity, male and female, is created in the image of God. According to Genesis—and Jesus—we are God's creation, not His offspring.

WHY JESUS TAUGHT IN PARABLES

A parable is a narrative used to teach truth; that is, it is an earthly story with a heavenly meaning. In literary form it is an extended metaphor, a figure of speech that makes an implied comparison between two objects that are poles apart from each other but have some characteristics in common.

"By employing parables in His teaching Jesus:

1. Aroused interest, attention, and inquiry;

2. Imparted unwanted truth without arousing prejudice;

3. Evaded the spies who pursued Him relentlessly;

4. Created in the minds of His hearers lasting impressions that would be renewed and intensified when the scenes presented in the parables again came to mind or to view;

5. Restored nature as an avenue for knowing God."[2]

We find the concept of God as Father in a different sense in the Old Testament, however. God calls Israel "my firstborn son" (Exod. 4:22), and Moses in his farewell song reminds the people, "Is he not your Father, your Creator, who made you and formed you?" (Deut. 32:6; see also Deut. 1:31; 8:5; Isa. 1:2; Jer. 31:9; Hosea 11:1). Here God is Father by virtue of His own sovereign choice and action.

When Jesus refers to God as His Father, He indicates a unique relationship, which we shall consider in the next chapter. But Jesus's use of God as "Father" extends beyond Himself; He tells us that God is also *our* Father. Thus, the prayer He taught us to pray, commonly known as the Lord's Prayer, although it is really *our* prayer, begins, "Our Father in heaven" (Matt. 6:9; compare with Luke's account, where the prayer begins simply, "Father," Luke 11:2).

Jesus's invitation to His disciples to address God as "our Father" radically reorients the concept of God. God is not remote, separated from us as far as heaven is from earth. Nor is God a supreme deity beyond our comprehension or approach. God is very close. He is our heavenly Parent. All that we see of love and goodness in human relations (and there is much that is *not* good and loving) is but a glimpse of the fatherhood of God.

Gone is the fear of a God who jealously watches for every failing. God is the Judge, but not in the terrifying aspect that too many Christians, in the past and still today, associate with God. But did Jesus really teach such a benevolent God, our Father? Indeed; notice how Jesus described the way God relates to us.

The Father Delights to Give

There is no need to rehearse our prayers in an effort to impress God, said Jesus. Many words will not commend us to the Father. "Your Father knows what you need before you ask him" (Matt. 6:8). So don't be afraid to come before God, and don't be hesitant to ask: "Ask and it will be given to you; seek and you will find; knock and the door will be opened to you. For everyone who asks receives; the one who seeks finds; and to the one who knocks, the door will be opened" (Matt. 7:7, 8).

God the Father is readier to give good gifts to us than any earthly father to his children: "Which of you, if your son asks for bread, will give him a stone? Or if he asks for a fish, will give him a snake? If you, then, though you are evil, know how to give good gifts to your children, how much more will your Father in heaven give good gifts to those who ask him" (Matt. 7:9–11). This directness of approach to God as Father is unmatched in Judaism.

The Father Knows Our Circumstances and Need

We live in an age when super-computers can store billions of pieces of information and recall them in seconds. How much greater is the mind of the Father! He tracks every person on earth. He knows where we live. He knows us by name. No earthly father ever watched over his children more tenderly and solicitously than our Father.

Jesus told us that the Father even watches the birds. "Look at the birds of the air," He said. "They do not sow or reap or store away in barns, and yet your heavenly Father feeds them. Are you not much more valuable than they? Can any one of you by worrying add a single hour to your life?" (Matt. 6:26, 27).

Luke adds this detail: "Are not five sparrows sold for two pennies? Yet not one of them is forgotten by God. Indeed, the very hairs of your head are all numbered. Don't be afraid; you are worth more than many sparrows" (Luke 12:6, 7).

In these times many people no longer believe in God. Among those who do, many have abandoned the concept of a God who takes a personal interest in every man and woman, young person, and child. They reason that the world is too big and society too complex to maintain beliefs such as that of a Supreme Being.

But that is just the sort of God that Jesus taught by word and by example. He told us about and showed us the Father. On the final evening of His earthly life, when the disciples were troubled because He told them He was about to leave them, Philip asked Him to show them the Father. Jesus answered, "Don't you know me, Philip, even after I have been among you such a long time? Anyone who has seen me has seen the Father. How can you say, 'Show us the Father'? Don't you believe that I am in the Father, and that the Father is in me? The words I say to you I do not speak on my own authority. Rather, it is the Father, living in me, who is doing his work" (John 14:9, 10).

Down through the centuries the burning questions of humanity have been Is there a God? And if there is, what is God like? Philosophers and thinkers have reasoned and speculated. The answers in many cases are elusive, merely demonstrating the truth of the saying in the Book of Job: "Canst thou by searching find out God?" (Job 11:7, KJV).

Jesus came and we now know the true answers in the age-long search. Yes, there is a God. And God is infinitely loving, compassionate, and caring. God is our Father in heaven. How can we know? Because Jesus has revealed Him. We have seen Jesus—infinite in love, compassionate, and caring. And in seeing Him, we have seen God.

The Father Provides for Our Every Need

Whether rich or poor, everyone has needs. If our finances are meager and we barely make ends meet from one paycheck to the next, the Father Who watches over the birds and clothes the grass of the field also tenderly watches over us. If we have more of this world's goods, we still have needs: we worry about our work, our families, our health, and what lies ahead.

Jesus taught us to trust the Father. He showed us how to live, committing every concern into the hands of a wise,

good, and kind Parent in heaven. "So do not worry, saying, 'What shall we eat?' or 'What shall we drink?' or 'What shall we wear?' For the pagans run after all these things, and your heavenly Father knows that you need them" (Matt. 6:31, 32).

Fear of the future chokes the joy out of the lives of many people, including Christians. Some who believe in the return of Jesus—that is, who are Adventists—anxiously dwell on the trials and troubles of the end times. Again, Jesus has a word for us all: "Therefore do not worry about tomorrow, for tomorrow will worry about itself. Each day has enough trouble of its own" (Matt. 6:34). And if we are called to suffer for our faith: "Whenever you are arrested and brought to trial, do not worry beforehand about what to say. Just say whatever is given you at the time, for it is not you speaking but the Holy Spirit" (Mark 13:11).

The Father Is the Heavenly Seeker

Jesus showed us a God who, contrary to what has often been taught about Him, is trying to get us all into heaven, not seeking evidence of our failings that would keep us from His presence.

Three wonderful parables, found in Luke 15, graphically reveal the seeking Father. These simple but moving stories all deal with the lost and the accompanying search. They move from the lost sheep to the lost coin to the lost son, rising in interest and intensity. Each underscores the *value* of what is lost—whether sheep, coin, or son—the *earnestness* of the effort to bring restoration and the *rejoicing* when the lost is found.

We should note the setting of these stories: "Now the tax collectors and sinners were all gathering around to hear Jesus. But the Pharisees and the teachers of the law muttered, 'This man welcomes sinners and eats with them'" (Luke 15:1, 2). What a tribute! To the religious teachers, Jesus's association with tax collectors and assorted sinners was a mark of contempt, but to everyone today who acknowledges that he or she is a sinner, it is a glorious badge of hope. Jesus, friend of sinners, wants to be *our* friend!

In telling these stories Jesus not only defended His actions against the charges of the critics but He revealed the Father. In effect, Jesus was arguing: "I act in this manner because this is how the Father acts."

The third story—the lost son—is frequently dubbed the Parable of the Prodigal Son. It is indeed about the wayward child, but its focus falls not on the son, but on his father. The story is more accurately termed as the Parable of the Prodigal Father, understanding "prodigal" to signify love abundant and overflowing to the point of recklessness.

These ideas express in parable form what Jesus conveyed to the night caller, Nicodemus: "For God so loved the world that he gave his one and only Son, that whoever believes in him shall not perish but have eternal life" (John 3:16).

A Righteous God

Jesus makes very clear that God is a moral God. He is our Father, not a sentimental grandfather who winks at sin. The Father delights to forgive and spares no effort to win back the lost. As He takes us to Himself, He purposes that we will be changed by His grace into loving, upright people who reflect His holy character.

Matthew 6 reveals that the prayer to our Father, which Jesus taught, includes the statement, "Forgive us our debts, as we also have forgiven our debtors" (v. 12). Jesus drove home the point by elaborating, "For if you forgive other people when they sin against you, your heavenly Father will also forgive you. But if you do not forgive others their sins, your Father will not forgive your sins" (vv. 14, 15).

Jesus told a powerful parable that emphasizes the change in behavior that accompanies the working of grace received in one's life. In this story, found in Matthew 18:21–35, we encounter a man who owes an enormous debt. The figure, ten thousand talents, boggles the mind. It is obtained by combining the largest number in the Greek language, ten thousand, with the largest unit of money known to the people. Today, we might roughly translate the debt as "millions of dollars," but even that fails to convey the vast size of what the man owed. What is being expressed is the utter impossibility of ever paying the debt—it was simply too large.

What a picture of sin! We are like this man, saddled with a debt that, even if we lived a thousand lives, could never be discharged. But God does not leave us in this hopeless state. He cancels the debt freely because He is a God who delights to forgive. This is grace, and we shall have much more to say about it in a later chapter.

But that isn't the end of Jesus's story. This man who has been forgiven so much turns around and oppresses a fellow servant who owes him a hundred denarii (a denarius was a day's wage; Matt. 20:2). The contrast falls between a debt of millions of dollars and one of a comparatively few dollars. The first servant was the beneficiary of incredible generosity, and he should have been changed by his deliverance. Instead, he behaved in a mean, grasping, cruel manner as if he had never been forgiven the huge debt. The result? He was excluded from the society of the forgiven. By his actions he demonstrated that he did not belong among those saved by grace.

Today, it isn't popular for preachers to speak about hell or the exclusion of the wicked from God's eternal kingdom. Jesus had no such qualms (see, for example, Matt. 5:20; 10:33; 11:20–24; 12:32; 18:6, 35). Jesus didn't teach universalism—that is, that God's love is so all-embracing that eventually everyone will be saved. For Jesus, this life is the place of decision where the course we choose will determine our eternal future (John 5:29).

The Father, according to the plainest words of Jesus, looks for genuine religion of the heart—not superficial acts, rituals, and formulas. To the woman by the well in Samaria the Master said, "God is spirit, and his worshipers must worship in the spirit and in truth" (John 4:24). In the Sermon on the Mount He called His followers to such living: "Be careful not to practice your righteousness in front of others to be seen by them. If you do, you will have no reward from your Father in heaven" (Matt. 6:1). He elaborated the point by giving three examples: almsgiving (vv. 2–4) without outward show to impress others, prayer (vv. 5–15) without attempting to gain the attention of others or of God by public display and multiplying words, and fasting (vv. 16–18) without appearing to others to fast.

Jesus had strong words for religious pretense, especially when accompanied by exploitation of the weak—such as religious teachers who used the device of "corban" to avoid their duty to care for parents (Mark 7:9–13) or teachers of the law who went around in long robes and made lengthy prayers but who robbed widows of their homes (Mark 12:38–40). By such teachings Jesus mirrored the character of the Father, who is a God of justice.

The God whom Jesus revealed comes to the defense of the weak. Another parable of Jesus tells about the plight of a poor widow who was denied her rights by an unjust judge. Because the widow persisted, the judge eventually relented.

"And will not God bring about justice for his chosen ones," said Jesus, "who cry out to him day and night?" (Luke 18:7).

My Father, Your Father

Just after Jesus rose from the dead, He sent a message through Mary Magdalene to the grieving members of the disciple band. "Go . . . to my brothers and tell them, 'I am ascending to my Father and your Father, to my God and your God'" (John 20:17).

My Father your Father, my God your God—how preciously close has Jesus made us to God. He has brought heaven down to earth and lifted us up to heaven. He who prayed so often and so earnestly to "My Father" or "Father" has made the connecting bridge so that we too can pray, "Our Father. . ."

We need not feel that we are on our own in a vast, alien universe. We have a heavenly Father who loves us. We are precious to Him and He will never leave or forsake us. He will supply our every need. What a God!

Yet we should notice a subtle distinction in Jesus's language about the Father. He refers to "My Father" and "your Father," but not to "Our Father" in any context that includes Himself. He taught *us* to pray "Our Father in heaven," but He did not pray that prayer. It is *our* prayer, not His.

Jesus is Son in a way that we are not children. Jesus is the special son and unique son. His divine Sonship is the basis of His mission, not its achievement. We are only children by adoption, as the apostle Paul makes clear (Rom. 8:23; Gal. 4:4–7). There is, and must always be, a qualitative difference between Jesus as the Son and us as children of the Father.

QUESTIONS FOR DISCUSSION

1. Why did Jesus teach in parables? How did it help His ministry?

2. What does the story of the lost son teach about sin, repentance, and God's love?

3. How do the three parables in Luke 15 answer the Pharisees' objection in verse 2?

What Jesus Taught about Himself

OBJECTIVES

- Investigate the awareness of Jesus of Nazareth concerning Himself.

- Study the theological interpretation of the Sonship of Jesus.

- Understand how Jesus viewed His relationship with the Father.

- Know that the forgiving power of Jesus is available for each of us.

SCRIPTURE

- John 1:1–18; Philippians 2:5–11; Colossians 1:15–20; 1 Timothy 3:16; Hebrews 1:1–4

It is of utmost importance to learn how Jesus understood Himself. If the most critical question of the ages is, "Who was Jesus of Nazareth?" we cannot hope to arrive at a valid answer without first probing the Master's self-understanding.

The world's three great monotheistic religions—Christianity, Islam, and Judaism—all go back to Abraham, but they diverge over the person of Jesus. To the Jews, Jesus was not the Messiah because He taught that the kingdom of God was about to come, but it did not come. He was therefore a false teacher. (We shall study more closely what Jesus taught about the kingdom in chapter 18.)

Muslims, unlike Jews, hold that Jesus was indeed the Messiah. They also believe that Jesus was born of the Virgin Mary and that He never sinned. He was, they assert, a prophet—but no more than a prophet. They take offense at the Christian doctrine of the Trinity because they understand it to teach three Gods—the Father, the Son, and the Holy Spirit. To Muslims, that is blasphemy. The founder of their religion called the Arabian tribes away from many gods to worship the one and only God, Allah.

Notice that neither Judaism nor Islam questions the humanity of Jesus of Nazareth. Nor was that ever an issue in His day. Only long after His death, toward the end of the first century AD, did some people begin to suggest that His humanity was only apparent, not real (those who took this position shared the ideas of false teaching known as Gnosticism).

The issue in Jesus's time and ever since has been whether Jesus was not *merely* human but *more than* human. That is why any study of His identity must begin with an examination of what He taught about Himself.

His Names

One of the most striking facts in this search for Jesus's self-understanding is that He avoided the designation "Messiah." When others called Him the Messiah, He did not deny it or contradict them, as when Peter at Caesarea Philippi, in answer to Jesus's question, "Who do you say I am?" replied, "You are the Messiah, the Son of the living God" (Matt. 16:15, 16). Likewise, when Jesus stood before the Sanhedrin and the high priest Caiaphas solemnly charged Him to declare if He were the Messiah, He stated, "You have said so" (Matt. 26:64).

Why did Jesus seek to avoid being known as the Messiah? Presumably because in His time the term had become loaded with political weight. Expectation among the Jews ran at white heat for a new king of the line of David who would lead the nation to victory and banish the occupying Roman armies.

Jesus *was* the Messiah, but not the Messiah of popular expectation. He would establish a kingdom, but it would be vastly different from what the people hoped for. He would rule as king, but in love, not by force.

The Master's preferred designation for Himself was "Son of Man." Scholars, seeking to probe Jesus's messianic consciousness, have endeavored to trace the roots of this term to a variety of non-biblical sources. We do not need to look so far afield, however: Jesus was immersed in the Hebrew Scriptures, not in the writings of other cultures. In the Old Testament we find "son of man" occurring prominently in the books of Daniel and Ezekiel.

In the apocalyptic prophecy found in Daniel 7, the "son of man" plays a key role: "In my vision at night I looked, and there before me was one like a son of man, coming with the clouds of heaven. He approached the Ancient of Days and was led into his presence. He was given authority, glory and sovereign power; all nations and peoples of every language worshiped him. His dominion is an everlasting dominion that will not pass away, and his kingdom is one that will never be destroyed" (7:13, 14).

Jesus seems to echo this passage as He describes His return to earth: "For the Son of Man is going to come in his Father's glory with his angels, and then he will reward each person according to what they have done" (Matt. 16:27).

The "son of man" references in the Book of Ezekiel do not carry the apocalyptic context of those in Daniel. Rather, they seem to highlight the person of the prophet Ezekiel as representative of the nation of Israel. Over and over, when the Lord speaks to Ezekiel, He addresses him as "son of man:" "Son of man, stand up on your feet and I will speak to you" (Matt. 2:1; see also 2:6, 8; 3:1, 3, 4, 10, 17, 25).

Apparently Jesus found this Old Testament term "son of man" with its apocalyptic overtones and suggestions of one truly human bearing a divine message more fitting than "Messiah" to describe His person and message. We find Him referring to "Son of Man" in at least four different types of sayings:

- *To indicate His humanity:* "The Son of Man came eating and drinking" (Matt. 11:19). Here "Son of Man" is equivalent to "man."

- *To indicate authority to forgive sins:* "But I want you to know that the Son of Man has authority on earth to forgive sins" (Mark 2:10).

- *To indicate His approaching sufferings and death:* "'We are going up to Jerusalem,' he said, 'and the Son of Man will be delivered over to the chief priests and the teachers of the law. They will condemn him to death and will hand him over to the Gentiles'" (Mark 10:33).

- *To indicate His coming in glory:* "For the Son of Man is going to come in his Father's glory with his angels" (Matt. 16:27).

Jesus the Son

Jesus preferred to refer to Himself as the Son of Man, but He did not deny the term "Son of God" when others applied it to Him (e.g., Matt. 8:29; John 1:49; 11:27). Frequently He referred to Himself simply as "the Son" in discourses that involved His relationship to the Father (see page 164).

The language of Sonship gave rise to much discussion after Jesus's death. For several centuries, followers of Jesus debated its meaning, with the issue reaching a climax in the general church council held at Nicea in AD 325.

After so many centuries the controversy still hasn't been laid to rest. Among Seventh-day Adventists, occasionally people arise vehemently advocating a position similar to that held by Arius at Nicea—that the Son was not eternally preexistent with the Father. These modern Adventist Arians appeal to some of the pioneers of Adventism, including James White, for support. It is a fact that James White and some others of our early leaders argued strongly against the doctrine of the Trinity, holding that it derived from the Roman Catholic Church, not the Scriptures.

Ellen G. White was an exception among the Adventist pioneers. Although for the first forty years or so of her ministry she did not specifically address the question of Christ's preexistence, in later writings she became very clear in affirming that He had no beginning but is coeternal with the Father. She makes the categorical statement, "In Him [Christ] was life, original, unborrowed, underived."[1] For most Adventists this statement and others of a similar nature from her pen helped settle the matter, but a small number continue to advocate the Arian view.

Anciently and still today, the term "only begotten" in John 3:16—God gave His "only begotten Son" (KJV)—causes misunderstanding. It suggests that the Son of God was begotten; that is, in some manner created or generated by the Father. Therefore, it is reasoned, God is actually the Father from whom the Son derived His existence at some point in time.

The Greek word translated as "only begotten" in the KJV and some other versions is *monogenēs*. Its true meaning is "unique" or "special"; it does not refer to the "begetting" (for that we have another Greek word) or creating of the Son. God has many sons, but only one *Son*. He didn't send an angel to pay the price of our redemption; He gave His unique one, who is coeternal with God.

We find the word *monogenēs* also used in the book of Hebrews, where it is translated as "one and only": "By faith Abraham, when God tested him, offered Isaac as a sacrifice. He who had embraced the promises was about to sacrifice his one and only son, even though God had said to him, 'It is through Isaac that your offspring will be reckoned'" (Heb. 11:17, 18). Now, Abraham was already the father of Ishmael when Isaac was born; later he had other sons through Keturah (see Gen. 25:1, 2). Isaac, the *monogenēs*, was not Abraham's only begotten son, but he was the son of the promise, the special son.

But what about the language of "Father" and "Son"? If it does not signify ontology—that is, descent or origin—what does it connote? It is equality of nature, shared essence, as Jesus's discussion with the Jewish leaders in John 5 makes clear. After Jesus healed the man by the pool of Bethesda on the Sabbath, He defended His actions by claiming that He was only doing what the Father already was doing. "In his defense Jesus said to them, 'My Father is always at his work to this very day, and I too am working.' For this reason they tried all the more to kill him; not only was he breaking the Sabbath, but he was even calling God his own Father, *making himself equal with God*" (John 5:17, 18; emphasis added). The Jews, therefore, understood Jesus's reasoning about Father and Son to be a claim of *equality* with God.

Elsewhere in the Gospels we occasionally find the language of Sonship used by Jesus in contexts that obviously do not mean origin, as when the Master gave James and John the nickname Boanerges, literately "sons of thunder" (Mark 3:17).

We find the language of the Sonship of Jesus also in the book of Hebrews. Here we learn that the Son is "the radiance of God's glory and the exact representation of his being," that the universe was made through Him, and that He sustains all things by His powerful word (Heb. 1:2, 3). The Son is directly addressed as deity in several passages:

> But about the Son he says,
> "Your throne, O God, will last for
>   ever and ever . . .
> Therefore God, your God, has set
>   you above your companions . . ."
> (Heb. 1:8, 9).

He also says,

> "In the beginning, O Lord, you laid
>   the foundations of the earth . . ."
> (Heb. 1:10).

When Jesus is called the Son, therefore, the terminology doesn't mean that Jesus derived His being from the Father at a point in time. Nor does it find its meaning in the incarnation of Jesus—that He became God's Son because of His birth as a human being. Rather, He is the *eternal* Son, from the beginning one with the Father. All that God is, the Son is—is, always has been, and always will be.

Ellen G. White has several significant statements regarding Jesus as the Son. Referring to the Incarnation, she observes, "In His incarnation He gained in a new sense the title of the Son of God. Said the angel to Mary, 'The power of the Highest shall overshadow thee: therefore also that holy thing which shall be born of thee shall be called the Son of God' (Luke 1:35, KJV). While the Son of a human being, He became the Son of God in a new sense. Thus He stood in our world—the Son of God, yet allied by birth to the human race."[2] That is, He already was the Son before His birth; now He became Son in a double or heightened sense.

The issue at the council of Nicea was far more than an argument among theologians. It wasn't an academic battle of hairsplitting of Greek words. It involved the very heart of Christianity because it concerned Jesus: Who *was* He? Who *is* He?

If the Son were an exalted being, one who existed before our world began but

Who Himself was created in time—that is, one less than fully and eternally God—He could not be our Savior. Only God could deliver us from the mess into which we have fallen, the sin problem. Only God could make a way of escape by taking our burden of guilt upon Himself.

When we come to Jesus—committing our lives to Him for now and for eternity—to whom do we make the commitment? Is it to God or to someone, however exalted, who is less than God? When Jesus forgives our sins, can we be certain that *God* has forgiven them? That is the ultimate issue that stems from Nicea but that pulsates beneath questions about Jesus in our times.

Father and Son

Jesus said, "I and My Father are one" (John 10:30, KJV). By this He meant unity of character, purpose, and action. That the Father and Son are separate entities and not merely manifestations or modes of God becomes apparent from the following passages:

- *The Son reveals the Father:* "Anyone who has seen me has seen the Father" (John 14:9).

- *The Son is the way to the Father:* "No one comes to the Father except through me" (John 14:6).

- *The Father sends the Son into the world:* "And the Father who sent me has himself testified concerning me" (John 5:37).

- *The Son comes from the Father and returns to the Father:* "Jesus knew that the Father had put all things under his power, and that he had come from God and was returning to God" (John 13:3).

- *The Son is in the Father and the Father in the Son:* "Believe me when I say that I am in the Father and the Father is in me" (John 14:11).

- *The Father loves the Son:* "The reason my Father loves me is that I lay down my life—only to take it up again" (John 10:17).

- *The Father knows the Son and the Son knows the Father:* "I am the good shepherd; I know my sheep and my sheep know me—just as the Father knows me and I know the Father" (John 10:14, 15).

- *The Son receives commands from the Father:* "I have authority to lay it [my life] down and authority to take it up again. This command I received from my Father" (John 10:18).

- *The Son prays to the Father:* "Father, save me from this hour. . . . Father, glorify your name" (John 12:27, 28).

- *The Son does exactly what the Father has commanded Him:* "The world may learn that I love the Father and do exactly what my Father has commanded me" (John 14:31).

- *As the Father works, so does the Son:* "My Father is always at his work to this very day, and I too, am working" (John 5:17).

- *The Son does nothing by Himself:* "Very truly I tell you, the Son can do nothing by himself; he can do only what he sees his Father doing, because whatever the Father does the Son also does" (John 5:19).

- *As the Father gives life to the dead, the Son also gives life:* "For just as the Father raises the dead and gives them life, even so the Son gives life to whom he is pleased to give it" (John 5:21).

- *The Father entrusts judgment to the Son:* "Moreover, the Father judges no one, but has entrusted all judgment to the Son" (John 5:22; see also v. 27).

- *He who does not honor the Son does not honor the Father:* "That all may honor the Son just as they honor the Father. Whoever does not honor the Son does not honor the Father, who sent him" (John 5:23).

- *As the Father has life in Himself, He has granted the Son to have life in Himself:* "For as the Father has life in himself, so he has granted the Son also to have life in himself" (John 5:26).

- *The Father testifies concerning the Son:* "I have testimony weightier than that of John. For the works that the Father has given me to finish—the very works that I am doing—testify that the Father has sent me. And the Father who sent me has himself testified concerning me. You have never heard his voice nor seen his form" (John 5:36, 37).

- *The Father is greater than the Son:* "My Father is greater than I" (John 14:28, KJV).

- *The Son prays to be glorified with the glory that He had previously with the Father:* "And now, Father, glorify me in your presence with the glory I had with you before the world began" (John 17:5).

- *All whom the Father gives to Jesus come to Him:* "All those the Father gives me will come to me, and whoever comes to me I will never drive away" (John 6:37).

All the preceding references come from the Gospel of John. Occasionally, however, we find parallels in the Synoptic Gospels, as in, "All things have been committed to me by my Father. No one knows the Son except the Father, and no one knows the Father except the Son and those to whom the Son chooses to reveal him" (Matt. 11:27; see also Luke 10:22).

Among these many references that indicate the unity of Father and Son in character, purpose, and action, two stand apart and call for explanation. When Jesus states that the Father is greater than He (John 14:28) and that the Father has granted for the Son to have life in Himself (John 5:26), He appears to introduce a qualitative distinction between Himself and the Father. These two statements are best accounted for in terms of the Incarnation when Jesus, as Paul says, "emptied" Himself, becoming truly human and living in total submission to the Father (see Phil. 2:5–11).

The Forgiving of Sins

Jesus, in statements like those listed on the previous page, claimed a closeness with the Father to which no ordinary person has right. Furthermore, He *acted* in a manner that corresponded with these claims. Thus, He defended His actions in healing the paralyzed man by the pool of Bethesda on the Sabbath by referring to similar actions of the Father (John 5:16–23). The Jews understood His words as making Himself equal to God.

Jesus's actions toward the man lowered through the roof on a stretcher provided a further and more controversial demonstration of His claims to divinity, as we read in Mark 2:1–12. When the man, brought by friends who sought a miracle from the Master, dramatically entered the scene, Jesus's first words were, "Son, your sins are forgiven" (v. 5). That created a stir in the crowded room, with the teachers of the law protesting, "Who can forgive sins but God alone?" (v. 7). To them, Jesus's words constituted blasphemy, the ultimate sin of taking upon oneself the prerogatives due to God alone.

Jesus could have avoided a lot of trouble for Himself by simply healing the man on the stretcher and making no mention of his sins. But the Master, who had come to earth to make men and women whole, knew that the man placed before Him had a twofold need of healing—spiritual as well as physical. Therefore He did not hesitate to announce that he was forgiven before performing the miracle of physical healing.

In concluding this chapter on what Jesus taught about Himself, we will notice a series of profound statements. These are His claims that commence with "I am."

The "I AM" Statements

The seven "I am" sayings found in the Gospel of John have no parallels in the world's religions. Here is a spiritual leader who does not merely hand down teachings about the way to ultimate reality—He proclaims *Himself* as that way.

The unique nature of the "I am" sayings of Jesus comes into sharp focus if we compare Jesus with the founder of another major religion, Gautama Sakyamuni (d. 483 BC). According to Buddhist lore, Gautama, a prince raised in his father's palace and heir to the throne, was shielded from pain and suffering for many years. But one day, leaving the palace, he encountered in turn a sick man, an old man, and a dead man, thus experiencing the reality of the human condition. The fourth sight followed—a monk, serene in bearing.

These "four passing sights" led the prince to renounce throne and family and embark on a quest for enlightenment. At length, after enduring hardship and self-mortification, he became the Buddha, the Enlightened One, and spent the rest of his life teaching the Noble Eightfold Path to all who were prepared to listen.

Jesus, on the other hand, did not *discover* the way to God. He didn't *develop* teachings that He then passed on to others. He didn't *point* to the way; He proclaimed that He Himself was the Way. He didn't just *teach* truth; He asserted that *He Himself* was the Truth.

The seven "I am" sayings of Jesus, simple in wording, warrant our prayerful meditation. They are above all else *personal*: they center on the person of Jesus and they address us personally. They demand that *each individual* make a decision about these amazing claims.

Here we can only touch upon the content of each of these sayings. I invite the reader to explore them quietly and alone.

"I am the Bread of Life" (John 6:35, 48)

Jesus made this claim in the synagogue at Capernaum. The previous day He had fed the multitude from five small barley loaves and two fishes; but when the crowd made a move to crown Him as their king, He summarily sent them home. Now, as they tracked Him down to the Capernaum synagogue, He delivered a sharp rebuke: "Very truly I tell you, you are looking for me, not because you saw the signs I performed but because you ate the loaves and had your fill" (John 6:26).

The people sought bread to fill their bellies; Jesus wanted to give them the real, spiritual bread. "For the bread of God is the bread that comes down from heaven and gives life to the world," He said (v. 33).

"I am the Light of the World" (John 8:12)

This claim came during Jesus's visit to Jerusalem during the Feast of Tabernacles.

The full statement reads, "I am the light of the world. Whoever follows me will never walk in darkness, but will have the light of life."

Ellen G. White has an interesting comment on this claim in the context of the Feast of Tabernacles:

> When He spoke these words, Jesus was in the court of the temple specially connected with the services of the Feast of Tabernacles. In the center of this court rose two lofty standards, supporting lampstands of great size. After the evening sacrifice, all the lamps were kindled, shedding their light over Jerusalem. This ceremony was in commemoration of the pillar of light that guided Israel in the desert, and was also regarded as pointing to the coming of the Messiah. At evening when the lamps were lighted, the court was a scene of great rejoicing. Gray-haired men, the priests of the temple and the rulers of the people, united in the festive dances to the sound of instrumental music and the chants of the Levites.[3]

John the Beloved tells us that Jesus is "the light of all mankind" (John 1:4), and Jesus Himself in the night discourse with Nicodemus pinpointed the sinful perversity of humanity: "This is the verdict: Light has come into the world, but people loved darkness instead of light because their deeds were evil" (John 3:19). When the Light shines on us, we stand exposed. The Light strips away our masks and reveals our inner rottenness—and thus our desperate need of divine help. When the Light shines on my life, how do I respond?

"I AM" (John 8:58)

Jesus had claimed to be the Light of the World at the Feast of Tabernacles; now He made a statement that went even further. He had been debating with the Jewish leaders concerning fathers. They claimed Abraham was their father, Jesus countered that God was His Father (John 8:33–42). Then Jesus said, "Very truly I tell you, before Abraham was born, I am" (John 8:58). Not "before Abraham was born, I was," but "before Abraham was born, I am." Only God can say "I am," because He alone always is, has been, and will be.

Jesus's words echoed those given to Moses at the burning bush: "I AM WHO I AM. This is what you are to say to the Israelites: 'I AM has sent me to you'" (Exod. 3:14). What a breathtaking claim by Jesus! No wonder the Jews attempted to stone Him. It is nothing less than the claim to be God, the eternal I AM. Anyone saying this is either a madman or an imposter. Unless He really is God.

"I am the Gate" (John 10:7–9)

We find this saying immediately after Jesus had healed the man born blind. That miracle had led to strong contention with the Pharisees, who insisted that the miracle could not be genuine or Jesus truly from God because He had healed the man on the Sabbath. Jesus countered that it was the Pharisees who were really blind (John 9:39–41).

In this context of genuine versus false teachers, Jesus presented an extended illustration of sheep, sheepfolds, and shepherds (John 10:1–18). Speaking of the door or gate to the sheepfold, He said, "Very truly I tell you, I am the gate for the sheep. All who have come before me are thieves and robbers, but the sheep have not listened to them. I am the gate; whoever enters through me will be saved. They will come in and go out, and find pasture" (John 10:7–9).

These words claim an exclusivity that rings strangely on modern ears. In today's world it has become the norm to accept all manner of religious leaders with their various teachings. Believing that all paths lead to the same end, many people assert that to teach only one correct way smacks of arrogance. But the words of Jesus cannot be brushed aside: "All who ever came before me were thieves and robbers" (v. 8). They make the ultimate claim to religious authority.

"I am the Good Shepherd" (John 10:11, 14)

In this fifth affirmation Jesus describes the tender love that He has for His people. He cares so much for them that He is even ready to lay down His life for them. By contrast, those who are merely hired hands regard shepherding as just a job. When danger appears, they abandon the sheep and flee (vv. 11–13).

The Good Shepherd knows His sheep and they know Him. The bond between them is close and intimate, like that between the Father and the Son (vv. 14, 15). The sheep are safe in the care of this Shepherd: He will keep them from every predator, and they will find eternal life (vv. 27–29).

The Good Shepherd has other sheep beyond the sheep pen of Judaism. He calls them also to Himself so that there will be "one flock and one shepherd" (v. 16). Here we find a reiteration of Jesus's claim to be the one true religious guide to humanity. Just as He asserted that He alone is the Gate to salvation, here He presents a picture of universality, where He gathers all who are saved to Himself.

"I am the Resurrection and the Life" (John 11:25)

Lazarus, brother of Martha and Mary, had died. Jesus had been notified of Lazarus's sickness, but He did not come. When at last after four days He arrived, Martha delivered a mild rebuke: "Lord, if you had been here, my brother would not have died" (John 11:21).

That was true. Jesus broke up every funeral He attended. In the presence of the Life-giver, death fled. Now He assured Martha, "I am the resurrection and the life. The one who believes in me will live, even though they die; and whoever lives by believing in me will never die" (John 11:25, 26).

Jesus called Lazarus from the tomb and he came out. His life was restored, but not to immortal life. That awaits the day when Jesus will return to earth with trumpet blast and all the dead in Christ will come forth. All who believe in Jesus now are united with His life and the grave will not be able to hold them. Do you believe in Jesus's life-giving power?

"I am the Way, the Truth, and the Life" (John 14:6)

This, the final of Jesus's "I AM" claims, sums up all the others. He doesn't just show us the way to God; He *is* the Way. He doesn't just reveal truth; He *is* the truth. In the ultimate analysis, truth is a person—Jesus. He doesn't just offer us life; He is Life. In Him is life—our life.

QUESTIONS FOR DISCUSSION

1. A historian wrote that if the Arian view had won the day at the Council of Nicea, Christianity eventually would have dwindled to nothing. Why would he suggest this? Do you agree with him?

2. Look up all the references to "Son of Man" in the Gospel of Mark. Group them according to the categories explained in this chapter.

3. Reflect upon the seven "I AM" statements in the Gospel of John. How does Jesus's claim differ from the claims of other founders of world religions?

17

What Jesus Taught about the Holy Spirit

OBJECTIVES

- Explore features of the Holy Spirit as they relate to the Father and the Son.

- Gain a clearer understanding of the nature and work of the Holy Spirit.

- Understand the function of the Holy Spirit in our daily lives.

- Obtain insights into the Holy Spirit from the life, ministry, and teachings of Jesus.

SCRIPTURE

- John 14–17

Of all the topics in the Bible, the Holy Spirit is the most mysterious. Here students must tread with extra caution, prayerfully and humbly setting aside their preconceptions and being ready to listen to the words of Scripture and accept them as they are.

We are accustomed to reasoning from data and drawing appropriate conclusion. *If* the data indicate this, *then* it follows that. . . . This approach, which works well for most topics, is inadequate when we attempt to understand God. God is too big for our little minds; He cannot be captured and confined by human logic. Only when human logic is informed by what God has revealed to us in the Bible can it be trusted.

Drawing inferences based on Scripture that go beyond it is dangerous. Christian history, especially in the early centuries, shows the chaos created by thinkers who, endeavoring to understand the nature of God, went beyond the clear statements of the Word. They developed, at great cost to Christian unity, a philosophical version of a truly biblical doctrine of the Trinity and then set about to purify the church of those who differed in understanding. The arguments from those long-past church councils surface even today and at times cause confusion.

As we embark on the material of this chapter, we do well to heed Ellen G. White's counsel: "The nature of the Holy Spirit is a mystery. Men cannot explain it, because the Lord has not revealed it to them. Men having fanciful views may bring together passages of Scripture and put a human construction on them, but the acceptance of these views will not strengthen the church. Regarding such mysteries, which are too deep for human understanding, silence is golden."[1]

The Holy Spirit in the Life and Ministry of Jesus

The Holy Spirit was associated with Jesus throughout the entire period of the Incarnation. Mary, espoused to Joseph, became pregnant through the Holy Spirit. No earthly man was involved in her conception. "She was found to be pregnant through the Holy Spirit. . . . What is conceived in her is from the Holy Spirit" (Matt. 1:18, 20).

When Jesus left the carpenter's bench in Nazareth and went to John the Baptist to commence His public ministry, the Holy Spirit descended on Him in the form of a dove as the Father's voice came from heaven saying, "This is my Son, whom I love; with him I am well pleased" (Matt. 3:17; see also Luke 3:22; John 1:32, 33).

Immediately following this experience, Jesus was led by the Spirit into the desert, where He endured the devil's temptations for forty days (Matt. 4:1, 2; Luke 4:1, 2). The wording in Matthew's account— "Then Jesus was led by the Spirit into the wilderness to be tempted by the devil"— calls for comment. At face value it suggests that Jesus *invited* temptation. This is an idea that directly contradicts our Lord's teaching in the prayer that He taught His disciples: "Lead us not into temptation" (Matt. 6:13). Did the Holy Spirit lead Jesus to do the opposite?

Not at all. The construction of the Greek text of Matthew 4:1 can be taken as indicating either *purpose* or *result:* that is, as either the Spirit leading Jesus into the desert for the *purpose* of His being tempted by the devil, or as the Spirit leading Jesus into the desert with the *result* that He was tempted by the devil. In view of Jesus's instruction in what we call the Lord's Prayer, I think the latter is the correct interpretation.

Jesus's ministry was enabled by the Holy Spirit. Luke tells us that He was "full of the Holy Spirit" (Luke 4:1) and that He returned to Nazareth in the power of the Spirit (Luke 4:14, 16). In the synagogue at Nazareth, Jesus read from Isaiah's prediction: "The Spirit of the Lord is on me, because he has anointed me to proclaim good news to the poor" (Luke 4:18), and then applied the passage to Himself. When answering the criticisms of the Pharisees against His ministry, He said, "But if it is by the Spirit of God that I drive out demons, then the kingdom of God has come upon you" (Matt. 12:28).

After the Ascension, when the apostle Peter brought the good news to Cornelius and his relatives and close friends, he summarized the Master's ministry thus: "God anointed Jesus of Nazareth with the Holy Spirit and power, and . . . he went around doing good and healing all who were under the power of the devil, because God was with him" (Acts 10:38).

Three of the four Gospel accounts draw to a close with emphasis on the Holy Spirit. In each case it is the risen Lord who speaks, and as He hands off His work to the apostles, He indicates that the Spirit is to be central in their mission.

Matthew's Gospel closes with the Great Commission: "Then Jesus came to them and said, 'All authority in heaven and on earth has been given to me. Therefore go and make disciples of all nations, baptizing them in the name of the Father and of the Son and of the Holy Spirit, and teaching them to obey everything I have commanded you. And surely I am with you always, to the very end of the age'" (Matt. 28:18–20). This passage plays a crucial role in our understanding of the nature of the Holy Spirit and relations among Father, Son, and Spirit. We shall return to it later in this chapter.

Luke's Gospel closes with Jesus instructing the disciples to wait in Jerusalem for the promised Gift: "I am going to send you what my Father has promised; but stay in the city until you have been clothed with power from on high" (Luke 24:49). The book of Acts, the companion volume to Luke's account, picks up where the Gospel leaves off (see Luke 1:1–4; Acts 1:1, 2). It tells us that the risen Lord, while eating with the apostles, said, "Do not leave Jerusalem, but wait for the gift my Father promised, which you have heard me speak about. For John baptized with water, but in a few days you will be baptized with the Holy Spirit" (Acts 1:4, 5).

The Acts narrative adds that Jesus told the disciples: "But you will receive power when the Holy Spirit comes on you; and you will be my witnesses in Jerusalem, and in all Judea and Samaria, and to the ends of the earth" (Acts 1:8).

John's Gospel supplies a treasure trove of instruction about the Holy Spirit. Especially during Jesus's Farewell Discourse— His words in private with His friends on that final Thursday night, found in John 14–17—Jesus shared precious, intimate details about the Holy Spirit and His work. After His resurrection the Lord came to the disciples and said, "'Peace be with you! As the Father has sent me, I am sending you.' And with that he breathed on them and said, 'Receive the Holy Spirit'" (John 20:21, 22).

Father, Son, and Holy Spirit

The words of Jesus give us unparalleled insights into the nature and work of the Holy Spirit. Without them our understanding would be severely curtailed. The Old Testament has but few, and undetailed, references to the Spirit. On the other hand, the New Testament writings other than the Gospels, while they make frequent mention of the Holy Spirit, do not emphasize the personal, intimate perspectives that Jesus shared with His closest friends on that last, fateful Thursday night.

We might highlight the significance of Jesus's insights like this: Jesus's words give us a view from *within*, from the stance of God, that only He could share. Jesus's statements that bear on the Holy Spirit occur in four places in the Farewell Discourse: John 14:16–18; 14:26; 15:26; and 16:7–15. We shall study each of these passages in order, searching the texts for understanding and praying that the same Spirit about whom we seek to learn more will open the eyes of our hearts.

John 14:16–18

> And I will ask the Father, and he will give you another advocate to help you and be with you forever—the Spirit of truth. The world cannot accept him, because it neither sees him nor knows him. But you know him, for he lives with you and will be in you. I will not leave you as orphans; I will come to you.

From this passage we discern the following aspects relative to the Holy Spirit:

1. *A new name is introduced—Paraclete, translated here as "Advocate."* The Greek *paraklētos*, literally "one called alongside," is difficult to convey in its full sense in translation. It is a rich word, positive and encouraging. Translations include "Comforter," "Counselor," and "Defender." We find Jesus using this word four times, all of them in the passages that we are studying here (John 14:16, 26; 15:26; 16:7).

That the Holy Spirit is indicated is clear from John 14:26, where Paraclete and Holy Spirit are equated.

2. *The Father gives the Paraclete/Holy Spirit to the disciples.*

3. *The Paraclete/Holy Spirit will be with them forever.* Jesus is about to leave them, but His place will be taken by the Paraclete.

4. *The Holy Spirit is also called the "Spirit of Truth."* This designation occurs two more times in Jesus's Farewell Discourse (John 15:26; 16:13).

"Truth" is an important term in the Gospel of John. In the Prologue we saw that Jesus, the Word made flesh, was "full of grace and truth" (John 1:14). In the debates between Jesus and the religious leaders, the key issue was this: Who is telling the truth? Jesus sets forth Himself as the One Who has come from God and Who bears the truth (see John 8:37–47). To His followers He announced Himself as truth personified: "I am . . . the truth" (John 14:6). And at the end of it all, as Pilate engaged Jesus in conversation, once again the central element concerned truth. Jesus stated, "In fact, the reason I was born and came into the world is to testify to the truth. Everyone on the side of truth listens to me" (John 18:37). To that statement Pilate could only frame a cynical reply, "What is truth?" (v. 38).

Jesus is no longer on this earth, but the Holy Spirit carries on His work of testifying to the truth. In some of the last letters of the New Testament, the three epistles of John dating from late in the first century AD, we see once again the conflict between truth and falsehood coming to a head as deceivers—in reality antichrists—infiltrated the church and led many Christians astray (see 1 John 2:18, 19, 22, 23). The aged apostle John assures the troubled believers, "But you have an anointing from the Holy One, and all of you know the truth" (1 John 2:20). "This is how we recognize the Spirit of truth and the spirit of falsehood" (1 John 4:6).

5. *The world neither sees nor knows the Holy Spirit*, but believers do, because the Spirit lives with them and is in them. Here we see the profound difference between the believer and the unbeliever. To the latter, the things of God and eternity are incomprehensible; they are foolishness and meaningless. But that's not so for the believer, for the Holy Spirit dwells with him or her and reveals them to the heart.

6. *The Paraclete coming to the believer and living in the heart is just like having Jesus present again.* Jesus comforted His followers: "I will not leave you as orphans [because He was about to go away]; I will come to you" (John 14:18). How privileged were the disciples to accompany the Master, to be with Him, to see His acts of loving ministry, and to hear His teachings. But we today may enjoy the same sort of fellowship with the Lord through the Holy Spirit, Who dwells within.

Christians, in speaking of the Holy Spirit, frequently use the pronoun "it." That is not correct. The Spirit is not a thing but a person. We all need to be careful of our language in referring to the Holy Spirit.

Because the nature of the Holy Spirit is so mysterious, some people visualize a force, power, or influence. All such concepts fall short and fail to do justice to Jesus's words in this passage. The Holy Spirit comes as Paraclete—a comforter, helper, and advocate—to teach and aid us in our Christian walk. He is far more than an influence; He is a Person and knowing Him is just like knowing Jesus.

John 14:26

> But the Advocate, the Holy Spirit, whom the Father will send in my name, will teach you all things and will remind you of everything I have said to you.

From this passage we learn more about the work of the Holy Spirit:

1. *The Father sends the Holy Spirit.* This thought parallels that in John 14:16, where the Father gives the Holy Spirit.

2. *The Father sends the Holy Spirit in Jesus's name.* In the Bible, the name of a person stands for the person themselves. Thus, God is frequently referred to simply as the Name. In the Farewell Discourse Jesus instructed His disciples to make their request in His name (John 14:13; 16:23, 24). To ask in His name is to imply His authority and power. Thus, when Jesus says in John 14:26 that the Father will send the Holy Spirit in His name, that name brings the saving, powerful efficacy of Jesus's person and work.

3. *The intimate connections between Father, Son, and Holy Spirit are evident.*

The Father sends the Holy Spirit in Jesus's name. At the same time, Father, Son, and Holy Spirit are separate and distinct, and yet one. That is to say, Jesus and the Holy Spirit are not separate phases or modes of being.

4. *The Holy Spirit "will teach you all things."* In this respect He carries on the ministry of Jesus, Who devoted much time to teaching the disciples.

5. *The Holy Spirit reminds the followers of Jesus's words.* This work of bringing into memory played a key role in the writing of the Gospels. The Holy Spirit continues this work among Jesus's followers today. When we are faced with temptations and trials, the Spirit reminds us of the sayings of Jesus. However, He is only able to do this for us as we have already taken the time to acquaint ourselves with Jesus's words by reading the Bible.

John 15:26

When the Advocate comes, whom I will send to you from the Father—the Spirit of truth who goes out from the Father—he will testify about me.

In this passage we see motifs repeated from the two passages in John 14: Paraclete, sending, and Spirit of Truth. But we also find new ideas:

1. *The Holy Spirit **goes out** from the Father.* This concept points to activity within God in which there is a movement.

2. *The Holy Spirit testifies about Jesus.* He is not focused on Himself but on Jesus: He exalts the Son, leads to the Son, and glorifies the Son (John 16:13, 14).

John 16:7–15

But very truly I tell you, it is for your good that I am going away. Unless I go away, the Advocate will not come to you; but if I go, I will send him to you. When he comes, he will prove the world to be in the wrong about sin and righteousness and judgment: about sin, because people do not believe in me; about righteousness, because I am going to the Father, where you can see me no longer; and about judgment, because the prince of this world now stands condemned.

I have much more to say to you, more than you can now bear. But when he, the Spirit of truth, comes, he will guide you into all the truth. He will not speak on his own; he will speak only what he hears, and he will tell you what is yet to come. He will glorify me because it is from me that he will receive what he will make known to you. All that belongs to the Father is mine. That is why I said the Spirit will receive from me what he will make known to you.

This passage reveals further vital aspects concerning the work of the Holy Spirit:

1. *The Paraclete will not come to the disciples unless Jesus goes away* (16:7); therefore it is for their good that Jesus will leave them. How can this be? Was the Holy Spirit not on earth before Jesus's departure? What about the era of the Old Testament? What about others during Jesus's lifetime who are said to have been led by the Holy Spirit—like John the Baptist (Luke 1:15), Elizabeth

(Luke 1:41), Zechariah (Luke 1:67), and Simeon (Luke 2:25)? We shall consider this puzzling statement of Jesus later in this chapter.

2. *The Paraclete convicts the world of guilt in regard to sin* because its people do not believe in Jesus. When the Master walked among humanity, people came face to face with the beauty of His person, which was full of grace and truth. He was the Light, and looking on Him each person was forced to make a choice whether to accept or reject Him.

3. *We discover insights into the fundamental nature of sin.* In the Bible sin is described in various ways, such as missing the mark and falling short in the Old Testament and as lawlessness (1 John 3:4), acting outside of faith (Rom. 14:23), or neglecting to do the right thing (James 4:17) in the New Testament. Here our Lord cuts to the bone: sin is not believing in Him.

In our world, people often make comments about what it takes to get to heaven. Usually these discussions come down to the good deeds we have done, and whether the good deeds outnumber the bad ones. But in this passage Jesus shows that the Judgment won't be so much about what we have done as about what we have done with God's Son. He is the Way and He alone—there is no other.

4. *The Holy Spirit also convicts concerning righteousness,* because Jesus has gone back to the Father and we no longer have that wonderful life to provide the standard of righteousness. But the Holy Spirit works on our conscience, calling us back to that standard as we read and reflect on accounts in the Gospels.

5. *The Holy Spirit also convicts the world regarding judgment.* The great controversy pits Christ against Satan, truth against lies, and love against evil. Satan, the accuser of Jesus in heaven and of His followers on earth, stands exposed in the light that streams from Calvary. Now all can see that the evil one, who promises life, is a deceiver and a murderer (John 8:44). Death, not life, clings to his person.

6. *The Holy Spirit guides the followers of Jesus into all truth.* This tells us that truth isn't static, fixed in concrete for all time. Revelation is progressive. As James Russell Lowell put it:

> New occasions teach new duties;
> Time makes ancient good uncouth.[2]

However, truth as it progresses doesn't contradict what has gone before; rather, it elaborates it.

7. *The Holy Spirit doesn't speak on His own.* He works in close cooperation with Father and Son. He takes from the Son and makes it known to the followers of Jesus. The Holy Spirit doesn't initiate truth; He always works in close relation to Jesus.

8. *The Spirit brings glory to Jesus.* He does not glorify Himself; He glorifies the Son.

During the history of the church, from time to time movements have arisen claiming, in the name of the Holy Spirit, to have new revelations of truth. Early in Christianity the Gnostics set out their deviant ideas with such arguments. Even today some Christians emphasize the Holy Spirit above Jesus. Such people need to take seriously Jesus's words in the Farewell Discourse. The Holy Spirit always brings us back to Jesus and His teachings; He does not introduce a new religion that goes beyond Jesus or that exalts Himself.

We should note what Jesus does *not* say about the work of the Holy Spirit in John 14–16. He does *not* say that the Spirit will endow everyone who truly believes in Jesus with a particular spiritual gift, such as ecstatic utterance, commonly known as "speaking in tongues." Spiritual gifts have their place (see Rom. 12:4–8; 1 Cor. 12:1–30), but Jesus makes no mention of them in His closing words to His followers.

The Name of the Father, Son, and Holy Spirit

Jesus's words in the Farewell Discourse clearly indicate two facts about the Holy Spirit: He is a Person and He is God.

The manner in which Jesus speaks of the Paraclete and His activities—personal pronouns, teaching, guiding, convicting, glorifying, testifying—preclude any concept of the Holy Spirit as merely a power, force, or influence. Over and over the Holy Spirit is placed in closest relation to the Father and the Son. The Spirit is distinguished from Father and Son, but He is with them and works with them to carry forward the ministry of Jesus. His relationship to Father and Son and His work makes manifest that the Holy Spirit is God just as the Father is God and the Son is God.

The words with which Matthew's Gospel ends—words given by the risen Lord—are highly significant. "Therefore go and make disciples of all nations, baptizing them in the name [singular] of the Father and of the Son and of the Holy Spirit" (Matt. 28:19). From this passage we hear again that there is only one God, not three gods, for God has only one name. But we also learn that the one God encompasses a "three-ness"—not that God appears or acts in three different modes but that God encompasses three personal distinctions.

Beyond this we cannot, and should not, venture. Christian thinkers, reflecting on the mystery of God, eventually formulated the doctrine of the Trinity. This term, which does not occur in the Scriptures, affirms two fundamental but mysterious facts: God is one, not three; and the one God is Father, Son, and Holy Spirit. Speculations concerning God's nature and endeavors to define it by recourse to Greek philosophical contexts, as did the theologians who developed the classical doctrine of the Trinity, are fraught with the danger of falling into error. Let us be content to live with the mystery: God is God, far beyond the capacity of our minds to comprehend. So while we have some knowledge provided by Scripture, we should not go beyond it and fall into speculation.

The Age of the Spirit

Although the Holy Spirit was manifested during Old Testament times and in the ministry of Jesus, the Master's death and resurrection ushered in a new era wherein the Spirit has come with new power. Jesus spoke of this era in the Farewell Discourse, but He had already forecast it during the Feast of Tabernacles: "On the last and greatest day of the festival, Jesus stood and said in a loud voice, 'Let anyone who is thirsty come to me and drink. Whoever believes in me, as Scripture has said, rivers of living water will flow from within them'" (John 7:37, 38). The apostle John explains what Jesus intended by this announcement: "By this he meant the Spirit, whom those who believed in him were later to receive. Up to that time the Spirit had not been given, since Jesus had not yet been glorified" (v. 39).

The descent of the Holy Spirit on the apostles on the day of Pentecost marked the dawning of a new age—one of the Spirit. The Holy Spirit's coming in power attested to Jesus's victory over death. Peter proclaimed this fact to the crowds gathered in Jerusalem for the festival: "Exalted to the right hand of God, he has received from the Father the promised Holy Spirit and has poured out what you now see and hear" (Acts 2:33). We live in that era—the age of the Spirit. Jesus's death and resurrection have released to every believer the fullness of the Paraclete.

The Holy Spirit and Mission

While the Holy Spirit as the Paraclete comforts, helps, and guides us, Jesus made clear that this divine Gift is especially intended for mission. After His resurrection He commissioned the disciples to carry on His work: "As the Father has sent me, I am sending you." Then He breathed on them and said, "Receive the Holy Spirit" (John 20:21, 22).

Their mission would extend to earth's farthest bounds, and it would be one empowered by the Holy Spirit: "But you will receive power when the Holy Spirit comes on you; and you will be my witnesses in Jerusalem, and in all Judea and Samaria, and to the ends of the earth" (Acts 1:8).

In the work of God, the Spirit alone brings people to new life in Christ. Jesus told Nicodemus that no one can enter the kingdom of God unless they are born again of the Spirit (see John 3:5–8). We do not "win" souls for Christ; only the Holy Spirit can do this work. Our role is to be men and women whom God the Holy Spirit can use to bring the good news with power. The Spirit works *in* us and *through* us. The kingdom advances, not because of our strength or skill, but through the Spirit's power.

1. How would you show from the Bible that the Holy Spirit is personal but also deity (God)?

2. Look up at least six different translations of the Bible and list how they translate *paraclete*. From these various translations, at what concept of *paraclete* do you arrive?

3. The Early Church was empowered to mission by the reception of the Holy Spirit. How is the same Holy Spirit impressing you to join this mission? Write down possible ways that you may be a Holy Spirit-empowered agency for His mission.

18

What Jesus Taught about the Kingdom of Heaven

<table>
<tr><td>OBJECTIVES</td><td>• Understand what Jesus meant by "the kingdom of heaven."</td></tr>
<tr><td></td><td>• Understand the nature of the kingdom in its tension of being already here and still to come.</td></tr>
<tr><td></td><td>• Grasp what it means to live as a citizen of Jesus's kingdom.</td></tr>
<tr><td>SCRIPTURE</td><td>• Matthew 5–7</td></tr>
</table>

To this day the Jewish people do not accept that Jesus of Nazareth was the Messiah. As we already indicated, the reason they give is simple: the kingdom didn't come. He proclaimed that it was about to come, but His words failed. Therefore, He was not the Messiah.

In the Synoptic Gospels, the kingdom motif is central to Jesus's proclamation. This is shown at least partially by the frequency with which it occurs: about fifty times in Matthew, fifteen in Mark, and forty in Luke. In John's Gospel the kingdom language occurs in only two places—Jesus's discourse with Nicodemus (John 3:3, 5) and His encounter with Pontius Pilate (John 18:36, 37).

A striking aspect of Jesus's use of kingdom language is that He never defines what He means by the kingdom, nor do any of His hearers ask for an explanation. This silence indicates that the people of Jesus's time already had an idea of what the kingdom meant, so Jesus did not need to elaborate when He used the term.

It (the kingdom) was the heart of His life and the object of His hopes. It provided the touchstone for all His piety and religious observances. The kingdom of God was not subject to the confusions and uncertainties of the changing political order. It was not a realm or an administrative system like that of the Romans, but simply and solely God's rule over His people Israel.

The question that divided Israel in Jesus's times, therefore, was not whether God ruled, but when and how His rule would be realized upon the earth. Would His decisive intervention in human affairs come through political developments involving Greece or Rome or Persia, or would it be a purely supernatural event? Could it be hastened by individuals "taking upon themselves the yoke of the kingdom of heaven" in prayer and good works? What would be the role of Israel as a nation? Would God raise up a messianic king of David's line to avenge past wrongs and restore Jewish political fortunes to their former eminence?[1]

A curious feature of Jesus's kingdom language is that it almost completely disappears after the Master's return to heaven. Although John the Baptist's message was "Repent for the kingdom of heaven has come near" (Matt. 3:2), and Jesus when He began to preach gave the identical emphasis (Matt. 4:17), we rarely find the kingdom mentioned elsewhere in the New Testament. The book of Acts tells us that the apostles went out preaching about the kingdom of God (Acts 8:12; 14:22; 19:8; 20:25; 28:23, 31), but in Paul's letters the term hardly occurs.

Instead of "kingdom," a new word comes to dominate in the New Testament—*ekklēsia*, which we commonly translate as the "church." Thus, although Jesus preached the kingdom of God, the church was the result. The kingdom, however, cannot be equated with the church.

In the Gospels we find both "kingdom of heaven" and "kingdom of God," and sometimes just "kingdom." "Kingdom of heaven" occurs exclusively in the Gospel of Matthew, whereas "kingdom of God" is found only five times in the original Greek (Matt. 6:33; 12:28; 19:24; 21:31, 43). In Mark, Luke, John, and Acts, "kingdom of heaven" does not occur—only "kingdom of God."

Did Jesus distinguish between the terms "kingdom of God" and "kingdom of heaven"? Apparently not. It seems impossible to make any significant difference between the two. We find the terms used interchangeably; for instance, Matthew tells us that when Jesus began to preach He proclaimed, "The kingdom of heaven has come near" (Matt. 4:17), whereas Mark records His message as "the kingdom of God has come near" (Mark 1:15). Again in Matthew 19:23, 24: "Then Jesus said to his disciples, 'Truly I tell you, it is hard for someone who is rich to enter the kingdom of heaven. Again I tell you, it is easier for a camel to go through the eye of a needle than for someone who is rich to enter the kingdom of God.'"

Of greater import is the *time* aspect of Jesus's kingdom sayings. They divide sharply along two lines: some indicate the kingdom as even now present or breaking in, whereas the others point to it as *future*. We shall look at each group of sayings in turn.

The Kingdom Already Here

Matthew sets forth John the Baptist as a preacher of the imminent kingdom.

"Repent ye: for the kingdom of heaven is at hand," he proclaimed from the wilderness of Judea (Matt. 3:2, KJV). It is a message of urgency: time is very short, God's wrath is about to fall, and the One mightier than John will soon appear.

As Jesus commences His ministry, He repeats that call: "Repent: for the kingdom of heaven is at hand" (4:17, KJV). His opening words in the Sermon on the Mount are: "Blessed are the poor in spirit, for theirs is the kingdom of heaven" (5:3). Indeed the whole sermon is about the kingdom. It is a manifesto of the privileges and responsibilities of its citizens. Clearly, the kingdom was not far in the future. The kingdom *even now* is dawning. Jesus is imparting instruction for the present time.

Matthew 12:24 (ESV) provides an especially telling scene. As the opponents of Jesus witness His mighty acts, they denigrate them with what appears to be a plausible objection—"It is only by Beelzebul, the prince of demons, that this man casts out demons." Jesus answers their challenge headlong. Will Satan then destroy himself? By whom do the sons of the Pharisees succeed in their exorcisms—also by Satan? Then comes the clincher: "But if it is by the Spirit of God that I drive out demons, then the kingdom of God *has come upon you*" (12:28). The statement is unequivocal. Jesus's miracles show that God's rule has broken through to humanity.

The inquiry of the Baptist from prison offers a parallel case. John wishes to know if Jesus really is the promised "one who is to come" (Matt. 11:3) or if that one is still in the future. Jesus's reply is significant. The disciples of John should report what they have seen and heard—the blind restored to sight, the lame walking, the lepers cleansed, the deaf hearing, the dead raised up, and the poor receiving the Good News. Once again the appeal is to Jesus's mighty works—the works of God's reign.

We find in Matthew 11 a further statement of the in-breaking of the kingdom. Says Jesus, "From the days of John the Baptist until now, the kingdom of heaven has been subjected to violence [or, "has been coming violently"]. . . . For all the Prophets and the Law prophesied until John" (vv. 12, 13). The verse as it has come down to us is obscure, but not in its teaching concerning the kingdom. Clearly, John is set forth as the *beginning* of the reign of God—the Old Testament revelation was "until John."

As with Jesus's miracles, so with His teachings. His preaching is specifically termed "the good news of the kingdom" (4:23; 9:35). Likewise, over and over He commences His parables with, "The kingdom of heaven is like . . ." (e.g., 13:24, 31, 33, 44). These parables do not refer primarily to the future. Rather, the reverse seems to be the case. Usually they set out the character and growth of that reign of God inaugurated by Jesus's ministry. Consider but one example— the parable of the sower. After Jesus has told the parable, He tells His disciples,

"To you it has been given to know the secrets of the kingdom of heaven" (13:11, ESV). Then, as He explains the parable, He reveals that the seed is the hearing of "the word of the kingdom" (v. 19, ESV). It seems beyond dispute that the application of the parable is not to some future realm. The accent is on the here and now. The kingdom is breaking in, and Jesus's preaching is the Good News of the fact.

Yet we must quickly add that Jesus was far more than a mere announcer. It was *in His person* that the kingdom was coming—in His mighty acts and teachings that God's reign was breaking upon the people who long had sat in the darkness and "shadow of death" (4:16). With the coming of Jesus, the kingdom had come.

The Kingdom to Come

Although God's reign was present in the work of Jesus Christ, it clearly has a future aspect also. The Lord's Prayer itself embodies this aspect. For two thousand years, Jesus's followers have prayed, "Thy kingdom come" (Matt. 6:10, KJV). By this they intend, "May Thy kingdom come," recognizing that God's reign is not yet manifested in fullness.

It has become fashionable among many scholars of the Gospels to set aside or diminish the futuristic aspect of the kingdom. They have set out a teaching of "realized eschatology"—that Jesus's life and ministry themselves removed the need of any future coming in of the reign.

But this interpretation cannot be made to square with the Lord's Prayer or, indeed, with the New Testament as a whole. And Matthew's Gospel, possibly more than any other document of the canon, preserves this future.

Often in Matthew's Gospel the themes of kingdom are interlinked with judgment, the latter unquestionably yet to come (13:24, 37–43). There are also passages that speak about the state of blessedness in the kingdom. Matthew 8:11 tells how "many will come from east and west and will take their places at the feast with Abraham, Isaac, and Jacob in the kingdom of heaven," while in 19:28 the Twelve receive this promise: "At the renewal of all things, when the Son of man sits on his glorious throne, you who have followed me will also sit on twelve thrones, judging the twelve tribes of Israel." The following chapter records the dispute among the Twelve as to who will receive the thrones in the places of honor—on either side of Jesus in His kingdom.

The strongest evidence for the kingdom yet to come still remains, however. We refer to the apocalyptic discourse of Matthew 24. Jesus sets out a series of indications in answer to His disciples' query, "What will be the sign of your coming and of the end of the age?" (24:3). He reveals that the end will be accompanied by cataclysmic upheavals of nature and celestial phenomena. It will be heralded by social disintegration, strife and bloodshed, and religious deceptions.

But, while Jesus gives *signs* of the end, no one knows its precise date—"not even the angels in heaven, nor the Son, but only the Father" (24:36).

Thus the Christian must remain continually ready. The end, although indicated by the collapse of the natural and social worlds, will catch people unawares, just as did the Flood. The keynote, then, must be, "Watch therefore, for you do not know what hour your Lord is coming. . . . Therefore you also be ready; for the Son of Man is coming at an hour you do not expect" (24:42, 44; NKJV).

Yes, God's reign broke in upon human existence with the coming of Jesus Christ. It invested the human lot with a meaning that the passing of the ages cannot dim. In that simple life of gentle and noble deeds, and above all in its strange ending—an execution on a Roman cross—divine power was manifest. God has come close to humanity in a unique manner, even as the Babe of Bethlehem was the Immanuel sign—"God with us" (1:23; see also Isa. 7:14).

But that life of grace did not exhaust the rule of God. Just as the kingdom did not come to an end with the tragedy of Calvary, so it was not fully encompassed by the Incarnation. The "already" of the gentle life of Jesus is balanced by the "not yet" of the future, glorious reign.

The Nature of the Kingdom

To Pilate Jesus said, "My kingdom is not of this world. . . . My kingdom is from another place" (John 18:36). Those critics of the Master—who argue that He could not be the Messiah because, while He proclaimed that the kingdom was near, it did not come—reveal a fundamental misunderstanding of the nature of His kingdom. It was not of this world; it was altogether other.

The Greek word translated "kingdom," *basileia*, does not have to signify an actual domain or political realm. It can as well be translated as "reign" or "rule." Thus, "kingdom of God" equals the "reign of God."

In Jesus's life and work, God's reign was breaking through. His ministry demonstrated that God had not left humankind alone—God had manifested His presence and power. The kingdom of God had already begun on earth.

Today, whenever someone accepts Jesus as Lord of their life—wherever He holds first place—there the kingdom or reign of God is manifested.

In this life, God's kingdom is as real as any government. It manifests itself, however, not with armies, weapons, and physical power but in the transformed lives of people who have taken Jesus as their Lord.

The kingdom is of infinite value. In light of it all, earthly wealth, prestige, and attainments pale into nothingness. It is, taught Jesus, like treasure hidden in a field or a precious pearl for which a person sells all his possessions (see Matt. 13:44–46).

God's kingdom grows silently and unobtrusively as a child, young person, or adult allows Jesus to be Lord. It is like the seed scattered on the ground that sprouts and grows, said the Master (Mark 4:26–29). No one can explain just how the change takes place.

Kingdom Living

The Gospels abound with words from Jesus that instruct us on how we become citizens of God's kingdom and how we are to live as its citizens. No portion, however, surpasses the magnificent instruction found in the Sermon on the Mount (Matt. 5–7). It has rightly been described as the magna carta—the great charter—of the kingdom of heaven. Because of limitations of space we can only give a summary treatment of this magnificent passage.

Citizens of the Kingdom of Heaven (Matt. 5:3–12)

Nine times Jesus pronounces a blessing, and nine times those singled out for blessing are the opposite of what the world values. The world praises power. It admires men and women who are "cool"—in charge, confident, self-sufficient, and feeling no need of God or others. But the kingdom of heaven values just the opposite:

- Not the proud and haughty but those who, broken like the rest of humanity, acknowledge their brokenness.

- Not the outwardly carefree and light-hearted, but those who enter into the sorrow of the world and confess their own failings.

- Not the aggressive and domineering, but people who are emptied of self so they can be filled by God.

- Not those who crave pleasure, fame, and wealth, but those who yearn to see right prevail.

- Not the cruel and heartless, but those who show mercy.

- Not those who lust for sex and power, but those who are wholly devoted to God.

- Not those who stir up strife, who rage, and who kill, but those who bring about reconciliation.

- Not slanderers and false accusers, but those who accept persecution with joy and gladness.

Making the World a Better Place (Matt. 5:13–16)

The values of Jesus's followers are utterly different from those of the world, yet they influence all around them for the better. They are like salt and light, improving life in this world and helping drive back the darkness.

Practicing a Better Righteousness (Matt. 5:17–48)

The righteousness (right living) that Jesus describes far outstrips the righteousness that the scribes and Pharisees sought to achieve by their rigorous attention to details of the Law. This righteousness goes beyond words and deeds—it reaches to the thoughts and motives of the heart. The religious teachers did not attempt to go so far in their quest for righteousness.

In the Sermon on the Mount, Jesus raises the bar of righteousness to impossible heights. Righteousness cannot be attained by mere human effort, but a power outside of humanity will be required. Those called to such a high standard, however, are utterly different from the Pharisees and religious teachers. They are meek and merciful; they are pure in heart and peacemakers. They are new people transformed in their hearts by the Lord Whom they serve.

Under the "better righteousness" that Jesus proclaimed in the Sermon on the Mount, the commandments of the Old Testament find deep spiritual meaning and are intensified. As the prophet Isaiah had foretold—"He will magnify the law, and make it honorable" (Isa. 42:21, KJV)—Jesus takes a series of examples from the Old Testament and shows their added meaning for citizens of the kingdom. Six times He says, "You have heard that it was said . . ." and six times He intensifies the command by stating "But I tell you . . ." (Matt. 5:22, 28, 32, 34, 39, 44):

- *Murder.* Jesus extends the sixth commandment of the Decalogue to embrace anger and words that denigrate and belittle. In case of a dispute, He tells us to take the first step in reconciliation, not waiting for the person who feels aggrieved to come to us. Reconciliation takes precedence over formal religious observance. He tells

us to leave our offering gifts at the altar and go at once to the offended party.

- *Adultery.* The rabbis counted only deeds in their quest for righteousness, but Jesus extended the seventh commandment to include lustful thoughts and looks. For Jesus, adultery imagined constitutes sin. (What a condemnation of what the media portray in our world!) He tells us that we should take the strongest measures to avoid sin. Any habit, no matter how dear to us, must be cut off if it leads to temptation.

  The Christian scholar, Origen, who lived AD 185–254, took these words of Jesus literally and castrated himself. But Jesus, whose whole ministry was about bringing healing and wholeness to broken men and women, surely didn't intend for us to pluck out our eyes, sever our hand, or mutilate our bodies in any way.

- *Divorce.* The Mosaic code permitted a husband to write a certificate of divorce and send away the partner who displeased him (note that this provision was gender specific; a wife could not divorce her husband in similar manner). The actual words in the Torah stated, "If a man marries a woman who becomes displeasing to him because he finds something indecent about her, and he writes her a certificate of divorce, gives it to her and sends her from his house" (Deut. 24:1).

The rabbis of Jesus's time argued over the stipulation "something indecent." The school of Hillel, the liberal side, were ready to grant divorce to a man whose wife displeased him merely by the food she prepared for him. The more conservative school of Shammai, however, opposed such easy divorce.

Here and elsewhere in Jesus's teachings, we find Him strongly upholding the sanctity and permanence of marriage. He cut through rabbinical speculations and went back to Eden (see Matt. 19:3–12).

- *Oaths.* The teachers of the law not only compiled lists of regulations, but also ways to circumvent them. Thus, they taught that if anyone swore by the temple, the oath could be set aside; but it could not be if they swore by the gold of the temple. That was likewise with the temple altar and a gift placed on it (see Matt. 23:16–22). But the kingdom calls us to lay aside all such theological nitpicking and honor our promises.

- *An eye for an eye.* The Mosaic code was designed to limit revenge. The punishment should be appropriate to the crime, and only judges could determine it (see Exod. 21:22–24; Lev. 24:19, 20; Deut. 19:21). Jesus, however, teaches a response to injury that reverses this system of strict justice. Instead of resisting an evil person, the citizen of the kingdom of heaven responds with non-violence (Matt. 5:39). Mahatma Gandhi, the father of free India, put this principle into practice. The British rulers ultimately had no answer and left India.

- *Love for enemies.* This final example of the better righteousness of the kingdom of heaven rises to impossible heights. Who can hope to love as Jesus loves? Love is beyond measure.

And not just loving those who return our love. This is love for the unlovable, who hate us and want to hurt us. A religion of dos and don'ts, a checklist religion, will never attempt to reach such an ideal.

This is love as the Father loves. He loves without discriminating between those who are evil and those who are good. This is love that surpasses human love.

It is in such a context that Jesus concludes His six examples of the righteousness of the kingdom with words that, taken by themselves, have troubled many earnest seekers: "Be perfect, therefore, as your heavenly Father is perfect" (Matt. 5:48). Note the "therefore." It is in light of the discussion of loving one's enemies that Jesus challenges, "Be perfect as your heavenly Father is perfect." As the Father loves impartially, so must we. We can never love to the *extent* or *depth* of His love, but we can by His grace experience a love that goes out to all people, both the lovely and the unlovely.

Some people have heard in Matthew 5:48 a call to sinless perfection. That idea, however, is foreign to the context that begins in verse 43. God indeed calls us to victory over sin, but that is not in view here. Sinless living is something negative—not sinning—but the call here is to something positive—to loving. Loving even our enemies is the call of the kingdom. And with God all things are possible.

Authentic Religion (Matt. 6:1–18)

The kingdom of God seeks people who are genuine in their religion. In our times, as in Jesus's time, a lot of professed followers play games with God. They fool others and perhaps fool themselves, but they don't fool God.

In the Sermon on the Mount, Jesus mentions three religious practices in which people played games with God—giving to the needy (Matt. 6:2–4), praying (vv. 5–15), and fasting (vv. 16–18). In each case the people performed these acts principally to impress others. They made loud announcements of their supposed generosity, stood on street corners where everyone would see them

praying, and disfigured their faces to draw attention to themselves when they fasted.

Jesus called these fakes "hypocrites"—actors. They weren't authentic; they were treating religion as a public stage in which they pretended to be something they were not. They sought to be honored by those who observed their fake piety. But that would be the only reward they would receive. "Truly I tell you," Jesus said, "they have received their reward in full" (Matt. 6:2, 16).

Authentic religion comes from the heart with silent, secret communion with the Father. Out of that heart proceed genuine prayer, worship, and loving acts of kindness to others. Jesus had more to say concerning prayer in the Sermon on the Mount. We shall take up this counsel in chapter 23.

Single-Minded Living (Matt. 6:19–24)

The values of citizens of the kingdom are focused on God and heaven, not on the world around them. For most people in the world, money takes priority: getting rich. A person doesn't need to have plenty of money to be preoccupied with it; a poor person can be just as greedy for more as a wealthy person.

Money itself isn't bad, but loving it is. Paul tells us, "Love of money is a root of all kinds of evil" (1 Tim. 6:10). But setting one's sights on wealth and building the life around it is a formula for ruin, now and eternally. Money lets us down: banks fail, the stock market collapses, and investments go bad.

Citizens of the kingdom seek to lay up treasure in heaven, where the banks never fail and the stock market never collapses. They put first investments in divine currency—a character that reflects the Master's. With eye single to the glory of God and loyalty to Jesus undivided, they live out their lives in this world. On the surface, many of their behaviors seem to be the same as those of the people around them, but they are, in reality, different. Whether they pray, give to the needy, handle finances, or do anything else, all they do proceeds out of a heart devoted to their Lord.

Trusting the Heavenly Father (Matt. 6:25–34)

Earlier in this book we noticed this passage when we studied what Jesus taught about God (chap. 15). God, incredibly caring and kind, knows all our needs and provides for them. He cares for the birds and clothes the flowers of the field with natural beauty. So, says Jesus, trust your heavenly Father to take care of you also. Don't worry, fret, or be anxious. Tomorrow will take care of itself. "Seek first his kingdom and his righteousness, and all these things will be given to you as well" (Matt. 6:33).

Relating to Others (Matt. 7:1–6)

As we live as citizens of the kingdom, the genuineness of our religion will be shown by how we relate to others. The previous six examples of kingdom living set forth a life of love that flows out in blessings—in forgiveness, reconciliation, generosity, purity, and affirmation of others.

Our Master warns us of two specific failings as we relate to others. First, we should avoid falling into the trap of fake religion—trying to impress others with our piety, as we noticed earlier. Second, we should not try to judge others. When we begin to focus on others, we become more and more conscious of their shortcomings and less conscious of our own failings. In our estimation we appear more favorable as they appear worse. And before long we have become hypocrites trying to remove a speck from a brother's eye when all the while a plank is in our own eye!

Bearing Fruit (Matt. 7:15–23)

As Jesus brings to a close the Sermon on the Mount, He underlines the great ideas with which He commenced the address. Just as in the nine Beatitudes He placed *being* ahead of *doing*—"Blessed *are* the poor in spirit . . . ," for example—now He turns to an illustration from trees. "Every good tree bears good fruit, but a bad tree bears bad fruit. A good tree cannot bear bad fruit, and a bad tree cannot bear good fruit" (Matt. 7:17, 18).

Jesus goes back to the heart, as He has throughout the Sermon on the Mount. The kingdom of heaven is all about *new* and thus *different* people because they have allowed Jesus of Nazareth to become their Savior and Lord. His transforming presence has changed them and is still changing them into His loving image.

Building for Eternity (Matt. 7:24–27)

The Sermon closes with a powerful appeal. Sung by little children, the words about the wise man and the foolish man pierce to our core, no matter what our age. They confront us with an existential question: "On what am I building my life? Is it on rock, or is it on sand?" Jesus is the Rock. Only the Rock will stand in the storms of life; all else will wash away. Only Jesus abides. And life joined to Him will last forever.

QUESTIONS FOR DISCUSSION

1. Are you familiar with a person who in your opinion practices the principles of the Sermon on the Mount? What practical implications do you notice in this person's life?

2. Why was Jesus so vehement in denouncing hypocrisy (note especially Matt. 23:1–39)?

3. John the Baptist and Jesus preached a message of repentance, for "the kingdom of God has come near" (Matt. 3:2; 4:17). But what, in fact, resulted was the beginning of the Christian Church. Is the church synonymous with the kingdom? Why do you think so?

19

What Jesus Taught about Grace

OBJECTIVES
- Discover what Jesus taught about grace.
- Understand from Jesus's teachings the relationship between grace and behavior.

SCRIPTURE
- Matthew 18:21–35; 20:1–16; 22:1–14; Luke 14:15–24; 15:11–32; 18:6–14

The seminar included trainers from a variety of professions and backgrounds. Over lunch the conversation turned to religion. The seminar presenter, a Jewish man, got the ball rolling.

"The problem I have with Christianity," he said, "is that it's too easy. Someone messes up big time. They say they are sorry and they're forgiven. Just like that." He snapped his fingers for effect. "It's too easy."

"I agree," a young man chimed in, getting up from a nearby table and sitting down with the presenter and his Adventist tablemate. "For Protestants, it's too easy. For Catholics you have to work through your punishment."

So what did Jesus teach about grace? The Protestant Reformation of the sixteenth century proclaimed four foundational principles: the Bible alone (*sola scriptura*), grace alone (*sola gratia*), faith alone (*sola fide*), and Christ alone (*solus Christus*). Were the Reformers correct?

If Jesus taught that the way to salvation rests wholly on God's goodness without any deeds on our part, that is an idea totally different from anything one can find in other religions. Wherever else we turn—whether to Buddha or Muhammed; to Hinduism, Taoism, or Shintoism; or to any other set of morals or precepts—the path to God always, without exception, requires some action by the seeker that qualifies him or her to receive the desired blessing from the deity.

But did Jesus in His teachings give no place to human action? Was the grace He preached a "cheap grace," as some have claimed? In order to sort out the truth among the various ideas and arguments on this topic, we need to study carefully both the teachings and the life of the Master. We notice immediately a curious fact: Jesus not once used the word for grace (Greek *charis*) in His ministry. What we find, however, is a series of parables, most of which begin, "The kingdom of heaven is like . . ."

These parables intrigue us. They are at once simple enough for a child to grasp; but the more we think about them, the greater the depths of truth we discover. Some of these parables surprise us, even shock us. They turn our world upside down.

Parables of Grace

Grace is a common theme in many of Jesus's parables. It would be useful to examine some of them.

Workers in the Vineyard

The most startling of Jesus's parables is the one dealing with day laborers in the vineyard, found in Matthew 20:1–16:

> For the kingdom of heaven is like a landowner who went out early in the morning to hire workers for his vineyard. He agreed to pay them a denarius for the day and sent them into his vineyard. About nine in the morning he went out and saw others standing in the marketplace doing nothing. He told them, "You also go and work in my vineyard, and I will pay you whatever is right." So they went.

> He went out again about noon and about three in the afternoon and did the same thing. About five in the afternoon he went out and found still others standing around. He asked them, "Why have you been standing here all day long doing nothing?"

> "Because no one has hired us," they answered.

> He said to them, "You also go and work in my vineyard."

> When evening came, the owner of the vineyard said to his foreman, "Call the workers and pay them their wages, beginning with the last ones hired and going on to the first."

> The workers who were hired about five in the afternoon came and each received a denarius. So when those came who were hired first, they expected to receive more. But each one of them also received a denarius. When they received it, they began to grumble against the landowner.

> "These who were hired last worked only one hour," they said, "and you have made them equal to us who have borne the burden of the work and the heat of the day."

> But he answered one of them, "I am not being unfair to you, friend. Didn't you agree to work for a denarius? Take your pay and go. I want to give the one who was hired last the same as I gave you. Don't I have the right to do what I want with my own money? Or are you envious because I am generous?"

> So the last will be first, and the first will be last.

The first half of the parable is wholly predictable; the second half bursts the shell of our expectations. Jesus at first paints a familiar scene. Men stand on street corners at accustomed sites for hiring. Depending on their needs for day laborers, bosses come by and hire them.

In Jesus's time the denarius, a silver coin, was considered wages for a full day's work. The men hired at 6 a.m. could expect to receive that as their reward for twelve hours of work. Others who were hired later in the day knew that their wages would be reduced according to the hours they put in.

So far, so good. Nothing unusual about this story. But now comes the surprise.

Evening arrives and at 6 p.m. the laborers hear the word to quit for the day. First surprise: the owner instructs the boss to pay the men who were hired last. That was unusual. The order for payment was the exact opposite. Second surprise: those hired last in the day each receive a denarius. They can hardly believe it—a full day's wages for only one hour of work!

The word travels like wildfire along the line of workers waiting to be paid. This owner is either fabulously rich or amazingly generous. Those hired earlier begin to figure out how much they will receive—even as much as twelve denarii for laboring the whole day. Their mouths salivate in expectation.

But surprise! Everyone receives exactly one denarius. The one-hour workers, three-hour workers, six-hour workers, nine-hour workers, and twelve-hour workers—everyone gets the same. It's just one denarius whether they worked the full day or only one hour.

Now the grumbling begins. The owner, with whom they were so happy only moments before, seems unfair. "'These men who were hired last worked only one hour,' they said, 'and you have made them equal to us who have borne the burden of the work and the heat of the day'" (v. 12).

Have you ever encountered an owner like this? I have not; I wonder if such an owner can be found anywhere. In our world people don't behave like this. This owner is at once incredibly generous and seemingly unfair. But the parable isn't about our world. Jesus commenced it with, "The kingdom of heaven is like . . ." It's a parable about God, not about people.

It teaches us that God doesn't treat us as we deserve. Instead, God treats us as we don't deserve. That's grace—not getting what we deserve.

Ellen G. White said it best: "Christ was treated as we deserve, that we might be treated as He deserves. He was condemned for our sins, in which He had no share, that we might be justified by His righteousness, in which we had no share. He suffered the death which was ours, that we might receive the life which was His."[1]

What about the question of fairness? Doesn't the Lord take note of faithful service? Indeed, He does. But the point of the parable is that, no matter how much faithful service we give, that service doesn't earn heaven's reward. Everyone who finds a place in the kingdom of heaven—from the thief on the cross, who accepted Jesus as Savior and Lord only a few hours before his death, to the apostle Paul, who served for thirty or more years—will be there because of the incredible generosity of God. That is, they will be saved by grace alone.

The Tax Collector and the Pharisee

Another parable of Jesus, regarding a tax collector and Pharisee, makes the same point. Here the scene changes from the workplace to the temple (see Luke 18:9–14):

> To some who were confident of their own righteousness and looked down on everyone else, Jesus told this parable:

> "Two men went up to the temple to pray, one a Pharisee and the other a tax collector. The Pharisee stood by himself and prayed: 'God, I thank you that I am not like other people—robbers, evildoers, adulterers—or even like this tax collector. I fast twice a week and give a tenth of all I get.'

> But the tax collector stood at a distance. He would not even look up to heaven, but beat his breast and said, 'God, have mercy on me, a sinner.'

> I tell you that this man, rather than the other, went home justified before God. For all those who exalt themselves will be humbled, and those who humble themselves will be exalted."

Luke supplies the setting of the parable: Jesus told it to people who were confident of their own righteousness and looked down on everyone else. This focus on themselves that led them to compare themselves with others reminds us of a feature of the previous parable. Here the Pharisee isn't content to simply pray to God, but spends time telling God how much better he is than the tax collector. He praises God because he is not like other men or the tax collector.

The element of comparison also plays a part in the story of the day laborers in the vineyard. When the owner hands out the wages at the end of the day, those hired first grumble, not because they didn't receive what they previously agreed upon, but because the owner of the vineyard brought all the laborers to the same level of compensation. "These who were hired last worked only one hour," they complained. "*You have made them equal to us* who have borne the burden of the work and the heat of the day" (Matt. 20:12; emphasis added).

This element common to both parables—comparing ourselves with others—reveals a failure to grasp the wonder of grace. When we realize how utterly unworthy we are to be granted a place in the kingdom of heaven and how infinite is the price paid for our redemption, all thought of comparing ourselves with others vanishes. We see not those around us but Jesus only.

Like the previous parable, this story carries a strong note of surprise. Jesus's listeners expect the Pharisee, scrupulous in religious practices, to receive the divine approval. The tax collector, a pawn of the Roman powers, was roundly despised. His actions condemned him in the eyes of his fellow Jews: he had sold his soul for the sake of money. But at the end of the story it is the tax collector whose prayer God hears. He, not the Pharisee, goes home right with God.

The people of Palestine despised tax collectors, but Jesus did not. He didn't despise anyone. No one was beyond the reach of the kingdom that was breaking in through the words and deeds of the Master. So, surprising as it must have seemed at the time, Jesus selected a tax collector, Levi Matthew, to be one of the Twelve. And later in Jericho He singled out Zacchaeus, the chief tax collector, for special favors.

Grace is marvelous and unfettered. It smashes human conventions and dashes human expectations. It throws open wide the doors to the kingdom to everyone poor in spirit who accepts the gift of salvation that the Lord freely offers.

The Prodigal Son

No doubt the best-known parable of Jesus is the one commonly known as the Prodigal Son. Because it deals with a family situation, it is also the most powerful. The story it tells is universal and timeless.

The parable is the third in a series of "lost and found" stories told by Jesus and recorded in Luke 15: the lost sheep, the lost coin, and the lost son. We noticed these parables in an earlier chapter when we studied what Jesus taught about God,

observing that the chief idea in all three is the portrayal of God as the heavenly Seeker who leaves no stone unturned to bring people back to Him.

In the third parable of the series, the grace aspect emerges with compelling clarity (Luke 15:11–32). The younger son has made ruin of his life. He has wasted away the inheritance that he rudely demanded though his father was still alive. He has abandoned the moral upbringing to which he had been privileged. He has disgraced the family name. Alone in a far country, penniless and

"The Return of the Prodigal Son"
by James Tissot

hungry, he has fallen to the lowest point imaginable for a Jew—to feeding pigs.

He comes to his senses and decides to go home. There he can ask for a job among the father's hired servants and at the least can have food to eat. As he wends his way back, he rehearses the speech he will make when he meets his father: "Father, I have sinned against heaven and against you. I am no longer worthy to be called your son; make me like one of your hired servants" (vv. 18, 19).

Clad in rags, dirty, and still smelling of the pigpen, he at last nears home. What sort of reception can he expect to receive? Will he be ordered off the property and told never to come back because he has been disowned? Will he receive a tongue-lashing from a furious father who refuses to listen to his speech?

Once again, surprise! While he is still a long way off, his father recognizes the wretched figure dragging himself along the road. Abandoning all decorum, the old man hitches up his robe about him and runs to meet his lost son. He throws his arms around him and kisses him.

The son begins the speech he has rehearsed over and over. Before he can complete it, however, his father cuts him off. The son is about to ask to be made a hired worker, but instead the father barks out orders to his servants: "Quick! Bring the best robe and put it on him. Put a ring on his finger and sandals on his feet. Bring the fattened calf and kill it. Let's have a feast and celebrate. For this son of mine was dead and is alive

again; he was lost and is found" (Luke 15:22–24).

What a marvelous picture of grace! The utterly unworthy is treated with all the privileges of a family member—not dealt with as he deserves but as he does not deserve. This is how God the heavenly Seeker desires to deal with us.

Most people end the story at this point—the young son is home at last and received back into the family circle with joyous celebration. But Jesus didn't stop there: He added a coda that further highlights the nature of grace.

Not everyone is glad to see the younger son back at home. Not everyone joins in celebrating. His older brother, coming home from a day in the fields, hears the music and laughter, inquires what is going on, and is furious at the news. He refuses to join the party: he won't even go in to greet his long-lost brother. Once again the father, abandoning protocol, casts aside dignity and goes out to plead with the older brother.

The older son whines about how unfair his dad is: "Slaving all these years . . . never did anything wrong . . . you never put on a party for me . . . blah, blah, blah." He refuses to acknowledge the younger son as his brother—he's "this son of yours" (v. 30).

But the father corrects him—"this brother of yours." And he justifies putting on the party: "We had to celebrate and be glad, because this brother of yours was dead and is alive again; he was lost and is found" (v. 32). Jesus's words echo those spoken earlier to the religious teachers: "I tell you that in the same way there will be more rejoicing in heaven over one sinner who repents than over ninety-nine righteous persons who do not need to repent" (v. 7).

In several respects this parable mirrors that of the day laborers in the vineyard. Both are surprising, even shocking. Both raise questions concerning justice and fairness. Both expose whiners—those who complain because they think God should have rewarded them for their works.

Ultimately, both parables, revealing the startling nature of grace, leave us with a searching personal question: "Could I, after giving years of what I consider to be faithful service, fail to make it into the kingdom of heaven?" To the Pharisees Jesus said, "Truly I tell you, the tax collectors and the prostitutes are entering the kingdom of God ahead of you" (Matt. 21:31). What would He say to His professed followers today?

The Banquet Parables

Two grace parables of Jesus have a banquet setting. Very similar in nature, they are the Wedding Banquet found in Matthew 22:1–14 and the Great Banquet in Luke 14:15–24. In both, guests are invited to a banquet but refuse to come. To take their place, the person putting on the banquet gives orders that anyone found on the street is to be brought to the feast. The parables differ in details. In Matthew's account it is a king who prepares the banquet, which is for his son's

"The Wedding Feast" by Eugène Burnand

wedding; in Luke, the person in charge is simply designated as "a man," and no mention is made of a wedding or his son. The parable in Matthew emphasizes the lack of respect displayed by the invited guests toward the king's servants who call them to the wedding—they mistreat them and kill them. Luke's story highlights the lame excuses that they put forward for their refusals to come to the banquet.

It seems likely that Jesus sometimes told the same story in different settings, changing details to suit His hearers. In the Wedding Banquet parable, the context from the previous chapter shows Jesus disputing with the chief priests and the elders of the people and predicting the removal of the covenant privileges from the Jewish people (see Matt. 21:28–46). In this light we understand the parable of chapter 22 to further emphasize the idea stated in Matthew 21:43—"Therefore I tell you that the kingdom of God will be taken away from you and given to a people who will produce its fruit."

The setting of the parable of the Great Banquet is quite different. Here Jesus is at the home of a prominent Pharisee and it is Sabbath (Luke 14:1). As the guests sit around the table, He gives the parable in response to a remark made by one of the guests: "Blessed is the one who will eat at the feast in the kingdom of God" (v. 15).

In both parables the grace aspect shines forth in the description of those who sit

THE WEDDING GARMENT

In several places in the Bible, the righteousness that God provides is likened to a clean garment. One of the most powerful scenes is found in the book of Zechariah, written to the people of God who had recently returned from exile in Babylon.

> Then he showed me Joshua the high priest standing before the angel of the LORD, and Satan standing at his right side to accuse him. The LORD said to Satan, "The LORD rebuke you, Satan! The LORD, who has chosen Jerusalem, rebuke you! Is not this man a burning stick snatched from the fire?"

> Now Joshua was dressed in filthy clothes as he stood before the angel. The angel said to those who were standing before him, "Take off his filthy clothes."

> Then he said to Joshua, "See, I have taken away your sin, and I will put fine garments on you."

> Then I said, "Put a clean turban on his head." So they put a clean turban on his head and clothed him, while the angel of the LORD stood by (Zech. 3:1–5).

Ellen White also wrote about the robe of righteousness: "By the wedding garment in the parable is represented the pure, spotless character which Christ's true followers will possess. . . . It is the righteousness of Christ, His own unblemished character, that through faith is imparted to all who receive Him as their personal Savior. . . . The robe, woven in the loom of heaven, has in it not one thread of human devising."[2]

down at God's table in the kingdom of God. They aren't the ones originally invited—that is, those who have been privileged with knowledge about God and His ways. No, they are just the opposite: "anyone you find," "the bad as well as the good" (Matt. 22:9, 10), "the poor, the crippled, the blind and the lame" (Luke 14:21). These are least likely of all people one expects to be present at a great banquet.

Grace stoops down to lift up the unworthy. Grace takes the poor, the crippled, the blind, and the lame and seats them at the king's table. For that is what we are. Each of us is poor, crippled, blind, and lame.

The parable in Matthew adds a significant detail that highlights grace:

> But when the king came in to see the guests, he noticed a man there who was not wearing wedding clothes. He asked, "How did you get in here without wedding clothes, friend?" The man was speechless.
>
> Then the king told the attendants, "Tie him hand and foot, and throw him outside, into the darkness, where there will be weeping and gnashing of teeth."
>
> For many are invited, but few are chosen. (Matt. 22:11–14)

What a magnificent illustration of righteousness by faith! This man was invited to the banquet, having been plucked off the streets, and was provided with clothes just right for the grand occasion. Everything he needed had been given him. But when the king came in, there he was—still in his old, dirty garments.

We too are invited to the King's banquet. But there's a problem: we don't have suitable clothes for the occasion. Jesus, however, provides just the dress or suit that we need. It fits us perfectly. It's the garment of His righteousness that replaces our filthy rags.

Transformed by Grace

Although we are saved by grace alone, bringing nothing of human works to provide merit, grace doesn't leave us the same. Grace transforms us into the likeness of Jesus, our Savior and Lord.

Several parables of Jesus teach the difference grace makes. The most striking is the story of the Unmerciful Servant (Matt. 18:21–35).

> Then Peter came to Jesus and asked, "Lord, how many times shall I forgive my brother or sister who sins against me? Up to seven times?"
>
> Jesus answered, "I tell you, not seven times, but seventy-seven times.
>
> "Therefore, the kingdom of heaven is like a king who wanted to settle accounts with his servants. As he began the settlement, a man who owed him ten thousand bags of gold was brought to him. Since he was not able to pay, the master ordered that he and his wife and his children and all that he had be sold to repay the debt.
>
> "At this the servant fell on his knees before him. 'Be patient with me,' he begged, 'and I will pay back everything.' The servant's master took pity on him, canceled the debt and let him go.

"But when that servant went out, he found one of his fellow servants who owed him a hundred silver coins. He grabbed him and began to choke him. 'Pay back what you owe me!' he demanded.

"His fellow servant fell to his knees and begged him, 'Be patient with me, and I will pay it back.'

"But he refused. Instead, he went off and had the man thrown into prison until he could pay the debt. When the other servants saw what had happened, they were outraged and went and told their master everything that had happened.

"Then the master called the servant in. 'You wicked servant,' he said, 'I canceled all that debt of yours because you begged me to. Shouldn't you have had mercy on your fellow servant just as I had on you?' In anger his master handed him over to the jailers to be tortured, until he should pay back all he owed.

"This is how my heavenly Father will treat each of you unless you forgive your brother or sister from your heart." (Matt. 18:21–35)

As we already indicated, ten thousand talents was a fabulous sum, almost beyond comprehension. How the servant accumulated such a debt also seems incomprehensible, as does his request to be given time to pay it off. How long did he hope to get? A series of lifetimes would not suffice. But the point Jesus wants to make is the enormous burden of sin: it is a crushing load from which we can never hope to be set free by human effort. What we cannot do for ourselves, God does for us. He simply cancels the debt; we are freely forgiven. This is grace—the kingdom of heaven.

But the story goes on. The servant, forgiven such an enormous debt, does not treat his fellow servant in kind. That servant's debt is a hundred denarii—one hundred days' wages. In comparison with the debt the first servant owed the king, this is a trivial amount. But instead of brushing it off, he comes down cruelly on his fellow, demanding every penny and throwing him into prison.

The first servant's actions showed that he didn't belong in the kingdom of heaven. He had received redeeming grace, but he hadn't allowed that grace to transform him. And he ended up outside the kingdom.

We find the same point, although made positively rather than negatively, in the last recorded parable of Jesus—the Sheep and the Goats, found in Matthew 25:31–46. In this parable we see Jesus triumphant, sitting on the throne of glory. The nations are arrayed before Him, and He divides them into those who will be received into the kingdom and those who will not.

Welcoming the favored ones, He commends them for their acts of kindness and love—feeding the hungry, giving drink to the thirsty, taking in the stranger, clothing the naked, and visiting the sick and the prisoner. In each case Jesus identifies Himself with the person helped: "I was hungry. . . . I was sick. . . . I was in prison."

The righteous are surprised. They ask: "Lord, when did we see *you* hungry . . . , thirsty . . . ?" (vv. 37–39). They had performed all their acts of kindness and love unselfconsciously. They hadn't done them to gain merit; they hadn't kept score of their good works. They produced good fruit because they were good, as Jesus taught in the Sermon on the Mount (Matt. 7:15–20). Saved by grace, they had been transformed into the likeness of Jesus and carried on His loving ministry to others.

The power of grace working in a person's life runs like a golden thread throughout Jesus's teachings. It is diffused through parable after parable, as in the story of the Sower and the Soils (Mark 4:2–20). The seed in good soil takes root and begins to grow, eventually producing a phenomenal harvest—thirty, sixty, even one hundred times. (The normal return was only about ten times.)

We see grace in the parable of the Growing Seed (Mark 4:26–29), in the Mustard Seed (Mark 4:30–32), in the Yeast (Matt. 13:33), and so on. Jesus's teachings are all about grace.

And what He taught by word, He taught by life. He was grace embodied; He was "full of grace" (John 1:14).

QUESTIONS FOR DISCUSSION

1. Some individuals believe that Christianity makes forgiveness too easy. Why do you agree or disagree with this statement?

2. You have always been a "good" son or daughter. Your brother, on the other hand, has messed up his life with drugs and alcohol. One day your aging parents inform you that they intend to divide their inheritance equally between you and your brother. Knowing that they already paid off a couple of heavy fines for him, how do you react to the news? Does the material of this chapter give you any guidance?

3. Is the landowner in Matthew 20 unjust or generous or both? Why?

4. Can the grace of God be forfeited? Provide some biblical evidence for your answer.

20

What Jesus Taught about Discipleship

OBJECTIVES	• Understand what is entailed in being a disciple of Jesus Christ.
	• Distinguish genuine discipleship from the false.
SCRIPTURE	• Matthew 4:18–22; 10:1–42; 16:21–27; 18:1–20

As it was in Jesus's time, the term "disciple" is widely used today. The pupil who devotes himself or herself to studying at the feet of a master in music, art, or another field is dubbed "a disciple" of that maestro.

People in Jesus's time were familiar with rabbis who went around teaching accompanied by students who hoped in time to become teachers of the law themselves. The Greek word for disciple, *mathētēs*, occurs more than 240 times in the Gospels. While it usually refers to followers of Jesus, occasionally we find it in other contexts, such as the disciples of John the Baptist (Matt. 14:12; John 1:35, 37; 3:25), disciples of the Pharisees (Matt. 22:16), or disciples of Moses (John 9:28).

We do not know how many disciples Jesus had, but their number was large. Luke twice refers to them as a "large crowd" (Luke 6:17; 19:37). Included among them were the apostles, known as "the Twelve" (Mark 3:14–19), and a group of seventy-two who went out on a special mission (Luke 10:1–20). Occasionally we find individual disciples mentioned by name, such as Joseph of Arimathea (Mark 15:43) and Cleopas (Luke 24:18). The five hundred brothers and sisters to whom Jesus appeared after His resurrection (1 Cor. 15:6) and the 120 people who gathered before Pentecost (Acts 1:15) should also be included among Jesus's disciples.

With discipleship being so common in the Judaism of the first century AD, was there a difference among the followers of Jesus? What did He expect of *His* disciples?

Before we can address this question, we need to consider the relation of the Twelve to the matter of discipleship. As we study the many references to disciples and discipleship in the Gospel accounts, we find surprisingly few references to the original band whom the Great Teacher had called and set apart. It becomes obvious that the Gospel writers aren't primarily concerned with a history of the Twelve as such. Rather, their concern is to show us what genuine discipleship entails and what distinguishes the true disciple from the false.

This point becomes clear as we realize that the Gospels do not limit discipleship to the Twelve. Three great passages found in Matthew's Gospel especially underline the conclusion: Matthew 10, 16, and 18.

In Matthew 10, the Twelve are first designated as "disciples" (v. 1), but immediately thereafter as "apostles" (v. 2). Jesus is about to send them out for some field experience. After being with Him and observing His methods of ministry, they are to try their own hand at the work. He tells them where they are to go, what they should take, what they are to do and preach, and how they are to react to favorable and unfavorable receptions.

But the instruction (vv. 5–15) goes far beyond the immediate situation facing the Twelve. It speaks of the opposition that the heralds of Jesus's message will face. They will be flogged, persecuted, and imprisoned—opposed even to the point of death (vv. 16–31). The Twelve did not meet this hatred during the ministry of Jesus. The teaching has rather become timeless in its application—pointing to the difficulties with the Jewish and Gentile worlds that faced the young Christian church in its early stages and reaching to embrace even us. That is, what begins as instruction to the Twelve develops into a full-blown account of discipleship for every Christian.

Two other passages dealing with the life of the disciple follow a similar course. In chapter 16 of Matthew, Peter remonstrates with Jesus against His predictions of the impending Passion (vv. 21–23). The Master first rebukes Peter for not understanding the nature of His mission, but the incident provides an occasion for the teaching that a cross stamps all genuine discipleship. Although in Matthew 16 Jesus begins by speaking to "his disciples," the instruction ends up couched in terms of "whoever" and "anyone" (vv. 24–26).

Matthew 18 provides the third example. Here the context is the question of the Twelve as to who is greatest in the kingdom of heaven. Jesus answers by setting a child in their midst and telling them that unless they become like the child they will not even find *entry* into the kingdom. Once again, however, the immediate situation leads to general instruction. From the child the subject matter merges into talk of the "little ones who believe in me" (v. 6, ESV) and on to "your brother and sister" (v. 15). The chapter becomes an important one for setting out the pattern of Christian personal relationships, or, we might say, relations between disciples of Jesus Christ.

From our quick look into Matthew 10, 16, and 18, it is clear that when Jesus talks about discipleship, He does not have merely the Twelve in view. Rather, the Twelve only provide the occasion for Jesus to explain discipleship. They are themselves the first disciples and (as we shall see) examples of discipleship.

If, then, discipleship is not to be confined to the Twelve, who *is* a disciple? What features would identify him or her today? We may conveniently approach these questions by considering in turn the disciple's relation to Jesus, the disciple as a learner, and the contrasts between the genuine and the false disciple.

The Relation to Jesus Christ

In Matthew 4, we find an interesting story about how Jesus related to His disciples. As Jesus was walking beside the Sea of Galilee, he saw two brothers, Simon called Peter and his brother Andrew. They were casting a net into the lake, for they were fishermen. "Come, follow me," Jesus said, "and I will send you out to fish for people." At once they left their nets and followed him.

Going on from there, he saw two other brothers, James son of Zebedee and his brother John. They were in a boat with their father, Zebedee, preparing their nets. Jesus called them, and immediately they left the boat and their father and followed him (vv. 18–22).

The account of the call to discipleship is gripping in its brevity. It pares the story to the bone: "He walked . . . He saw . . . He said . . . They left . . . and followed."

It is a drama enacted in high-speed sequence, highlighting the principal players. The scene hinges on *command* and *response*. The word of Jesus comes as command, not as invitation, and the fishermen respond immediately without reasoning, bargaining, or discussion: "At once they left their nets. . . . Immediately they left the boat and their father, and followed him" (vv. 20, 22).

Now the unique relation of disciple and Master begins to come into focus. The disciple is one who has made a distinct break with the past to follow Jesus. Matthew 19:27 crystallizes the idea: "We have left everything to follow you!"

What personal dynamics and drawing power flowed out from the Teacher of Galilee? Who can read the minds of the fishermen as they abandon their nets—and a whole way of life? We cannot read their minds, nor should we attempt to. Suffice to notice that down the ages people have heard a voice—a call—and have cast aside the settled, the secure, and the established to follow that same Master into the great unknown.

Thus the relationship is unique. The disciple is tied to *Him*—not to a program, philosophy, or organization. *He* has called and they have left all to follow *Him*.

That is why Christianity, more than any other religion to which a questing spirit has turned, centers on a person. That is why, as no other faith does, it rests on historical events. Take away Jesus Christ, and Christianity must dwindle away. Discipleship then loses its very foundation and collapses into legalism or philosophy.

A *closeness* of personal relationship exists between Jesus and disciple. The disciples' view of Jesus differs greatly from the view of the crowd. It comes across vividly in the way they address Him: over and over they call Him *kyrios* (Lord), whereas to the others He is no more than *didaskalos* (Teacher; compare Matt. 8:25; 9:28; 14:30; 16:22; 17:4 with 22:16).

Jesus is their Lord. They are *followers* of Him. If one word preeminently describes the personal relationship of discipleship, it is followers. In Matthew's Gospel, "follow" is used a total of twenty-four times, with at least fourteen times referring to discipleship. We see clearly the attractive power of Jesus.

Following Jesus means sharing in the *mission* of Jesus. He, the Lord of the mission, says to all as He said to those He called by the lake, "Come, follow me, and I will send you out to fish for people" (Mark 1:17). His closing words before the Ascension underscore mission: "Go . . . make disciples . . . baptizing . . . teaching" (Matt. 28:18–20).

The position of a follower offers a mixed blessing. At times the consequences are pleasant; at other times they are painful.

On the one hand, following Jesus brings a closeness to Him. All through Matthew's Gospel, the disciples are continually *with* Him. Where He goes, they go; as the tremendous and finally tragic events of the ministry unfold, they are always *there*. "Then he got into the boat and his disciples followed him" (Matt. 8:23). They are present to hear His words—some are addressed to them (e.g., the Sermon on the Mount, 5:1). They see His miracles. They hear the forecast of His rejection. They dine by His side at the Supper, their final meal together before His death. They are with Him at the arrest in the Garden. And the very last words of the Gospel are addressed to them.

On the other hand, they share the hardships of Jesus's ministry. To the would-be disciple, the scribe who is quick to promise, "Teacher, I will follow you wherever you go," Jesus replied, "Foxes have dens and birds have nests, but the Son of Man has no place to lay his head" (Matt. 8:19, 20).

Again, in the great discourse on discipleship, the perils and pains of the follower come into sharp focus, as we have already noticed. "If the head of the house has been called Beelzebul, how much more the members of his household! . . . Anyone who loves their father or mother more than me is not worthy of me; anyone who loves their son or daughter more than me is not worthy of me" (Matt. 10:25, 37).

Pleasure and pain are the lot of the follower. The famous saying of Matthew 11:28–30 combines both ideas. It is the *yoke* to which the disciple bends his neck—not a very pleasant idea. But it is no ordinary yoke; "my yoke is easy, and my burden is light."

Notice a final point concerning the unique relationship at the heart of Christian discipleship: *imitation*. Following Jesus is essentially a recapitulation of His life and words. Matthew 10 emphasizes this aspect. The disciples must bear the same message that Jesus preached: "The kingdom of heaven has come near" (v. 7). They go in His name and in that name repeat the mighty deeds of His ministry—healing the sick, raising the dead, cleansing the lepers, exorcising the demons. They go out as His representatives. "Anyone who welcomes you welcomes me" (v. 40). And, in the Great Commission that closes the Gospel, it is not their own words but "everything I have commanded you" that they are to teach people to obey, as they, like their Lord before them, "make disciples" (Matt. 28:19, 20).

Sharer of His secrets, companion in His labors, participant in His sufferings—this is the disciple of Jesus Christ. He or she enjoys a relationship closer than the ties of blood and dearer than links of race, country, education, or profession. Listen as the Lord of the disciple describes it:

> Then Jesus' mother and brothers arrived. Standing outside, they sent someone in to call him. A crowd was sitting around him, and they told him, "Your mother and brothers are outside looking for you."
>
> "'Who are my mother and my brothers?' he asked."
>
> Then he looked at those seated in a circle around him and said, "Here are my mother and my brothers! Whoever does God's will is my brother and sister and mother" (Mark 3:31–35).

The Disciple as a Learner

Despite the closeness of the disciples to Jesus, they had much to learn. Indeed, the Lord had not called them to follow Him because they had shown spiritual maturity. Just as the Twelve were undistinguished in Jewish society, so the Gospel writers underscore their continuing weakness.

The most dramatic demonstration of their spiritual frailty occurs in the Garden of Gethsemane. Jesus had sought to prepare them for the coming conflict with His adversaries, but at the time of testing they all "deserted him and fled" (Matt. 26:56). Yet the story has prepared us for this great act of disappointment. Repeatedly Jesus has rebuked their lack of faith: "You of little faith" (Matt. 6:30; 8:26; 14:31; 16:8). Also, the stronger reproof: "You unbelieving and perverse generation . . . how long shall I stay with you? How long shall I put up with you?" (Matt. 17:17).

We find the disciples rebuking the mothers who brought their children to the Lord for a blessing (Matt. 19:13). We see them striving among themselves, angry lest James and John gain places of precedence among them (Matt. 20:24). Despite the Lord's warnings of their impending failure and His admonition to "watch and pray," they all fall asleep in Gethsemane. And the mob that comes out armed with swords and clubs to arrest Jesus is led by Judas, one of the disciples' number (Matt. 26:40–50).

Jesus's own designations of His followers likewise accent their continuing weakness. "Little ones," He calls them, and even "little children" (Matt. 10:42; 18:6, 10, 14; 11:25). These affectionate terms show at once His tender regard for them and their utter dependence upon Him.

And He *is* concerned for them. They are weak, but they are learners in the finest school humans may attend—the school of Jesus Christ. To these same "little children" is given the hidden things of God—secrets that "the wise and learned" might have had (Matt. 11:25). These "little ones" are identified with Him, and God notes every act done to help them. They are like the teacher of the law of Matthew 13:52, who "has become a disciple in the kingdom of heaven."

The account of feeding the five thousand illustrates sharply this aspect of frailty. Jesus has spent the day healing the sick in a lonely place where a great crowd has gathered to seek His aid and see His mighty acts. But the day is ending, and the disciples grow restless. It is time for the meeting to break up and for Jesus to send the people home to supper. But when they at last give voice to their feelings, they receive a surprising reply, "They do not need to go away. You give them something to eat," Jesus says (Matt. 14:16). He tosses the ball back into the disciples' court! His words seem as impossible today as they are unexpected. Yet eventually the disciples *do* give the crowd their supper. They receive the broken bread and fish from Jesus's hands and distribute them to the multitude. From being weak and doubting, they become partners with Jesus.

Such is the life of the disciples. Their weaknesses are great. They possess no "holier than thou" faith or experience in which they may boast. The pressure of what Paul calls "the flesh" (Rom. 8:5) is always there with its striving for the top place, its misunderstanding of the meaning of the cross, its roughness, and its cowardice. How much disciples need their Lord! But the Lord knows them and has called them as they are with all their deficiencies. That Lord Who has called is with them always, even to the end of the age. And so, by continual association with the Lord and continual exposure to the living words of the Teacher, those of "little faith" (Matt. 8:26), though weak and in need, are ever learning.

True Versus False Discipleship

While the Gospels have much to say on the subject of discipleship, they also occasionally sound a discordant note. Here and there they tell us that not all discipleship is genuine. A person may claim to be a follower of Jesus but be rejected by the Lord Himself.

This idea comes into view very clearly in Matthew 7 and 25. In the first passage we find people who address Jesus as "Lord" and recount their prophesying, exorcism, and many other "mighty works." But the awful sentence falls upon them: "I never knew you. Away from me, you evildoers" (7:23).

The second passage relates the parable of the sheep and the goats—the disposition of humanity at the last great assize. Once again we catch the element of *surprise*. Those who are on the left, who hear the fateful word, "Depart from me, you who are cursed, into the eternal fire prepared for the devil and his angels" (25:41), are stupefied that Jesus should thus judge them.

From these passages we can see several negative characteristics in a definition of discipleship. Most obvious, of course, is that of *profession*. Merely taking the name of the Lord does not in itself qualify one to be a disciple. It is Jesus Who designates the disciple.

Second, *Christian service* in itself does not prove discipleship. From a human viewpoint, surely exorcising, working miracles, and prophesying give evidence of a relationship with the Lord—but not in God's sight. Even those who are supremely confident of their standing with the Lord may hear the terrible words "I never knew you" (7:23).

Finally, Jesus's denunciation of the religious leaders of His day makes clear that *outward show* does not characterize the true disciple. Indeed, those who most display their piety are least likely to be the Lord's.

So much for pseudo-disciples. But can we go beyond what we have already discovered in this chapter to further characterize the genuine? What *positive* features of true discipleship do the Gospels set out? We briefly note five features that mark genuine discipleship.

Discipleship and Practical Christianity

"This is to my Father's glory, that you bear much fruit, showing yourselves to be my disciples" (John 15:8).

Discipleship is *lived* out rather than preached. Just as grapes don't grow on thorns nor figs on thistles, so a living relationship with the Lord will bring its good "fruit." Indeed, the genuine followers of Jesus may live largely unnoticed by their fellows, even by brothers and sisters in the church. They do not keep any score of their good deeds. They are not trying to win "brownie points" with the Lord. But day by day their discipleship shows, and the Lord takes note. Every one of those "little nameless, unremembered acts of kindness and of love"[1] described by the poet William Wordsworth—the food to the hungry, the visit to the sick, the help to the prisoner—gives evidence that they are followers of Jesus Christ.

Discipleship and Humility

Disciples understand that desiring applause from the crowd, grasping for the spoils of office, and all those subtle words and deeds by which people seek to put down another and raise oneself have no place in the kingdom of God. "Not so with you," says the Lord. "Instead, whoever wants to become great among you must be your servant, and whoever wants to be first must be your slave—just as the Son of Man did not come to be served, but to serve, and to give his life as a ransom for many" (Matt. 20:26–28). If the Lord took the lowest position, so also must His followers.

Discipleship and God's Will

Not the disciples' estimate but God's will is their passion, for only those who do the will of the Father enter the kingdom. Says the Lord, "Whoever does the will of my Father in heaven is my brother and sister and mother" (Matt. 12:50). So the divine will is exalted above human ideas of right and wrong, of greatness and servitude.

Discipleship and Jesus's Words

"Whoever has ears, let them hear" (Matt. 13:9). Those in the common crowd hear, but hear not; they see, but see not; but to the disciple is "given to know the secrets of the kingdom of heaven" (Matt. 13:11, ESV). To disciples alone is given the scene of glory on the Mount of Transfiguration and to them the mysterious words, heavy with portent, of the coming sufferings of their Lord. The knowledge that they gain is not a ground for boasting, even as it does not entitle them to a part in the kingdom. Rather, it is a privilege that they receive as a result of the closeness of their relationship with the Lord.

Just as we share our confidences with our friends, so the Lord shares His secrets with those who are closest to Him.

Discipleship and Love

"By this everyone will know that you are my disciples, if you love one another" (John 13:35). Without love, all else falls short; with love, all else is made complete.

We may now see clearly how the concept of discipleship found in the Gospels applies in our day.

The Disciple Today

In our times Christianity is a big business. The assets of the churches are enormous. If you can preach well enough, you can make a lot of money—and fast. At the same time we see a rash of charismatic manifestations. Healings, and even speaking in tongues, have become respectable. The emphasis is on the Spirit.

At such a time as this, the biblical concept of discipleship seems especially relevant. If Jesus's words mean anything, they tell us that genuine discipleship cannot be gauged by outward manifestations. I may be a famous preacher, winning many souls for the Lord, raising the sick with my prayers, and having devils yielding to my command. But God may not call me a disciple!

On the other hand, I may be considered a model citizen. I'm in good and regular standing in church and I support all worthwhile community projects. People like me are the backbone of the nation—honest, hardworking, and law abiding. But the words may fall upon my shocked ears, "I never knew you."

Is that possible, with all of those good works and powerful displays of the Spirit? Yes, says Matthew's Gospel—possible and likely, for *God* alone knows the genuine disciples (see Matt. 7:22, 23). He alone designates them, and the divine decision brings with it many surprises. In its essence, discipleship involves something that humans cannot see. We may fool our friends, even our spouse and children, but *discipleship involves the heart.* God alone can read it. He knows how it has responded to His call. He knows how deceitful it is. But His call has come. With some that call has fallen like seed on the good ground. It has sprung up to bear good fruit.

The question is, "Have I, like those of old, left all to follow Him? Have I so yielded my will and my ways over to His plan that my life is no longer my own?" Yielded. Perhaps we need to be reminded that, even in these days, the follower of Jesus will find pain as well as pleasure as he or she seeks to walk in Jesus's footsteps.

But His word still has power. That voice is still heard—and many, like those fishermen by the Sea of Galilee, immediately leave their boats and nets to follow. Their Master is King in humility, so why should they seek great things for themselves? They are weak, but He is a Mighty Teacher—and they are ready to learn. And most and best of all, to Him they say from the heart, "Lord!"

QUESTIONS FOR DISCUSSION

1. List all the characteristics of discipleship—both positive and negative—that you find in this chapter. In light of this list, do you think that it is easy or difficult to be a follower of Jesus? Give reasons for your answer.

2. Is it possible to be a *secret* disciple of Jesus?

3. What does being a disciple of Jesus mean today?

21

What Jesus Taught about the Sabbath

<table>
<tr><td>OBJECTIVES</td><td>• Learn the role of the Sabbath in Jesus's life and teachings.</td></tr>
<tr><td></td><td>• Reflect on the Sabbath miracles of Jesus.</td></tr>
<tr><td>SCRIPTURE</td><td>• Mark 1:21–31; 3:1–6; Luke 13:1–17; 14:1–6; John 5:1–15; 9:1–41</td></tr>
</table>

The Sabbath played a major role in the life, ministry, and teachings of Jesus of Nazareth. Sabbath-keeping was part of His lifestyle, He gave important instruction in addresses on the Sabbath, and the Sabbath early became the focus of strong conflict that developed between Him and the religious leaders.

The Gospels record seven miracles that Jesus performed during Sabbath hours. None of these was of an "emergency" nature; all could have been put off at least until the next day. It seems obvious that the Master intentionally performed these acts knowing that they would antagonize His enemies and add fuel to the bitter feelings that already were smoldering. In fact, we read that on some occasions His healing on the Sabbath resulted in the teachers of the law and Pharisees plotting to kill Him.

In several ways, consideration of the Sabbath focused on differences between the religion that Jesus had come to announce and the Judaism of the day. Jesus sharply disagreed with the way to God as taught by the religious leaders—but not with the religion of the Old Testament as such. He took issue with the preoccupation with externals that so often missed the heart of righteousness as He understood, taught, and lived it.

The Judaism of the first century AD had been drastically influenced by the Babylonian exile six centuries earlier. The unthinkable had happened: Yahweh had permitted Israel's foes to sweep down and destroy the beloved city with its magnificent temple. According to the prevailing theology, such could never happen: Israel would be delivered at the eleventh hour, as she had been so often in the past.

Now, in captivity without king, city, or temple, the Jews struggled to regroup. Out of reflection on their brokenness, they took to heart the warnings of the prophets whose messages they had failed to heed. They singled out idolatry and Sabbath-breaking as major sins that had led Yahweh to reject them. Their attention focused on the Torah that God had given them as a mark of the covenant people.

Under the guidance of experts in the law, like Ezra, they now sought to codify religion in a manner that would put a "hedge" around the Torah—that is, that would seek to protect it from being transgressed as formerly. Religious teachers gave their lives to the intense study of the law, with different schools of interpretation taking form. A body of commentary on the Torah was developed; in Jesus's time it was still oral, but in later centuries it was written down as the Mishnah (AD 200) and later the Talmud (the Palestinian Talmud, c. AD 400, and the longer Babylonian Talmud, c. AD 600, comprising seventy volumes).

By Jesus's time the Jews had scattered across the vast reach of the Roman Empire. Although often grouped in small communities, they succeeded in retaining a distinct identity. Their religion set them apart by two features in particular: they worshiped only one God in a world of many deities, and they observed the Sabbath every week.

The scribes' preoccupation with the law resulted in their giving special emphasis to the Sabbath. They expanded the simple stipulations of the fourth commandment of Exodus 20:8–11 into a list of regulations for Sabbath-keeping. These regulations sought to legislate one's total conduct from food preparation to travel. In the Talmud, the tractate "Shabbat" identifies thirty-nine categories of activity prohibited on the Sabbath.

But the many prohibitions that developed also allowed for means of circumventing them. For instance, a Sabbath day's journey came to be defined as a distance of two thousand cubits (about three thousand feet), but a person could travel farther by, prior to the Sabbath, laying down a cache of food at the end of the permitted distance. Then, after eating the food, he or she could be considered to commence a new Sabbath day's journey.

These and other minutiae relative to the law were, of course, not part of the Torah that Yahweh had given to Moses. They were totally of human devising, and Jesus showed no regard for them.

Jesus's teaching and practices relative to the Sabbath make clear that His mission encompassed far more than a reformation of the Judaism that He found. His message of the kingdom of heaven announced a new understanding, system, and religion. Although Christianity was cradled in Judaism, He foretold that it would burst out of rabbinic Judaism, just as new wine could not be contained in old wineskins (see Matt. 9:17).

In this chapter we shall first look at Jesus's own Sabbath observance. Then we shall take up His seven Sabbath miracles, noting the impact of several. Finally, we shall draw together summary conclusions that crystallize what Jesus, by word and deed, taught about the Sabbath.

Jesus's Sabbath Observance

Jesus kept the seventh-day Sabbath. No other conclusion can be warranted from a reading of the four Gospel accounts.

His enemies accused Jesus of breaking the Sabbath (see John 5:16–18; 9:16). The issue, however, involved not the fourth commandment of the Decalogue, but the regulations that had been attached to the Sabbath in the oral law. Jesus did not observe them any more than He kept the requirements for ceremonial purity that the teachers of the law and Pharisees demanded. But when the issue was the law of God, which includes the Sabbath commandment, there was nothing Jesus could be accused of (John 8:46).

In later centuries, and up to today, Christians would debate over which day should be observed for worship—Saturday or Sunday. Many, contrary to the Scriptures, would even term Sunday as "Sabbath." All such considerations are totally foreign to the Gospels.

In Jesus's life and teachings the question of Saturday or Sunday not once arose—there was no debate as to which day was the day of rest. The issue was not Sabbath-keeping but *how* the Sabbath should be kept. Jesus, untrained by rabbinical standards, taught with authority a view of the Sabbath that differed radically from that held by the religious teachers.

Luke tells us that "He went to Nazareth, where he had been brought up, and on the Sabbath day he went into the synagogue, *as was his custom*" (Luke 4:16; emphasis added). In several other references the Gospel writers locate Jesus on Sabbath where observant Jews would be found—in the house of worship (Matt. 12:9; Mark 1:21; 3:1; 6:2; Luke 4:31; 6:6; 13:10). Often we find Jesus in a teaching situation in the synagogue.

Jesus's practice of observing the Sabbath corresponded with His teachings regarding the Torah that had been given by Yahweh. He made clear that He had not come to abrogate the prior revelation of the divine will. In the Sermon on the Mount He stated, "Do not think that I have come to abolish the Law or the Prophets; I have not come to abolish them but to fulfill them. For truly I tell you, until heaven and earth disappear, not the smallest letter, not the least stroke of a pen, will by any means disappear from the Law until everything is accomplished. Therefore anyone who sets aside one of the least of these commands and teaches others accordingly will be called least in the kingdom of heaven, but whoever practices and teaches these commands will be called great in the kingdom of heaven" (Matt. 5:17–19).

Isaiah had predicted that the Messiah would "magnify the law, and make it honorable" (Isa. 42:21, KJV). This is precisely what Jesus did by life and by teachings. Immediately following the statement from Matthew 5:17–20 calling for a better righteousness than that taught by the Pharisees and scribes, Jesus gave six examples of what He meant: "For I tell you that unless your righteousness surpasses that of the Pharisees and the teachers of the law, you will certainly not enter the kingdom of heaven" (v. 20).

Murder: "You have heard that it was said to the people long ago, 'You shall not murder, and anyone who murders will be subject to judgment.' But I tell you that anyone who is angry with a brother or sister will be subject to judgment. Again, anyone who says to a brother or sister, 'Raca,' is answerable to the court. And anyone who says, 'You fool!' will be in danger of the fire of hell.

"Therefore, if you are offering your gift at the altar and there remember that your brother or sister has something against you, leave your gift there in front of the altar. First go and be reconciled to them; then come and offer your gift.

"Settle matters quickly with your adversary who is taking you to court. Do it while you are still together on the way, or your adversary may hand you over to the judge, and the judge may hand you over to the officer, and you may be thrown into prison. Truly I tell you, you will not get out until you have paid the last penny."

Adultery: "You have heard that it was said, 'You shall not commit adultery.' But I tell you that anyone who looks at a woman lustfully has already committed adultery with her in his heart. If your right eye causes you to stumble, gouge it out and throw it away. It is better for you to lose one part of your body than for your whole body to be thrown into hell. And if your right hand causes you to stumble, cut it off and throw it away. It is better for you to lose one part of your body than for your whole body to go into hell.'"

Divorce: "It has been said, 'Anyone who divorces his wife must give her a certificate of divorce.' But I tell you that anyone who divorces his wife, except for sexual immorality, makes her the victim of adultery, and anyone who marries a divorced woman commits adultery."

Oaths: "Again, you have heard that it was said to the people long ago, 'Do not break your oath, but fulfill to the Lord the vows you have made.' But I tell you, do not swear an oath at all: either by heaven, for it is God's throne; or by the earth, for it is his footstool; or by Jerusalem, for it is the city of the Great King. And do not swear by your head, for you cannot make even one hair white or black. All you need to say is simply 'Yes' or 'No'; anything beyond this comes from the evil one."

Eye for Eye: "You have heard that it was said, 'Eye for eye, and tooth for tooth.' But I tell you, do not resist an evil person. If anyone slaps you on the right cheek, turn to them the other cheek also. And if anyone wants to sue you and take your shirt, hand over your coat as well. If anyone forces you to go one mile, go with them two miles. Give to the one who asks you, and do not turn away from the one who wants to borrow from you."

Love for Enemies: "You have heard that it was said, 'Love your neighbor and hate your enemy.' But I tell you, love your enemies and pray for those who persecute you, that you may be children of your Father in heaven. He causes his sun to rise on the evil and the good, and sends rain on the righteous and the unrighteous. If you love those who love you, what reward will you get? Are not even the tax collectors doing that? And if you greet only your own people, what are you doing more than others? Do not even pagans do that? Be perfect, therefore, as your heavenly Father is perfect" (Matt. 5:20–48).

Thus, the gospel of the kingdom that Jesus proclaimed in no way abolished "the Law or the Prophets" (Matt. 5:17). It abolished the righteousness of the teachers of the law and Pharisees, not the revelation of the divine will given through Moses. With the examples from the Ten Commandments, it went beyond a score-card of rules to matters of the heart; it pierced to motivations, inner thoughts, and desires.

Nor did the followers of Jesus understand Him to have abolished the Sabbath. On that Friday evening after the final agonizing hours on the cross when He breathed His last, they ceased from their labors as "the Sabbath was about to begin . . . and rested on the Sabbath in obedience to the commandment" (Luke 23:54, 56).

Matthew, in the closing words of his account, records the Great Commission of the risen Lord to the disciples: "All authority in heaven and on earth has been given to me. Therefore go and make disciples of all nations, baptizing them in the name of the Father and of the Son and of the Holy Spirit, and teaching them to obey everything I have commanded you. And surely I am with you always, to the very end of the age" (Matt. 28:18–20).

The teaching of Jesus includes the Sabbath. It wasn't something that He brushed aside or treated lightly; rather, He made a point of drawing attention to what Sabbath-keeping—the Sabbath-keeping of the kingdom of heaven—is really like. He did so, knowing that His words and actions would arouse intense opposition and hasten the day of His death.

As a follower of Jesus Christ, I observe the Sabbath because He did and because He taught His followers how to keep it. Followers of Christ also keep the Sabbath because it was instituted at creation, given by God as a blessing to humanity (Gen. 2:1–3); kept by the Patriarchs and Israelites prior to Sinai (Gen. 26:5; Exod. 16:23); formulated as one of the Ten Commandments (Exod. 20:4–7); and maintained in the New Testament.

The Sabbath Miracles of Jesus

It is not possible to provide a strict chronology or ordering of events in the ministry of Jesus. We cannot, therefore, be sure of the exact order of Jesus's seven Sabbath miracles.[1]

The Invalid at Bethesda (John 5:1–15)

This first Sabbath miracle, performed fairly early in Jesus's ministry, is wonderfully instructive for the insights it provides into both the Sabbath and the kingdom of heaven.

First, we note the *intentionality* of Jesus. Here is an invalid who has been paralyzed for thirty-eight years. By no stretch of the imagination could he be considered an emergency case. But Jesus will not put off the healing by even one day. He takes the initiative, not even waiting for the man to ask for help. "Do you want to get well?" He asks (v. 6). Then, with instructions that ensure that the healing will draw public attention, He tells the invalid, "Get up! Pick up your mat and walk" (v. 8).

The man does so, and soon the religious leaders accost him. "It is the Sabbath; the law forbids you to carry your mat," they charge (v. 10).

He replies, "The man who made me well said to me, 'Pick up your mat and walk'" (v. 11).

Now the stage is set for a confrontation on the meaning and purpose of the Sabbath.

Second, we see contrasting views of the nature of *religion*. The Jews can only see a violation of Sabbath law; they don't discern the miracle of healing. They don't ask to see the person who performed this wonderful act. They have only one interest: "Who is this fellow who told you to pick it up and walk?" (v. 12).

The religion of Jesus—the religion of the kingdom—puts high value on people and their welfare. Other religions set up systems of works, rites, and regulations, and they become the center.

Third, we notice the basis on which *Jesus defended His actions*. "My Father is always at his work to this very day," He said, "and I, too, am working" (v. 17). That is, Jesus was only carrying on the work of the Father. The Father is always doing good—always healing. His activities do not cease when the sun sets on Friday evening (see Lev. 23:32).

It was a bold argument. The Jewish leaders at once realized what it implied: an intimacy with God that no ordinary human being dared to claim. Jesus "was even calling God his own Father, making himself equal with God" (John 5:18). Now they became determined to kill Jesus. They decided that He was both a Sabbath-breaker and a blasphemer. It was still early in Jesus's ministry, but from this moment on He would need to be on His guard when He came to Jerusalem.

The Demoniac in the Synagogue (Mark 1:21–28)

Jesus has left Judea and is commencing His ministry in Galilee. He is in Capernaum, the headquarters for His work in the north, and it is Sabbath. Jesus is just where we expect to find Him—in the synagogue and teaching. Suddenly the

Sabbath calm is shattered by the loud cry of a crazy man: "What do you want with us, Jesus of Nazareth? Have you come to destroy us? I know who you are—the Holy One of God" (v. 24).

The Jews don't recognize Jesus for who He is; nor do His disciples yet. But the demons do. They have girded for battle. But Jesus commands sternly, "Be quiet! Come out of him!" The demon shakes the man violently and, shrieking, comes out of him (v. 25).

We do not read of anyone finding fault with Jesus for this miracle. Apparently the teachers of the law had not yet begun to dog Jesus's footsteps in Galilee. Instead, the exorcism amazes everyone and news about Jesus spreads far and wide. For the erstwhile demoniac, it has been a day of liberation.

Peter's Mother-in-law (Mark 1:29–31)

This miracle immediately followed the previous one. It was the only Sabbath healing performed in a private setting; these two miracles in Capernaum were the only ones of the seven that did not result in controversy.

The Man with a Withered Hand (Mark 3:1–6)

At the conclusion of this Sabbath healing we read that "the Pharisees went out and began to plot with the Herodians how they might kill Jesus" (v. 6). The alliance of Pharisees and Herodians was a most unusual one. The Herodians favored the ruling house of Herod, which the Pharisees did not because the founder of the dynasty, Herod the Great, was Idumean, not Jewish. But these two parties, normally at odds with one another, now banded together to get rid of Jesus.

We discern how dangerous it was for Jesus to heal publicly on the Sabbath. His actions challenged the religious system with its preoccupation with regulations; He was a non-conformist upsetting the status quo. He refused to conform to non-biblical traditions; God's will alone guided His life and actions.

Obviously, Jesus could have waited until after Sabbath hours to heal the man with the shriveled hand and avoided much trouble for Himself. The problem of the man's hand hadn't just come on—the hand had been useless to him for some time, perhaps years. Nor was it pain that led him to seek Jesus's help. The man had simply come to worship on the Sabbath, and in the synagogue he encountered the Master.

The dynamics of the scene arrest our attention. In this house set apart for study and worship, the minds of some people were far from worship. When they saw Jesus enter, they immediately foresaw a possible occasion to accuse Him of Sabbath-breaking: Would He heal the man with the shriveled hand?

Jesus sized up the situation and became angry at the perversion of true religion in the scene about to unfold. Taking the initiative, He called on the man to stand up so everyone could see him. Turning to the religious teachers waiting to find fault, He challenged, "Which is lawful on the Sabbath: to do good or to do evil, to save life or to kill?" (v. 4). Jesus's words cut through the religious red tape of the Sabbath traditions. He went to bedrock, returning to first principles. He laid truth bare.

Faced with truth so sharply, His enemies found nothing they could bring in reply. Jesus "looked around at them in anger and, deeply distressed at their stubborn hearts, said to the man, 'Stretch out your hand.'" He did so and in a moment the hand was completely restored (v. 5).

Every religion that does not care about human needs and sufferings is a pseudo religion. "The gospel places a high value upon humanity as the purchase of the blood of Christ, and it teaches a tender regard for the wants and woes of man."[2]

The Man Born Blind (John 9:1–41)

We have already studied this event in some detail, so here we will merely note the chief ideas relative to the Sabbath.

Unlike some of His other miracles, Jesus didn't simply heal the blind man by a word, as He did with Bartimaeus of Jericho (Mark 10:46–52). Here in Jerusalem He made mud from saliva, put it on the man's eyes, and told him to go wash in the Pool of Siloam. These actions seemed intentionally to challenge the rabbinical restrictions concerning the Sabbath and ensured that the healing would not only become widely known but become

a point of sharp dispute over the nature of Sabbath observance.

In the simple but enthralling account, the healed man bests all the arguments of Jesus's enemies with an irrefutable testimony: "One thing I do know. I was blind but now I see" (John 9:25). Questioned repeatedly about how the miracle happened, he continues to reiterate the sequence: a man named Jesus made mud, put it on his eyes, and told him to go to Siloam and wash. He did so, and then he could see (vv. 11, 15, 27).

Rabbinical law forbade kneading or mixing on the Sabbath. By making the mud with which Jesus anointed the blind man's eyes, He was in violation of the Sabbath code. His act of anointing likewise transgressed the tradition, which only permitted anointing of a usual type.

This was the second Sabbath miracle that Jesus performed in Jerusalem. The earlier one, for the invalid at Bethesda (John 5:1–18), had resulted in plots to kill Him. Now, some eighteen months later, the healing of an unnamed beggar born blind made the Pharisees even more decided in their opposition. Their hostility extended to the man whom Jesus had healed: they threw him out of the synagogue.

The Woman with Curvature of the Spine (Luke 13:10–17)

This miracle follows a scenario familiar from the previous Sabbath miracles: a person present in the synagogue who has had an affliction for eighteen years,

Jesus making a public display of the act of healing He intends to perform, the restoration of wholeness in a moment of time, opposition from the religious leaders, and Jesus exposing with startling clarity the hypocrisy of the Sabbath regulations as He shows the true meaning of the holy day.

The scene is gripping and powerful. A woman has curvature of the spine: her body is bent at a right angle and she walks with eyes on the ground, unable to lift her head to the heavens. The synagogue ruler, indignant because Jesus heals on the Sabbath, instead upbraids the people (by inference the woman), telling them not to come for healing on the Sabbath. And Jesus, Who came to this world to set people free, refuses to delay the woman's release from infirmity by even one day, showing that the pseudo-Sabbath observance of the synagogue ruler assigns higher value to an ox or a donkey than to a human being.

The Man with Fluid Retention (Luke 14:1–6)

This malady of the body's cells retaining excessive amounts of fluid was previously known as dropsy; today we know it as edema. Quite likely the man's body was swollen from the fluid, as the text suggests: "There in front of him was a man suffering from abnormal swelling of his body" (v. 2)—the man was too obvious to escape notice.

The setting of this Sabbath miracle differs from the others. It was not in the synagogue but in the home of a prominent Pharisee. Although an invited guest, Jesus was being carefully watched. His accusers were never far away but were always waiting for some word or act that they could turn against Him.

Jesus speaks first. He asks the Pharisees and experts in the Law, "Is it lawful to heal on the Sabbath or not?" They don't utter a word (vv. 3, 4). He heals the man and sends him away. He makes an argument similar to one from an earlier Sabbath healing: "If one of you has a child or an ox that falls into a well on the Sabbath day, will you not immediately pull it out?" The spies are silent, as are Pharisees and law experts. Jesus's logic is irrefutable (v. 5).

Seven Sabbath miracles were performed for seven people in need with wasted bodies, derangement, fever, shriveled limbs, blindness, curvature of the spine, and edema. The parade of woe sounds familiar to us. The only difference is Jesus. He, the Liberator, sets free each person on the Sabbath day. Even at risk of His life.

Lord of the Sabbath

In Mark 2, Jesus's clearest teaching concerning the nature of the Sabbath and His relation to it was given one Sabbath in an encounter with the Pharisees:

> One Sabbath Jesus was going through the grainfields, and as his disciples walked along, they began to pick some heads of grain. The Pharisees said to him, "Look, why are they doing what

is unlawful on the Sabbath?" He answered, "Have you never read what David did when he and his companions were hungry and in need? In the days of Abiathar the high priest, he entered the house of God and ate the consecrated bread, which is lawful only for priests to eat. And he also gave some to his companions." Then he said to them, "The Sabbath was made for man, not man for the Sabbath. So the Son of Man is Lord even of the Sabbath." (vv. 23–28)

The rabbis had gathered together hundreds of requirements for observing the Sabbath and called for meticulous observance of them. "The Mishnah lists 39 primary, or major, types of labor prohibited on the Sabbath day. . . . The first 11 of these were steps leading to the production and preparation of bread: sowing, plowing, reaping, binding sheaves, threshing, winnowing, selecting (sorting what was unfit for food from what was fit), grinding, sifting, kneading, and baking."[3] Jesus's disciples, by picking some heads of grain, were in violation of the rabbinical Sabbath laws.

Jesus's reply to the accusations of Sabbath-breaking point to the fundamental nature of this day set apart by Yahweh. "The Sabbath was made for man, not man for the Sabbath," He stated (v. 27). That understanding was 180 degrees opposed to the view of the religious leaders, whose myriad of prohibitions showed that in their thinking the Sabbath was of more importance than humanity.

The Master illustrated this truth by reference to an example out of the Old Testament. Normally only the priests ate the showbread used in the sanctuary services; but when David and his men were hungry and in need, they were given the only food on hand—the consecrated bread (1 Sam. 21:2–7). Thus, the situation of human need took precedence over the laws pertaining to the sanctuary.

Jesus's closing words in this incident state precisely His relation to the Sabbath: "So the Son of Man is Lord even of the Sabbath" (Mark 2:28). He and He alone instructs us on what is appropriate in Sabbath observance. We His followers don't need lists of dos and don'ts. We have Jesus—the basic principles He gave us in the Old Testament, His example of Sabbath-keeping, and His teachings about the Sabbath—and He is sufficient.

Just as fellow humans should not attempt to dictate Sabbath practices beyond what the Bible clearly indicates, they also should not attempt to meddle with the day itself. Jesus the Creator instituted the Sabbath at the end of the creation week (Gen. 2:1–3). He blessed it and set it apart. In human flesh He restored it to its rightful place. No one has authority to change what He, Lord of the Sabbath, has put in place.

Declared a day of liberation, day of rest ("Sabbath" means "cessation"), and day of our Lord Jesus Christ, the Sabbath is *our* day. God made it for you and for me that we may fellowship with Him.

1. Bearing in mind that "Sabbath" means "rest," what do Matthew 11:28–30 and Hebrews 4:9, 10 show us concerning Jesus and the Sabbath?

2. Some Christians argue that Sunday, the day of Jesus's resurrection, has replaced the Sabbath as the day of worship. What evidence do you find in Jesus's own words that He expected His followers to continue to keep the Sabbath? (Hint: Note especially Mark 2:28 and Matthew 24:20.)

3. What do Jesus's Sabbath miracles teach us about how to keep the Sabbath?

22

What Jesus Taught about the End

OBJECTIVES
- Discover what Jesus taught about the end of the world.

- Gain an understanding of biblical apocalyptic.

- Learn how we should live in expectation of Jesus's Second Coming.

SCRIPTURE
- Matthew 24:1—25:46

All four Gospel writers record that, just prior to the events that led to Jesus's crucifixion, He spent time with those who were closest to Him—His friends the disciples. Throughout His ministry, His words went out to all who chose to listen. During the first few days of the Passion Week, He maintained a highly public presence as He disputed in the temple with Pharisees, Sadducees, teachers of the law, and Herodians. But now, with the shadow of the cross casting its pall, He gave a private discourse to the Twelve.

He didn't intend His words for a general audience. Only those who belonged, who loved Him and whom He loved dearly, qualified to receive this discourse. Jesus wanted to speak to them about the days ahead when they would be on their own. The Master sought to prepare them for a new and dangerous future.

While Matthew, Mark, Luke, and John all record Jesus's final, private discourse with His friends, John's account differs considerably from the others. Matthew 24, Mark 13, and Luke 21 cover the same ground. Mark reports that Jesus sat on the Mount of Olives opposite the temple and told Peter, James, John, and Andrew what they could expect after He had left them.

His remarks sprang from an exchange that occurred as they walked out of the temple for the final time on that Tuesday (possibly Wednesday) evening. One of the disciples, noticing the huge foundations of the superb structure (consisting of blocks more than 25 feet by 8 feet [7.6 x 2.4 m]), commented, "Look, Teacher! What massive stones! What magnificent buildings!" (Mark 13:1).

But Jesus replied, "Do you see all these great buildings? Not one stone here will be left on another; every one will be thrown down" (v. 2).

Imagine the consternation of the disciples. Such a calamitous event must surely mean the end of all things. So a little while later, as they sat on the Mount of Olives with the sun's last rays gleaming from the gold leaf and white marble of the temple opposite them, they asked Jesus, "Tell us, when will these things happen? And what will be the sign that they are all about to be fulfilled?" (v. 4). Jesus opened up a window on the future, foretelling not merely the destruction of the temple but also the end of the age when He would return.

John, however, passes over in his account all this material, apparently concluding that the other writers have covered it sufficiently. Instead, he focuses on Jesus's last moments with the disciples, on the Thursday night just before His capture. In a long discourse that also deals with the future (John 13–17), Jesus comforts His friends and promises that He will continue to be with them through the coming of the Paraclete, the Holy Spirit. In Mark 13 we learn of events in the world, while in John 13–17 we hear of the life of the disciples after Jesus leaves earth.

His final words—the discourse we find in the Synoptic Gospels and that in John's account—contain precious instruction. They are Jesus's parting legacy to us, His friends, who belong at His side.

Apocalypse: The End Is Near!

Mark 13, like Matthew 24 and Luke 21, comprises apocalyptic material. The word comes from the Greek *apokalupsis*, which occurs also in Revelation 1:1—"The revelation *[apokalupsis]* of Jesus Christ, which God gave him to show his servants what must soon take place." Thus, the root meaning of apocalypse is an unveiling, or a revealing of the future. The entire book of Revelation, called by many the Apocalypse, deals with what would take place in the future from a first-century perspective, but Revelation is not the only book of apocalyptic in the Bible. Long before it, the book of Daniel sketched future events in ways that Revelation echoes and elaborates.

While Daniel and Revelation furnish the clearest examples of apocalyptic writings, we find chapters elsewhere in Scripture that reflect its characteristics—for example, Isaiah 24, Joel 2, and Zechariah 14 in the Old Testament. In the New Testament we have 1 Thessalonians 4 and 2 Thessalonians 2. Apocalyptic is a particular form of biblical prophecy that prominently features the end of the world.

As we have already learned from Mark 13, apocalyptic is private discourse—divine instruction for God's people who face an uncertain future. It's meant to give them insight into what would lie ahead and assurance that the Lord would be with them and bring all things to a happy conclusion. So we find scattered throughout apocalyptic writings hints and suggestions that God did not intend such material for a general audience but for those close to God who will read and understand. "But you, Daniel, close up and seal the words of the scroll until the time of the end. Many will go here and there to increase knowledge" (Dan. 12:4). "He who has an ear, let him hear what the Spirit says to the churches" (Rev. 2:7, 11, 17, 29; 3:6, 13, 22). "This calls for wisdom. If anyone has insight, let him calculate the number of the beast" (Rev. 13:18).

In apocalyptic writings the revelation of the future often comes encoded in symbols. Daniel saw a vision of a great image (Dan. 2); King Nebuchadnezzar dreamed of a tree suddenly cut down (Dan. 4); a bloodless hand wrote mysterious words on the palace wall (Dan. 5); first in a dream (Dan. 7) and then in a vision (Dan. 8) the prophet beheld a series of beasts that represented the rise and fall of nations. In Revelation the future unfolds through a series of vivid scenes, both in heaven and on earth, with the forces of evil portrayed as fantastic, rapacious beasts, and the forces of good marshaled as armies under the banner of Jesus Christ, Whose most common title in the book is "the Lamb."

The Bible is not the only place in which one finds apocalyptic writings. In the two centuries just before Jesus the Jews produced a series of apocalypses such as 2 Esdras and the Psalms of Solomon, while a little later some Christians apart from John the revelator wrote apocalypses that the church did not consider inspired and left out of the canon of Scripture (e.g., the Shepherd of Hermas).

During the past two millennia of Christian history, the church largely neglected the apocalyptic writings of Scripture. As it settled down with the conversion of the Roman emperor Constantine, the focus shifted from a coming kingdom of God to one right here and now. As church and state joined hands, the church looked ahead to the millennium, which would in due course result on this earth. Eventually, of course, that dream collapsed. With the Enlightenment of the seventeenth and eighteenth centuries, religion found itself on the defensive before the advance of reason. People now believed that knowledge and education would solve the problems of society as humanity, which, having evolved from the slime, would continue to improve. There seemed no need for divine intervention such as the Second Coming of Christ and the end of the world. Apocalyptic was for pessimists and ignoramuses.

In such a milieu—the unbridled optimism about the inevitability of human progress—the Seventh-day Adventist movement was born. With our revival of study of long-neglected biblical apocalyptic, especially the prophecies of

Daniel and Revelation and our message that time was running out for the world, we seemed to be doomsayers and a crazy voice in the wilderness. But we painted our convictions right into our name—Seventh-day Adventists—and flung them in the face of a scoffing society.

How times have changed! The rosy future of the early twentieth century crashed in flames as World War I—a conflict between supposedly Christian nations—engulfed humanity in a global nightmare. And that was only the beginning of a violent, bloody century that brought hatred, torture, unspeakable cruelty, violence, and fear. Humans learned to live with the threat of global annihilation as atomic weapons hung over their heads. Now, to add to that danger, we find ourselves in the midst of global terrorism and new threats from chemical and biological weapons.

Our language has changed. Apocalypse has become a household word. But it isn't the apocalypse of John and the other Bible writers, in which Jesus reveals the future to His friends and gives them assurance of encouragement for the hard times ahead. Rather, today "apocalypse" means that the end is coming—through war, an asteroid impact, or an invasion from outer space. It is apocalypse without Jesus and without hope.

At such a time as this, the Adventist message has never been more relevant. It offers hope, comfort, and assurance that Jesus is in control: He, not warmongers or asteroids or aliens, will ring down the curtain on human history. He assures us that we can put our hand in His—the hand that was nailed to the cross for us—and He will never let us go.

That's the message of Matthew 24, Mark 13, and Luke 21. Because these three passages cover the same ground, we will give detailed study to Mark's record.

Interpreting Mark 13

Unlike the books of Daniel and Revelation, Mark does not feature symbols, beasts, and calculations. In just one place Jesus refers to Daniel: "When you see 'the abomination that causes desolation' standing where it does not belong . . . then let those who are in Judea flee to the mountains" (Mark 13:14; see also Dan. 9:27; 11:31; 12:11; Matt. 24:15). His prediction found fulfillment in the invasion of Israel by imperial Rome, when Titus captured Jerusalem and destroyed the temple in AD 70.

Throughout Mark 13, the emphasis falls on the need for Jesus's followers to be on guard against deception and dangers of various kinds:

- "Watch out that no one deceives you" (v. 5).

- "Many will come in my name, claiming, 'I am he,' and will deceive many" (v. 6).

- "You must be on your guard. You will be handed over to the local councils" (v. 9).

- "If anyone says to you, 'Look, here is the Messiah!' or, 'Look,

there he is!' do not believe it"
(v. 21).

- "False messiahs and false prophets will appear and perform signs and wonders to deceive, if possible, the elect" (v. 22).

- "So be on your guard; I have told you everything ahead of time" (v. 23).

- "Be on guard! Be alert! You do not know when that time will come" (v. 33).

- "Therefore keep watch" (v. 35).

- "What I say to you, I say to everyone: 'Watch!'" (v. 37).

Thus the theme of Mark 13, sounded again and again, is *alertness*. As we wait for Jesus to return, we must stay awake, keep ready for action, and stand at our post. The time between Jesus's ascension and His Second Coming will pose three types of dangers for His followers: first, false messiahs and false prophets performing signs and miracles, who lead people into thinking that the end has already come; second, persecution, hatred, and difficulty that cause faith to waver and friends to turn their backs and betray; and finally a gradual loss of anticipation of Jesus's return so that His coming takes us by surprise.

As Jesus sat with Peter, James, John, and Andrew on the Mount of Olives that evening, He looked across the sweep of human history to the end of time. We see in a specific reference to that event that He clearly intended to

cover the period ending in His second advent: "At that time people will see the Son of Man coming in clouds with great power and glory. And he will send his angels and gather his elect from the four winds, from the ends of the earth to the ends of the heavens" (vv. 26, 27). Likewise, Mark 13 contains numerous references to "the end" and expectations of it (vv. 7, 8, 10, 13, 29, 32, 35).

The disciples' question, however, dealt with the destruction of the temple. Jesus's comment that the day would come when not one stone would remain upon another must have stunned them. They wanted to know more. "Tell us," they asked him, "when will these things happen? And what will be the sign that they are all about to be fulfilled?" (v. 4).

Jesus's preview of the future from the Mount of Olives thus covers two concerns: the signs of the fall of Jerusalem and those of the end of the world. To the disciples with their foreshortened view of history, the events were coterminous—the end of the temple must surely signify the close of human history on the planet. Matthew's account of their question makes this clear: "'Tell us,' they said, 'when will this happen, and what will be the sign of your coming and of the end of the age?'" (Matt. 24:3).

In interpreting Mark 13, therefore, we need to keep in view the double foci of the passage. Some verses relate primarily to the fall of Jerusalem and the destruction of the temple in AD 70, while others clearly designate events leading up to the

Second Coming. Several verses leave us in doubt as to the schema in which they best fit. Possibly they apply in both the first century and later.

While we cannot claim an exact analysis of the chapter, the following outline seems persuasive:

1. *An overview of the future (vv. 5–8)*

- Warnings

- Wars

- Rumors of wars

- National and international conflicts

- Earthquakes

- Famines

2. *Living in troubled times (vv. 9–13)*

- Christ's followers arrested and flogged

- Witnessing before governors and kings

- The gospel preached to all nations, despite the persecution

- The Holy Spirit supplying words when we find ourselves put on trial

3. *Signs of the impending fall of Jerusalem (vv. 14–23)*

- The "abomination that causes desolation" (Roman armies entering the temple [see Luke 21:20])

- Necessity for rapid flight from Jerusalem

- Days of distress

- False messiahs and false prophets

- Signs and wonders of great power to deceive

4. *Signs of the end of the world (vv. 24–29)*

- Sun darkened

- Moon not giving light

- The stars falling

- Heavenly bodies shaken

- The Son of Man coming with great power and glory

- A lesson from the fig tree

5. *The critical quality: watchfulness (vv. 30–37)*

- This generation to see it

- Christ's words never to pass away

- The day and hour unknown

- A lesson from the householder who goes away

- Ready at all times to meet the Master

We could wish for a neatly ordered series listing events and signs extending from that evening on the Mount of Olives through the fall of Jerusalem, across the long ages, and culminating in the return of Christ. But Jesus didn't set out to give a lesson on "history in advance." He wanted to provide *spiritual preparation* for His friends, as they would face an uncertain future. And God in His wisdom knows best. We would probably misuse a list of signs and events that told us just when to expect the Second Coming. Many of us would put off the needed preparation until the last minute.

What we have, then, isn't a chart of the future that provides us with superior knowledge in which we can take pride. (Who wouldn't love to have such a chart?) Rather, we have a spiritual road map useful for any time and place between now and the Second Advent. As we hear of wars and rumors of wars; as false christs and false prophets arise, even working miracles; as nations and superpowers threaten and clash; as earthquakes strike with increasing frequency and severity; as famine stalks large areas of the world; as God's people suffer abuse, false arrest, flogging, imprisonment, and death itself; and as the gospel message goes onward and forward to earth's remotest bounds—in all these events, we know that His coming is near. Observing the fig tree teaches us that summer is about to burst over the world.

In light of this analysis of Mark 13, we may better grasp a verse that long has puzzled students of the Scriptures:

"Truly I tell you, this generation will certainly not pass away until all these things have happened" (v. 30). Some Adventists understood Jesus here to say that the generation that sees the signs in

the heavens—sun darkened, moon darkened, stars falling (Matt. 24:29)—would live to see His return. For a time they could cling ever more tenuously to that interpretation, but now no more. Far too many years have passed. That generation is long since dead and buried.

Did Christ's words fail? Not at all. The answer lies in the double foci of the chapter. "This generation" applies not to the time before the Second Coming but to the disciples' era. Surely "*this* generation" designates their generation. And Jesus is warning them, "Listen! The destruction of the temple is near at hand. People now living will witness it." Immediately following, He makes the prediction that His words will never pass away, and concludes with the exhortation to watch.

Parables of the Second Coming

The three parables found in Matthew 25 follow on without a break from Jesus's discourse on the End. In the original text, no suggestion of a change in subject can be found (chapter and verse breaks were added much later, only in the thirteenth and sixteenth centuries, respectively).

Each of these parables sheds light on how the followers of Jesus are to live as they await His return. Each contributes a particular aspect to our understanding. Taken together, they form a powerful trio of unsurpassed value to the earnest Christian in every century.

At the same time, the parables share a note of solemn warning. With each we note the idea of the *dividing* of humanity at the End of all things. Not all those who profess Jesus find entry into the eternal kingdom: five of the ten girls have no part in the wedding feast, one of the men who received the talents is strongly rebuked because of his laziness and is cast out into the darkness, and the "goats" are consigned to eternal fire.

The lesson comes through unequivocally: Jesus did not teach universalism (the view that everyone will be saved at last). While His grace is measureless and free, every person must individually make a decision in favor of the kingdom.

In the parable of the ten girls, the accent falls on *readiness*. Five look ahead and make preparation; five do not. When the test comes at midnight, only those with lamps still burning go into the wedding feast.

The parable of the talents, on the other hand, emphasizes *individual accountability*. To everyone is given abilities—to some many, to others fewer. But whether we have received many or few, we each have at least one "talent." This life is our opportunity to improve what we have. So for the follower of Jesus, this life—so filled with wonder and joy—also has a serious side. We only get one chance; we don't go around another time.

The theme of judgment, implied in the first two parables, becomes explicit in the third. In a scene reminiscent of that in Revelation 20:11–13, in which all who have ever lived stand before the great white throne, here all the nations are gathered before the Son of Man seated on His glorious throne. And the multitude is divided. Some go into eternal bliss and others into eternal damnation.

In the great judgment, the actions done in this life shape the decision pronounced upon each person. These actions, whether by commission or omission, reveal whether each person has yielded to God's transforming grace and has, even though to a lesser degree, lived or not lived a life that reflects the life of Jesus.

Living Jesus's Counsel

Today we are in the waiting time. We Adventists—who arose from the expectation of Jesus's return on October 22, 1844—are still here. How shall we then live until the Advent? How do we go on living with expectations?

Sad to say, some are so frustrated over what they perceive to be a delay in Jesus's return that they are Adventists in name only. They hear sermons on the Second Coming and join in the great chorus of the church, "We Have This Hope," but the soon return of Jesus no longer shapes their lives in a significant way. They have become like the people described in Ezekiel 33:32—"Indeed, to them you are nothing more than one who sings love songs with a beautiful voice and plays an instrument well, for they hear your words but do not put them into practice."

How different is the Adventist life sketched by Jesus in Mark 13! Here the Master portrays a people who eagerly await His coming, an anticipation that brightens even times of persecution and difficulty. They observe the signs, which, like the fig tree, show that the end is near. And they maintain an attitude of watching and waiting, living on the knife-edge of time, and leaning into the future, which is God's.

If some Adventists have suffered spiritual burnout, others fall into the opposite camp. They spend time and energy trying to figure out just *when* Jesus will come. Employing charts, calendars, and calculations, they arrive at a specific or implied date for the Second Coming.

But Jesus said, referring to His Second Coming, "But about that day or hour no one knows, not even the angels in heaven, nor the Son, but only the Father" (Matt. 24:36). After His resurrection, the disciples inquired, "Lord, are you at this time going to restore the kingdom to Israel?" (Acts 1:6). His response was, "It is not for you to know the times or dates the Father has set by his own authority" (v. 7).

Ellen White preached on Acts 1:6, 7 in a sermon in Lansing, Michigan, in 1891. As she had consistently counseled throughout her long ministry whenever Adventists began to get excited over dates for the Second Coming, she again warned against all such calculations. In effect, she said we have more important ways to spend our efforts—to live every day for the glory of the Master by building up His kingdom. And her words are still worth remembering in our day, more than one hundred years later: "You will not be able to say that He will come in one, two, or five years, neither are you to put off His coming by stating that it may not be for ten or twenty years."[1]

Eschatological fever draws a crowd and sells books. But it is unbiblical and irresponsible, because ultimately it leads to spiritual burnout after the dates pass without Jesus's return.

How then shall we live as we await the Advent? We can continue in loving, active service to others, sharing the blessed hope and ministering to the poor, hungry, downtrodden, and needy. Every morning we can wake to praise God for the new day and for life with meaning and purpose. And we can work at the post that He has given us, filling each moment with the hope, joy, and peace He puts within us.

How then shall we live? By being persons who are fully alive—to His glory.

QUESTIONS FOR DISCUSSION

1. Compare the three accounts of Jesus's apocalyptic discourse in Matthew 24, Mark 13, and Luke 21. What similarities do you find? What differences?

2. What is meant by "eschatological fever"? How can we eagerly await Jesus's coming without making this mistake?

3. Reflect on the parables of the Second Coming in Matthew 25. What is the message of each of the three parables?

4. How does prosperity, self-centeredness, and egoism diminish our eschatological expectations?

23

What Jesus Taught about Prayer

OBJECTIVES
- Learn principles of prayer from Jesus's own prayer life.
- Study Jesus's teaching concerning prayer.
- Examine the prayer Jesus taught His disciples—The Lord's Prayer—for insights into the nature of prayer.

SCRIPTURE
- Matthew 6:5–15; Luke 11:1–13; John 17:1–26

Jesus was a praying person. This fact, like nothing else about His life, shows that He was truly human. For Him, prayer was both a necessity and a privilege.

> Jesus Himself, while He dwelt among men, was often in prayer. Our Saviour identified Himself with our needs and weakness, in that He became a suppliant, a petitioner, seeking from His Father fresh supplies of strength, that He might come forth braced for duty and trial. He is our example in all things. He is a brother in our infirmities, "in all points tempted like as we are;" but as the sinless one His nature recoiled from evil; He endured struggles and torture of soul in a world of sin. His humanity made prayer a necessity and a privilege. He found comfort and joy in communion with His Father. And if the Saviour of men, the Son of God, felt the need of prayer, how much more should feeble, sinful mortals feel the necessity of fervent, constant prayer.[1]

From cradle to grave the Master's life was bathed in prayer. Before His birth we find both Zechariah and Mary lifting up their voices in praise to God (Luke 1:46–55, 67–79). The infant Jesus, brought into the temple to be presented to the Lord, becomes the object of thanksgiving to God as the devout Simeon and Anna recognize in Him the long-awaited Deliverer of Israel (Luke 2:25–38). And Jesus's final words, uttered as He hung dying on the cross, are an anguished cry to the Father (Matt. 27:46; Mark 15:34; Luke 23:46).

Jesus's Prayer Life

Luke tells us, "But Jesus often withdrew to lonely places and prayed" (Luke 5:16). During much of His public ministry, He was surrounded by crowds. Often they pressed upon Him, pushing to get closer to hear Him or obtain healing. At times He and the Twelve did not even find time to eat. But Jesus frequently went apart to a quiet place. There in solitude He lifted up His being to the Father in close communion.

Thus, we learn that *Jesus practiced prayer as a habit*. No matter how busy He was or how weary from a life of ceaseless giving to others, He took time to talk with the Father.

Second, we learn that Jesus sought a *quiet place* for prayer away from the crowds, noise, and distractions—this is where He went to pray.

Mark's account includes a statement about Jesus's prayer life that, although brief, is pregnant with meaning: "Very early in the morning, while it was still dark, Jesus got up, left the house and went off to a solitary place, where he prayed" (Mark 1:35).

The context indicates that it was a Sunday morning—a very early morning before dawn—when this incident took place. The previous day, a Sabbath, had been packed with activity. Jesus taught in the synagogue in Capernaum, cast out a demon from a possessed man, and then went to the home of Simon Peter and Andrew. Told about Peter's mother-in-law who lay sick with a fever, He immediately went to her and healed her. After sunset, the whole town gathered at the door of the home, bringing the sick. And Jesus healed them (see Mark 1:21–34).

We don't know what time it was when the last of the crowd had left and Jesus was able to get some rest, but it must have been late. Nevertheless, before others in the house had begun to stir the next morning, Jesus was long since gone. He left in the dark and, in a lonely place, all alone He prayed.

Jesus's prayer life shows us the importance of *individual prayer*. He prayed with the Twelve, but He frequently withdrew for private, one-on-one conversations with the Father. We also may benefit greatly by joining with other believers in prayer, but nothing can take the place of personal prayer in a quiet place, with no one but the Lord present to see and hear.

Jesus liked to go to the mountains to pray. We find several references to His going to a mountain to talk with His heavenly Father (Matt. 14:23; Mark 6:46; Luke 6:12; 9:28, 29).

While Jesus practiced prayer on a regular basis, at special times His prayer life took on added intensity. Several moments in His life and ministry assumed deep significance.

At His Baptism

It was at His baptism that Jesus consecrated Himself to the mission for which He had come to earth. "When all the people were being baptized, Jesus was baptized too. And as he was praying, heaven was opened and the Holy Spirit descended on him in bodily form like a dove" (Luke 3:21, 22).

In Selecting the Twelve

Jesus chose the twelve apostles from His many disciples. On this occasion Jesus not only prayed, but spent the entire night in prayer, seeking divine guidance: "One of those days Jesus went out to a mountainside to pray, and spent the night praying to God. When morning came, he called his disciples to him and chose twelve of them" (Luke 6:12, 13).

As the Climax of His Work Approached

With the shadow of the cross looming large, Jesus again went to pray on a mountain. This time He took with Him Peter, James, and John—not all Twelve, but those closest to Him. As He prayed, the appearance of His face changed, and His clothes became bright as a lightning flash. Two glorious beings, Moses and Elijah, appeared with Him and spoke about the work He would accomplish in Jerusalem. It was a glimpse of heaven—a reminder of what Jesus had left behind and of what awaited Him beyond the agony of the cross.

We know only the barest facts about this unique encounter. Unfortunately, Peter, James, and John, weary from the tramp up the high mountain, fell asleep. They awakened only in time to catch the end of Jesus's conversation with Moses and Elijah and to hear the Voice that came from the cloud that enveloped them, saying, "This is my Son, whom I have chosen; listen to him" (Luke 9:28–36; see also Matt. 17:1–8; Mark 9:2–8).

When He Met Some Greeks

A number of Greeks had come to worship during Passover (John 12:20–33). During His years of ministry Jesus frequently referred to "the hour," still future, when He would complete the mission for which He had been born: "My hour has not yet come" (John 2:4); "my time is not yet here" (John 7:6); "my time has not yet fully come" (John 7:8); "my appointed time is near" (Matt. 26:18). Now, during the final week of His life, He said, "The hour has come for the Son of Man to be glorified" (John 12:23).

Some Greeks, probably Greek-speaking God-fearers, had come to Jerusalem for the Feast. They had heard about Jesus and wanted to meet Him. And, through the intervention of Andrew and Philip, they not only met Jesus but became witness to a remarkable scene. Seeing these seekers after truth, Jesus glimpsed the multitude from all over who would come to the gospel. The Greeks were a foreshadowing of the harvest of souls that would be won from the earth.

But before the harvest must come the cross. "Very truly I tell you, unless a kernel of wheat falls to the ground and dies, it remains only a single seed. But if it dies, it produces many seeds" (John 12:24). Jesus would cast Himself into the furrow of the world's needs, and, by dying, bring forth an abundant return.

The cross lay just ahead. Before the sun set on Friday afternoon of that week, scourged and bleeding, He would breathe His last. Jesus shrank from the experience that faced Him and He cried out, "Now my soul is troubled, and what shall I say? 'Father, save me from this hour'? No, it was for this very reason I came to this hour. Father, glorify your name" (vv. 27, 28).

And for the third time the Voice came from heaven, "I have glorified it, and I will glorify it again" (v. 28).

In Gethsemane

On Thursday night, the city, bathed in a full moon, is sleeping. But in the Garden of Gethsemane the Son of Man agonizes in prayer. The woes of a universe gone wrong roll upon His shoulders, and He feels the horror of the darkness of separation from the Father. He prays that, if it is possible, the dreadful experience might be removed. His sweat falls like great drops of blood on the ground (see Luke 22:44). But He yields His all to the Father's will: "not my will, but yours be done" (v. 42). There is no other way; the cup cannot be taken from Jesus if humanity is to be saved. He will go to the cross.

In this, the hour of His deepest need, Jesus seeks the support of His friends. He takes the whole group with Him, and then singles out Peter, James, and John and asks them to stay by as He endures the life-and-death struggle for the fate of humanity. Once again those closest to

Him let Him down. They sleep, while Jesus agonizes. The Savior of the world must drink the cup of woe all by Himself.

At the baptism, the Voice had come to reassure Jesus. On the Mount of Transfiguration it came again, strengthening Him for what lay ahead. In the temple it came a third time as Jesus caught a glimpse of the result of His mission. But no voice comes in the Garden of Gethsemane. Jesus agonizes while an angel strengthens Him in the silence of the night.

Jesus clings to God. He hangs on by the fingernails of faith. This is prayer in its most elemental form.

Once, the Twelve observed Jesus praying. When He had finished, one of them requested, "Lord, teach us to pray, just as John taught his disciples" (Luke 11:1). In the Garden, as nowhere else in His ministry, Jesus taught them—and us—to pray.

Prayer in the Teachings of Jesus

In His teachings Jesus often spoke about prayer. He Whose life was refreshed and energized by communion with the Father shared precious instruction.

God Welcomes Our Prayers

He waits to hear and answer; we don't have to try to get His attention or convince Him of our need.

"Which of you, if your son asks for bread, will give him a stone?" Jesus asked. "Or if he asks for a fish, will give him a snake? If you, then, though you are evil, know how to give good gifts to your children, how much more will your Father in heaven give good gifts to those who ask him?" (Matt. 7:9–11).

When we come to God in prayer, we do not come fearfully, wondering what will happen. No, as the book of Hebrews puts it, we come "boldly unto the throne of grace" (Heb. 4:16, KJV). All that is good among human fathers—all the love, compassion, understanding, tender regard—is but a faint glimmering of what our heavenly Father is like.

We Should Pray in Jesus's Name

Jesus's name is the most powerful in the universe. It bears the signature of His victory on Calvary. To pray in that name is to claim all that the name represents—Savior, Lord, High Priest, Friend, Advocate, Son of Man.

On that last Thursday night Jesus told His dearest earthly friends, "Very truly I tell you, my Father will give you whatever you ask in my name. Until now you have not asked for anything in my name. Ask and you will receive, and your joy will be complete" (John 16:23, 24).

In His own prayer that night just before He was arrested, Jesus also prayed for His disciples—and not just for the Twelve, but for those who would believe on Him in years to come: "I pray also for those who will believe in me through

"Grace" by Eric Enstrom

their message, that all of them may be one, Father, just as you are in me and I am in you" (John 17:20, 21). That prayer includes all believers. So when you and I pray, we come in the name of Him who prayed for us already in the garden.

We Shouldn't Hesitate to Ask

Nothing that disturbs our peace is too big for God, or too little. "Ask," said Jesus, "and it will be given to you; seek and you will find; knock and the door will be opened to you. For everyone who asks receives; the one who seeks finds; and to the one who knocks, the door will be opened" (Matt. 7:7, 8). How much have we missed simply because we didn't ask? Perhaps we didn't take the time, or didn't think the Lord would care enough to grant our petitions.

Jesus Tells Us to Persevere in Prayer

We need to keep on praying—not trying to persuade God, but to change ourselves. Persevering in prayer—wrestling with God—leads us to examine our lives so that we may come into conformity with God's plan for us. Prayer doesn't change God; it changes us.

The Master told a parable along these lines. Luke at the outset gives us its purpose: "Then Jesus told his disciples a parable to show them that they should always pray and not give up" (Luke 18:1). The parable goes like this:

> In a certain town there was a judge who neither feared God nor cared what people thought. And there was a widow in that town who kept coming to him with the plea, "Grant me justice against my adversary."
>
> For some time he refused. But finally he said to himself, "Even though I don't fear God or care what people think, yet because this widow keeps bothering me, I will see that she gets justice, so that she won't eventually come and attack me!"
>
> And the Lord said, "Listen to what the unjust judge says. And will not God bring about justice for his chosen ones, who cry out to him day and night? Will he keep putting them off? I tell you, he will see that they get justice, and quickly. However, when the Son of Man comes, will he find faith on the earth?" (Luke 18:2–8)

Most of Jesus's parables teach by similarity, as in "The kingdom of heaven is like . . ." This one, however, makes the point by contrast. God isn't like the crooked judge; no, He is just the opposite. But if the judge, unjust as he was, at last yielded to the widow's pleading, how much more will a just Father hear the cries of His people as they persist in prayer?

God Listens to and Answers Prayer

To the Father of the demon-possessed boy at the foot of the Mount of Transfiguration, Jesus said, "Everything is possible for one who believes" (Mark 9:23), and to blind Bartimaeus of Jericho, "Your faith has healed you" (Mark 10:52). The disciples had tried to heal the demon-possessed boy but had failed. Coming to Jesus privately after the public embarrassment, they wanted to know what had gone wrong. He replied, "Because you have so little faith. Truly I tell you, if you have faith as small as a mustard seed [an exceedingly tiny seed], you can say to this mountain, 'Move from here to there' and it will move. Nothing will be impossible for you" (Matt. 17:20, 21).

As doubts and fears beset us, we may feel as though we have almost no faith at all. Mustard-seed faith indeed! However, if we *act* on that little faith—if the mustard seed is planted in the ground—great things beyond our wildest imaginings can happen. *But* that's only if we go ahead and sow the mustard seed.

Prayer Must Come from the Heart

In the Sermon on the Mount, Jesus blasted the religious leaders around Him whose chief concern in prayer was to impress their fellows. "Hypocrites," Jesus called them—actors playing religious games. They impressed others, but they didn't impress God. "Truly I tell you," He said, "they have received their reward in full" (Matt. 6:5). The only reward they would get was the praise of people here on earth.

In contrast, the way to pray according to Jesus is to "go into your room, close the door and pray to your Father, who is unseen. Then your Father, who sees what is done in secret, will reward you" (Matt. 6:6). Here Jesus condemns prayer made for outward show. He does not condemn sincere group prayer per se, as we learn from instruction He gave the disciples on a later occasion: "Again, truly I tell you that if two of you on earth agree about anything they ask for,

THE LORD'S PRAYER

Matthew 6:9–13	Luke 11:2–4
Address:	
Our Father in heaven,	Father,
Kingdom Petitions:	
hallowed be your name,	hallowed be your name,
your kingdom come,	your kingdom come.
your will be done, on earth as it is in heaven.	[omitted from older manuscripts]
Disciple Petitions:	
Give us today our daily bread.	Give us each day our daily bread.
And forgive us our debts,	Forgive us our sins,
as we also have forgiven our debtors.	for we also forgive everyone who sins against us.
And lead us not into temptation, but deliver us from the evil one.	And lead us not into temptation.

it will be done for them by my Father in heaven. For where two or three gather in my name, there am I with them" (Matt. 18:19, 20).

Jesus not only shared general instruction about prayer; He shared a model prayer. His prayer, usually known as the Lord's Prayer, should be called the "Disciples' Prayer," because it was given to them. If any prayer of Jesus qualifies as the "Lord's Prayer," it is His high-priestly petition found in John 17:1–26.

Jesus's Model Prayer

We find two versions of the prayer that Jesus taught His disciples—one in Matthew 6:9–13 and the other in Luke 11:2–4. These prayers show some variations, but they contain the same elements and in the same order. The fact that these versions were given in different settings—Matthew's as part of the Sermon on the Mount and Luke's in response to the disciples' request for Jesus to teach them how to pray—probably accounts for the differences.

We will focus on the longer version, found in Matthew's Gospel. As we examine it, the following outline emerges:

The address:
"Our Father in heaven"

Three kingdom petitions:
"Hallowed be your name"
"Your kingdom come"
"Your will be done on earth as it is in heaven"

Three disciple petitions:
"Give us today our daily bread"
"Forgive us our debts, as we also have forgiven our debtors"
"Lead us not into temptation, but deliver us from the evil one"

The conclusion familiar to most Christians who recite the model prayer—"For yours is the kingdom and the power and the glory forever, Amen."—is not found in the earliest manuscripts of the New Testament and therefore is probably not original.

Looking at each of these elements in Jesus's model prayer, we note the following aspects:

"Our Father in heaven": This address makes clear that this prayer is for the disciples to utter, not Jesus; Jesus always addressed the Father as "Father" or "My Father," once as "Holy Father" (John 17:11), but never as "our Father." Jesus and the disciples spoke in Aramaic; the New Testament, however, is written in Greek. What Aramaic word did Jesus use for the Father in this model prayer? We cannot be sure, but it is possible, even likely, that He used the familiar term "Abba" because this is what He employed in His agonizing prayer in the Garden of Gethsemane. The Gospel writer Mark, who elsewhere gives us the actual Aramaic words spoken by Jesus (see Mark 5:41; 7:34; 15:34) describes the scene in Gethsemane: "Going a little farther, he fell to the ground and prayed that if possible the hour might pass from him. '*Abba*, Father,' he said, 'everything is

possible for you. Take this cup from me. Yet not what I will, but what you will'" (Mark 14:35, 36).

Abba expresses warm closeness as in "my Father" or even "Daddy." We find it used in two other places in the New Testament, both in a context of prayer:

- "The Spirit you received does not make you slaves, so that you live in fear again; rather, the Spirit you received brought about your adoption to sonship. And by him we cry, '*Abba*, Father'" (Rom. 8:15).

- "Because you are his sons, God sent the Spirit of his Son into our hearts, the Spirit who calls out, '*Abba*, Father'" (Gal. 4:6).

The language of *Abba* reveals how deeply personal and close is, first, Jesus's relationship to the Father, and, second, our relationship to God. We come as little children crying *"Abba*—Daddy." We come confidently, without hesitation, because we know that we are loved.

Whether or not Jesus intended for us to understand the *Abba* terminology in the model prayer, the term "Father" itself carries much of the same meaning. It was the address that Jesus used in His own prayers; He teaches us to do the same.

God, the Father of Jesus, is also our Father. He is our Father "in heaven." With this reminder the model prayer takes us out of our everyday realm. As we lift heart and voice, we, although still on this earth, enter the courts of glory. How frequently our prayers fail to include this element! We come to God bowed down with cares and eager to unload a shopping cart full of requests. As we mention each item, the earthly environment continues to press down upon us.

The Kingdom Petitions

Before presenting personal requests, Jesus teaches us to first pray for the kingdom and its concerns. Only after the three kingdom petitions does the model prayer take up our needs and desires.

How rarely do God's people follow the model. Burdened and stressed, we rush to lay our petitions before the Lord. This isn't wrong per se, but we might benefit greatly from focusing first of all on the kingdom. Perhaps in its light the matters that so press us down might pale in their significance.

"Hallowed be your name": The first kingdom petition asks that God's name might be respected. To "hallow" is to treat as holy. With this petition, we ask that God might be honored and revered.

This prayer embraces the entire world: we seek the day when God will be worshiped and adored from pole to pole. It also applies to us with a personal thrust, however: may God's name be hallowed in our lives.

We live in a profane world. People everywhere take the Lord's name carelessly in jest or oath. The media, especially the entertainment industry, continually profanes the name of God, oblivious to the third of the Ten Commandments:

"You shall not misuse the name of the LORD your God, for the LORD will not hold anyone guiltless who misuses his name" (Exod. 20:7). Right here is my chief complaint about Hollywood. Apart from the violence and sex, which I find objectionable, even worse is the frequent profanation of God's name in the movies. Such language degrades the way in which the Christian regards God.

"Your kingdom come": Jesus proclaimed that the kingdom of heaven was even now breaking in among society, and indeed it was, as we noticed earlier in chapter 18 of this book. But He also taught that the full coming of the kingdom was still future. That kingdom will be open, not secret, and glorious, not silent. In praying "Your kingdom come," we express our desire to see God's reign realized over all the earth, which implies the Second Coming of Jesus in glory (for example, Matt. 16:27).

"Your will be done, on earth as it is in heaven": When tragedy strikes, people often blame God. They question why God didn't intervene to save a dying child or prevent a natural disaster. Often they suggest that God must be a monster because He doesn't prevent pain and suffering when He has the power to do so. But God is not responsible for evil. He gave us a free will. He allows things to happen and sin to work itself out so that humans can see the absurdity of evil while He pursues His redemptive goals. We live on a planet in rebellion, where a war is being waged between Christ and Satan. This war takes victims—each of us! The third kingdom petition looks forward to the day when the long conflict will be over—when peace and love will fill the earth without a discordant note. It also has a personal reference: "May Your will be done in *me*." In this context it is a prayer of submission to the Father, Who knows what is best for us.

The Disciple Petitions

The three disciple petitions mentioned in the model prayer are meant to be representative, not exhaustive. We each come before the Lord and talk to Him as to a friend, laying out all that pleases us and all that concerns us.

"Give us today our daily bread": The first disciple petition requests provision for the necessities of life. No mention of wealth nor of luxury—just "daily bread." This petition reminds us of the prayer found in the book of Proverbs:

> Give me neither poverty nor riches,
> but give me only my daily bread.
> Otherwise, I may have too much and
> disown you
> and say, "Who is the LORD?"
> Or I may become poor and steal,
> and so dishonor the name of my
> God (Prov. 30:8, 9)

In our greedy, materialistic age, this is an apt prayer for followers of Jesus.

"Forgive us our debts, as we also have forgiven our debtors": This is not a one-time petition. We are constantly in need of forgiveness because we constantly fall

from the path of God's will. Until we reach the heavenly kingdom, we need to realize our need of the grace of forgiveness and pray this prayer.

Sin is a heavy debt. It is like the crushing weight of the ten thousand talents—a sum almost beyond imagination—that Jesus mentioned in His parable of the two debtors (Matt. 18:23–33). But the God of grace freely cancels all our debts. God's action produces reciprocal action in us. We live in grace, forgiving others as God forgave us. That is why this petition for forgiveness adds "as we also have forgiven our debtors" (Matt. 6:12; see also vv. 14, 15).

"And lead us not into temptation, but deliver us from the evil one": This petition asks for divine guidance. It seeks strength from above to meet every situation. For tests will come (the word for "temptation" is the same as that for "test"). Some tests we foresee; others we do not. Without warning we find ourselves thrown into a fiery furnace, struggling to survive spiritually. But even there the One Who "looks like a son of the gods" (Dan. 3:25) will be by our side. God promises:

> When you pass through the waters,
> I will be with you;
> and when you pass through the rivers,
> they will not sweep over you.
> When you walk through the fire,
> you will not be burned;
> the flames will not set you ablaze.
> (Isa. 43:2)

In the wording of the model prayer most familiar to many Christians, the third disciple petition closes with "but deliver us from evil." The NIV translation, "deliver us from the evil one," is truer to the original text. Our warfare ultimately isn't against generalized evil but against the prince of darkness—the foe of Christ and all His followers.

The three disciple petitions—for daily needs, for forgiveness, and for divine guidance—encompass the range of the Christian's needs. They cover past, present, and future. With them we place ourselves in the care of a loving Father.

QUESTIONS FOR DISCUSSION

1. What part did prayer play in the life and ministry of Jesus?

2. Does Jesus's model prayer provide a detailed pattern for us to follow, or does it instead provide general principles? Give reasons for your answer with reference to the model prayer.

3. What are some practical ways that could enhance your prayer life based on Jesus's prayer habits?

24

What Jesus Taught about Power, Sex, and Money

<table>
<tr><td>OBJECTIVES</td><td>• Learn the startling teachings of Jesus about power, sex, and money.</td></tr>
<tr><td></td><td>• Discern the radical nature of Jesus's words and actions concerning the use of force.</td></tr>
<tr><td>SCRIPTURE</td><td>• Matthew 5:1–48; Mark 9:14—10:31</td></tr>
</table>

Many years ago I read a book titled *Men of Power* by Albert Carr. I remember well the parade of characters—mostly generals and heads of state—that passed through its pages grasping for control, people who were manipulative, ruthless, cruel. Power—of the gun, personality, and pride—took these individuals to the highest posts in their nation and enabled them to rule as unchallenged dictators.

That book told the stories of men whom the world called great. But with all the Napoleons, Charlemagnes, and Stalins the author presented, none named could hold a candle to the greatest man of all time: Jesus Christ.

Jesus commanded no army and won no laurels on the battlefield. But He has influenced countless millions across the face of the planet and continues to do so. At His word they have gone forward into battle—but not with tanks and mortars, missiles, and grenades. Yet in His name and by His power they wage warfare every bit as real.

Want a man of power? I give you a champion, the King of Kings and Lord of Lords, who by gentleness and kindly deeds wins the world to Himself. He did not send angels or humans in front of Him to be cannon fodder for the enemy, but went on ahead of us all, dying the death that was ours on Calvary's tree in order to give us the life that was His.

The passages for this chapter will reveal that Jesus of Nazareth completely reversed the standards of the world and will provide startling answers in two other areas that still play major roles in the lives of men and women today—sex and money.

Power

Scholars of primitive religions tell us that the worship of Stone Age peoples centered in *mana*, power. They sought to tap life forces that would cause the crops to grow and the women to bear children. Superstition is the attempt to manipulate for one's interests and well-being—through supposedly efficacious words, acts, or rituals—the *mana* that lies all around us.

Christianity is about power. "I am not ashamed of the gospel," the apostle Paul said, "because it is the power of God that brings salvation to everyone who believes" (Rom. 1:16). Here is the power—God's power. Not power through politicking and scheming or through vaulting ambition and single-minded ruthlessness. Our need is not human power, but *God's* power. Human power, in fact, gets in the way of divine power. The paradox of Christianity lies in this cosmic truth: "My grace is sufficient for you, for My strength is made perfect in weakness" (2 Cor. 12:9, NKJV). And from the human side: "For when I am weak, then I am strong" (v. 10).

Heaven's doors open to the soul that feels and acknowledges its powerlessness. In the Sermon on the Mount, Jesus said, "Blessed are the poor in spirit, for theirs is the kingdom of heaven" (Matt. 5:3). Without distorting the text we could paraphrase it, "Blessed are those who aren't hungry for power, for theirs is the kingdom of heaven." Ellen G. White put it well in a quotation that is one of my favorites: "To him who is content to receive without deserving, who feels that he can never recompense such love, who lays all doubt and unbelief aside, and comes as a little child to the feet of Jesus, all the treasures of eternal love are a free, everlasting gift."[1]

Jesus's disciples were slow to learn this truth, just as we are today. In Mark 9 we find them arguing as they walked along about who was the greatest. Oh, how blind! When they had the greatest Person in their midst, how could they look away from Him and stoop to comparing themselves with each other?

Jesus took the Twelve apart and sat them down. "Anyone who wants to be first," He said, "must be the very last, and the servant of all" (v. 35). Taking a child in His arms, He said: "Whoever welcomes one of these little children in my name welcomes me; and whoever welcomes me does not welcome me but the one who sent me" (v. 37).

The Master identified with the powerless. Here He did so with a child—surely the most powerless element in society during His life on earth. Elsewhere He equated Himself with those who were blind, deaf, paralyzed, or disabled; with women, considered second-class citizens; with lepers, outcasts from society; and with Samaritans and other Gentiles, those outside the pale of the chosen.

By word and deed Jesus upended the pyramid built by the social order of His day. That pyramid rested on power, as it still does in our time. Human beings strive to rise higher while struggling, sweating, trampling on those below them, and clawing their way to the top. But Jesus takes the pyramid and stands it on its head. Instead of rising by trampling others down, and instead of gaining success by standing on the shoulders of the powerless, He bears the weight of the entire world—the world of the powerless—on His shoulders.

In spite of Jesus's crystal-clear teaching about power, the disciples didn't get it. In Mark 10 we find James and John, the sons of Zebedee, asking Him for a favor—the best seats in His kingdom, one on His right and the other on His left (v. 37). Again He tried to set them and the others straight. "You know that those who are regarded as rulers of the Gentiles lord it over them, and their high officials exercise authority over them," He said. "Not so with you. Instead, whoever wants to become great among you must be your servant, and whoever wants to be first must be slave of all" (vv. 42–44). Then He capped off the discussion with a statement that summarized His mission to a lost earth, one that has become a Christian classic: "For even the Son of Man did not come to be served, but to serve, and to give his life as a ransom for many" (v. 45).

Only, perhaps, when the disciples saw Jesus give His life on Calvary's tree did they begin to understand the radical nature of His teaching about power. Too often the church has set aside His teaching. The ways and practices of the power-hungry world have invaded the church and corrupted it into a political institution marred by intrigue and vainglory. Christians too often today put business before religion, rationalizing that in the dog-eat-dog modern marketplace, the teachings of Jesus about power lead only to failure.

Jesus's words in the Sermon on the Mount are perhaps His most quoted sayings. In practice, however, they are massively neglected, even by those who claim to be His followers.

Look at them again:

Blessed are the poor in spirit . . .
Blessed are those who mourn . . .
Blessed are the meek . . .
Blessed are those who hunger and
    thirst for righteousness . . .
Blessed are the merciful . . .
Blessed are the pure in heart . . .
Blessed are the peacemakers . . .
Blessed are those who are persecuted . . .
Blessed are you when people insult
    you . . . (Matt. 5:3–11)

And what about the teachings that follow? "You have heard that it was said, 'Eye for eye, and tooth for tooth.' But I tell you, do not resist an evil person. If anyone slaps you on the right cheek, turn to them the other cheek also. And if anyone wants to sue you and take your shirt, hand over your coat as well. If anyone forces you to go one mile, go with them two miles. Give to the one who asks you, and do not turn away from the one who wants to borrow from you" (Matt. 5:38–42).

"You have heard that it was said, 'Love your neighbor and hate your enemy.' But I tell you, love your enemies and pray for those who persecute you" (Matt. 5:43, 44). These words of Jesus have perplexed Christians for centuries. Surely the Master didn't expect His followers to take them literally? But He did. That is how He lived and how He reacted to beatings, torture, and taunting.

But how could society function if it tried to follow these teachings? The Sermon on the Mount isn't a blueprint for any earthly society. It isn't about the kingdoms of the world but about "the kingdom of heaven," as its opening words tell us (Matt. 5:3). That kingdom is already here and we, Jesus's followers, are called to live by *its* principles, not those of the world. Radical? Indeed.

Across the centuries and still today some people take seriously Jesus's words.

His living presence transforms their lives: they regard every human being as a valuable a child of God. Those whom the world ignores or despises they accept in Jesus's name, and by His grace they reach out in loving ministry to the poor, the hungry, the broken, the helpless—the powerless. And they transform the world.

In this world power intertwines and interacts with sex and money. Power leads to sex and money, while sex and money themselves are power. What did Jesus teach about the other two members of the axis of power—sex and money?

Sex

Mark tells us that the Pharisees set a trap for Jesus, asking Him publicly, "Is it lawful for a man to divorce his wife for any and every reason?" (Matt. 19:3). The question was loaded politically, because the ruler over Galilee, Herod Antipas, had divorced his wife and married Herodias, wife of his brother Philip.

John the Baptist had come to grief over this very matter. The fearless preacher of repentance had not minced his words, condemning the marriage of Antipas and Herodias, the latter who had divorced her husband to marry Antipas. It was a public scandal that incensed the people, but John paid with his life for voicing what everyone was saying in private.

Now the Pharisees were trying to snare Jesus. If Jesus replied, "Sure, divorce is OK," He would run against public sentiment. But if He said—as they probably hoped He would—"This marriage is a disgrace and abomination," word would get back to Antipas, who would soon put Jesus behind bars. Jesus, however, didn't give a yes-or-no reply. Instead, He took the discussion back to first principles, and in so doing cast the Pharisees' question in a radically new light.

> The question put to Jesus in the passage before us must be set in its ancient context to be appreciated fully. In ancient Judaism, divorce was a right only for husbands; women were legally the property of their husbands and had no power to end the marriage. Further, there was never any question about whether a man might be free to end his marriage by divorce, the only concern reflected in the ancient rabbinic tradition being that a man give proper official certification of the divorce to his wife. There was a difference of opinion between two major schools of ancient rabbinic thought about what were the legitimate causes for divorcing a woman, one school insisting that the only valid reason was sexual impurity in the wife, and the other arguing that the wife could be sent away simply if the husband grew tired of her. The latter view was dominant, no doubt because it was more convenient for a husband.[2]

Note that the playing field wasn't level for men and women. Jewish law and practice almost put women in the role of chattels—things (not persons) that their husbands could discard at a whim. Sad to say, in many societies today such a view of women still prevails. And even in the supposedly enlightened culture of the West, with its laws to safeguard women's rights, the practice often falls short. Society at all levels, beginning with Hollywood, casts women in the role of sex objects for lustful males to use and then toss aside.

Jesus, however, would take us back to God's original purpose. He quoted the Creation account (Gen. 1:26, 27), in which God made us in His image, male and female. Together we bear the divine stamp. One gender is not to have lordship over the other, but only mutuality and equality. Next Jesus referred to the divine intent for marriage given in Eden: "For this reason a man will leave his father and mother and be united to his wife, and the two will become one flesh" (Matt. 19:5; see also Gen. 2:24). Becoming "one flesh" rules out of court any view that permits a man or a woman to sever the marriage relationship casually.

Under the laws of Moses a Jewish husband could easily divorce his wife without even going to court (Matt. 19:7). But Jesus set aside such provisions, which, He said, were merely an accommodation to fallen human beings (Mark 10:5). What He called for was a radical approach that seems to have been without precedent in Jewish thought.

In pointing His hearers back to the Edenic ideal of relations between men and women, Jesus went even further. "Anyone who divorces his wife and marries another woman commits adultery against her" (that is, *against his wife*; v. 11). Hurtado notes, "This idea is apparently totally unparalleled in ancient Judaism, where adultery was understood only as an offense committed against another man, either by seducing a man's daughter and depriving him of a marriageable girl, or by violating a husband's exclusive sexual rights with his wife."[3]

Thus, Jesus underscored the importance of women in marriage. His teaching, radical for first-century Judaism, speaks to our day with no less compelling power. Abused women, battered women, neglected women, discarded women—the litany of crimes against women stretches to lengths that only God knows.

Jesus has the answer to the appalling situation of our times. Politicians and social workers try hard, and I applaud their efforts, but the problem, manifested in cruel and abusive acts, ultimately is one of the heart. Only Jesus can change that, and He does as individuals yield their will to Him and He makes them over in His image.

Money

A man ran up to Jesus and fell on his knees before Him, Mark tells us (Mark 10:17). Matthew and Luke also record the incident, and from their accounts we learn additional details: the individual was young (Matt. 19:20), and he was a ruler or leader (Luke 18:18).

It is a sad story, made all the more poignant because of a detail that we find only in Mark's Gospel: "Jesus looked at him and loved him" (Mark 10:21). Many of His encounters with individuals had happy endings, but this one did not. We cannot read the story without a stab of pain at what might have been. The young man had so much going for him—energy, enthusiasm, responsibility, respect, and religious devotion. He might have become a pillar of the early church, but it never happened. At Jesus's words—which cut to the quick of his spiritual experience—his "face fell. He went away sad" (v. 22). *He missed out on a chance to be with Jesus.*

What Jesus called for seemed too radical for him. It is still radical and too revolutionary for many people today. Usually we focus on Jesus's instruction to the young man to sell everything he had, give the proceeds to the poor, and follow Jesus. But before this He said something that stopped the young man in his tracks and that pointed to his spiritual poverty.

The young man approached Jesus with a dramatic flourish. He ran up to Him, fell on his knees before Him, and asked, "Good teacher, . . . what must I do to inherit eternal life?" (v. 17).

But Jesus brushed aside the flowery opening: "Why do you call me good? No one is good—except God alone" (v. 18). It was a rebuke, softly worded but nonetheless a reprimand. Only God is truly good. Was the young man, thinking to praise Jesus, prepared to acknowledge Him as more than man—as God? His flattering words in fact fell far short of the reality of the God-man before Whom he knelt.

And Jesus's soft rebuke had additional ramifications. The young man thought as society in his day did, as we also too often reason—he divided people into "good" and "bad." For Jesus, however, the distinction was artificial, because *everyone*, whether "good" or "bad," is a lost sheep whom He came to seek and rescue. What mattered—and still matters—is not whether one is a Pharisee or a tax collector, a Nicodemus or a Mary Magdalene. All, regardless of social standing, require the grace of God. Jesus spoke of the need of grace and of the kingdom—God's rule. But more than that, He inaugurated the kingdom. In that kingdom we find no "good" or "bad," because we are all "bad." But we all are saved by grace.

Despite all his sterling qualities, the young man was far from the kingdom. People would have called him "good"—no doubt he'd heard that appellation frequently because of his scrupulous attempts to keep the law—and perhaps that framed his opening line to Jesus: "Good teacher . . ."

Jesus, Who reads the heart, understood just what it would take to change the man's thinking and bring him into the kingdom—expose the paucity of all his previous efforts at righteousness so that he could receive God's gift of eternal life. But to obtain the gift he must first give all away.

"You still lack one thing [and how big a thing that one was!]," Jesus said. "Sell everything you have and give to the poor, and you will have treasure in heaven. Then come, follow me" (Luke 18:22).

The young man had come to the crossroads of life. He looked down an avenue that stretched strange and uncertain into a future without the security and privilege that wealth buys. It was a road brightened by only one element—the presence of Jesus. Then he glanced in the opposite direction at the continuation of what he had known and loved, a path that guaranteed a safe and comfortable life. Sorrowfully he turned away from Jesus, unable to bring himself to take the step that led to true life.

Let us be clear as to the story's intent. Jesus does not here advocate poverty as an ideal, just as He does not introduce a social program for the redistribution of wealth. The point is this: the call of Jesus demands our all. He wants our all (be it little or much), or nothing at all.

Having recognized this central idea, however, Jesus's words speak directly to the issue of possessions in the lives of His followers. After the young man went away, Jesus said to the disciples, "How hard it is for the rich to enter the kingdom of God!" (Mark 10:23). His comment amazed the disciples. The theology of the day taught that acquisition of wealth demonstrated divine favor. On the other hand, the poor had God's curse upon them.

But Jesus, who spoke for and reached out to the poor, the sick, and the marginalized, directly countered this theology that was so comforting to the rich, the well, and the prominent. He said again, "How hard it is for the rich to enter the kingdom of God! Indeed, it is easier for a camel to go through the eye of a needle than for someone who is rich to enter the kingdom of God" (Luke 18:24–25).

Radical words! No wonder church leaders and theologians through the centuries have tried to escape their plain thrust, inventing such fanciful interpretations for the eye of a needle as a gate or hole in the wall of Jerusalem. Today many would argue that riches per se are no problem, but only as they become our god or are used for selfish or evil purposes.

Hear again Jesus's radical words: Riches *themselves* are a problem. The more possessions we accumulate, the harder it will be to make it into the kingdom. Christ's words aren't just for the millionaires and billionaires. They are for all of us, especially if we live in the affluent West. Uncomfortable as His words are, we must face them if we would claim to be followers of Jesus.

History, both ancient and modern, testifies to the truth of Jesus's observation. From its inception "the poor, and the maimed, and the halt, and the blind" (Luke 14:21, KJV), rather than those who are affluent, have claimed Christianity. It was so in the first century of the church and is equally so today. Where people feel rich, well fed, and in need of nothing, they most often turn away at the crossroads of life and follow the path of the rich young ruler. However, when they are down and out, struggling to survive or seeking a better life, they are most ready to say yes to the call of the Master, "Come to me, all you who are weary and burdened, and I will give you rest" (Matt. 11:28).

The three—power, sex, money—intertwine and interact. Power leads to sex and money, while sex and money themselves are power. All three continue to shape the world, as they always have. But Jesus the radical Messiah upends our thinking about them. His ideas are so different, and the life He calls us to so at odds with the current thinking, that we must cross over from this world (while still in it) and come under His rule as members of His kingdom.

QUESTIONS FOR DISCUSSION

1. Did Jesus intend for us to understand the Sermon on the Mount literally? Give reasons for your answer, referring to the biblical text.

2. Does the path of non-resistance to evil advocated by Jesus lead to people who are passive and weak, or does it lead to strength?

3. What does Jesus's teaching about money tell us about how we should handle possessions?

4. In matters of ethics, can a Christian have one mind-set in church and in private but another mind-set at the marketplace and in public?

PART III

HIS PASSION

Surely he took up our pain
    and bore our suffering,
yet we considered him punished by God,
    stricken by him, and afflicted.
But he was pierced for our transgressions,
    he was crushed for our iniquities;
the punishment that brought us peace was on him,
    and by his wounds we are healed.

—Isaiah 53:4, 5

25

From "Hosanna!"
to "Crucify Him!"

<table>
<tr><td>OBJECTIVES</td><td>

• Grasp the importance of events and the chronological order of the final week of Jesus's life.

• Understand why Jesus's actions took on a different character during the Passion Week.

</td></tr>
<tr><td>SCRIPTURE</td><td>

• Matthew 21:1–11; Mark 11:1–11; Luke 14:28–44; John 12:1–19

</td></tr>
</table>

After ten chapters spent studying the principal teachings of Jesus of Nazareth, we take up His story again. His mission in Galilee completed, He was on the way south with His disciples. The route He took was circuitous; He timed the journey to arrive at its destination just in time for the Feast of Passover.

Inevitably, inexorably, the footsteps of Jesus led to Jerusalem. Hailed by the crowds in Galilee but dogged by religious leaders who suspected Him and sought to do Him harm, the Master knew that the climax of His mission would occur in Judea. Jerusalem summoned Him.

In Luke we find Jesus telling the disciples, "In any case, I must press on today and tomorrow and the next day—for surely no prophet can die outside Jerusalem" (Luke 13:33). While the other Gospels do not include a similar statement, we find occasions on which Jesus takes the disciples aside and tells them what awaits Him in Jerusalem (Matt. 16:21; Mark 9:30, 31; 10:32–34). With each occasion the instruction becomes more detailed and specific. The final passage in the series leaves an indelible picture:

> They were on their way up to Jerusalem, with Jesus leading the way, and the disciples were astonished, while those who followed were afraid. Again he took the Twelve aside and told them what was going to happen to him. "We are going up to Jerusalem," he said, "and the Son of Man will be delivered over to the chief priests and the teachers

of the law. They will condemn him to death and will hand him over to the Gentiles, who will mock him and spit on him, flog him and kill him. Three days later he will rise." (Mark 10:32–34)

What a portrait of Jesus. He knew where He was headed and He knew what would happen there—Jerusalem killed prophets! But He set His face like flint, just as Isaiah had predicted: "Because the Sovereign LORD helps me, I will not be disgraced. Therefore have I set my face like flint, and I know I will not be put to shame" (Isa. 50:7).

The disciples, however, were filled with foreboding. Their troubled minds went beyond the usual failure to grasp Jesus's meaning. Now they sensed that something terrible was going to happen in Jerusalem. Down from Galilee they walked, following the valley of the Jordan until they reached Judea. They came to Jericho, some 800 feet (244 m) below sea level, with the Dead Sea nearby. The road ahead winds steeply up through the mountains. At the top, at its destination, lies Israel's capital, only 22 miles (35 km) away, but necessitating a climb of more than 3,000 feet (914 m).

The book of Psalms contains a series of songs of ascent (Pss. 120–134). Three times each year—at Passover, Pentecost, and Tabernacles—all Jewish males were required to journey to Jerusalem, and they sang these songs as they made their way to the holy city: "Jerusalem is built like a city that is closely compacted together. That is where the tribes go up—the tribes of the LORD—to praise the name of the LORD according to the statute given to Israel" (Ps. 122:3, 4).

Today you make the trip by car. Even so, the road is steep and taxing as it winds through dry, brown hills. Occasionally you see the tents of Bedouin with their animals, but there is no other sign of life. Perhaps halfway up you come across an ancient inn, dating back to the time of Jesus, and remember His story of the traveler on the lonely road who fell among thieves but who was rescued by a passing Samaritan and taken to a roadside inn.

Then, suddenly, you are climbing out of the hills and looking on settlements. You see the holy city laid out just ahead with the gold of the Dome of the Rock gleaming in the sunlight. Jesus walked up this road. He did so resolutely with jaw set firm and face straight. The disciples followed behind, wondering and whispering among themselves.

On the Mount of Olives, where the road turned down to the city, they looked over Jerusalem. The city wasn't as big as it is now, and the Dome of the Rock wouldn't yet exist for hundreds of years. But it was a beautiful city, intriguing and fateful. And dominating it was the huge temple complex, one of the wonders of the ancient world.

Jesus and His disciples probably arrived on the Friday before Passover. The seven days that stretched ahead would be decisive for the Master, for the Twelve, and for the world. It would be a week marked by amazing high points and incredible low ones. The crowd that shouted "Hosanna!" on Sunday would cry out "Crucify Him!" on Friday. It was also a week made bright by three acts of love—two by women and one by Jesus Himself. It was a week of intrigue and plotting, betrayal, struggle, agony, and rejection.

And it was a week of death—of suicide and execution. One week after Jesus arrived in Jerusalem, on the next Friday, He would hang suspended between earth and sky on a Roman cross.

The final week of Jesus's life would bring His mission to a climax. All the Gospel writers trace its events day by day, devoting space far out of proportion to the rest of the life of Jesus. Matthew, Mark, Luke, and John want us to read and reflect on what happened that week. They don't want us to be like the Twelve who didn't get it. The events on Sunday were filled with interest with surprising elements:

- Jesus deliberately draws attention to Himself.

- He uses force to drive the merchants and money changers from the temple.

- He curses a fig tree because He doesn't find fruit on it, so that the fig tree withers.

Is this the same Jesus with Whom we became acquainted earlier in the Gospels? How can He act in a manner so out of character with what we know and expect of Him?

The Gospel of Matthew gives eight of its twenty-eight chapters to this single week, Mark six of sixteen, Luke six of twenty-four, and John no less than nine of its twenty-one. Because of this disproportionate treatment, the Gospels with some merit have been called accounts of Jesus's Passion with long introductions.

These four records of the Passion Week are powerful: they grip the reader as the story of Jesus comes to a tragic yet glorious climax. We should study them carefully and prayerfully, reflecting on their message and remembering Ellen G. White's admonition:

> It would be well for us to spend a thoughtful hour each day in contemplation of the life of Christ. We should take it point by point, and let the imagination grasp each scene, especially the closing ones. As we thus dwell upon His great sacrifice for us, our confidence in Him will be more constant, our love will be quickened, and we shall be more deeply imbued with His spirit. If we would be saved at last, we must learn the lesson of penitence and humiliation at the foot of the cross.[1]

The Order of Events

All four Gospels include the same major events of the Passion Week. However, they do not tell the story with exactly the same order, so we cannot be sure that we know just what happened on each day. We can only suggest a particular order.

We begin the study of this climactic week with the day following the Sabbath. By biblical reckoning—sunset to sunset—this day begins on what we call Saturday night.

THE FINAL EVENTS IN THE LIFE OF JESUS

Friday	Jesus arrives in Bethany
Saturday night	The anointing at Bethany
Sunday	Judas decides to betray Jesus
	The triumphal entry
	Retirement to Bethany
Monday	Cursing the fig tree
	Second cleansing of the Temple
	Retirement to Bethany
Tuesday	The fig tree withers
	Jesus's last day in the temple
	Retirement to the Mount of Olives
	Jesus teaches the disciples about the end
	Judas concludes the betrayal plot
Wednesday	In retirement
Thursday	Preparation for the Passover
	The Lord's Supper
	Gethsemane
Friday	Jesus before the Sanhedrin
	Jesus tried by Pilate and Herod
	Judas commits suicide
	Jesus scourged and crucified
	Jesus dies
	Jesus buried in the tomb of Joseph of Arimathea
Saturday	Jesus rests in the tomb
	Religious leaders visit Pilate

The Anointing at Bethany

On that Saturday night an unusual event occurred at a dinner given in Jesus's honor. A woman poured a pint of expensive perfume over Jesus's feet, wiping His feet with her hair. That act, and the conversation about it that followed, would have far-reaching consequences.

Matthew, Mark, and John record the event. Their accounts are so similar as to ensure that the same incident is portrayed: the anointing takes place shortly before the Passover, and in Bethany; a woman anoints Jesus's feet with expensive perfume and wipes them with her hair; and her act is criticized by the disciples, but Jesus defends her (see Matt. 26:6–13; Mark 14:1–9; John 12:1–8).

Matthew and Mark do not name the woman, but John states explicitly that she was Mary, the sister of Martha and Lazarus. On the other hand, Matthew and Mark tell us that the anointing took place in Bethany at the home of "Simon the Leper" (Matt. 26:6; Mark 14:3). John omits the man's name, simply indicating that the event took place in Bethany.

The most significant difference concerns the *timing* of the event. John, whom we noticed in earlier chapters to provide precise information, makes clear that the anointing took place "six days before the Passover" (John 12:1), that is, on Saturday night. Matthew and Mark, however, seem to locate the event two days before the Passover (Matt. 26:2; Mark 14:1). How can that be?

As we study carefully the context of the event in each of these Gospels, the apparent discrepancy disappears. In both Matthew's and Mark's accounts, the larger setting is the plot of the chief priests and scribes to kill Jesus. They want to get rid of Jesus, but He is constantly in the midst of a crowd. Then an unexpected solution falls into their hands—Judas comes to them and offers to deliver Jesus to them privately.

How did this development come about? Matthew and Mark break the chronological order to show us the links in the story of Jesus's betrayal. The account of the anointing at Bethany backtracks in time to give the reason for Judas's decision to go to Jesus's enemies. Both Matthew and Mark signal that they are inserting the anointing narrative by telling us that the event took place in Bethany, not Jerusalem.

With this background we catch the element of intrigue that lies behind the seemingly straightforward story of that Saturday night in Bethany. On one hand, Mary's act demonstrates wholehearted devotion to the Master—pure nard to express her pure love. The perfume was

The Gospel writers focus on Jesus and only mention other people as they play a part in the story of Jesus. This means that we are given only incidental details of the people around Jesus. Since each writer tells the story according to the particular portrait of the Master that he develops, we find "gaps" in the story that often intrigue us.

One of the most interesting examples involves the anointing of Jesus by the woman. Who was she? Do we have hints as to her identity? And was there only one anointing, or were there two instances?

John identified the woman as Mary—presumably the sister of Lazarus and Martha, who are specifically identified. In the Gospel of Luke the woman is simply called "a woman who had lived a sinful life in that town." Who was this woman with a notorious reputation? We cannot be certain, but the evidence points to Mary of Magdala. She was a woman with a past: Luke informs us Jesus had cured her of demon possession (Luke 8:1, 2). All four Gospel writers inform us of her devotion to Jesus at the cross and afterward (Matt. 26:7; Matt. 27:56; Mark 15:40, 47; Luke 24:9, 10; John 20:1, 10–18). If the "sinful woman" was in fact Mary of Magdala, Luke protected her identity because of her past life. When John wrote much later, presumably she was no longer living, so he felt clear to name her.

rare and expensive—three hundred denarii would be equivalent to $30,000–$50,000 in today's U.S. currency. But she loved deeply and gratefully, heedless of the cost.

Judas grumbled. He could only think about all the money that perfume might have contributed to the disciples' kitty. He was the treasurer; he held the money bag. And, John tells us, he was a thief and used to raid the kitty from time to time (John 12:6). For Judas, Jesus's defense of Mary was the last straw. He had experienced months of disappointment and growing frustration over Jesus's failure to exert Himself as the popular political Messiah that he and the other disciples were waiting for.

Following Jesus's public rebuke, Judas came to a decision. He would take matters into his own hands. He would force Jesus's hands by maneuvering Him into circumstances where He would be forced to act. Now Jesus faced increased danger, not only from the chief priests and religious leaders, but from within the circle of those closest to Him. Now one of the Twelve had become a mole.

The Triumphal Entry

On Sunday morning Jesus sends two of His disciples into a village (probably Bethany, or maybe Bethphage) with a strange order. "You will find a colt tied there," He says. "Untie it and bring it here. If anyone asks you, 'Why are you doing this?' say, 'The Lord needs it and will send it back here shortly'" (Mark 11:2, 3; see also Matt. 21:2, 3).

The disciples left and found a colt tied in the street by a doorway. They loosed the colt, and when some of the people standing around asked them what they were doing, they answered just as Jesus had told them. Then, tingling with excitement, they brought the colt to Jesus. After they threw their coats on the animal, Jesus got on. For the first and only time in His adult life, of which we have record, He rode instead of walked. And they began to descend the Mount of Olives to Jerusalem.

All four Gospel writers record the incident (Matt. 21:1–11; Mark 11:1–11; Luke 19:29–44; John 12:12–15). It's essentially the same in all four accounts. As they went along, more and more people joined them, until a huge crowd was following Jesus. People threw their cloaks on the road; others cut branches from trees and palms and spread them in front of Jesus.

Closer and closer they came to Jerusalem, and still the crowds swelled. Those before and behind shouted out, "Hosanna!" (which means, in Hebrew, "Lord, save us, we pray," based on Ps. 118:25).

> "Blessed is he who comes in the name
>   of the Lord!"
> "Blessed is the coming kingdom of
>   our father David!"
> "Hosanna in the highest heaven!"
>   (Mark 11:9, 10)

For six hundred years the Jews had been a subject people. But the prophets had foretold that another great king like

David would arise and lead them to victory. The prophet Zechariah had described just what that day would be like:

> Rejoice greatly, Daughter Zion!
> Shout, Daughter Jerusalem!
> See, your king comes to you,
> righteous and victorious,
> lowly and riding on a donkey,
> on a colt, the foal of a donkey. . . .
> He will proclaim peace to the nations.
> His rule will extend from sea to sea
> and from the River [that is, the Euphrates] to the ends of the earth.
> (Zech. 9:9, 10)

The most interesting part about this triumphal entry on Palm Sunday was that Jesus set it up. He orchestrated it. All along He had taken a low-key approach, avoiding publicity and dampening enthusiasm. But on the Sunday before He died He reversed Himself by getting the colt and riding it down the king's way to Jerusalem, letting the crowd honor Him as king in act and words. He encouraged the popular expectation that He was the long-awaited Messiah, the new Son of David. Everybody went wild. Peter and the disciples? It was the biggest day of their lives.

But the crowd that shouted "Hosanna!" on Palm Sunday would cry out "Crucify Him! Crucify Him!" on Friday morning. The disciples who jubilated with the crowd on Sunday would run away on Friday. And Peter, who boldly intended to suffer or die with Jesus if need be, would wilt before a servant girl's questions and three times deny that he even knew Jesus.

But what was going on that Sunday morning? Why did Jesus, Who throughout His work in Galilee had made strong efforts to avoid publicity, now suddenly reverse Himself? Or did He? I find Ellen G. White's comment on the Master's actions particularly helpful:

Never before in His earthly life had Jesus permitted such a demonstration. He clearly foresaw the result. It would bring Him to the cross. But it was His purpose thus publicly to present Himself as the Redeemer. He desired to call attention to the sacrifice that was to crown His mission to a fallen world. While the people were assembling at Jerusalem to celebrate the Passover, He, the antitypical Lamb, by a voluntary act set Himself apart as an oblation. It would be needful for His church in all succeeding ages to make His death for the sins of the world a subject of deep thought and study. Every fact connected with it should be verified beyond a doubt. It was necessary, then, that the eyes of all people should now be directed to Him; the events which preceded His great sacrifice must be such as to call attention to the sacrifice itself. After such a demonstration as that attending His entry into Jerusalem, all eyes would follow His rapid progress to the final scene.[2]

The fact is, Jesus *was* the fulfillment of Zechariah's prophecy of the Messiah. He was Israel's true and rightful King, Whose rule—one day—would stretch from pole to pole. While He was not the Messiah of popular expectation, He was the Messiah of God's appointment. By calling for a colt, riding it into Jerusalem, and doing nothing to discourage the celebration of the disciples and the crowd, He proclaimed for all to see that He fulfilled the ancient predictions.

In Galilee the situation called for a low-key approach. Jesus tried to dispel notions that He was merely a miracle worker and a traveling exorcist. Though He was such things, He was far more—the Son of God. The sights and sounds of blind people healed, deaf people rejoicing, and multitudes fed from a few loaves and fishes got in the way of His message. Like people today, most of the Galileans couldn't see beyond outward appearances.

Now on Palm Sunday He had come to the final, fateful week of ministry. He wanted all eyes to focus on what He was about, as White noted. He also intended to leave no doubt as to Who He was. Later, after the climactic events of that Friday and the following Sunday, the disciples and others would go over the scene point by point. As their eyes opened to His true person and mission, they would also discern how He—in a manner totally unexpected from the popular anticipation—fulfilled the Scriptures that prophesied about Him.

Mark tells us, "Jesus entered Jerusalem and went into the temple courts. He looked around at everything, but since it was already late, He went out to Bethany with the Twelve" (Mark 11:11). On the morrow, however, He would come back to the temple. He would throw down the gauntlet to the religious establishment at the locus of its authority. By doing so He would cause an inevitable backlash and seal His doom.

QUESTIONS FOR DISCUSSION

1. Compare and contrast the four accounts of Jesus's anointing in Matthew, Mark, Luke, and John. Do they all refer to the same event? If so, how do you explain the differences in the accounts?

2. Look up all the references to Judas Iscariot in the Gospels. What hints of his future betrayal of Jesus do you find? Do Ellen White's comments about him (see *Desire of Ages*, chapter 76, "Judas") shed light on what led to his tragic end?

3. Consider the different groups in Jerusalem: the pilgrims, the Jewish leaders, and the disciples. How do you think each felt about the triumphal entry?

26

Messiah versus the Temple

OBJECTIVES	• Learn about the role of the temple at the time of Jesus.
	• Understand Jesus's purpose in cursing the fig tree.
	• Grasp the import of Jesus's challenge to the religious establishment by His actions and teachings in the temple.
SCRIPTURE	• Matthew 21:18–46; Mark 11:12—12:44; Luke 19:45—21:4

The events covered in this chapter probably took place on the Monday and Tuesday of the Passion Week. By word and deed Jesus signaled finality in the work that He had come to earth to do, and finality for the continued existence of both the temple and Jerusalem. The first day, Monday, began with an act of Jesus that seemed altogether out of character.

Jesus and the Fig Tree

According to Mark's account, Jesus cursed the fig tree on His way from Bethany to Jerusalem. It seems He was hungry. Apparently He hadn't eaten breakfast. Noticing a leafy fig tree in the distance, He understandably looked to find fruit on it. Green figs ordinarily appear in early spring, before the leaves appear. The fruit ripens in June, but this was a tree out of season—it was only late March or April. But the fig tree proved to be a big disappointment: it had plenty of leaves but no fruit.

"May no one ever eat fruit from you again," Jesus pronounced (Mark 11:14). Then He went on to Jerusalem before returning to Bethany that evening. As Jesus and the Twelve went again to Jerusalem the next morning, they saw the fig tree withered down to the roots. Peter, remembering the incident from the previous morning, observed, "Rabbi, look! The fig tree you cursed has withered" (v. 21).

Critics of the Bible point to this event as evidence that Jesus was a human just like us, subject to loss of temper. They see Him acting out of disappointment and pique. However, a careful reading of the incident in the light of its context and Jesus's earlier teachings gives a quite different understanding.

First, we find this story in Matthew's Gospel as well as Mark's (Matt. 21:18–22). Neither writer displays any embarrassment or tries to water it down. Each obviously considered it important enough to include in his account.

Second, we must remember that the cursing of the fig tree took place during the Passion Week. Every word and act of Jesus during those days deserves our closest scrutiny. Nothing is superfluous; everything is freighted with significance. Since the incident did not occur in full view of the crowds (only the disciples witnessed it), clearly Jesus intended that it should teach them a vital lesson.

Third, the cursing of the fig tree is a prophetic sign-act; that is to say that Jesus delivered a message through an action that embodied it (for examples in the Old Testament, see Jer. 13:1–11; Ezek. 4:1–13).

Fourth, Jesus's act links directly with a short but powerful parable of a barren fig tree that He told earlier during His ministry (Luke 13:6–9). Each year the owner of the vineyard came seeking fruit, only to be disappointed—the fig tree had leaves but no fruit. So he told the gardener to give the fig tree one more year. Then, if it failed to bear fruit, he should cut it down. The fig tree symbolized unrepentant Israel (see also Isa. 5:1–7), and the parable indicated that judgment was coming against them.

Two details from Jesus's cursing of the fig tree drive home the lesson that He sought to convey to His disciples. The fact that the tree had leaves but no fruit meant that it would not bear any fruit at all. Mark notes that "it was not the season for figs" (Mark 11:13), so Jesus did not really expect to find ripe figs on it. The tree was a fake, just as the religious leaders of Israel had become all show without the fruit of righteousness that the Lord expected of His people.

Mark mentions that by the next morning the fig tree had withered from the roots. Such a rapid loss of life surely was unusual: one morning it was covered with leaves, but by the next morning it was totally dead. Thus the incident points us away from a purely natural event with natural causes to divine judgment that hangs over unrepentant people.

In Mark's telling of the story he places the cleansing of the temple squarely between the cursing and the sighting of the withered tree the next day. He records no other teaching or act of Jesus that day apart from the dramatic act in the temple.

The connection between the prophetic sign-act and the temple is surely not coincidental. The rot lay at the center of the nation's worship. Under many corrupted religious leaders, the temple had become a hollow show, with scrupulous concern for ritual but a place where love of money (on the part of the priests) supplanted love for God. So far from God's plan and will had the temple services departed—so bankrupt of true spirituality—that the priestly class who organized and led them failed to recognize the Lord of the temple when He came to His own. And not merely did they not recognize Him, but they set about to murder Him! Despite abundant leaves, this tree would never bear fruit. And it would be smitten by the divine hand, withering to the roots.

Messiah Comes to His Temple

The temple that Jesus knew—in which He was dedicated as an infant, where at age twelve He met with the teachers of the law, and into which He entered on Palm Sunday—was much larger than Solomon's temple. Herod the Great replaced and enlarged the temple built under Zerubbabel when the Jews returned from exile in Babylon, and the work was still going on during Jesus's ministry.

One would expect that those who served in the temple would provide models of spirituality for Israel. In Jesus's day, however, the exact opposite was the case. The high priestly office had become embroiled in politics and money-grubbing; it was sold to the highest bidder.

We cannot be sure when Jesus drove out the merchants and money changers. Matthew's and Luke's accounts suggest that it happened on the Sunday evening after the triumphal entry (Matt. 21:12, 13; Luke 19:45, 46), but Mark puts it on the following day. Of that Sunday Mark simply tells us, "Jesus entered Jerusalem and went into the temple courts. He looked around at everything, but since it was already late, he went out to Bethany with the Twelve" (Mark 11:11).

Since Mark gives a graphic description of Jesus's cleansing the temple the next day, his account more likely presents the correct order of events. Matthew and Luke telescoped the visits of Sunday evening and Monday. According to Hurtado, "ancient Jewish evidence indicates that there had been markets for the purchase of sacrificial animals on the Mount of Olives overlooking the Temple for some time, under the jurisdiction of the Jewish Council (Sanhedrin). In about AD 30 or so, the high priest seems to have authorized the setting up of similar businesses in the Temple precincts, and this is very likely what Jesus was protesting."[1]

Mark's description of Jesus's actions rivets us: "Jesus entered the temple courts and began driving out those who were buying and selling there. He overturned the tables of the money changers and the benches of those selling doves, and would not allow anyone to carry merchandise through the temple courts" (11:15, 16).

Jesus didn't just drive out animals. He expelled the merchants, pushed over tables (sending coins rattling everywhere), and overturned benches. He physically prevented anyone from carrying goods through the temple. What was going on with Jesus? What happened to the shepherd of Isaiah's prophecy?

> He tends his flock like a shepherd:
> He gathers the lambs in his arms
> And carries them close to his heart;
> He gently leads those that have
> young. (Isa. 40:11)

Jesus fulfilled those words during His ministry in Galilee. But the Scriptures had also predicted another side to the Messiah:

> "Then suddenly the Lord you are seeking will come to his temple. . . . But who can endure the day of his coming? Who can stand when he appears? For he will be like a refiner's fire or a launderer's soap. He will sit as a refiner and purifier of silver; he will purify the Levites and refine them like gold and silver." (Mal. 3:1–3)

Jesus didn't act out of character when He threw out merchants and money changers and took charge of traffic in the temple courts. He was Lord of the temple. Its services were supposed to point to *Him*. And the religious establishment had defiled the temple, turning it into "a den of robbers" (Mark 11:17), supplanting true worship by moneygrubbing, It was time for Jesus to don the role of refiner.

The Jesus that emerges in this scene changes our preconceptions, two of them in particular. First, the image of "gentle Jesus, meek and mild" simply won't cut it. Here we see a strong and angry Jesus who takes over and uses force. It is a portrait of the Master that has found far too small a place in Christian reflection and art, both anciently and still today.

Second, manipulation of spiritual activities for financial benefit infuriates the Master. Jesus and mammon don't mix—never have and never will. What must He feel today when His name gets invoked in the same breath as appeals for money to make the preacher rich? How would He react to bingo, bazaars, and bake sales in our "temples"? Let's beware of taking Jesus lightly. He is still the refiner who comes to His temple.

Challenged by the Religious Hierarchy

The Messiah had come to His temple, but He found it a hostile place, full of plotting bent on His murder. It had become the heart of a religious system gone to seed, in which ritual had banished spirituality, and filthy lucre counted for more than pleasing God. When the Messiah came to His temple, it wasn't just the Messiah *in* His temple; it was the Messiah *versus* the temple.

The first group to confront Jesus, perhaps as soon as He arrived—"while Jesus was walking in the temple courts"—comprised the leaders, "the chief priests, the teachers of the law and the elders" (Mark 11:27). Their challenge did not involve the rightness or wrongness of Jesus's actions. They simply appealed to authority. "By what authority are you doing these things?" (Mark 11:28). No doubt they had in mind the events of the day before when Jesus had driven out the merchants and money changers.

The leaders' challenge finds echoes in every age wherever functionaries of a religious system place the system itself above issues of truth and right. We find it as far back as the Old Testament when God called Amos, a shepherd of Tekoa, to go to Samaria with a message against the calf worship at Bethel. Amaziah the priest of Bethel tried to intimidate the prophet: "Get out, you seer! Go back to the land of Judah. Earn your bread there and do your prophesying there. Don't prophesy anymore at Bethel, because this is the king's sanctuary and the temple of the kingdom" (Amos 7:12, 13).

But Amos wasn't cowed by the effort to put him in his place; nor did Jesus back off. To the question of authority He posed a counter question: "I will ask you one question. Answer me, and I will tell you by what authority I am doing these things. John's baptism—was it from heaven, or of human origin? Tell me!" (Mark 11:29, 30).

It wasn't an evasive response. In the answer to Jesus's question lay the answer to the leaders' question: the One behind both Jesus and John the Baptist was God. Both spoke at divine direction. They were not only messengers of God's will, but they were linked in mission with John the forerunner of the Messiah and Jesus the Messiah Himself.

By Jesus's counter question, He challenged the religious hierarchy to come clean about their opinion of John. That put them on the spot. If they affirmed the Baptist's divine calling, they would be forced to acknowledge Jesus, of Whom John spoke also. But to deny John publicly—the encounter took place in full view and hearing of others in the temple courts—would incur the anger of the people, who looked on the Baptist as a prophet.

Of course, the leaders rejected both John and Jesus. Bound up in robes of self-righteousness and self-importance, they could brook no challenge to their position as the spiritual hierarchy. But to reveal their thinking would be politically incorrect, so they evaded Jesus's question by replying, "We don't know" (Mark 11:33).

Jesus replied, "Neither will I tell you by what authority I am doing these things" (v. 33). In effect: "You have your answer. You rejected John, and now you reject Me."

"We don't know." How much more evidence would it take—how many more miracles and words of life—before they would know? There would never be enough to convince them, because they had closed their eyes and shut their ears to God. Wrapped in robes of their own weaving, they retreated before the truth into the safety of the system.

A Searching Parable

The leaders had confronted Jesus with a challenge. Now He told a parable in their hearing. Although a crowd was present (Mark 12:12), everyone could discern the thrust of the words: it was a message aimed squarely at the leadership.

Jesus's hearers were familiar with the Song of the Vineyard in the book of Isaiah: "I will sing for the one I love a song about his vineyard: My loved one had a vineyard on a fertile hillside. He dug it up and cleared it of stones and planted it with the choicest vines. He built a watch-tower in it and cut out a winepress as well. Then, he looked for a crop of good grapes, but it yielded only bad fruit" (Isa. 5:1, 2). Jesus retold the story, giving it a new twist. Whereas in Isaiah the emphasis falls on the failure of the vineyard, representing Israel, to produce fruit, now the focus shifts to the tenants of the vineyard, who do not appear in Isaiah's version.

In Jesus's parable the tenants behave disgracefully. They ill-treat the succession of servants that the owner dispatches to them, beating some, insulting others, and even killing several. And the tenants never send any fruit to the owner. Why do the tenants act so brazenly? Because they fail to recognize their place—that they aren't the owners but mere tenants. They have usurped the rights of the owner.

Jesus's parable cut the religious leaders to the quick. They would have loved to seize Him on the spot, but they were afraid of the crowd. His words struck home because their attitude toward the temple and religious affairs mirrored that of the tenants. While failing to produce the fruit of righteousness, they had forgotten that God was the object of the temple worship and Israel's religion.

The parable now rises to a climax. The owner "had one left to send, a son, whom he loved. He sent him last of all, saying, 'They will respect my son'" (Mark 12:6). But the tenants, blind to reality in their self-absorption, instead saw the son's arrival as an opportunity to seize the inheritance for themselves.

"So they took him and killed him, and threw him out of the vineyard" (v. 8). Their reaction is incredible, even at the level of story. Our sense of justice rises up in indignation at the wickedness of the tenants and in astonishment at their self-delusion. How could they be so stupid? Did they think they could get away with murder?

If the tenants' actions amaze and repulse us, what shall we say of the application? What colossal stupidity and blindness of self-delusion led to the religious leaders treating the Son of God in the very same way: "They took Him and killed Him, and threw Him out of the vineyard" (v. 8)? Jesus spoke these words on Tuesday. Three days later the religious establishment would take and kill Him outside the city of Jerusalem.

An Unholy Plot by an Unholy Alliance

The religious leaders went away, but continued to scheme. "Keeping a close watch on him, they sent spies, who pretended to be sincere. They hoped to catch Jesus in something he said, so that they might hand him over to the power and authority of the governor" (Luke 20:20). Works of darkness make strange bedfellows. Normally the Pharisees and Herodians were poles apart in ideology. But both groups hated Jesus sufficiently to lay aside their differences in a common cause.

They approached Him with words of flattery. "Teacher," they said, "we know that you speak and teach what is right, and that you do not show partiality but teach the way of God in accordance with the truth" (v. 21).

These flowery but totally insincere phrases were designed so that Jesus would let down His guard and say something they could use against Him. Then came the question, so harmlessly couched but loaded: "Is it right to pay the imperial tax to Caesar or not? Should we pay or shouldn't we?" (Mark 12:14, 15).

Either way—however Jesus replied— they had Him. If He said no, the Herodians could report it to Pontius Pilate, and Jesus would be in big trouble. But if He said yes, the Pharisees could accuse Him of going along with the hated Roman occupation.

The annual tax levied by Rome especially vexed the Jews. Not only did it demonstrate their subject status, but it had to be paid in Roman money. The common coin, the denarius, bore the likeness of the emperor with the inscription "Tiberius Caesar, Augustus, Son of Divine Augustus"—that is, as a semidivine being. Such a claim was blasphemous and greatly offended the Jews.

Jesus met the seemingly difficult situation in masterly fashion. Cutting through the claptrap, He flung a question back at His enemies: "You hypocrites, why are you trying to trap me?" (Matt. 22:18). Then He asked them to hand Him a denarius.

"Whose image is this? And whose inscription?" He asked (Matt. 22:20),

holding up the coin and forcing them to reveal their hypocrisy.

"Caesar's," they mumbled, squirming before the crowd.

Then came the classic statement, "So give back to Caesar what is Caesar's, and to God what is God's" (Matt. 22:21). By it Jesus established a legitimate but specific role for the state. He separated Himself from those in His time or any time who use violence or other means to overthrow government in order to establish a theocracy. But He likewise distanced Himself from any and all efforts to elevate the state to divine claims—as the inscription on the denarius implied.

A Trick Question

One more group of people tried to embarrass Jesus. The Sadducees approached with a stock question and motives every bit as slippery as those of the previous critics.

Since the Sadducees left no writings, our knowledge of them is more limited. They denied the resurrection (Luke 20:27), and Luke notes that in addition they rejected the existence of angels and

Silver denarius, a day's salary for a common worker

Shekel, worth four denarii

spirits (Acts 23:8). The Sadducees were "a minority religio-political Jewish party of New Testament times representing the wealthy, aristocratic, liberal, secular-minded wing of Judaism. . . . They had a strong concern f or the secular affairs of the nation, willingly accepted public office, and exerted an influence far beyond that which their numbers would seem to warrant."[2]

The Sadducees apparently accepted only "the Law"—the first five books of the Bible—as inspired. Yet, strange as it seems, they held the high priesthood during the time of Jesus. How far had Jewish spiritual affairs fallen! The leaders of Israel's worship at the temple were secular individuals whose focus fell on events in this life instead of the hereafter.

Relishing debate with the Pharisees, who affirmed the resurrection, the Sadducees liked to embarrass them with a story from the Apocrypha of the woman who married seven brothers in succession. They now put it to Jesus, not with any intent to learn truth, but to make fun of Him and any belief in an afterlife. The punchline seemed to make their argument unassailable: "At the resurrection whose wife will she be, since the seven were married to her?" (Mark 12:23).

But Jesus didn't squirm. Instead He replied, "Are you not in error because you do not know the Scriptures or the power of God? When the dead rise, they will neither marry nor be given in marriage; they will be like the angels in heaven" (vv. 24, 25). Then He quoted Exodus 3:6, in which the Lord calls Himself "the God of Abraham, the God of Isaac, and the God of Jacob" as biblical proof that the dead will rise (v. 26).

In several books of the Old Testament—notably Job, Psalms, Isaiah, and Ezekiel—we find allusions to the resurrection. However, the Sadducees apparently did not accept the inspiration of such books. Hence Jesus quoted from the portion that they did accept—the Law, or Pentateuch. By doing so He called upon a biblical proof that, so far as is known, the Sadducees had never discerned.

In Luke's account of the same incident we find these additional words: "He is not the God of the dead, but of the living, *for to him all are alive*" (Luke 20:38; emphasis added). That is, although Abraham, Isaac, and Jacob—and indeed, all the righteous ones of the ages—die and

Half shekel, worth two denarii

rest in the grave, they are bound up in the life of God. And that life will inevitably call them forth from the tomb at God's appointed time (see Col. 3:3, 4).

So, Jesus said, the Sadducees really didn't understand the very Scriptures in which they took pride, nor did they know God's power—His ability to change the present world order of marriages, births, and deaths. The Sadducees had made this life the measuring stick of the future, but in doing so had neglected God. How true this still is!

Concerning the future world order, Ellen G. White writes:

> There are men today who express their belief that there will be marriages and births in the new earth, but those who believe the Scriptures cannot accept such doctrines. The doctrine that children will be born in the new earth is not a part of the "sure word of prophecy." The words of Christ are too plain to be misunderstood. They should forever settle the question of marriages and births in the new earth. Neither those who shall be raised from the dead, nor those who shall be translated without seeing death, will marry or be given in marriage. They will be as the angels of God, members of the royal family.[3]

A Sincere Question

The day was wearing away, but Jesus received yet another question. It came from a scribe, and unlike the previous ones it arose from a true heart. "You are not far from the kingdom of God," Jesus said to the inquirer at the close of the conversation (Mark 12:34).

The person who posed the question was a teacher of the law. Members of the group devoted themselves to the study of the Scriptures and had high respect for their learning. We might conclude that a life devoted to the study of the Word would result in godliness, but it does not necessarily follow. True, the Word has power to transform, but only if the heart is open to the divine influence. When people study the Bible primarily to acquire knowledge, they can become learned teachers far from the kingdom of God. And the acclaim that one receives from others closes the heart even more tightly against God's will. Thus it was in Jesus's day and still is. Some of the leading scholars of the Bible today make no profession of following Jesus Christ, the Lord of the Word.

In the Gospels, therefore, we find the scribes as a class united with those who oppose Jesus and eventually want Him out of the way. Jesus directed some of His sharpest criticisms against the "teachers of the law and Pharisees, hypocrites" (see Matt. 23, especially vv. 13, 15, 23, 25, 27, 29). And here, as His last day of public teaching drew to a close, Jesus said:

> Watch out for the teachers of the law. They like to walk around in flowing robes and be greeted with respect in the marketplaces, and have the most important seats in the synagogues and the places of honor at banquets. They devour widows' houses and for a show make

lengthy prayers. These men will be punished most severely. (Mark 12:38–40)

While Jesus condemned the scribes as a class, He did not dismiss them out of hand. His ear was open to any individual who was ready to listen to Him, regardless of what group they might belong to. And so when one of the teachers of the law raised a sincere question, Jesus commended him for his honest search to know and follow God's will.

The scribe's question raised a matter that the Jews frequently discussed: "Of all the commandments, which is the most important?" (Mark 12:28). The Jews counted 613 commandments in the Torah and understandably looked for an organizing principle or center for all of them.

The scribe in question had been listening intently to Jesus's debate with the Sadducees. Noting that Jesus "had given them a good answer" (v. 28), he decided to raise the longstanding question as to the heart of the law—not to try to trap Him but out of a sincere desire to hear His response.

Jesus replied by quoting two passages from the Torah. He designated the first one He cited, which we find in Deuteronomy 6:4, 5, as "the most important." "Hear, O Israel: The LORD our God, the LORD is one. Love the LORD your God with all your heart and with all your soul and with all your strength." Then he quoted Leviticus 19:18: "Love your neighbor as yourself."

So the center of the law is in the heart. As with all 613 commandments, the law ultimately reaches beyond what we can reduce to rules, for love cannot be spelled out. It was the same point Jesus elaborated in the Sermon on the Mount when He called for a righteousness that surpasses that of the Pharisees and the teachers of the law (Matt. 5:20).

The final comment by Jesus in this encounter with the teacher of the law leaves us wondering. "You are not far from the kingdom of God," the Master commended him (Mark 12:34). But "not far" is still outside. Did the scribe eventually open his heart all the way and become a follower of Jesus? How I would like to know!

"And from then on no one dared ask him any more questions" (Mark 12:34). Jesus had silenced them all—priests, elders, Pharisees, Sadducees, Herodians, and teachers of the law. But there still remained one final question to close off the day. With this one, however, Jesus would turn the tables.

The Final Question

Jesus asked one more question. Through it He challenged the teachers of the law as "the large crowd listened to him with delight" (Mark 12:37). But His query involved far more than matters of interpretation. It was the ultimate question for the teachers of the law, for the crowd, and for us today.

"'Why do the teachers of the law say that the Messiah [Christ] is the son of David?' He asked. 'David himself calls him "Lord." How then can he be his son?'" (vv.

Prutah, worth 1/64 of a denarius

35, 37). Jesus, here quoting Psalm 110:1, showed that it wasn't sufficient merely to call the Messiah the Son of David. The Messiah would be more than David's descendant: He would be his Lord, one far greater than the ancient Israelite king.

Through this discussion Jesus pointed to a more important subtext, specifically the issue of Who He was. For years rumors and whispers about the preacher-healer from Galilee had stirred the people. Could the long-awaited Messiah have come? And just a couple days before, Jesus had ridden into Jerusalem in triumph with the crowd hailing Him as the Messiah.

Now He in effect confronted the teachers of the law and the crowd: "You say I am the Messiah, but do you realize who Messiah will be? Not just the Son of David, but Lord of David!"

Here we have the incident at Caesarea Philippi replayed. "'Who do people say the Son of Man is?' . . . 'But what about you?' . . . 'Who do *you* say I am?'" (Matt. 16:13–15).

It was Jesus's final question because it is the ultimate one that haunts men and women in every age. That's because Jesus is the Man Who won't go away. Reject Him we may, spit on His face, turn our backs on Him—but He is still *there*.

A Gift of Love

The Master had had a long and trying day. Conservative critics, liberal critics, and political critics had all sought to embarrass Him before the crowds in the temple or to garner material that they could use against Him in court. But Jesus had deflected each thrust with grace and Scripture-laced skill. Now, as He was about to leave the temple for the last time, He encountered someone at the lowest rung of the social order but who ranked high on heaven's list.

As He sat by the temple treasury and watched the crowd putting in their money, He noticed a poor widow, trying not to be seen, drop in two *lepta*—two copper coins, the smallest in circulation, worth less than a penny in today's currency. The widow quickly slipped away unnoticed and unappreciated by all—except Jesus.

"Calling his disciples to him, Jesus said, 'Truly I tell you, this poor widow has put more into the treasury than all the others. They all gave out of their

Bronze lepton, worth 1/128 of a denarius

wealth; but she, out of her poverty, put in everything—all she had to live on'" (Mark 12:43, 44). Commentators and preachers customarily focus on the smallness of the widow's gift, but Jesus regarded it in just the opposite terms. For Him, it was a magnificent gift, huge and sacrificial. Not how little—but how much!

After the widow dropped in the two *lepta*, she had nothing left. Nothing in the bank. No credit card. No stash of cash under the bed. She gave her last money, little as it was but big as it was. And nobody noticed that her gift was so great. Nobody—except Jesus. He still notices today.

QUESTIONS FOR DISCUSSION

1. Study the Parable of the Two Sons, found only in Matthew (21:28–32). How does it fit with Jesus's answer about authority in verses 23–27?

2. How do Jesus's cursing of the fig tree, His cleansing of the temple, and the parable of the tenants all teach the same truth? What is that truth?

27

The Last Thursday

<table>
<tr><td>**OBJECTIVES**</td><td>• Trace the events of the last Thursday of Jesus's life.</td></tr>
<tr><td></td><td>• Understand the meaning of the Last Supper.</td></tr>
<tr><td></td><td>• Grasp what so distressed Jesus about His experience in the Garden of Gethsemane.</td></tr>
<tr><td>**SCRIPTURE**</td><td>• Matthew 26:1–5, 14–46; Mark 14:10–42; Luke 22:1–46; John 13:1–38; 18:1–11</td></tr>
</table>

We come at last to the climax of Jesus's ministry. For this end was He born—born to die! He was "the Lamb slain from the foundation of the world" (Rev. 13:8, KJV). The manger in Bethlehem foreshadowed the cross.

In one sense we are all born to die. Death is the great inevitable in human experience. "The living know that they shall die," as Ecclesiastes tells us (9:5, KJV). Because we come into a world cursed and blighted by the Fall of the race, our life is a one-act play—beautiful, often comic, but always tragic. Every life ends the same way in this drama.

But the Babe of Bethlehem would face death not as any human being before or since. He would confront death, wrestle it to the ground, and vanquish it. By His dying He would set humanity free, by His suffering He would release joy, and by His despair He would bring hope.

The moment of His dying would be at once tragic and glorious, combining defeat and victory, extinction and salvation. All heaven and all humanity held its breath then.

The final portions of all four Gospel accounts focus on those hours. In this chapter we feel the rush of events as the gathering storm of hatred and opposition reaches crisis point. First, however, we shall pause to notice how John writes concerning the Passion Week.

John's Account of the Passion Week

The broad outline of events of the Passion Week is the same in all four Gospels: the week begins with the triumphal entry into Jerusalem on the Sunday and ends with

Jesus resting on the Sabbath in Joseph's new tomb after having been crucified and buried on Friday.

As elsewhere, John passes by information already noted in the three earlier Gospels and instead supplies additional details. Thus, John's account makes no mention of Jesus cleansing the temple, the cursing of the fig tree, or the series of confrontations in the temple between Jesus and the religious teachers, the poor widow and her gift of love, or Jesus's private instruction to the disciples about the destruction of the temple and events far into the future.

On the other hand, if we possessed only the Synoptic Gospels, our understanding of this final week of Jesus's life on earth would be greatly diminished. In the thickening plot to get rid of Jesus, we wouldn't be aware that the raising of Lazarus from the dead played a major role because of the huge and continuing interest that it aroused (see John 12:9–11, 17–19). Nor would we know about the Greeks who had come up to Jerusalem for Passover, and the Father's voice that came from heaven as Jesus, seeing in the Greeks a foretaste of the harvest that would result from His mission, spoke concerning His impending death (see vv. 20–36).

John makes no mention of the "This is my body . . . this is my blood" formula that we find in the Synoptic Gospels, but he alone informs us that during the Master's final meal with His friends, He washed their feet. Further, John gives us a vivid picture of the interaction between Jesus and Judas at that final meal, closing the dramatic account with poignant words as Judas went out: "And it was night" (John 13:30).

Then follows Jesus's final discourse, given privately, just to the Eleven (Judas having left). Occupying four full chapters of the Gospel (John 14–17), it contains precious spiritual instruction to which the followers of Jesus have often turned over the centuries for hope, counsel, and comfort. We studied much of this material in considering Jesus's teaching about the Holy Spirit (chap. 17).

Beyond these differences in content between John's Gospel and the Synoptics is a marked change of *time*, signaled by the words "glory" and "glorify." As he wrote, the aged apostle looked back over the years to that time many years before when he was privileged to walk and talk with the Word Who "became flesh," having seen His glory, "full of grace and truth" (John 1:14). As he came to the Passion Week—the climax of Jesus's life and ministry—he saw it suffused with light. Even in the midst of betrayal, scourging, and agony, Jesus was fulfilling the Divine will. He was saving the world; He was the Lamb of God slain for us all. Thus, in chapters 12 through 21 of his Gospel, John uses the words "glory" and "glorify" more than twenty times. In John's account, more than anywhere else in the Bible, we find the *meaning* behind the story of Jesus.

Before leaving this discussion of John's account and transitioning the other three, we should notice an item that has led to extended, ongoing debate among scholars of the Scriptures. The point is interesting but does not, in the final analysis, affect our understanding of the Passion Week.

The issue is this: Precisely when did Jesus die in relation to the Passover? According to the Law, the Passover lamb was to be slain on the fourteenth day of the first month of the Jewish calendar, that is, on Nisan 14, and eaten with bitter herbs and unleavened bread the following evening, that is, Nisan 15 (see Exod. 12:1–16). According to John's account, the crucifixion took place on "the day of Preparation of the Passover" (John 19:14), that is, on Nisan 14 (Matt. 26:17, 20, 26, 34, 47; 27:1, 2, 31; Mark 14:12, 16, 17; Luke 22:7, 8, 13–15; John 13:2, 4, 30; 14:31; 18:1–3, 28; 19:16). But the Synoptic accounts—not John's—call the Last Supper a Passover meal (Matt. 26:17, 20; Mark 14:12, 16, 17; Luke 22:7, 8, 13–15).

Thus John's Gospel places the official celebration of the Passover meal

twenty-four hours later than the Last Supper. This puts it on Friday night, which would be Nisan 15 and the correct day according to the stipulation in Exodus 12:1–16.

The Passover lamb pointed to Jesus, "the Lamb of God who takes away the sin of the world" (John 1:29). Paul calls Jesus our Passover lamb: "For Christ, our Passover lamb, has been sacrificed" (1 Cor. 5:7).

Jesus died on Friday afternoon of Nissan 14, the very time when the Passover lamb was to be slain. Jesus could not have eaten the actual Passover meal on the previous night; it was impossible for Him to die at the designated hour and yet eat the Passover meal, which came on the following night. John's account is correct concerning the date of Jesus's death while the Synoptic gospels are not wrong regarding Jesus's celebration of the Last Supper with His disciples.

We return now to the events of the last Thursday as they unfolded.

Intrigue

In considering the life of Jesus, especially its final events, we easily fall into the mistake of failing to give full weight to its grim reality. We have heard the Passion recited perhaps scores of times and even seen reenactments, and its familiarity may cause us to think of it as merely a story and assume an element of unreality, like a Hollywood production.

Further, Scripture makes clear that behind the scenes God was directing the drama to its appointed conclusion. As we already noted, three times Jesus tells His disciples point-blank that He will be betrayed, mocked, rejected, and killed in Jerusalem, but that He will rise again from the dead. Repeated references to events happening to fulfill prophecy add to the sense of divine inevitability in the Passion.

Let's be perfectly clear: the events of the Passion were terribly and grimly real for Jesus. Although God predicted what would happen, the risk of failure and eternal loss did not decrease one whit. Jesus struggled and was tested to the limit. Jesus could have quit; He could have failed.

Thus, while the Godhead's eternal plan to win back a lost world worked itself out, every moment in the drama was pregnant with possibilities for good or bad choices. God was working out a divine plan, but other plans were also being hatched and put in place.

"Then the chief priests and the elders of the people assembled in the palace of the high priest, whose name was Caiaphas, and they schemed to arrest Jesus secretly and kill him" (Matt. 26:3–4). It had been their plan for some time. During the previous months their resolve had hardened. Without doubt the crowd's acclamation on Palm Sunday made them determined to act without delay. Time was running out. They had to put the upstart peasant from Galilee out of the way before He did more damage to their authority. Jesus threatened the whole religious establishment that centered on the temple and that provided them with power and prestige.

So for the enemies of Jesus the question was not what to do, but how and when. Gladly would they have openly arrested Him, but that wouldn't have worked—Jesus had the support of the crowds. "Not during the festival," they said, "or there may be a riot among the people" (Matt. 26:5).

Their problem was that Jesus was constantly in the midst of a crowd. Each morning He walked into the city, and each evening He departed. Probably many other pilgrims—including those from Galilee—were doing the same thing. Nights Jesus spent outside the city—not in a village like nearby Bethany, where they might have tracked Him down, but in the open (see also John 7:53–8:1).

Then an unexpected solution fell into the hands of His enemies. One of Jesus's close associates sought them out and offered to make a deal. He would lead them to Jesus at a time and place away from the crowds. "Then Satan entered Judas, called Iscariot, one of the Twelve. And Judas went to the chief priests and the officers of the temple guard and discussed with them how he might betray Jesus. They were delighted and agreed to give him money. He consented, and watched for an opportunity to hand Jesus over to them when no crowd was present" (Luke 22:3–6).

The chief priests and teachers of the law were planning their moves, and so was Jesus. He avoided exposing Himself to a quick, quiet arrest. Not only did He spend nights outside the city from Sunday through Wednesday, but when Thursday came He kept secret the location for the Passover meal.

The disciples, wondering what the plan was, asked Jesus, "Where do you want us to go and make preparations for you to eat the Passover?" Jesus's reply showed that He already had made a private arrangement: "Go into the city, and a man carrying a jar of water will meet you. Follow him. Say to the owner of the house he enters, 'The Teacher asks: Where is my guest room, where I may eat the Passover with my disciples?' He will show you a large room upstairs, furnished and ready. Make preparations for us there" (Mark 14:12–15).

Had Jesus said, "Look for a woman carrying a jar of water," that would have been no help. In that society *women* carried the water. But a man with a water jar? That would be a clear signal. Jesus did not tell them to say anything to the man. Rather, they were simply to follow him to the house where they would find the large upper room laid out for Passover. Clearly, Jesus had friends in Jerusalem—friends beyond the Twelve who would work secretly with Him to provide a place for Passover and keep it confidential.

John's Gospel sheds further light on the intrigue surrounding Jesus's time in Jerusalem. We read that on an earlier occasion "Jesus hid himself, slipping away from the temple grounds" (John 8:59), and that as Passover drew near, "the chief priests and Pharisees had given orders that anyone who found out where Jesus was should report it so that they might arrest him" (John 11:57).

In light of this cat-and-mouse aspect of the last days of Jesus's life, Judas's treachery becomes all the more reprehensible. No wonder Jesus's enemies were "delighted" when Judas came to them (Luke 22:5). Had Judas all along planned to betray his master, or did something happen to tip the scales?

The Last Supper

Jesus looked forward to the last meal with His friends and declared, "I have eagerly desired to eat this Passover with you before I suffer" (Luke 22:15). The "hour" that Jesus had spoken about many times and for which He now steeled Himself was about to break over Him. These moments with the Twelve would be their last time together until after the Resurrection. And then, of course, the Twelve would become the Eleven—Judas would be no more.

The disciples knew nothing of all this. Although Jesus had repeatedly tried to prepare them for the crisis in Jerusalem, they remained confused, unable to break out of the shell of preconceived messianic notions.

"While they were eating, Jesus took bread, and when he had given thanks, he broke it." Giving it to His disciples, He said, "Take and eat; this is my body" (Matt. 26:26). Then, picking up the cup, He offered a prayer of thanks and handed it to them. They all drank from it, and Jesus said, "This is my blood of the covenant, which is poured out for many" (v. 28).

All four Gospels record Jesus's final meal with His friends. The accounts in Matthew, Mark, and Luke are quite similar. From John, however, we learn that Jesus washed the disciples' feet (John 13:1–17), and we find no mention of the "This is my body . . . this is my blood" formula. As elsewhere, John apparently passes over information already noted in the three earlier Gospels and instead supplies additional details.

Luke's account of the Supper includes Jesus's admonition: "Do this in remembrance of me" (Luke 22:19), and the early Christians did so. Some twenty years later Paul wrote to Christians in Corinth, and his letter makes clear that they gathered together to observe the Lord's Supper (1 Cor. 11:20). However, Paul was displeased over their conduct at the Supper. They combined the actual Supper (the bread and the wine) with a more extensive meal, as Jesus did on that last Thursday night. In Corinth, however, some members ate well while others had nothing. Paul counseled them to take their meal at home before the Supper and so avoid the abuse of Christian fellowship (vv. 21–34).

The Last Supper has become a rite of the Christian church. Known as Communion, or the Lord's Supper, it is observed by almost all who take the name of Jesus (with a few exceptions, such as the Salvation Army). In the large body of believers that in time became known as the Roman Catholic Church, the Supper assumed major importance. By the end of the second century we can discern two trends converging: the movement to regard ministers of the gospel as priests, and the Lord's Supper—administered only by a priest—as having sacramental value. In time, the teaching of the Mass emerged full-blown, wherein the priest, by pronouncing the words of the institution, becomes creator of the Creator, as the wafer (bread) becomes—so it is taught and believed—the actual body of Christ and the wine His actual blood.

Did not Jesus say to the Twelve, "This is my body . . . this is my blood"? Indeed.

But He obviously did not mean the words literally. Picture the scene. Jesus was reclining around the table with His friends. When He broke the bread and passed the cup, He was *there*, separate and apart from the bread and the wine. He and the Twelve *knew* that the bread wasn't His body or the wine His blood. Instead, by partaking of them they were choosing to identify themselves with Him in His passion. If we simply go back to that Thursday night and think through the scene and Jesus's words, we must realize how far from the original intent the teachings of the Mass have come.

Note 1 Corinthians 10:16—"The cup of blessing which we bless, is it not the communion of the blood of Christ? The bread which we break, is it not the communion of the body of Christ?" (NKJV). Consider also 1 Corinthians 11:23–26, which declares the bread and wine to be a remembrance of the death of Jesus. The book of Hebrews argues emphatically that Christ died once for all—He is not sacrificed again and again every time someone celebrates the Lord's Supper. "Nor did he enter heaven to offer himself again and again, the way the high priest enters the Most Holy Place every year with blood that is not his own. Otherwise Christ would have had to suffer many times since the creation of the world. But he has appeared once for all at the culmination of the ages to do away with sin by the sacrifice of himself" (Heb. 9:25, 26).

Gethsemane

Just outside the eastern wall of Jerusalem in the Kidron Valley, below the Mount of Olives, lies a grove of olive trees. Its name, *Gethsemane*, means in Hebrew "olive press." The garden probably had a press for extracting oil that lent its name to the site.

As we have seen, Jesus was a man of prayer. Throughout the Gospels we find Him communing with the Father, often spending the entire night in prayer. When He visited Jerusalem, the garden became for Him a retreat from the demands of the crowd and the intrigues of foes. It was a quiet place and hallowed spot. But on this Thursday night, this last night of the Savior's earthly life, He found no repose here. Gethsemane became for Him the "olive press" indeed as events crushed, squeezed, and wrung dry His soul.

"Gethsemane"—the word conjures up countless paintings, sermons, and meditations. Jesus's struggle in the olive grove outside Jerusalem just prior to His arrest has moved Christians for two thousand years and still grips our interest today. Perhaps as nowhere else in the Gospels we see here the humanity of Jesus laid bare, showing His closeness to us. We also sense mystery as we wonder why He agonized to such an extent that night.

All four Gospel writers record the event—Matthew, Mark, and Luke in accounts closely parallel (Matt. 26:36–46; Mark 14:32–42; Luke 22:39–46) and John in a variant form (John 17:1–18:2).

We find another voice in the book of Hebrews in which the writer, arguing strongly for the true humanity of Jesus, observes, "During the days of Jesus' life on earth, he offered up prayers and petitions with fervent cries and tears to the one who could save him from death, and he was heard because of his reverent submission. Son though he was, he learned obedience from what he suffered" (Heb. 5:7, 8).

The language in Hebrews is very strong, both in translation and in the original Greek. Jesus did not pray silently: He pleaded with God through "fervent cries and tears." We know what He prayed for, because even though the disciples kept dozing off, they couldn't help hearing His imploring words: "*Abba*, Father, . . . everything is possible for you. Take this cup from me. Yet not what I will, but what you will" (Mark 14:36). The cup of woe, separation, and desolation was leading Him to feel godforsaken, as it contained the sins of fallen humanity.

Once, when James and John came to Jesus seeking the best seats in the kingdom, He asked them, "Can you drink the cup?" (Mark 10:38). In their foolish self-confidence they replied, "We can" (v. 39). But they could not. Only in part would they as followers of Jesus eventually share His experience.

Jesus's cup was His and His alone. Only He could drink it and become the Sin Bearer for a lost world. And praise God, He *did* drink it. He lifted it high and drained it to the dregs, taking the last sin of the last sinner on Himself. Jesus, the book of Hebrews tells us, *tasted death* for everyone (Heb. 2:9).

In Gethsemane that cup trembled in the hands of a man—yes, the God-man, but a man nonetheless. His humanity shrank from the ordeal. He sought a way out—provided it was from God. But there was no other way.

Of all the words written about Gethsemane, none seems to lift the veil on its mystery and speak to the heart more than those by Ellen White:[1]

> Turning away, Jesus sought again His retreat, and fell prostrate, overcome by the horror of a great darkness. The humanity of the Son of God trembled in that trying hour. He prayed not now for His disciples that their faith might not fail, but for His own tempted, agonized soul. The awful moment had come—that moment which was to decide the destiny of the world. The fate of humanity trembled in the balance. Christ might even now refuse to drink the cup apportioned to guilty man. It was not yet too late. He might wipe the bloody sweat from His brow, and leave man to perish in his iniquity. He might say, Let the transgressor receive the penalty of his sin, and I will go back to My Father. Will the Son of God drink the bitter cup of humiliation and agony? Will the innocent suffer the consequences of the curse of sin, to save the guilty? The words fall tremblingly from the pale lips of Jesus, "O My Father, if this cup may not pass away from Me, except I drink it, Thy will be done."

Peter

Mark 14 records that a crisis broke, and all the disciples failed miserably. Jesus in His hour of extremity sought the companionship and support of praying friends. But they slept.

He warned them that the hour of testing was upon them, and that they needed to watch and pray. Instead they ignored His words. When the mob came and seized Jesus, His disciples deserted Him and fled.

Although all the disciples failed, Peter's performance was especially shameful. At the Supper he had been so confident: "Even if all fall away, I will not" (v. 29). And when Jesus told Peter that he would disown Him three times that very night, the disciple brushed the possibility aside, asserting emphatically, "Even if I have to die with you, I will never disown you" (v. 31).

Yet he did. Within only a few hours, Peter's resolve collapsed like a sand castle swept away by a mighty wave. Confronted by a servant girl, he denied that he knew Jesus, and then repeated it again and again, eventually lacing his betrayal of the Master with profanity. This was Peter at his worst. It is us at our worst. How quickly we make promises, and how quickly we break them. How fair are our words of loyalty to Jesus, but how base our actions of betrayal.

The beloved John was there in the upper room when Jesus had predicted, "You will all fall away" (v. 27). He joined the others in insisting that they would never desert Him. But when they all turned their backs on Jesus in Gethsemane and fled, John ran away too.

But here's the difference between John and Peter: John entered the courtyard of the high priest—in fact, it was he who got Peter admitted (John 18:15, 16)—but he did not publicly deny Jesus. He did not try to conceal his association with his Master. Peter's failure was a base act—no way to deny it. He, so often ready to speak for the rest, failed the rest. And above all, he failed his Master.

So far will self-confidence take us down the path of ruin. We think that we are strong enough to withstand the assaults of the enemy and that nothing can shake our loyalty to Christ. But we cannot foresee what even a day may bring. Only by living as Paul did—"I have been crucified with Christ and I no longer live, but Christ lives in me. The life I now live in the body, I live by faith in the Son of God, who loved me and gave himself for me" (Gal. 2:20)—can we be guarded against denying the Master. And only as we realize and put into practice "for when I am weak, then I am strong" (2 Cor. 12:10) can Jesus supply grace sufficient for every situation.

"Grace"—that's the final word in Peter's story. He failed miserably, but Jesus brought him back. When the cock crowed and Jesus turned and looked at him, Peter broke down and wept (Mark 14:72). Jesus brings hope to those who break down and weep. He offers us another start—a second chance.

There are two betrayals in this story. One man plotted with Jesus's enemies to betray Jesus and did. One man never expected to betray Jesus—that was furthest from his intent—but also did. One man ended in a suicide. The other died following his Lord, crucified as He was.

QUESTIONS FOR DISCUSSION

1. Has anyone else ever suffered like Jesus did in Gethsemane? Explain your answer.

2. What was the year of Jesus's death? Look up *The Seventh-day Adventist Bible Commentary*, vol. 5, 251–254 concerning the date of Jesus's death.[2]

3. Contrast the betrayal of two of Jesus's disciples, Judas and Peter. Why are the results of their unfaithfulness different?

The Judge on Trial

OBJECTIVES

- Follow Jesus through the long night of trial in the hands of His enemies.

- Grasp the issues involved in the religious and civil charges brought against Jesus.

- Compare and contrast the experiences of Peter and Judas.

SCRIPTURE

- Matthew 26:57–75; 27:11–26; Mark 14:53—15:15; Luke 22:63—23:25; John 18:12—19:16

The setting for this chapter in the story of Jesus seems incongruous: the Judge of the universe being tried by creatures of His hand! Early in His ministry Jesus had declared, "Moreover, the Father judges no one, but has entrusted all judgment to the Son" (John 5:22). Who are they, then, who take it upon themselves to put the Son of God on trial?

These enemies will one day stand in the dock of God's tribunal. They, together with the rest of humanity, will need to give an accounting to the Son, who will be their judge. Of one aspect of that assize we may be sure: they will receive a fairer hearing than the one they gave Jesus. He, the Judge of all the earth, will do right (Gen. 18:25). They weren't concerned about right and justice; they sought only one outcome—Jesus's condemnation. All the sham proceedings and sham witnesses were manipulated to achieve this end. For them, the outcome of the trial of Jesus was clear before the first word was spoken—they wanted Jesus eliminated.

The events of this late Thursday and early Friday produced incredible ironies. We find in this chapter a pagan ruler trying hard to save Jesus while the religious leaders, ostensibly the spiritual guardians, wanted Him dead. This same ruler will call Jesus "King of the Jews" while His own people shout, "Crucify Him!" (Mark 15:13). The ruler, sensing that Jesus is innocent, offers to release Him, but the crowd calls out for a murderer, Barabbas, instead.

In this night of trial, as in the events of Friday after the day dawned, we see evil unmasked in all its hideousness. The age-long foe of Jesus in the great controversy between good and evil, working through human beings, hurls all his hellish weapons against the suffering Son of God, now seemingly so helpless. Jesus stands alone. All His friends have run away, and two of the Twelve publicly betray Him. No one, not even the beloved John, remains loyal.

Jesus will endure this long, sleepless night of beatings, mocking, scorn, and lying accusations—totally alone. Yet He is not alone. As heaven looks down and weeps while Satan and his legions rejoice, the Lamb of God hangs on by faith in His Father's love.

Arrested in the Garden

They came in the night to take Jesus. Night suited their schemes, for they were bent on murder. Night hid their actions from the throngs of pilgrims who had come to Jerusalem for Passover and who would have forestalled the evil plans.

Jerusalem slept. The light of a full moon beamed down on the city, bathing all in a sacred calm. But while most people rested, perhaps dreaming of the slaying of Passover lambs the next day, some people were wide awake. In the palace of the high priest Caiaphas, plans were afoot. This was the night that priests and religious teachers had long awaited. This night their thoughts and talk were not about sacred things, but instead about murder. This night they would seize Jesus and send Him on the path to death. The annoying carpenter from the north, this troublesome miracle-worker, would be forever removed as a threat to their power. They had it all worked out, and it could not fail. One of Jesus's own, one of the Twelve, would lead them to their prey.

They came to Jesus in a large band— soldiers, priests, teachers of the law. Why so large a contingent to seize only one man? The numbers suggest that they were afraid. Once before they had ordered the temple guards to arrest Jesus, but the guards returned empty-handed (see John 7:32, 45–49). They wanted to avoid a repeat of that fiasco.

Perhaps, despite their denials and disclaimers about Jesus, they were also secretly apprehensive as to how this Man might respond when they tried to seize Him. It was said that in Galilee He had turned water into wine, fed thousands of people from just five barley loaves and two small fish, and had calmed the angry waters. What if . . . ? They came armed to the teeth: swords, clubs, spears. How little they understood of the life and teachings of the Prince of Peace!

Jesus knew they were coming for Him. He saw the flashes of light from their lamps and torches, and He heard the sound of their approaching footsteps as they made their way through the olive grove. But He didn't move, run, or hide. Instead He went out to face them. "Who is it you want?" He asked them (John 18:4).

"Jesus of Nazareth," they replied.

"I am He" (v. 5).

And at that, "they drew back and fell to the ground" (v. 6). Ellen G. White, commenting on this event not mentioned in the Synoptic Gospels, informs us that an angel momentarily came between Jesus and the mob.[1] Even with this signal of divine approval of Jesus, however, the mob quickly regained their feet to pursue their murderous plot.

Now occurred the most heinous act of the whole heinous evening. Judas, who had led the crowd to the Garden, stepped forward. "Rabbi!" he greeted Jesus. Then he kissed Jesus repeatedly (the Greek verb used implies that this was no brief, casual kiss).

"Judas, are you betraying the Son of Man with a kiss?" responded the Master (Luke 22:48). I wonder how Judas felt when he heard those words—spoken in sadness, spoken in love. Did his heart want to break? Did he want to fall at Jesus's feet and beg for forgiveness?

Jesus's other disciples didn't betray their Lord like Judas, but they massively failed the test. They had slept when they should have stayed awake and joined Jesus in prayer; now, when the crisis burst upon them, they were caught unprepared.

Peter, who earlier that same night had boasted that he would never forsake his Lord, now reacted with irrational bravado. Drawing a sword, he began to flail around. All he succeeded in doing was cutting off the ear of Malchus, a servant of the high priest.

"Put your sword away!" Jesus commanded. "Shall I not drink the cup the Father has given me?" (John 18:11). "All who draw the sword will die by the sword. Do you think I cannot call on my Father, and he will at once put at my disposal more than twelve legions of angels?" (Matt. 26:52, 53). A Roman legion consisted of about six thousand foot soldiers and twelve horsemen.

Jesus's words and actions gave the decisive answer concerning where He stood as to the use of force. He refused to defend Himself and forbad His followers to attempt to do so.

It was all too much for boastful Peter. Now embarrassed, confused, and disheartened, he took to his heels and ran. The other ten fled with him. Jesus was left alone with the murderous mob. They tied Him up and led Him away.

Jesus and Caiaphas

In the time of Jesus, the Jews were a people subject to Rome. They had to pay taxes to Rome, suffer the indignity of being ruled by a Roman governor, and have Roman soldiers on their soil. They did not have the authority to execute offenders. The Romans permitted them to have authority in matters of their religion, but they restricted capital punishment to the jurisdiction of the governor.

Jesus's enemies, therefore, could not simply arrest Jesus, try Him before their court (the Sanhedrin), and then execute Him (which would be by stoning). They had to obtain the death sentence from

Pontius Pilate, the Roman governor for the province of Judea and Samaria.

All four Gospels describe two different types of trial that Jesus faced in the early hours of Friday. The first focused on religious concerns, with the Sanhedrin sitting as a court. Here the intent wasn't to determine Jesus's guilt or innocence—the religious leaders had already agreed to have Him executed—but rather to arrive at charges that they could present to the people. Jesus enjoyed a high level of popular support, especially in Galilee. Now, at Passover, hundreds of thousands of pilgrims had crowded into Jerusalem, and many of them came from Galilee.

The enemies of Jesus, determined to eliminate Him, realized that they had to act carefully. Prior to the Passion Week, they had decided to postpone any attempt to

"The Sanhedrin in Session"

arrest Jesus until after the festival, but unexpectedly Jesus had fallen into their hands. If the crowd perceived their real intent, a riot might have ensued with Jesus set free by popular demand.

This concern on the part of the religious leaders that their plot might backfire perhaps accounts for the seeming uncertainty of their actions after they had Jesus in custody. They seem not to have agreed on a well-thought-out plan before they put Jesus on trial.

The soldiers with their commander and Jewish officials first took the Master to Annas, who was the father-in-law of Caiaphas the high priest. Annas had been high priest but was removed from office by Vilerius Gratus, the Roman procurator (governor) who ruled over Judea and Samaria. Annas was highly regarded, with many of the Jews considering him to be the rightful high priest. In course of time, five of his sons and his son-in-law Caiaphas became high priest.

Annas, however, did not succeed in establishing Jesus's guilt, so He was next taken to the palace of Caiaphas (see John 18:24). John reminds us that this wily individual was the same "one who had advised the Jewish leaders that it would be good if one man died for the people"

(John 18:14; see also John 11:49, 50). Cunning and conniving, Caiaphas was more concerned with political matters than leading the nation spiritually.

Recent archeological discoveries around Jerusalem have shed light on the high priesthood in the time of Jesus. Excavations have revealed that the priests lived luxuriously in large homes with mosaic floors. Interestingly, artifacts from these homes include large stone vessels for holding water to be used in purification rites. At a different site—one for

> **CAIAPHAS**
>
> Appointed high priest about AD 18 by the Roman procurator Valerius Gratus and deposed about AD 36, Caiaphas was son-in-law of the former high priest Annas, with whom he is occasionally mentioned (Luke 3:2; Acts 4:6). Caiaphas took part in the court procedures against the apostles Peter and John (Acts 4:6), as well as those against Jesus. An ossuary bearing the name "Joseph son of Caiaphas" has been discovered. It may contain the bones of the high priest Caiaphas.

burying—remains have been uncovered that very likely are those of Caiaphas.

How far the high priesthood had fallen from its inception in the time of Moses. Now it had become as much a political office as a spiritual one. The office was powerful and lucrative, and therefore much sought after. The century prior to Jesus recorded political maneuvering, scheming, and even murder as candidates for high priest vied with one another to secure the coveted appointment.

The Roman procurator had the last word on the appointment of the high priest. As in the case of Annas, he could intervene and have him deposed. This meant that the high priest, whoever he might be, must necessarily be politically astute and keep close to the governor.

So they faced each other in court, Jesus and Caiaphas. One man, clothed in fine garments and with fawning attendants at the ready, was primarily a secular, political creature. He belonged to the Sadducees, which meant that he believed in neither angels nor resurrection. Jesus could expect no concern for justice from this individual. Yet this same Caiaphas, out of a twisted sense of religiosity, was scrupulous about ceremonial purity. He and his fellows later that morning wouldn't enter the governor's palace lest they become defiled and not be able to eat the Passover meal (see John 18:28). They didn't want to get their hands dirty, but they had no compunctions about trumping up charges against Jesus.

The high priest begins to question Jesus about His disciples and His teaching. "I have spoken openly to the world," Jesus replies. "I always taught in synagogues or at the temple, where all the Jews come together. I said nothing in secret. Why question me? Ask those who heard me. Surely they know what I said" (John 18:20, 21).

But Caiaphas didn't want to call as witnesses those people who had heard Him speak. They would have had nothing negative to say about Jesus. Jesus's words were a telling rebuke of how Caiaphas was conducting the trial. Sensing the dynamic, one of the officials standing nearby slapped Jesus in the face. "Is this the way you answer the high priest [that is, to expose his hypocrisy]?" he demanded (v. 22).

"If I said something wrong, testify as to what is wrong," Jesus replied. "But if I spoke the truth, why did you strike me?" (v. 23). Why indeed? When evil meets the truth, its only recourse is violence.

So far the arraignment wasn't going as planned. Next Caiaphas called up false witnesses, but they did no better. When you try to find something against One Who always tells the truth, Who is Truth, what can you come up with?

Getting frustrated, Caiaphas stands up and says to Jesus, "Are you not going to answer? What is this testimony that these men are bringing against you?" (Mark 14:60).

Jesus remains silent. Now Caiaphas tries one final gambit. He will attempt to have Jesus incriminate Himself.

"I charge you under oath by the living God. Tell us if you are the Messiah, the Son of God" (Matt. 26:63).

And to this challenge Jesus does speak. "You have said so. . . . But I say to all of you: From now on you will see the Son of Man sitting at the right hand of the Mighty One and coming on the clouds of heaven" (v. 64).

Jesus tells the truth—always. He *is* Truth. He would not stay silent, even though the answer gave Caiaphas just what he has been seeking. Jesus's reply took all who heard back to the vision found in the seventh chapter of the prophet Daniel: "In my vision at night I looked, and there before me was one like a son of man, coming with the clouds of heaven. He approached the Ancient of Days and was led into his presence. He was given authority, glory and sovereign power; all nations and peoples of every language worshiped him. His dominion is an everlasting dominion that will not pass away, and his kingdom is one that will never be destroyed" (Dan. 7:13, 14). By identifying Himself with the Son of Man of Daniel's prophecy, Jesus in effect made Himself God by claiming divine glory and divine prerogative.

Jesus's answer amazed Caiaphas. From Jesus's own lips came blasphemy far beyond any that the high priest had hoped to hear. Caiaphas ripped his clothes in a display of shocked horror. "He has spoken blasphemy! Why do we need more witness? Look, now you have heard the blasphemy. What do you think?"

And they all cried out, "He is worthy of death" (Matt. 26:65, 66).

Then they surrounded Jesus. In a studied effort to humiliate the Master—in a procedure that sociologists refer to as a degradation ritual—they spit on Him, punched Him, taunted Him.

Others slapped Him and said, "Prophesy to us, Messiah. Who hit you?" (v. 68).

The farce of a religious trial was over. All that remained for the religious leaders

BREAKING THE RULES

"In spite of their desire to give the impression that they were following due process, the Sanhedrin broke many of its own rules that would eventually be encoded in the Mishnah. In capital cases, for example, a guilty verdict required a second sitting of the court on the following day, both sittings had to take place during the daytime, and neither could be on the eve of a Sabbath or a festival. . . . One modern expert has documented nine legal errors in Jesus' trial."[2]

was to find charges by which Jesus could be successfully accused before the Romans.

Jesus and Pilate

Both individuals who presided at Jesus's trials—Caiaphas the high priest and Pontius Pilate at the civil trial—failed lamentably in their duties. The former totally abandoned all attempts to ensure that justice was done; he and his fellows determined that Jesus should die before proceedings began.

Pilate, on the other hand, quickly saw through the machinations of the Jewish religious leaders. He wanted to release Jesus and tried several times to find a way to do so. Finally, however, he gave up all efforts at fair play and yielded to the demands of the Jews.

Pilate's vacillating actions in the trial of Jesus stand in contrast to his usual behavior as recorded by both Jewish and

History records Pilate, Roman prefect of Judea AD 26–56, as inflexible, stubborn, and harsh. He offended the Jews by having his soldiers march into Jerusalem carrying standards to which images of the emperor were attached. He shocked the Jews further by using money from the Temple treasury to pay for the construction of an aquaduct to bring water into Jerusalem. Pilate crushed opposition ruthlessly.

Complaints concerning his cruelty were taken to the emperor, and led to Pilate being banished to Gaul (now France). He is said to have ended his life there by suicide.

Because of his role in the crucifixion of Jesus, the figure of Pontius Pilate exerted a continuing fascination for many Christians. Over the centuries a large body of legendary literature grew up in several languages. The most surprising and extreme development was in the Coptic tradition, where by the Middle Ages Pilate was hailed as a saint.

An inscription unearthed at Caesarea in 1961 identifies Pilate as "prefect of Judaea." Prior to this find he was understood to have the title of procurator. His responsibilities as prefect embraced maintaining law and order, collecting taxes, construction works, and deciding major (capital) crimes.

Roman writers. They portray him as a vindictive person with a furious temper, inflexible and cruel. We find Pilate mentioned in the Gospels in one other place before the Passion Week: "Now there were some present at that time who told Jesus about the Galileans whose blood Pilate had mixed with their sacrifices" (Luke 13:1). History doesn't shed light on this incident, but the writers of the time recorded similar atrocities at Pilate's hand.

Pilate was governor for Judea, Samaria, and Idumea. The governor's palace was located in Caesarea Maritima; Pilate did not live in Jerusalem. However, during the three big festivals of the Jewish year—Passover, Pentecost, and Tabernacles—he moved to that city in order to be on hand if a disturbance broke out with the many pilgrims who had come to worship.

According to the Jewish writer Philo, Pilate was responsible for "continual murders of people untried and uncondemned."[3] But when the Jews brought Jesus and demanded His execution, Pilate hesitated. As we study the accounts by Matthew, Mark, Luke, and John, we find Pilate making four successive efforts to set Jesus free.

First effort: Pilate quickly concluded that the Jewish authorities were attempting to use the power of Rome for their own purposes: he knew that it was out of envy that the chief priests had "handed Jesus over to him" (Mark 15:10). The religious leaders hurled accusations against Jesus—subverting the nation, opposing paying taxes to Rome, and claiming to be a king (Luke 23:2). When the governor questioned Jesus personally, however, he determined that Jesus's kingdom was not a threat to Caesar, because it was "not of this world" (John 18:36). Pilate was ready to release Jesus, but the chief priests vehemently objected.

Second effort: Learning that Jesus was from Galilee, Pilate tried to refer the trial to Herod Antipas, who was in Jerusalem at that time. This was the same King Herod who was responsible for the shameful execution of John the Baptist. For a long time Herod had wanted to see Jesus; now he hoped to have Jesus perform a miracle for his entertainment. But Jesus wasn't about to put on a magic show to please this dissolute monarch. He refused to say a word. Herod still wanted "some fun," so he "and his soldiers ridiculed and mocked Jesus. Dressing Him in an elegant robe, they sent Him back to Pilate" (Luke 23:11). The ball was back in Pilate's court.

Third effort: Pilate attempted to play upon the sympathies of the crowd. He had Jesus flogged—an excruciating punishment administered with a whip embedded with pieces of bone and metal in the lashes. The whipping tore the flesh from the body, exposing the bones; victims of flogging often died under its brutality.

So Pilate once more went out to the crowd. He said to the Jews: "'Look, I am bringing him out to you to let you know that I find no basis for a charge against him.' When Jesus came out wearing the crown of thorns and the purple robe, Pilate said to them, 'Here is the man!'" (John 19:4–5).

It didn't work. The mob wanted more than the sight of blood. They shouted, "Crucify! Crucify!" (v. 6). Pilate had gone down a path from which he could not retreat. He had publicly declared Jesus's innocence, yet he had subjected the Master to the fearful flogging. The bloodthirsty mob understood well what it all meant. The governor had shown himself to be weak, without moral backbone.

Fourth effort: Pilate tried the expedient of falling back on the Roman custom of releasing a prisoner from among the Jews at Passover time. He put up a radical insurrectionist named Barabbas, a man feared even by the Jews, as the choice over Jesus, leaving it to the crowd to choose. But the ruse misfired: to Pilate's surprise, they shouted out for Barabbas instead of Jesus.

"What shall I do, then, with Jesus who is called the Messiah?" Pilate asked.

"Crucify him!"

"Why? What crime has he committed?"

"Crucify him!" they cried even louder.

And Pilate caved in to the crowd. He set Barabbas free, and handed Jesus to the soldiers to be crucified (Matt. 27:22–26).

Peter and Judas

All of Jesus's disciples failed Him when the test came. Two failed in massive, public ways. And they were leaders among the Twelve.

Judas was perhaps the most intelligent member of the group. Certainly the others thought highly of him: they entrusted him with the finances. Judas was the "might have been." He might have been leader of the Twelve. He might have become a powerful influence for good in the early church. He might have had a gospel or epistle named for him in the New Testament.

But we will never have a "Gospel of Judas" or letters of Judas. Other apostles have had their names given to thousands of baby boys in many lands—think of all the Peters, Johns, Philips, and Matthews. But people do not name their children after Judas. That name, which might have been acclaimed in Christian history, has instead gone down in infamy.

Filled with remorse, Judas tried to return the thirty pieces of silver to the chief priest. "I have sinned," he cried out, "for I have betrayed innocent blood!" Then he threw the money into the temple, went out, and hung himself (Matt. 27:3–5).

Peter also failed his Lord—dismally and publicly. Three times he claimed that he never knew Jesus. Filled with remorse when the cock crowed, Peter remembered Jesus's warning to him given only hours before—the warning to stay alert and be on guard. His heart was cut to the quick; he went out and wept bitterly (Matt. 26:75).

But Peter, unlike Judas, didn't commit suicide. He came back. Back to a walk with the Lord. Back to acceptance by the other members of the band of disciples. Back to new and far greater service. How Peter came back—what brought a ray of hope in his darkest hours—will be a topic for us to consider later in this book. It is a wonderfully encouraging story of hope.

QUESTIONS FOR DISCUSSION

1. Only Matthew mentions the dream of Pilate's wife (Matt. 27:19) and Pilate washing his hands (v. 24). What do you learn from these incidents?

2. What made the difference between Peter and Judas?

Calvary

OBJECTIVES
- Learn the events of the day that Jesus died.

- Understand why all four Gospel writers devote so much attention to the death of Jesus Christ.

- Grasp the meaning and role of Jesus's death on the cross from the perspective of the plan of redemption.

SCRIPTURE
- Matthew 27:32–61; Mark 15:21–47; Luke 23:26–56; John 19:17–42

All roads lead to Calvary as the focal point of history. Everything before converges toward it, and everything afterward lies in its shadow. It is, as the apostle wrote, "the culmination of the ages" (Heb. 9:26).

It poses the supreme question of all time: Who was this Man who died there? During the course of centuries the Romans crucified thousands, but this cross was different. On that Friday—Good Friday to Christians—the crosses on either side of Jesus held impaled felons. We don't know their names, and history takes no notice of them. It's the cross in the center—*His* cross—around which the drama swirls. To believers, Calvary supplies the ultimate understanding of the ages. It answers such vital questions as these: Who was Jesus of Nazareth? What is God like? What is good, and what is evil?

Secular history provides almost no information about Jesus. The little that Roman writers noticed about Him was that Jesus was a Jew Who was crucified when Pontius Pilate governed Judea.

Matthew, Mark, Luke, and John tell us far more. For each of them, the events of Good Friday form the climax of the faith account of Jesus. They do not attempt to minimize the story. Nor do they reveal any hint of embarrassment that the One they confessed as Lord died as a common criminal, or make any effort to excuse or explain what happened. Their tone foreshadows that of Paul: "But God forbid that

I should glory, save in the cross of our Lord Jesus Christ, by whom the world is crucified unto me, and I unto the world" (Gal. 6:14, KJV).

Jesus was beaten so badly that He collapsed under the weight of the cross. The Romans conscripted Simon of Cyrene to carry it to the place of execution outside the gates of the city. There Jesus was stripped of all His clothing, fastened to the cross by nails hammered through His wrists and ankles, and lifted up for the final experience of humiliation and agony.

Even Jesus's clothes were no longer considered His possessions. The soldiers divided the garments into four parts—one for each soldier. For the *chitōn*, the long undergarment that was seamless and woven in one piece, they cast lots.

Jesus's enemies, triumphant at last over the One who had eluded them for so long, stood around the cross. They taunted Him, daring Him to save Himself. Eventually they had had enough of their callous sport and left Jesus to wait out His final hours alone. But Jesus wasn't left totally alone, as His mother Mary and the other faithful women remained. Of those disciples who had been closest to Him, the Twelve, only John the Beloved remained; the others had all fled, except for Judas, who had hung himself earlier in the day.

The Seven Words from the Cross

The accounts of the crucifixion in the four Gospels agree in the big picture but show individual variations in detail. By piecing the story together from all of them, we learn that Jesus uttered seven sayings as He hung on the cross. In Christian history these have come to be known as "the seven words from the cross":

1. "Father, forgive them, for they do not know what they are doing" (Luke 23:34). This was possibly the first of the seven "words," uttered as the spikes were being hammered through Jesus's wrists and feet.

2. "Woman, here is your son," spoken to His mother, and "Here is your mother," spoken to John (John 19:26, 27). In spite of the excruciating pain, Jesus's heart went out to Mary, who would be left alone.

3. "You will be with me in paradise," spoken to the criminal hanging alongside who expressed a measure of faith (Luke 23:43).

4. "My God, my God, why have you forsaken me?" (Matt. 27:46; Mark 15:34). Matthew and Mark record this cry of dereliction, reproducing the actual Aramaic words in which Jesus spoke. The words are a quotation from the great Davidic psalm of suffering (Psalm 22:1).

5. "I am thirsty" (John 19:28).

6. "It is finished" (John 19:30).

7. "Father, into your hands I commit my spirit" (Luke 23:46).

Mark tells us that "it was the third hour when they crucified him" (15:25,

NKJV), which is 9:00 a.m. "When the sixth hour [noon] came, darkness fell over the whole land until the ninth hour [3:00 p.m.]." This is when Jesus uttered the terrible cry, "My God, my God, why have you forsaken me?" (vv. 33, 34).

Shortly after, Jesus gave a "loud cry" and breathed His last (v. 37). Presumably, then, Jesus died about 3:30 p.m.—the very time when the lambs for Passover were being slaughtered. He, God's Passover Lamb, died right on time.

As Jesus suffered and died, heaven wept. How could it be—the King of heaven beaten and bloodied, insulted, scorned, humiliated, suffering, forsaken? But while heaven wept, the powers of darkness rejoiced. The cross was Satan's trump card in the contest with Jesus; he reasoned that Jesus would never consent to such a horrible end. Now he had his age-long enemy in his grasp—He Whom he first tried to challenge and usurp in the heavenly courts.

At Calvary, a parade of characters passes across the stage, and each of them invites our reflection. Pilate, the cruel official, who, strangely enough, became a saint in the Coptic tradition; Barabbas, who got off scot-free, in some ways a type of us; Simon of Cyrene, who carried Jesus's cross; the soldiers, who gambled for His clothing; the centurion, who watched over the scene and, observing how Jesus died, exclaimed, "Surely this man was the Son of God" (v. 39)—the only human Mark identifies in his Gospel as using this expression of Jesus

(everywhere else it's God and demons who call Jesus "Son of God").

Instead, let us turn our eyes on Jesus alone. Let us join the women as they watch from a distance. What do they see? What does Calvary mean?

Golgotha

Jesus was brought to the place called Golgotha (which means The Place of the Skull). There He was offered wine mixed with myrrh, but He did not take it. Then He was crucified (Mark 15:22–24).

The Romans did not invent the cross. That dubious honor probably belongs to the Phoenicians. But the Romans employed it for centuries to effectively deter opposition to their empire. They erected tens of thousands of crosses to enforce Roman rule.

The cross suited their purposes ideally. It was preeminently a means of public execution. The Romans paraded the opponents of the Pax Romana through the streets carrying their cross or part of

"The Church of the Holy Sepulchre"

"Rocky Escarpment Resembling a Skull,"
located northwest of the Church of the Holy Sepulchre

it. Passersby would see and shudder. The place of execution itself was a public one where crowds could see the fate of someone who dared to rise up against Rome. And death came slowly. The victim might linger for days, nailed or tied to the cross, until exposure and loss of body fluids finally brought merciful release.

The Romans employed the cross extensively, but no Roman citizen was ever to be crucified. The cross was a symbol of shame and humiliation—too horrendous for a citizen of Rome. The apostle Paul, for example, a Roman citizen, was not crucified. He was put to death with the sword. But Jesus of Nazareth, lacking Roman citizenship, could be crucified—and He was.

The spotless Son of God hung upon the cross, His flesh lacerated with stripes; those hands so often reached out in blessing, nailed to the wooden bars; those feet so tireless on ministries of love, spiked to the tree; that royal head pierced by the crown of thorns; those quivering lips shaped to the cry of woe. And all that He endured—the blood drops that flowed from His head, His hands, His feet, the agony that racked His frame, and the unutterable anguish that filled His soul at the hiding of His Father's face—speaks to each child of humanity, declaring, It is for thee that the Son of God consents to bear this burden of guilt; for thee He spoils the domain of death, and opens the gates of Paradise. He who stilled the angry waves and walked the foam-capped billows, who made devils tremble and disease flee, who opened blind eyes and called forth the dead to life,—offers Himself upon the cross as a sacrifice, and this from love to thee. He, the Sin Bearer, endures the wrath of divine justice, and for thy sake becomes sin itself.[1]

A Roman Cross

"The written notice of the charge against him read: THE KING OF THE JEWS" (Mark 15:26).

The people had come out to watch Him die. Fishermen jostled for a place with merchants, and priests elbowed out housewives for a better view. Some knew Him well; others hardly at all. Many had come just to see the sight and watch Him die. A number laughed and joked as the execution proceeded. A few wept—but they had to do it unobtrusively. The Romans would instantly crucify anyone who showed sympathy for the victim. The execution would take quite a while—certainly several hours—so they sat down on the grass and rocks to wait.

Soldiers were there too. Some of them stood on duty. After a while someone started a game of chance. An execution was nothing new to them—they had witnessed similar scenes many times before. Yet this public dying was different. How could these people have known that before the day's end the officer in charge would declare, "Truly this man was the Son of God" (v. 39, KJV)? How could they realize that the execution they were carrying out would become the symbol of a new religion?

With the crowd we stare at Jesus as He hangs dying on the cross. We wonder, *How has He come to this?* "Stop this gross miscarriage of justice!" we want to shout out. "Who is responsible for this diabolical act?" And as we watch Him, answers slowly come. Of course—the Romans were responsible! Roman authorities gave the orders for His death, and they nailed Him to a Roman cross.

Legally, it was a Roman execution. The Jews did not execute by crucifixion but stoned offenders to death. But first-century Palestine was under the subjugation of Rome, and the Jews no longer had authority to issue the death decree (John 18:31). A Roman governor signed the death warrant. "Don't you realize I have power either to free you or to crucify you?" Pontius Pilate asked Jesus (19:10).

The sign that Pilate had placed over Jesus's head served as a terrible witness to the power of Rome to deal with anyone who entertained any ideas of insurrection. Its message was: "This is what happens to anyone who tries to make himself a king!"

Each of the Gospels records the wording on the execution sign with slight variations understandable from eyewitness testimony:

> Matthew: "THIS IS JESUS, THE KING OF THE JEWS" (27:37).
> Mark: "THE KING OF THE JEWS" (15:26).
> Luke: "THIS IS THE KING OF THE JEWS" (23:38).
> John: "JESUS OF NAZARETH, THE KING OF THE JEWS" (19:19).

The central message of the sign is identical in all four accounts: "The King of the Jews." From the standpoint of the Romans, this was the key issue and the grounds for the execution of Jesus of Nazareth.

A Jewish Cross

"What shall I do, then, with the one you call the king of the Jews?" Pilate had demanded of the crowd.

"Crucify him!" they shouted.

"Why? What crime has he committed?" Pilate insisted.

But they yelled even louder, "Crucify him!" (Mark 15:12–14).

Jesus died on a Roman cross, but it was at the instigation of His own people. The cross of Jesus is more than a legal execution—it is a cross of rejection. "He came to that which was his own, but his own did not receive him" (John 1:11). When Pilate declared his innocence of the blood of Jesus, the crowd shouted out: "His blood is on us and on our children!" (Matt. 27:25). So the inscription on the cross, "The King of the Jews" (Mark 15:26), throbs with pathos.

But were the Jews Christ-killers? While the tragic rejection of Jesus as their King by their leaders is a historic fact, this does not mean that the Jews have been cursed by the Lord. When we turn back to the Gospel accounts of Jesus's crucifixion, we notice such statements as these: "When the chief priests and the Pharisees heard Jesus's parables, they knew he was talking about them. They looked for a way to arrest him, but they were afraid of the crowd because the people held that he was a prophet" (Matt. 21:45, 46).

The enemies of Jesus laid plans to take Him by stealth. "But not during the Festival," they said, "or there may be a riot among the people" (Matt. 26:5). And at the mockery of a trial before Pilate "the chief priests and the elders persuaded the crowd to ask for Barabbas and to have Jesus executed" (Matt. 27:20).

The members of the religious hierarchy had to persuade some of the populace to support their demands. If we speak of Christ-killers, we should limit the term to the ecclesiastical leaders, not to the Jews as a people. The disciples of Jesus support such a view: "The chief priests and our rulers handed him over to be sentenced to death, and they crucified him" (Luke 24:20).

The death of Jesus, then, does not give theological warrant for anti-Semitism. And have we forgotten Jesus's own prayer from the cross: "Father, forgive them, for they do not know what they are doing" (Luke 23:34)? Surely His petition is not to remain eternally unanswered. The cross is legally a Roman one. Religiously, it signifies His rejection by the leaders of His own people. And yet it represents even more. It is a divine cross.

A Divine Cross

When Pilate in the judgment hall boasted of his authority, Jesus gave him a surprising answer. "You would have no power over me if it were not given to you from above," He said (John 19:11). Also, in the Garden of Gethsemane at the time of His arrest—as the disciples prepared to defend Him—He commented, "Do you think I cannot call on my Father, and he will at once put at my disposal more than twelve legions of angels?" (Matt. 26:53). Such ideas drastically alter our conception of the cross. It was clearly more than a miscarriage of Roman justice and more than a tragic Jewish failure. In some way God was in and behind the death of Jesus.

Jesus, in fact, expected the cross. Months before He bore it, He had spoken of His death at Jerusalem. Throughout His ministry He alluded to "my hour" or "my time" that was "not yet" (John 7:6, 30; 8:20). Constantly He looked forward to the final events of His life. As He entered upon His last week, He knew what its end would be. "The hour has come for the Son of Man to be glorified," He said (John 12:23). And then, "I, when I am lifted up from the earth, will draw all people to myself" (v. 32). So in a sense neither the Romans nor the Jews killed Jesus. Neither Pilate nor the chief priests could have had power over Him unless He had permitted them.

Through the centuries the Romans erected tens of thousands of crosses. But this one stands alone in its uniqueness. It was an execution—but much more. God was working out a divine plan in the death of Jesus. "Christ died *for our sins*" was the affirmation of the first Christians

(1 Cor. 15:3; emphasis added). He tasted death *for everyone*—so they believed and preached (Heb. 2:9, 10).

Now we begin to understand why the cross is shrouded in divine mystery. The physical sufferings, though intense, were the least of Jesus's woes. Acute mental and spiritual anguish battered His being. His agonizing cry of desolation—"My God, my God, why have you forsaken me?" (Mark 15:34)—was the cry of a soul that looks into the maw of eternal nonexistence.

So the cross is a divine one. Through its terrible suffering Jesus died vicariously, that is, in our place. He was not being *punished* by God, for God had sent Him (John 3:16). Rather, through that cross God was "reconciling the world to himself" (2 Cor. 5:19).

My Cross

"For what I received I passed on to you as of first importance: that Christ died for our sins according to the Scriptures" (1 Cor. 15:3).

The apostle Peter declared of Jesus that "'He committed no sin, and no deceit was found in his mouth.' When they hurled their insults at him, he did not retaliate; when he suffered, he made no threats. Instead, he entrusted himself to him who judges justly. 'He himself bore our sins' in his body on the cross, so that we might die to sins and live for righteousness; 'by his wounds you have been healed'" (1 Pet. 2:22–24).

The entire New Testament teaches that Christ died for *our* sins, not for His own. Jesus is God's Lamb, "who takes away the sin of the world" (John 1:29). He is God's righteousness, given to us freely and received by faith as a gift (Rom. 3:21–25). And He is God's wisdom, Whose cross is foolishness to the Greeks and a stumbling block to the Jews but has divine power to save all who believe (1 Cor. 1:18–25).

Long before Jesus came, Isaiah had foretold Him as the Suffering Servant.

> Surely he took up our pain
>   and bore our suffering,
> yet we considered him punished by
>   God,
>   stricken by him, and afflicted.
> But he was pierced for our transgres-
>   sions,
>   he was crushed for our iniquities;
> the punishment that brought us peace
>   was on him,
>   and by his wounds we are healed.
> We all, like sheep, have gone astray,
>   each of us has turned to our own
>   way;
> and the Lord has laid on him
>   the iniquity of us all. (Isa. 53:4–6)

Would we condemn the Romans? We must protest their flouting of elemental justice in the death of Jesus. But we condemn ourselves too.

Would we call the Jews Christ-killers? Certainly not! We grieve at the tragic rejection of Jesus by their leaders. Perhaps they were representatives of us all. We would have done no better. Each of us also would have crucified Him. In fact, we *did* crucify Him, as He died for *our* sins.

"Were you there when they crucified my Lord?" challenges the old spiritual. And now we know that we were. His cross is every person's cross, for everyone is a sinner. It is our cross too. That is why the story of Calvary haunts humanity to this day.

But the good news of Christianity is that His cross *was* my cross. It no longer is mine. He took it in its shame, disgrace, humiliation, and despair. And in doing so, He transformed it from a curse into a blessing—from darkness into light, from despair into hope, and from a symbol of death into one of life.

Who killed Christ? The biblical answer is almost too shocking to repeat: I killed Christ! But it does not leave me despairing, because the cross is also the climax of a divine plan—it is my salvation. Through His death we find life.

Why Have You Forsaken Me?

"And at three o'clock in the afternoon Jesus cried out in a loud voice, '*Eloi, Eloi, lama sabachthani?*' (which means, 'My God, my God, why have you forsaken me?')" (Mark 15:34). Although on earth people mocked and taunted the Man on the center cross, leaving just a few women to weep, in heaven the songs were hushed. The Father's heart suffered with the anguish of the Son, and angels looked on in wonder at the measures to which divine love would go in order to win back a lost world.

Around noon, a strange darkness fell over Jerusalem. It was as though inanimate nature, suffering with its Creator, cast a veil over His final hours. Jesus was silent for a long while. Then He uttered a terrible cry: "My God, my God, why have you forsaken me?" (v. 34).

Let those who assume that Christ could not have failed contemplate that moan from the cross. Let those who reason that Jesus's sufferings were not real because He was God and knew that everything would end in triumph contemplate it as well. It is the cry of someone forsaken by God—the sob of dereliction and despair.

And when the devil comes with his allurements—the pleasures of sin that excite our senses and make the way of Jesus seem hard and dry—let us each remember that piercing wail from the darkness. Forever it tells how terrible is evil and how marvelous is the love of God.

Jesus, Who had enjoyed unbroken communion with the Father, now felt forsaken. Why?

> Upon Christ as our substitute and surety was laid the iniquity of us all. He was counted a transgressor, that He might redeem us from the condemnation of the law. The guilt of every descendant of Adam was pressing upon His heart. The wrath of God against sin, the terrible manifestation of His displeasure because of iniquity, filled the soul of His Son with consternation. . . .
>
> Satan with his fierce temptations wrung the heart of Jesus. The Savior could not see through the portals of the tomb. Hope did not present to Him His coming forth from the grave a conqueror, or tell Him of the Father's acceptance of the sacrifice. He feared that sin was so offensive to God that Their separation was to be eternal. Christ felt the anguish which the sinner will feel when mercy shall no longer plead for the guilty race. It was the sense of sin, bringing the Father's wrath upon Him as man's substitute, that made the cup He drank so bitter, and broke the heart of the Son of God.[2]

"It Is Finished"

From John's account we learn that Jesus's last words were "It is finished" (John 19:30). What sort of utterance was this? Was it a groan of relief—"It's over at last"—or was it a triumphal declaration that Jesus had won the decisive battle for our salvation? Surely the latter. There was rejoicing in heaven at the victory of Jesus.

> Now have come the salvation and the
>   power
>   and the kingdom of our God,
>   and the authority of his Messiah.
> For the accuser of our brothers and
>   sisters,
>   who accuses them before our God
>   day and night,
>   has been hurled down. (Rev. 12:10)

Jesus's last words on the cross have led evangelical Christians to speak of "the finished work of Christ." Some Christians dislike this language because it can be used to set aside the ongoing high-priestly ministry of Jesus in the heavenly courts. However, in several senses, we can legitimately comfort ourselves in the fact that Christ's parting shout signaled a decisive moment in time.

Jesus Offered a Complete and Final Sacrifice. With that cry, the veil of the Jerusalem temple was torn asunder. The system of sacrifices and offerings given anciently to Israel came to an end. All the multiplied deaths of animals in themselves could not atone for sin. They had educated the people of God in the plan of salvation by pointing forward to the Lamb of God, Who would take away the sin of the world (John 1:29).

We commemorate the dying of Jesus as we share in the Lord's Supper. But the bread and the wine are merely symbols to help us reenact Christ's last meal. They are not Christ's flesh and blood, for He died *once for all*, an all-sufficient sacrifice (Heb. 9:26, 28).

Jesus Unmasked the Character of the Devil. The cross was Satan's final and most powerful weapon. He thought that the Majesty of heaven would never stoop to such humiliation. But He did, revealing the matchless power of love. And thereby the devil exposed himself. He is a murderer and a liar who, despite his claims and deceptions, will stoop to any lengths to accomplish his ends, even killing God if he could.

Jesus Sealed Our Salvation. The war goes on, but its conclusion is not in doubt. Christ won the decisive battle. Satan is a defeated foe. He wounded Christ's heel, but Calvary struck the death blow to his head (see Gen. 3:15). "It is finished" (John 19:30) gives us strength in our struggles now and assurance of our eternal life in Him.

Forgiveness at the Cross

When the centurion, who stood there in front of Jesus, heard His cry and saw how He died, he said, "Surely this man was the Son of God" (Mark 15:39). They bound Jesus, but they could not restrain His power to set people free. They nailed Him to a cross, but even as He hung dying He extended forgiveness to people around Him.

Consider the three people who found salvation in Him that day—Simon of

Roman Centurion

Cyrene, the felon by His side, and the centurion.

Simon encountered Jesus seemingly by chance. He happened to be passing by when Jesus, hauling the crossbeam on the way to Golgotha, stumbled and fell beneath its weight. As Simon paused in sympathy, the soldiers conscripted him to carry the heavy beam. By chance? No. God's timing is exquisite; He put Simon at that spot at that moment. And Simon not only relieved Jesus's burden but became a believer. Thus Jesus could take Simon's own burden and make him free.

The dying thief seemed the unlikeliest candidate for heaven. His life lay in ruins, with only a few grains of sand left in his life's hourglass. Who could entertain hope for such a hardened criminal? But God saw differently. He never writes off any individual—no matter how hopeless or steeped in sin he or she may appear. If the felon on the cross could find salvation on Good Friday, so can *any* person we may meet. The power of Jesus's love, touching a human heart in its hour of extremity, can roll back the past and bring new life.

Even as Jesus was dying, he extended grace to the stranger passing by, the criminal in his death throes, and even a Roman officer. The centurion saw beyond the broken body dying on the cross; he saw Someone totally different from any criminal he had ever seen being executed. Seeing *how* Jesus died—especially the final "It is finished!"—he confessed faith in Jesus as the Son of God.

When the soldiers came to break Jesus's legs, they found that He was already dead. The two criminals crucified with Jesus were still alive, however; the soldiers broke their legs.

Jesus had died as a criminal, so normally His body would not have been given a decent burial. Joseph of Arimathea, a prominent person in the city and a secret follower of Jesus, now came forward openly. He went to Pilate and requested Jesus's body and, having received it, placed it in his privately owned tomb. A rock was rolled over the entrance and soldiers assigned to guard the sepulchre (Mark 15:43–46).

The women who had endured the long day's vigil observed as Jesus's body was placed in the tomb. They then went home and prepared spices and perfumes with which they intended to anoint the Master's body after the Sabbath.

So Jesus lay in Joseph's tomb—it was a cave cut from the rock. His body grew cold. All through the Sabbath hours, Mary's Son slept the sleep of death.

QUESTIONS FOR DISCUSSION

1. The chief priests and teachers of the law mocked Jesus as He hung on the cross: "He saved others, but he can't save himself" (Mark 15:31). How did they unwittingly express a profound truth with this statement?

2. Study Psalm 22 and list all the statements that prefigured the sufferings of Jesus on Calvary. On what kind of note does the psalm close?

3. Who was responsible for Jesus's death? Was it the Jews, Romans, God, us?

He Is Risen!

OBJECTIVES	• Explore the biblical record concerning the resurrection of Jesus.
	• Examine the evidence and arguments that support the factuality of Jesus's resurrection.
SCRIPTURE	• Matthew 28:1–20; Mark 16:1–20; Luke 24:1–49; John 20:1–31; 21:1–25

If the followers of the Jesus of Nazareth Who was crucified under Pontius Pilate did not believe that He rose from the dead, Jesus would be at best a footnote in history. There would be no Gospels and no Christian church. Nor would this book exist. The Romans during the course of their history executed by crucifixion scores of thousands of men and women. Only one victim came back to life.

In the Roman Empire the province of Judea-Samaria was notorious for being a hotbed of revolutionaries. The New Testament mentions several—Barabbas, jailed for committing murder during an uprising (Luke 23:18, 19); Theudas, who gathered a band of some four hundred followers (Acts 5:36); Judas the Galilean, who led a group of followers in revolt (Acts 5:37); and an unnamed Egyptian who started an uprising with four thousand terrorists (Acts 21:38). Some of the revolting leaders claimed to be the Messiah—most notably Bar Kochba, whose uprising against Rome brought down the unmitigated wrath of the Empire. These revolutionaries aimed to restore the Jewish kingdom. But only one King of the Jews—listed as such by the inscription over His head on the cross—was resurrected.

We cannot overstate the importance of the material of this chapter. If Jesus did not rise from the dead, all that He did and taught in that wonderful, unsurpassed life ultimately counts for nothing.

No wonder, then, that critics from the beginning of Christianity have tried to discredit the biblical accounts of the Resurrection. Stories were quickly made up to account for the missing body—some said that Jesus's disciples had stolen His body while the guard at the tomb slept (Matt. 28:11–15), while the pagan Porphyry in the third century charged that belief in the Resurrection rested on the words of some hysterical women. Still in our times the reliability of the Bible witness has been attacked.

Dead people don't come back to life: this is the argument. If someone did, it would be a miracle. But miracles don't happen—everything has a natural explanation. Or does it? If Jesus did rise from the dead, the discussion is no longer one of philosophy but of history. We are in the realm of *fact*, not conjecture or feeling. So let us examine the facts as a historian would. What do the Gospel writers tell us, as well as other writers of the New Testament, and do these accounts pass scrutiny?

First, a word about the "burial" of Jesus. The Jewish practice was quite different from what most people understand when they hear the word. Most Jewish burials in Palestine during Jesus's time followed a two-stage method. The body was first washed and totally wrapped in cloths with spices and perfume in the wrapping. Later, when all the flesh had decomposed, the bones would be collected, folded up, and put into a box called an ossuary. This would be stored in a loculus, a niche at the back of the tomb, or in some other convenient place.

Thus, burial did not involve a hole dug in the ground with dirt covering the body. The spices and perfume were essential to mitigate the odor of the rotting flesh. In Israel today, when a new road is built or construction projects begin, ossuaries often come to light.

This method of burial made it easy for anyone interested to find out if a body was still in the tomb. They had only to gain access to the tomb to see for themselves. It also made it easy for grave robbers to plunder the tomb for valuables placed with the body, or to steal the corpse. These considerations will be significant as we weigh the evidence for Jesus's resurrection.

Events of the First Sunday

It is very difficult, perhaps impossible, to reconstruct the exact sequence of events surrounding Jesus's resurrection. All four Gospel writers give separate accounts that do not point back to a common source. Each selects incidents that fit his overall presentation. And Mark's Gospel ends abruptly, leaving us with a question.

Having noted these differences, we should immediately observe that the four accounts are remarkably unified in their presentation of the main outline of what happened.

Appearances to the Women

All four writers record women as the first witnesses to the Resurrection.

Matthew

Mary Magdalene and "the other Mary" go to the tomb at dawn on Sunday morning. There is a violent earthquake; an angel of the Lord comes down from heaven and rolls away the stone. The guards are terrified at his appearance.

The angel says to the women, "Do not be afraid, for I know that you are looking for Jesus, who was crucified. He is not here; he has risen, just as he said. Come and see the place where he lay. Then go quickly and tell his disciples, 'He has risen from the dead and is going ahead of you into Galilee. There you will see him.' Now I have told you" (Matt. 28:5–7).

The women hurry away to tell the disciples. On the way Jesus meets them. "Greetings," He says. They worship Him and He says, "Do not be afraid. Go and tell my brothers to go to Galilee; there they will see me" (v. 10).

Mark

After the Sabbath, Mary Magdalene, Mary the mother of James, and Salome buy spices with which to complete the anointing of Jesus's body begun on the Friday afternoon. They go to the tomb very early on Sunday morning. On the way they wonder, "Who will roll away the stone from the entrance of the tomb?" (Mark 16:3).

But when they come to the tomb, they discover the stone already rolled away. They enter and see a young man dressed in white sitting to their right. They are alarmed. "Don't be alarmed," he said. "You are looking for Jesus the Nazarene, who was crucified. He has risen! He is not here. See the place where they laid him. But go, tell his disciples and Peter,

> **THE ENDING OF MARK'S GOSPEL**
>
> The oldest manuscripts of the Gospel of Mark end at 16:8, with the women afraid and fleeing the empty tomb of Jesus. That seems to be an abrupt end to this Gospel. Several other endings to the Gospel can be found, so we cannot be absolutely certain just where Mark intended to close. Ultimately, the question is interesting but not vital to our understanding. None of the proposed endings change the essential idea that Jesus rose from the dead and appeared to various people.

'He is going ahead of you into Galilee. There you will see him, just as he told you'" (vv. 6, 7). The women run from the tomb.

Luke

The account parallels those of Matthew and Mark. Bearing spices for the burial, the women come very early to the tomb. They find the stone rolled away; when they enter the tomb they find it empty. Suddenly two men in gleaming clothes appear beside them. The women are terrified but the men say, "Why do you look for the living among the dead? He is not here; he has risen! Remember how he told you, while he was still with you in Galilee: 'The Son of Man must be delivered over to the hands of sinners, be crucified and on the third day be raised again'" (Luke 24:5–7).

The women leave the tomb and tell the Eleven and all the others what they have seen and heard. But no one believes their tale, which seems "like nonsense." Peter, however, goes to the tomb and sees the strips of cloth lying there. He goes away wondering (see vv. 1–12).

As we consider these three accounts, we find they are agreed in all the essential facts. The differences in details are such as might be expected from different eyewitnesses and impart a sense of verisimilitude.

John

When we turn to the account in the fourth Gospel, we find repeated that pattern we observed earlier: John seems to assume that the reader is aware of the Synoptic accounts and, instead of repeating them, adds new information. The focus here is on Mary Magdalene. She comes very early to the tomb ("while it was still dark") and sees that the stone has been removed from its entrance. Running to Peter and "the other disciple," she exclaims, "They have taken the Lord out of the tomb, and we don't know where they have put him" (John 20:2). Peter and John run to the tomb. John arrives first, looks in, sees the strips of linen lying there, but doesn't go in. Peter arrives and goes in, and then John enters. Seeing the strips of linen and the burial cloth that had been around Jesus's head lying folded up and separate from the linen, John believes.

The disciples go back home, but Mary stands weeping outside the tomb. She stoops down and looks into the tomb, and there she sees two angels dressed in white and sitting where the body had lain. When the angels ask her why she is weeping, she replies, "They have taken my Lord away, and I don't know where they have put him" (v. 13). Then she turns around and sees Jesus standing there, but she doesn't recognize Him.

"Woman, why are you crying? Who is it you are looking for?"

"Sir [thinking Jesus is the gardener], if you have carried him away, tell me where you have put him, and I will get him."

"Mary."

"Rabboni" (vv. 15, 16).

Then Jesus tells Mary not to detain Him, for He hasn't yet returned to the Father. Instead, she is to go to the disciples and tell them, "I am returning to my Father and your Father, to my God and your God" (v. 17).

Mary gives the news to the disciples: "I have seen the Lord" (v. 18).

The striking aspect of these four accounts is the role they assign to women. All agree that one or more women came to the tomb very early on Sunday morning and discovered that the body of Jesus had disappeared. They all agree that the risen Jesus appeared to women before He was seen by the Eleven. This feature of the Gospel accounts is of major import. In the ancient world, among both pagans and Jews, women were not considered credible witnesses in the law court. Thus, these four accounts strongly suggest that they were based on solid historical evidence. No one would have fabricated a story about women as witnesses for the resurrection of Jesus.

Appearance to Peter

Upon meeting the women at the tomb that Sunday morning and instructing them to tell the disciples that Jesus had risen from the dead, the angel specifically mentioned Peter: "But go, tell his disciples and Peter" (Mark 16:7).

The Sabbath just past must have been the worst of Peter's life as over and over his mind retraced the events in the courtyard of Caiaphas when he so cowardly denied his Lord, and then the ordeal of Jesus dying on the cross. Now, Sunday morning, the women bring a message from the risen Lord that He wants to meet the disciples—including Peter!

Jesus did meet Peter one-on-one that same day. We don't know when or where, or what transpired, but we can be sure that it happened. Sunday night when Cleopas and his companion returned from Emmaus to Jerusalem they found the Eleven and others gathered together and saying, "It's true! The Lord has risen and has appeared to Simon" (Luke 24:33, 34). The apostle Paul, writing to the believers in Corinth in the early AD 50s, lists in order the post-Resurrection appearances of Jesus; he mentions the meeting with Peter first (1 Cor. 15:3–7).

I wish Peter had shared with us what transpired at that meeting. Perhaps it was too intimate—painful and yet wonderful—to put on paper. No doubt the disgraced leader poured out his shame and his sorrow in his abject brokenness. And Jesus extended compassion, hope, and forgiveness. From here on he would be a new Peter, one on whom the Lord could depend to help build His church.

With this meeting Peter found reconciliation with his Lord. But one matter remained to be resolved—reconciliation with the other members of the original Twelve. By publicly denying Jesus, Peter had forfeited the right to be considered one of their number. Jesus would attend to this "unfinished business" in His own time and way.

Appearance on the Road to Emmaus

Luke records another appearance of Jesus on the day He rose from the dead (Luke 24:13–35). In this meeting the persons privileged to see the risen Lord weren't prominent disciples—certainly not members of the Twelve. One was named Cleopas; the other's name is not even mentioned. We do not know anything else about these two men on the road. It is clear, however, that they were sincere followers of Jesus: "We had hoped that he was the one who was going to redeem Israel" (v. 21), they shared with the Stranger Who had come up and joined them.

Deep in thought, conversing about the events of that fateful Passover when Jesus had died, they didn't recognize that it was Jesus walking with them. Is this a pattern on that first day? Jesus comes to Mary as she weeps by the tomb. She is weeping for Jesus, but she doesn't recognize Him. Cleopas and his companion are talking about Jesus—their heads are full of Him—and they don't recognize that He is walking with them.

What is going on here? Simply this: the followers of the Lord didn't expect Him to come back to life. Jesus had tried to tell them beforehand about His betrayal, sufferings, and death, and had said straight out, "Three days later he [the Son of Man] will rise" (Mark 9:31; 10:34), but they didn't get it. In fact, they disputed among themselves what "rising from the dead" could mean (Mark 9:10). Surely not an *actual* resurrection—dead people don't come back to life!

The Stranger gave Cleopas and his friend a short Bible study about the Messiah. "Did not the Messiah have to suffer these things and then enter his glory?" He concluded (Luke 24:26).

Suddenly, they had reached Emmaus. How quickly the journey (about 8 miles [13 km] from Jerusalem) had passed. Jesus acted as if He were going farther, but they urged Him to stay the night with them. He consented, and then something wonderful happened. As they sat together for the evening meal and Jesus took the bread, gave thanks, and began to give it to them, suddenly they recognized that voice, that blessing, that breaking of bread. It was Jesus! Then He vanished. Cleopas and his friend felt their hearts bursting. They got up from the table and, late in the day as it already was, hurried back to Jerusalem.

Sunday Night Appearance

Cleopas and his friend hadn't finished their excited recounting of what they had experienced when suddenly there was Jesus in the midst of the group. John records that the disciples had locked the door for fear of the Jews, but that didn't keep out the risen Lord.

Everyone was startled and frightened. Was it a ghost? But Jesus reassured them, "Peace be with you!" (Luke 24:36; John 20:19). He showed them His hands and His feet. They could still scarcely believe that it was Jesus, so He asked them for something to eat. They brought a piece of broiled fish and He ate it in their presence.

Then Jesus explained to them from the Scriptures how the Christ was to suffer and rise from the dead on the third day. They were to become witnesses of all that had happened, proclaiming repentance and forgiveness of sins first in Jerusalem and then to all nations. But first, they were to stay in Jerusalem until the Gift promised by the Holy Father would be sent to them (see Luke 24:36–49; John 20:19–23).

Reflections of the First Post-Resurrection Appearances

Several conclusions seem warranted from these accounts of the first day:

First, the tomb was empty. Mary Magdalene came early and found it empty; so did the other women. Peter and John arrived shortly after them and confirmed Mary's report: the body was gone. The grave cloths, however, were not: they remained folded in two parts. This argues against body snatchers, who wouldn't have taken time to unwind the wrappings.

Second, Jesus appeared the same day to several people: Mary Magdalene; Mary, the mother of James; Salome; Peter; Cleopas and his companion; and the Eleven and other assembled disciples. Names and places of these appearances are given, along with the words spoken by the risen Lord.

Third, at each meeting the reaction of the followers of Jesus—shock, fear, amazement, disbelief—was such as to indicate that they had not expected Jesus to rise from the dead. The big doubter among them was Thomas, who was absent from the Sunday night meeting. Told that they had seen the Lord, he demurred, "Unless I see the nail marks in his hands and put my finger where the nails were, and put my hand into his side, I will not believe" (John 20:25).

Fourth, the risen Lord was the same Jesus they knew and loved. But yet He was different: He now could pass through a locked door into a room; He could vanish suddenly.

Later Appearances of the Risen Lord

To Thomas

One week after Jesus met with the disciples behind the locked door, the disciples gathered together again. Although they again had locked the door, Jesus came and stood among them. This time Thomas was present, and Jesus singled him out: "Put your finger here," He said. "See my hands. Reach out your hand and put it into my side. Stop doubting and believe."

"My Lord and my God!" Thomas exclaimed (John 20:27, 28).

Thomas is often faulted for his lack of faith, but there is another side to the matter. Thomas was open in his doubts—he wanted sufficient evidence, seeing for himself rather than simply accepting what the others reported. Presented with the evidence, he immediately acknowledged that it was Jesus.

Critics of the story of the Resurrection frequently portray the disciples as ignorant, gullible people who were quick to believe that they had seen a ghost. The Gospel records paint an altogether different picture of them knowing about ghosts but more inclined to discount the report of Jesus's rising from the dead than to accept it. In this light, Thomas's reactions to the first report from the Sunday night and then a week later provide a strong answer to the critics.

In Galilee

Jesus, through the angel, had instructed the disciples to go to Galilee, where He would meet with them. Why Galilee? Because this, His home country, was the place where He spent most of His life and where the common people knew and loved Him. Before returning home to heaven, He went home to Galilee.

We don't know much about what happened when the Eleven went back to Galilee. The Gospels record two appearances of Jesus there, and both are highly significant for the story of the Resurrection.

One meeting was on a mountain that Jesus had designated. There Jesus gave them the great commission, which we shall come back to in the last chapter of this book (Matt. 28:16–20).

Matthew mentions only the Eleven, but Paul, apparently referring to the same event, indicates that the number was far larger: "More than five hundred of the brothers and sisters at the same time, most of whom are still living, though some have fallen asleep" (1 Cor. 15:6).

Paul's brief description carries heavy weight. A meeting with more than five hundred people abolishes the argument raised by critics that Jesus's so-called appearances were hallucinations of a few simple-minded followers. And the fact that most of those present to witness the event were still alive some twenty years later provides a historical frame of reference to guarantee the authenticity of what had happened.

The other appearance in Galilee takes up the whole concluding chapter of John's Gospel. The scene of the lake, the fishermen, the catch of fish, and even many of the same characters (Peter, James and John, Nathanael) is like a flashback to the beginning of Jesus's ministry. They had fished all night but had caught nothing. Then Jesus said, "Throw your net on the right side of the boat and you will find some" (John 21:6). They did so, and their nets captured a haul of large fish.

It meant breakfast on the shore with the risen Lord serving as chef and waiter. What a delightful scene—a time of love, joy, fellowship. But Jesus had more in mind. The time had arrived for an important development in the life and future mission of the disciples. Ever since his betrayal on that fateful Thursday night, Peter's standing had been in question. Although he had made reconciliation with the Master, the others in the group still had questions about him.

Peter no doubt had the same questions. Not surprisingly, when the Eleven went back to Galilee, he did what he felt comfortable doing. "I'm going out to fish," he announced. And so others joined him and they went fishing. That could have been the future for Peter— fishing. Back to where he began. Back to where—after his betrayal—he belonged.

But Jesus, full of grace and truth, had other plans and saw a different future for Peter. After breakfast, in the presence of the others, He put a question to Peter: "Simon son of John, do you truly love me more than these?" (John 21:15).

Three times, the same question: "Do you love me?"

The words cut to Peter's heart. At first he answered quickly, "Yes, Lord, you know that I love you," but by the third time he was hurting badly.

Three public denials. Three public confessions. And after each confession Jesus declared: "Feed my lambs. . . . Take care of my sheep. . . . Feed my sheep" (vv. 15–17).

Three denials. Three confessions. Three affirmations.

Jesus wanted Peter in ministry building up the church, not fishing. And He wanted the other disciples to hear His "welcome back" to Peter. What a tender, compassionate, forgiving, and reinstating Lord!

To James

Paul, listing people to whom the risen Lord appeared, includes "then he appeared to James" after mentioning the group of more than five hundred. Presumably this James was the brother of John, a son of Zebedee. We have no other mention or information about this appearance apart from Paul's cryptic reference (1 Cor. 15:7).

Acts, the companion volume to Luke's Gospel, tells us that Jesus appeared to the apostles "over a period of forty days and spoke about the kingdom of God." By these meetings Jesus "presented himself to them and gave many convincing proofs that he was alive" (Acts 1:3)—that is, that He was indeed the same Jesus Who had been put to death on the cross.

Thus, the resurrection of Jesus was not only attested by a series of individuals and groups totaling in all more than five hundred people, but by the frequency of appearances of the risen Lord to the Eleven. These appearances, Luke informs us, included table fellowship (Acts 1:4).

During these visits with the apostles, Jesus instructed them to wait in Jerusalem for the Gift He had previously spoken about to them. "For John baptized with water, but in a few days you will be baptized with the Holy Spirit. . . . You will receive power when the Holy Spirit comes on you; and you will be my witnesses in Jerusalem, and in all Judea and Samaria, and to the ends of the earth" (Acts 1:5, 8).

One day Jesus led the Eleven out of the city, over the summit of the Mount of Olives, and to its eastern slope to the vicinity of the village of Bethany. He lifted up His hands in blessing, and while blessing them He was taken up into heaven before their very eyes. Eventually a cloud of angels hid Him from their sight and they were left alone, gazing intently into the sky (Luke 24:50, 51; Acts 1:9).

Their Lord had gone. He had returned to the place from which He had come more than thirty years before. This event, known as the Ascension of Jesus, marked the end of His many post-Resurrection appearances of the forty days. It was not, however, the end of the Jesus story.

1. How would you answer the following objections to Jesus's resurrection?

   a. He didn't come back to life—His body was taken away by His followers (see Matt. 28:11–15).

b. He didn't really die on the cross; He only appeared to die. In the coolness of the tomb, He revived, threw off the grave cloths, and walked out on His own.

c. His followers so much wanted Jesus to come back from the dead that they imagined that they saw Him alive.

2. What were the Jewish burial practices?

3. What are the similarities and differences between the Gospel acccunts of the Resurrection? Piece them together to get a full picture of what happened.

Story without End

OBJECTIVES
- Learn the work of Jesus after His return to heaven.
- Trace events on earth after Jesus left.
- Feel motivated to carry on the mission of Jesus.

SCRIPTURE
- Hebrews 2:17—3:6; 4:14—5:11; 6:19—8:6; 9:1—10:18

Just as the birth of Jesus was not the beginning of His life, so His death did not mark its close. The Son of God existed eons before He was formed in Mary's womb, even from eternity, and He will exist into the eternal future. His story in its entirety is boundless from whichever direction we approach it.

Our focus in this book has been on the earthly phase of that eternal existence—on the thirty-three or so years when He left heaven and took on humanity. In this concluding chapter, we will take note of what the Bible tells us about His activities after He returned to the Father. Our treatment will, of necessity, be brief—a summary rather than a detailed exposition.

Jesus After the Ascension

The New Testament indicates at least four aspects of the heavenly work of Christ.

His Exaltation

Speaking to the Jews gathered in Jerusalem for Pentecost, Peter proclaimed, "God has raised this Jesus to life, and we are all witnesses of it. Exalted to the right hand of God, he has received from the Father the promised Holy Spirit and has poured out what you now see and hear" (Acts 2:32, 33). Many years later the apostle Paul echoed Peter's sentiments: "Therefore God exalted him to the highest place and gave him the name that is above every name, that at the name of Jesus every knee should bow, in heaven and on earth and under the earth, and every tongue acknowledge that Jesus Christ is Lord, to the glory of God the Father" (Phil. 2:9–11).

Jesus returned to the Father as Victor over sin, death, and the devil. He had met headlong every weapon that Satan had thrown at Him, and had emerged triumphant—beaten and bloodied, but victorious. The book of Revelation portrays Him as the slain and yet victorious Lamb before Whom all heaven bows in wonder and praise: "You are worthy to take the scroll and to open its seals, because you were slain, and with your blood you purchased for God persons from every tribe and language and people and nation" (Rev. 5:9).

The apostle writing to the Hebrews tells us that "after he had provided purification for sins, he sat down at the right hand of the Majesty in heaven" (Heb. 1:3). This "sitting down" does not indicate cessation or rest, but rather formal installation. When Jesus returned to the Father, He was acknowledged and acclaimed for accomplishing the divine mission for which He came to earth. The "right hand" indicates the place of favor and privilege. The reference goes back to Psalm 110:1. "The LORD says to my lord: 'Sit at my right hand until I make your enemies a footstool for your feet.'" This word from the Psalms, referred to by Peter in the sermon at Pentecost (Acts 2:34, 35), became the most frequently quoted portion of the Old Testament in the writings of the New.

According to Peter, the verification of Jesus's exaltation in heaven was shown by an event on earth—the outpouring of the Holy Spirit (vv. 3, 4). "Therefore," he argued, "let all Israel be assured of this:

God made this Jesus, whom you crucified, both Lord and Messiah" (v. 36).

His High-Priestly Ministry

While the New Testament mentions in several places that the risen Lord makes "intercession" for us in heaven (Rom. 8:34, KJV), this work receives major consideration in the book of Hebrews, where the argument is developed that the Son, by virtue of His being God and also becoming a man, is qualified to be the Bridge—the Mediator between God and humanity. He is unique, being the one and only true High Priest Who has ever been or Who ever will be. And because He offered up not bulls, goats, or oxen but Himself as the once-for-all and all-sufficient Sacrifice for our sins, He has not just fulfilled the typical services of the Levitical system but has made purification for our sins.

> For this reason he had to be made like them, fully human in every way, in order that he might become a merciful and faithful high priest in service to God, and that he might make atonement for the sins of the people. Because he himself suffered when he was tempted, he is able to help those who are being tempted (Heb. 2:17, 18).

> Now the main point of what we are saying is this: We do have such a high priest, who sat down at the right hand of the throne of the Majesty in heaven, and who serves in the sanctuary, the true tabernacle set up by the Lord, not by a mere human being (Heb. 8:1, 2).

Day after day every priest stands and performs his religious duties; again and again he offers the same sacrifices, which can never take away sins. But when this priest had offered for all time one sacrifice for sins, he sat down at the right hand of God (Heb. 10:11, 12).

Besides always living to intercede for His people (Heb. 7:25) and providing timely help for them when they are tested (Heb. 2:18), Jesus guides the work of the church. The book of Revelation pictures Him as walking among the lampstands, which represent the seven churches, and holding in His right hand seven stars, which are the angels (messengers) of the seven churches (Rev. 1:12–20). He sends out angels to minister to His people (Heb. 1:14). He is the Leader of the hosts of heaven in the warfare with Satan. Although He won the decisive battle on Calvary, the controversy still rages (Rev. 12:7–12).

The Old Testament draws a sharp distinction between the office of high priest and the monarchy. Those who served as high priest were born to the position: only direct descendants of Aaron, who was of the tribe of Levi, were qualified for the office. Israel's kings, however, were selected in a different manner. The first of the line was Saul, chosen by God from the tribe of Benjamin. He was succeeded by a man who brought the nation to its pinnacle and who was revered by all later generations as the ideal—King David, youngest son of Jesse, from the tribe of Judah.

As the Jews of the period leading up to the birth of Jesus chafed under the yoke of Rome and eagerly awaited the coming of the Messiah, they were conscious of the division of authority—civil and spiritual. Some writings predicted that not one but two Messiahs would appear—one political and one religious.[1]

The same Old Testament that had drawn a sharp line of separation also contained hints of a day when Israel's king would also be the high priest. Psalm 110, much quoted for its opening verse, also contained this idea: "The LORD has sworn and will not change his mind: 'You are a priest forever, in the order of Melchizedek" (v. 4). Melchizedek, a shadowy figure from outside the line of Abraham who blessed the patriarch, was king of Salem (Jerusalem) and also "Priest of God Most High" (Gen. 14:18–20). The Book of Hebrews, elaborating on Psalm 110:4, argues that Jesus, Who was not born from the tribe of Levi and therefore not qualified to be an Aaronic priest, is priest nevertheless, but of a different and higher order—the order of Melchizedek (Heb. 6:20–7:28).

Judgment

Jesus's high priestly work embraces two phases. The first corresponds with the daily work of intercession in the Old Testament sanctuary. The second, typified by the annual Yom Kippur—Day of Atonement—is a work of judgment that comes at the close of the age. Jesus, while on earth, taught that the Father had placed judgment in His hands (John 5:22). Daniel foresaw the time of judgment when one like the Son of Man came to the Ancient of Days and the Judgment began (Dan. 7:13, 14). Likewise, the apostle Paul told the Athenians as he addressed them on Mars Hill, "For He [God] has set a day when he will judge the world with justice by the man he has appointed. He has given proof of this to everyone by raising him from the dead" (Acts 17:31).

From study of the prophecies of Daniel and Revelation, we Seventh-day Adventists understand that the time of judgment commenced in 1844.[2] Soon the work will be completed and the next, climactic act in the Great Controversy will take place.

Second Coming

Jesus's return to this earth has been guaranteed by His victory on Calvary. There He won the decisive battle in the Great Controversy; there He assured that He would one day reign as King of Kings and Lord of Lords. He promised, "I will come again, and receive you unto myself" (John 14:3, KJV). Jesus always keeps His promises; He will keep this promise also.

When Jesus ascended from the Mount of Olives, the disciples stood gazing up into the sky until the cloud of angels took Him from their sight. Suddenly they became aware that two men dressed in white were standing beside them. These men said, "Men of Galilee, why do you stand here looking into the sky? This same Jesus, who has been taken from you into heaven, will come back in the same way you have seen him go into heaven" (Acts 1:10, 11).

Jesus went into heaven in plain sight, not secretly. The disciples had been speaking with Him, and they saw Him leave before their eyes. That is how He will come again—in person, visibly, and audibly. John described what His coming will be like:

> "Look, he is coming with the clouds,"
> and "every eye will see him,
> even those who pierced him";
> and all peoples on earth "will mourn
> because of him."
> So shall it be! Amen. (Rev. 1:7)

Likewise the apostle Paul: "For the Lord himself will come down from heaven, with a loud command, with the voice of the archangel and with the trumpet call of God, and the dead in Christ will rise first. After that, we who are still alive and are left will be caught up together with them in the clouds to meet the Lord in the air. And so we will be with the Lord forever" (1 Thess. 4:16, 17).

Almost two thousand years have passed since Jesus went back to heaven. We measure time by our short lifespan of seventy or eighty years, but with God a thousand years are like only a day (2 Pet. 3:8). The lapse of time to us seems long, but not to God. He has the world in His hands; He is Lord of time and space. He is working out His plan, and His timing is meticulous. He will bring about the Second Coming of Jesus "in His own time" (1 Tim. 6:15).

When Jesus comes back, it won't be like the first advent. Then He came as a helpless, dependent baby; the second time He will come in glory, accompanied by myriads of heavenly angels (Matt. 24:30, 31). The righteous dead will be resurrected and the wicked destroyed by the brightness of His coming (2 Thess. 2:8, KJV). Then the resurrected righteous along with the living righteous will be caught up to meet the Lord in the air (1 Thess. 4:13–17).

"So we will be with the Lord forever" (v. 17). The Lamb will be our Shepherd. He will lead us to springs of living water. And "God will wipe away every tear from their eyes" (Rev. 7:17).

> And the years of eternity, as they roll, will bring richer and still more glorious revelations of God and of Christ. As knowledge is progressive, so will love, reverence, and happiness increase. The more men learn of God, the greater will be their admiration of His character. As Jesus opens before them the riches of redemption and the amazing achievements in the great controversy with Satan, the hearts of the ransomed thrill with more fervent devotion, and with more rapturous joy they sweep the harps of gold; and ten thousand times ten thousand and thousands of thousands of voices unite to swell the mighty chorus of praise.[3]

Back on Earth

The followers of Jesus heeded His command to wait in Jerusalem until they received the Holy Spirit Whom He had promised. And the Spirit did come—like wind and fire. On the day of Pentecost they were all together when suddenly they heard the sound of a violent wind filling the house where they were gathered. Then what looked like fire came and rested on each person. Everyone began to speak in other tongues by the power of the Spirit (Acts 2:1–4). It was a vivid, personal demonstration that the risen Lord had sent the Gift that He had promised. A new era had begun—the age of the Spirit.

Empowered by the Spirit, the followers of Jesus went everywhere proclaiming the gospel. They started right where they were in Jerusalem, and then spread out in ever-widening concentric circles to Judea, Samaria, and then beyond.

Their preaching had a simple, compelling message: Jesus Christ had risen from the dead as the Savior of all people. Apart from Jesus, no one had broken the bonds of the grave. Jesus of Nazareth, crucified by order of Pontius Pilate and buried in the tomb, was alive! The apostles had seen Him and testified to the fact. And there was a second factor that reinforced their witness—the Holy Spirit. The Spirit's presence—empowering their words, convicting the hearers of sin, and working miracles—was proof that Jesus was truly the long-awaited Messiah of the Jews.

The message of the good news about the risen Jesus was unstoppable. It spread like the wind. It won over men and women steeped in evil, priests and

Pharisees, doubters, mockers, and guards sent to arrest the apostles. It won over a young man who seemed the unlikeliest convert. Brilliant in intellect and fanatical in opposing the new message, he was the epitome of those opposed to followers of the Way, as the Jesus people were first called. But Jesus saw great things for this young Pharisee—a future that no believer and certainly no other Pharisee could imagine. Jesus met him on the road to Damascus, where he was headed with letters of authority from the religious leaders in Jerusalem to seize followers of the Way, tie them up, and drag them to Jerusalem for punishment.

In piercing light Saul of Tarsus fell to the ground as he heard a voice: "Saul, Saul, why do you persecute me?"

"Who are you, Lord?"

"I am Jesus, whom you are persecuting. Now get up and go into the city, and you will be told what you must do" (see Acts 9:4–6).

Saul, blinded from the brilliance of the light, had to be led by the hand. For three days he neither ate nor drank. Then Ananias, a disciple who lived in Damascus, came to him and placed his hands on him, saying, "Brother Saul, the Lord—Jesus who appeared to you on the road as you were coming here—has sent me so that you may see again and be filled with the Holy Spirit" (v. 17). Then Saul could see again. He was baptized, ate some food, regained his strength—and became Paul.

Almost immediately Paul began to preach in the synagogues that Jesus was the Son of God. His was an astonishing conversion that baffled the Jews. Before long they plotted to kill him, but Paul got wind of the plan and made his escape.

The conversion of Saul of Tarsus marked a turning point for the young church. He became its most powerful advocate, even though he was not one of the Twelve. Because of his advanced education—he had sat at the feet of a great scholar, Gamaliel—he was able to refute all the arguments advanced by Jewish critics of the movement.

The Lord selected this intelligent, earnest young man and worked on him and with him to prepare him to be the pre-eminent apostle to the larger world beyond the borders of Judaism. For several years the followers of Jesus had limited their proclamation to Jews and converts to Judaism. They continued to worship in the temple in Jerusalem or in the synagogues, retaining the customs with which they had been raised.

Likewise, the officials of the Roman Empire regarded the Way as just another sect of Judaism. This had advantages for the Christians, as they soon became known, for Judaism was an officially recognized religion of the Empire. Its followers were granted privileges, such as exemption from military service.

Paul was privileged in an additional respect—he was born in Tarsus and thereby was automatically a Roman citizen. This was no small status to claim in the days when Rome ruled from the British Isles to the Middle East.

The Lord had prepared the world for the coming of Christ and the spread of the new religion in His name. The vast expanse of the Empire was united in language (Latin spoken, Greek written), enabling the gospel to be communicated easily to the majority of the people who lived under the rule of Rome. Likewise, the Romans constructed a network of roads (hence the saying "all roads lead to Rome") that enabled easy, rapid travel for Paul and other emissaries of the cross. During the previous century, Pompey had cleared the seas of pirates, another factor facilitating the spread of the gospel.

Under the empowering of the Spirit, Paul pressed farther and farther west. He became missionary extraordinaire, always on the move, fearless, undaunted. Though imprisoned, flogged, exposed to death, lashed, stoned, beaten with rods, shipwrecked, constantly in danger—from the Jews, Gentiles, and bandits, both in the city and in the country—he never flagged and never turned back.

Pursuing a deliberate strategy, he planted churches in the major cities and continued to move on. Chiefly as a result of his tireless labors, the Christian church grew rapidly.

And it changed significantly. In its early phase, its members came wholly from Jews and converts to Judaism. By the AD 60s, when Paul was executed in Rome, it was a mixture of people from both Jewish and Gentile backgrounds. As the century wore on and into the next, the Gentile wing of the church grew ever larger until the original Jewish side shrank in proportion and significance.

Paul's training in the law, coupled with his experience as apostle to the Gentiles, gave him unique insights into the nature of the religion founded by Jesus. He came to see that, while the new was continuous with the old in important respects, it had vital elements of discontinuity. Jesus had predicted the inevitable parting of the ways when He spoke of the new wine that would bust out of the old wineskins (see Matt. 9:17).

Due to Paul's extraordinary labors, with large numbers of Gentile converts flocking into the church, a key issue came to a head: What should be expected of the Gentile believers? Should they in effect become Jews in religious practices when they accepted Jesus? Specifically, should males adopt the mark of the covenant, that is, circumcision?

This issue led to a sharp division among the early Christians, with those who had belonged previously to the Pharisees arguing vehemently that Gentiles must observe the law in order to be saved. The leaders of the church, who were based in Jerusalem with James, the brother of Jesus, considered to be the head, decided to call a church council.

The proceedings of this gathering, recorded in Acts 15, reveal the heat of the debate and the decision that emerged: Gentile converts would *not* be required to be circumcised. The council decided to write a general letter to be shared with them by the hands of Paul, Barnabas,

Judas Barsabbas, and Silas. In this epistle, they reiterated the council's decisions not to burden Gentile believers with any requirements other than abstention from food offered to idols, from eating blood, from the meat of strangled animals, and from sexual immorality.

This letter, together with the council that authorized it, cleared the way for the Gentile church to proceed unencumbered. It ensured what was already becoming more and more obvious: Christianity would no longer be a sect of Judaism—it would be a religion in its own right.

For their part, the Jews more and more wanted a clear separation from the Christians. They forced the issue for Jewish Christians by writing into the synagogue service prayers that pronounced a curse on followers of Jesus. This ensured that Christians would not only be unwelcome to worship in the synagogues but that they could not join in the service with a clear conscience.

So the story of the risen Lord did not end. It will not end. The good news spread from land to land and from sea to sea. Even though the centuries passed, and even though a "falling away" came into the church in both teachings and practice, the Lord always had a remnant who remained faithful to Him, loving Him above all else on earth and putting loyalty to Him above comfort, material benefits, and even life itself.

For Seventh-day Adventists, the word "remnant" is filled with precious connotations. For us, especially, we hear in it echoes of Revelation 12:17—"And the dragon was wroth with the woman, and went to make war with the remnant of her seed, which keep the commandments of God, and have the testimony of Jesus Christ" (KJV). We see ourselves in the end-time remnant, called into being by the risen Lord, and commissioned to take the everlasting gospel to "every nation, tribe, language and people" (Rev. 14:6) just prior to the Second Coming of Jesus.

Yes, the story goes on. It goes on in our day as people from around the circle of the earth hear the good news by radio, television, printed page, or the Internet and bow at the feet of Jesus as their Savior and Lord.

The story has no end and can have no end. In heaven we will someday sing with the heavenly beings, proclaiming without end: "Worthy is the Lamb that was slain to receive power, and riches, and wisdom, and strength, and honour, and glory, and blessing." "Blessing, and honour, and glory, and power, be unto him that sitteth upon the throne, and unto the Lamb for ever and ever" (Rev. 5:12, 13, KJV).

The Story and Us

The question that faces each of us as we come to the end of this book, not of the story, is this: Am I part of that story? Jesus invites each one of us to make His story our story. He invites us to simply receive Him, permitting Him to be our best Friend, Savior, and Lord.

"To all who did receive Him," wrote John the Beloved, "to those who believed in his name, he gave the right to become children of God" (John 1:12). Whoever you are, and wherever you live, this is your destiny. And mine. We're invited to become a daughter or a son of God!

Jesus calls us as He called James, John, Peter, and Andrew long ago by the lakeside. "Follow me," He says. It's an invitation that is at once a command. For He is the risen Lord.

"Then Jesus came to them and said, 'All authority in heaven and on earth has been given to me. Therefore go and make disciples of all nations, baptizing them in the name of the Father and of the Son and of the Holy Spirit, and teaching them to obey everything I have commanded you. And surely I am with you always, to the very end of the age'" (Matt. 28:18–20).

We are to carry on that life and ministry of Jesus. "As the Father has sent me, I am sending you," He tells us (John 20:21). He sends us to be His hands, His feet, His voice of hope, and His healing touch.

That is our destiny. What a privilege and what joy!

And then we will experience this: "The throne of God and of the Lamb will be in the city, and his servants will serve him. They will see his face, and his name will be on their foreheads" (Rev. 22:3, 4).

"Amen. Come, Lord Jesus" (v. 20).

QUESTIONS FOR DISCUSSION

1. What is Jesus doing now?

2. In the story of Jesus of Nazareth, what impresses you the most? Why?

ADDITIONAL READING

Jesus of Nazareth is written from a Seventh-day Adventist perspective. Some of the additional readings listed here may not share an Adventist perspective in every respect, and may be based on presuppositions or theological interpretations that are not always in agreement with those of the author or publishers of this book. However, such readings may, on general matters such as geography, culture, economy, history, and exegesis, provide useful information to enrich understanding of the life and times of our Savior. In providing these readings, the publishers assume that readers will be aware of this point and will make use of these readings accordingly.

Chapter 1: His Land and Times

From Adventist Writers

Johnston, Robert Morris. "How Rabbinic Literature Illuminates the New Testament." *Shabbat Shalom* 52, no. 2 (2005): 30–33.

McVay, John K. "Why Are There Four Gospels?" In *Interpreting Scripture: Bible Questions and Answers,* edited by Gerhard Pfandl, 73–78. Silver Spring, MD: Biblical Research Institute, 2010.

White, Ellen G. "The Chosen People" (chapter 2). *The Desire of Ages.* Mountain View, CA: Pacific Press, 1898. https://egwwritings.org/?ref=en_DA.27¶=130.61.

_______. "The Fullness of the Time" (chapter 3). *The Desire of Ages.* Mountain View, CA: Pacific Press, 1898. https://egwwritings.org/?ref=en_DA.31¶=130.82.

From Other Writers

Aberbach, Moshe. *Labor, Crafts and Commerce in Ancient Israel.* Jerusalem: Hebrew University Magnes Press, 1994.

Blomberg, Craig L. "Historical Background for Studying the Gospels." In *Jesus and the Gospels: An Introduction and Survey,* 2nd ed., 8–86. Nashville: Broadman and Holman, 2009.

Cohen, Shaye. *From the Maccabees to the Mishnah.* 3rd ed. Louisville, KY: Westminster John Knox Press, 2014.

Ferguson, Everett. "Parties and Sects." In *Backgrounds of Early Christianity*, 3rd ed., 513–534. Grand Rapids, MI: Eerdmans, 2003.

_______. "Society and Culture." In *Backgrounds of Early Christianity*, 3rd ed., 48–147. Grand Rapids, MI: Eerdmans, 2003.

Horsley, Richard A. *Archaeology, History, and Society in Galilee: The Social Context of Jesus and the Rabbis.* Valley Forge, PA: Trinity Press International, 1996.

Stemberger, Günter. *Jewish Contemporaries of Jesus: Pharisees, Sadducees, Essenes.* Minneapolis: Fortress Press, 1995.

Strauss, Mark L. "Part Two: The Setting of the Gospels." In *Four Portraits, One Jesus: An Introduction to Jesus and the Gospels,* 93–170. Grand Rapids, MI: Zondervan, 2007.

Walker, Peter. *Jesus and His World.* Downers Grove, IL: InterVarsity Press, 2003.

Yancey, Philip. "Background: Jewish Roots and Soil." In *The Jesus I Never Knew,* 47–66. Grand Rapids, MI: Zondervan, 1995.

Chapter 2: Can We Trust the Gospels?

From Adventist Writers

Blomberg, Craig L. *The Historical Reliability of the Gospels.* 2nd ed. Downers Grove, IL: IVP Academic, 2007.

Davidson, Richard M. "Biblical Interpretation: B. Historical Context." In *Handbook of Seventh-Day Adventist Theology,* edited by Raoul Dederen, 70–74. Vol. 12. Hagerstown, MD: Review and Herald, 2000.

Paroschi, Wilson. "Archaeology and the Interpretation of John's Gospel: A Review Essay." *Journal of the Adventist Theological Society* 20, nos. 1–2 (2009): 67–88.

White, Ellen G. *Selected Messages.* Vol. 1, 15–23. Washington, DC: Review and Herald, 1958. https://egwwritings.org/?ref=en_1SM.15¶=98.35.

From Other Writers

Barnett, Paul. *Is the New Testament Reliable? A Look at the Historical Evidence.* Downers Grove, IL: InterVarsity Press, 1992.

Bauckham, Richard. *Jesus and the Eyewitnesses: The Gospels as Eyewitness Testimony.* Grand Rapids, MI: Eerdmans, 2006.

Blomberg, Craig L. *The Historical Reliability of the Gospels.* 2nd ed. Downers Grove, IL: IVP Academic, 2007.

______. "The Historical Trustworthiness of the Gospels." In *Jesus and the Gospels: An Introduction and Survey,* 365–382. Nashville: Broadman and Holman, 1997.

Bock, Darrell L. "The Four Gospels: Distinctive Voices and How We Got Them." In *Jesus According to Scripture: Restoring the Portrait from the Gospels,* 2nd ed., 1–108. With Benjamin I. Simpson. Grand Rapids, MI: Baker Academic, 2017.

Boyd, Gregory A., and Paul Rhodes Eddy. *Lord or Legend? Wrestling with the Jesus Dilemma.* Grand Rapids, MI: Baker Books, 2007.

Keener, Craig S. *The Historical Jesus of the Gospels.* Grand Rapids, MI: Eerdmans, 2009.

Mykytiuk, Lawrence. "Did Jesus Exist? Searching for Evidence Beyond the Bible." *Biblical Archaeology Review* 41, no. 1 (January/February 2015): 44–51, 76.

Roberts, Mark D. *Can We Trust the Gospels? Investigating the Reliability of Matthew, Mark, Luke, and John.* Wheaton, IL: Crossway Books, 2007.

Strauss, Mark L. "The Historical Jesus." In *Four Portraits, One Jesus: An Introduction to Jesus and the Gospels,* 347–524. Grand Rapids, MI: Zondervan, 2007.

Strobel, Lee. "Examining the Record." In *The Case for Christ: A Journalist's Personal Investigation of the Evidence for Jesus,* 19–130. Grand Rapids, MI: Zondervan, 1998.

Van Voorst, Robert E. *Jesus Outside the New Testament: An Introduction to the Ancient Evidence.* Grand Rapids, MI: Eerdmans, 2000.

VanderKam, James C. *An Introduction to Early Judaism.* Grand Rapids, MI: Eerdmans, 2001.

Chapter 3: The Eternal Word

From Adventist Writers

Dederen, Raoul. "Christ: His Person and Work." In *Handbook of Seventh-Day Adventist Theology,* edited by Raoul Dederen, 160–163. Vol. 12. Hagerstown, MD: Review and Herald, 2000.

Gulley, Norman R. "Redemption: Life, Death, Resurrection." In *Systematic Theology: Creation, Christ, Salvation,* 393–478. Berrien Springs, MI: Andrews University Press, 2012.

White, Ellen G. "'God with Us'" (chapter 1). *The Desire of Ages.* Mountain View, CA: Pacific Press, 1898. https://egwwritings.org/?ref=en_DA.19¶=130.21.

______. "God's Love for Man" (chapter 1). *Steps to Christ.* Mountain View, CA: Pacific Press, 1892. https://egwwritings.org/?ref=en_SC.9¶=108.21.

From Other Writers

Bock, Darrell L. "Introducing Jesus in John's Gospel: The Word Incarnate and the First Witnesses." In *Jesus According to Scripture: Restoring the Portrait from the Gospels,* 2nd ed., 519-527 . With Benjamin I. Simpson. Grand Rapids, MI: Baker Academic, 2017.

Griffith-Jones, Robin. "From the Beginning to the End." In *The Four Witnesses: The Rebel, the Rabbi, the Chronicler, and the Mystic,* 285–316. San Francisco: HarperSanFrancisco, 2000.

Hobbs, Herschel. "The Period of Preparation." In *The Illustrated Life of Jesus,* 16–21. Nashville: Holman Bible Publishers, 2000.

McCready, Douglas. "The Writings of John." In *He Came Down from Heaven: The Preexistence of Christ and Christian Faith,* 135–162. Downers Grove, IL: InterVarsity Press, 2005.

Rissi, Mathias. "John 1:1–18 (the Eternal Word)." *Interpretation* 31, no. 4 (October 1977): 394–401. *ATLA Religion Database with ATLASerials*, EBSCO*host*. Accessed July 7, 2017.

Chapter 4: God with Us

From Adventist Writers

Davidson, Richard. "Christmas Festival of Lights." *Andrews University Seminary Studies* 44, no. 2 (2006): 197–201.

Dederen, Raoul. "Christ: His Person and Work." In *Handbook of Seventh-Day Adventist Theology*, edited by Raoul Dederen, 160–163. Vol. 12. Hagerstown, MD: Review and Herald, 2000.

Gulley, Norman R. "Redemption: Life, Death, Resurrection" (section "The Humanity of Jesus"). In *Systematic Theology: Creation, Christ, Salvation*, 421–431. Berrien Springs, MI: Andrews University Press, 2012.

White, Ellen G. "Unto You a Saviour" (chapter 4). *The Desire of Ages*. Mountain View, CA: Pacific Press, 1898. https://egwwritings.org/?ref=en_DA.43¶=130.120.

______. "The Dedication" (chapter 5). *The Desire of Ages*. Mountain View, CA: Pacific Press, 1898. https://egwwritings.org/?ref=en_DA.50¶=130.149.

______. "'We Have Seen His Star'" (chapter 6). *The Desire of Ages*. Mountain View, CA: Pacific Press, 1898. https://egwwritings.org/?ref=en_DA.59¶=130.188.

______. "As a Child" (chapter 7). *The Desire of Ages*. Mountain View, CA: Pacific Press, 1898. https://egwwritings.org/?ref=en_DA.68¶=130.235.

______. "The Passover Visit" (chapter 8). *The Desire of Ages*. Mountain View, CA: Pacific Press, 1898. https://egwwritings.org/?ref=en_DA.75¶=130.269.

From Other Writers

Bock, Darrell L. "The Birth and Childhood of Jesus." In *Jesus According to Scripture: Restoring the Portrait from the Gospels*, 2nd ed., 117–145. With Benjamin I. Simpson. Grand Rapids, MI: Baker Academic, 2017.

Brown, Raymond. *The Birth of the Messiah: A Commentary on the Infancy Narratives in the Gospels of Matthew and Luke*. Rev. ed. New York: Doubleday, 1993.

Graham, Daryn Robert. "Dating the Birth of Jesus Christ." *Reformed Theological Review* 73, no. 3 (December 2014): 147–159.

Hobbs, Herschel. "The Birth and Childhood of Jesus." In *The Illustrated Life of Jesus*, 22–41. Nashville: Holman Bible Publishers, 2000.

Moody, Dale. "On the Virgin Birth of Jesus Christ." *Review and Expositor* 50, no. 4 (October 1953): 453–462.

Yancey, Philip. "Birth: The Visited Planet." In *The Jesus I Never Knew*, 27–46. Grand Rapids, MI: Zondervan, 1995.

Chapter 5: Man with a Mission

From Adventist Writers

Gulley, Norman R. "Redemption: Life, Death, Resurrection" (section "Incarnational Nature"). In *Systematic Theology: Creation, Christ, Salvation*, 431–459. Berrien Springs, MI: Andrews University Press, 2012.

Mueller, Ekkehardt. "Why Did the Spirit of God Lead Jesus into the Wilderness (Mt 4:1)?" *Reflections: A BRI Newsletter*, April 2003, 4–5.

Reeve, Teresa L. "Rite from the Very Beginning: Rites of Passage in Luke 1–4 and Their Function in the Narrative of Luke-Acts." *Andrews University Seminary Studies* 49, no. 2 (2011): 243–259.

White, Ellen G. "The Baptism" (chapter 11) *The Desire of Ages*. Mountain View, CA: Pacific Press, 1898. https://egwwritings.org/?ref=en_DA.109¶=130.432.

———. "The Temptation" (chapter 12). *The Desire of Ages*. Mountain View, CA: Pacific Press, 1898. https://egwwritings.org/?ref=en_DA.114¶=130.458.

———. "The Victory" (chapter 13). *The Desire of Ages*. Mountain View, CA: Pacific Press, 1898. https://egwwritings.org/?ref=en_DA.124¶=130.509.

From Other Writers

Bock, Darrell L. "Preparation: Birth, John the Baptist, and the Temptations." In *Jesus the God-Man: The Unity and Diversity of the Gospel Portrayals*, 5–14. Grand Rapids, MI: Baker Academic, 2016.

———. "The Backdrop to Jesus's Ministry: John the Baptist, Jesus's Baptism and Temptations." In *Jesus According to Scripture: Restoring the Portrait from the Gospels*, 2nd ed., 156–159, 160–161. With Benjamin I. Simpson. Grand Rapids, MI: Baker Academic, 2017.

Guthrie, Donald. *Jesus the Messiah: An Illustrated Life of Christ*, 39–46. Grand Rapids, MI: Zondervan, 1972.

Hardin, Leslie T. "Casting Down Temptation." In *The Spirituality of Jesus: Nine Disciplines Christ Modeled for Us*, 39–51. Kregel, 2009.

Hobbs, Herschel. "The Time of the Beginning." In *The Illustrated Life of Jesus*, 43–68. Nashville: Holman Bible Publishers, 2000.

Laymon, Charles M. "The Baptism; The Temptation." In *The Life and Teachings of Jesus*, rev. ed., 99–120. New York: Abingdon, 1962.

Yancey, Philip. "Temptation: Showdown in the Desert." In *The Jesus I Never Knew*, 67–82. Grand Rapids, MI: Zondervan, 1995.

Chapter 6: The Cousins

From Adventist Writers

Miller, James E. "The Birth of John the Baptist and the Gospel to the Gentiles." *Andrews University Seminary Studies* 31, no. 3 (1993): 195–197.

Warren, Mervyn A. "John the Baptizer and Jesus Christ: When Symbol Meets Substance." *Journal of the Adventist Theological Society* 4, no. 1 (1993): 94–102.

White, Ellen G. "The Voice in the Wilderness" (chapter 10). *The Desire of Ages.* Mountain View, CA: Pacific Press, 1898. https://egwwritings.org/?ref=en_DA.97¶=130.361.

______. "'He Must Increase'" (chapter 18). *The Desire of Ages.* Mountain View, CA: Pacific Press, 1898. https://egwwritings.org/?ref=en_DA.178¶=130.791.

______. "Imprisonment and Death of John" (chapter 22). *The Desire of Ages.* Mountain View, CA: Pacific Press, 1898. https://egwwritings.org/?ref=en_DA.214¶=130.981.

From Other Writers

Bock, Darrell L. "The Backdrop to Jesus's Ministry: John the Baptist, Jesus's Baptism and Temptations"; "Introducing Jesus in John's Gospel: The Word Incarnate and the First Witnesses"; "The Book of Signs: Before the Hour." In *Jesus According to Scripture: Restoring the Portrait from the Gospels*, 2nd ed., 148–156, 527–530, 546–548. With Benjamin I. Simpson. Grand Rapids, MI: Baker Academic, 2017.

Bowens, Lisa M. "The Role of John the Baptist in Matthew's Gospel." *Word & World* 30, no. 3 (2010): 311–318.

Burnett, Clint. "Eschatological Prophet of Restoration: Luke's Theological Portrait of John the Baptist in Luke 3:1–6." *Neotestamentica* 47, no. 1 (2013): 1–24.

Kershner, Shannon Johnson. "John the Baptist—the Holy Homemaker." *Journal for Preachers* 35, no. 1 (2011): 40–43. *ATLA Religion Database with ATLASerials*, EBSCO*host.* Accessed July 20, 2017.

Williams, Catrin H. "John (the Baptist): The Witness on the Threshold." In *Character Studies in the Fourth Gospel: Narrative Approaches to Seventy Figures in John*, edited by Steven A. Hunt, D. Francois Tolmie, and Ruben Zimmermann, 46–60. Tübingen, Germany: Mohr Siebeck, 2013.

Chapter 7: Lord of the Temple

From Adventist Writers

Gonzalez, Eliezer. "Jesus and the Temple: Understanding the Teaching of the New Testament." *Ministry* 85, no. 1 (2013): 10–12.

Nichol, Francis D., ed. "Maps and Charts Illustrating the Life and Ministry of Jesus." In *Seventh-day Adventist Bible Commentary*, 229–232. Vol. 5. Washington, DC: Review and Herald, 1980.

Papaioannou, Kim. "The Heavenly Temple in the Gospel of John." *Ministry Magazine* 87, no. 4 (April 2015): 20–23.

White, Ellen G. "'We Have Found the Messiah'" (chapter 14). *The Desire of Ages*. Mountain View, CA: Pacific Press, 1898. https://egwwritings.org/?ref=en_DA.132¶=130.544.

———. "At the Marriage Feast" (chapter 15). *The Desire of Ages*. Mountain View, CA: Pacific Press, 1898. https://egwwritings.org/?ref=en_DA.144¶=130.621.

———. "In His Temple" (chapter 16). *The Desire of Ages*. Mountain View, CA: Pacific Press, 1898. https://egwwritings.org/?ref=en_DA.154¶=130.676.

Winkle, Ross E. "The Jeremiah Model for Jesus in the Temple." *Andrews University Seminary Studies* 24, no. 2 (1986): 155–172.

From Other Writers

Bock, Darrell L. "The Book of Signs: Before the Hour, The Book of Glory: The Farewell Discourse and the Johannine Passion Account—the Hour Has Come." In *Jesus According to Scripture: Restoring the Portrait from the Gospels*, 2nd ed. 536–543, 678–680. With Benjamin I. Simpson. Grand Rapids, MI: Baker Academic, 2017.

Griffith-Jones, Robin. "Joy of Man's Desiring: Jerusalem and Jesus." In *The Four Witnesses: The Rebel, the Rabbi, the Chronicler, and the Mystic*, 21–42. San Francisco: HarperSanFrancisco, 2000.

Guthrie, Donald. *Jesus the Messiah: An illustrated Life of Christ*, 47–56. Grand Rapids, MI: Zondervan, 1972.

Hoskins, Paul M. *Jesus as the Fulfillment of the Temple in the Gospel of John*. Eugene, OR: Wipf and Stock, 2007.

Klink, Edward W. III. "The Bridegroom at Cana: Ignorance Is Bliss." In *Character Studies in the Fourth Gospel: Narrative Approaches to Seventy Figures in John*, edited by Steven A. Hunt, D. Francois Tolmie, and Ruben Zimmermann, 233–237. Tübingen, Germany: Mohr Siebeck, 2013.

Leithart, Peter J. "John." In *The Four: A Survey of the Gospels*, 213–238. Moscow, ID: Canon Press, 2010.

Perrin, Nicholas. *Jesus the Temple*. London: SCPK Publishing, 2010.

Chapter 8: A Man for All People

From Adventist Writers

Aldridge, Edlyn. "Waiting by the Pool of Bethesda." *Adventist Review* 189 (April 2012): 24–26.

Davidson, Jo Ann. "John 4: Another Look at the Samaritan Woman." *Andrews University Seminary Studies* 43, no.1 (2005): 159–168.

General Conference Ministerial Association. "The Pool at Bethesda." *Elder's Digest* 18, no. 3 (July-September 2012): 17.

White, Ellen G. "Nicodemus" (chapter 17). *The Desire of Ages*. Mountain View, CA: Pacific Press, 1898. https://egwwritings.org/?ref=en_DA.167¶=130.739.

______. "At Jacob's Well" (chapter 19). *The Desire of Ages*. Mountain View, CA: Pacific Press, 1898. https://egwwritings.org/?ref=en_DA.183¶=130.815.

______. "'Except Ye See Signs and Wonders'" (chapter 20). *The Desire of Ages*. Mountain View, CA: Pacific Press, 1898. https://egwwritings.org/?ref=en_DA.196¶=130.882.

______. "Bethesda and the Sanhedrin" (chapter 21). *The Desire of Ages*. Mountain View, CA: Pacific Press, 1898. https://egwwritings.org/?ref=en_DA.201¶=130.907.

From Other Writers

Attridge, Harold W. "The Samaritan Woman: A Woman Transformed." In *Character Studies in the Fourth Gospel: Narrative Approaches to Seventy Figures in John*, edited by Steven A. Hunt, D. Francois Tolmie, and Ruben Zimmermann, 268–281. Tübingen, Germany: Mohr Siebeck, 2013.

Bock, Darrell L. "The Book of Signs: Before the Hour." In *Jesus According to Scripture: Restoring the Portrait from the Gospels*, 2nd ed. 543–546, 548–555. With Benjamin I. Simpson. Grand Rapids, MI: Baker Academic, 2017.

Culpepper, R. Alan. "Nicodemus: The Travail of New Birth." In *Character Studies in the Fourth Gospel: Narrative Approaches to Seventy Figures in John*, edited by Steven A. Hunt, D. Francois Tolmie, and Ruben Zimmermann, 249–259. Tübingen, Germany: Mohr Siebeck, 2013.

Griffith-Jones, Robin. "Nicodemus: 'Born Again from Above.'" In *The Four Witnesses: The Rebel, the Rabbi, the Chronicler, and the Mystic*, 326–330. San Francisco: HarperSanFrancisco, 2000.

Guthrie, Donald. *Jesus the Messiah: An Illustrated Life of Christ*, 57–59. Grand Rapids, MI: Zondervan, 1972.

Judge, Peter J. "The Royal Official: Not so Officious." In *Character Studies in the Fourth Gospel: Narrative Approaches to Seventy Figures in John*, edited by Steven A. Hunt, D. Francois Tolmie, and Ruben Zimmermann, 306–313. Tübingen,

Germany: Mohr Siebeck, 2013.

Michaels, J. Ramsey. "The Invalid at the Pool: The Man Who Merely Got Well." In *Character Studies in the Fourth Gospel: Narrative Approaches to Seventy Figures in John,* edited by Steven A. Hunt, D. Francois Tolmie, and Ruben Zimmermann, 337–346. Tübingen, Germany: Mohr Siebeck, 2013.

Chapter 9: The Galilean

From Adventist Writers

White, Ellen G. "The Call by the Sea" (chapter 25). *The Desire of Ages.* Mountain View, CA: Pacific Press, 1898. https://egwwritings.org/?ref=en_DA.244¶=130.1120.

———. "'He Ordained Twelve'" (chapter 30). *The Desire of Ages.* Mountain View, CA: Pacific Press, 1898. https://egwwritings.org/?ref=en_DA.290¶=130.1369.

From Other Writers

Bock, Darrell L. "The Initial Portrait of Jesus's Galilean Ministry: Teaching, Healing, and Controversy; Introducing Jesus in John's Gospel: The Word Incarnate and the First Witnesses." In *Jesus According to Scripture: Restoring the Portrait from the Gospels,* 2nd ed. 169–171, 196–197, 531–533. With Benjamin I. Simpson. Grand Rapids, MI: Baker Academic, 2017.

Connick, C. Milo. *"Call and Training of the Twelve." In Jesus: The Man, the Mission, and the Message,* 2nd ed. 169–171. Englewood Cliffs, NJ: Prentice-Hall, 1974.

Hobbs, Herschel. "The Great Galilean Ministry." In *The Illustrated Life of Jesus,* 69–114. Nashville: Holman Bible Publishers, 2000.

Manning, Gary T. Jr. "The Disciples of John (the Baptist): Hearers of John, Followers of Jesus." In *Character Studies in the Fourth Gospel: Narrative Approaches to Seventy Figures in John,* edited by Steven A. Hunt, D. Francois Tolmie, and Ruben Zimmermann, 127–132. Tübingen, Germany: Mohr Siebeck, 2013.

Chapter 10: Jesus and Conflict

From Adventist Writers

Reynolds, Edwin. "What Is the Unpardonable Sin?" In *Interpreting Scripture: Bible Questions and Answers,* edited by Gerhard Pfandl, 270–272. Silver Spring, MD: Biblical Research Institute, 2010.

Rice, George E. "Luke 4:31–44: Release for the Captives." *Andrews University Seminary Studies* 20, no. 1 (1982): 23–28.

White, Ellen G. "Days of Conflict" (chapter 9). *The Desire of Ages*. Mountain View, CA: Pacific Press, 1898. https://egwwritings.org/?ref=en_DA.84¶=130.316.

______. "'Is Not This the Carpenter's Son?'" (chapter 24). *The Desire of Ages*. Mountain View, CA: Pacific Press, 1898. https://egwwritings.org/?ref=en_DA.236¶=130.1076.

______. "Who Are My Brethren?" (chapter 33). *The Desire of Ages*. Mountain View, CA: Pacific Press, 1898. https://egwwritings.org/?ref=en_DA.321¶=130.1538.

______. "Ministry" (chapter 47). *The Desire of Ages*. Mountain View, CA: Pacific Press, 1898. https://egwwritings.org/?ref=en_DA.426¶=130.2068.

From Other Writers

Bock, Darrell L. "More Galilean Ministry: Miracles, Mission to the Outcasts, and Discipleship in the Face of Opposition"; "From Kingdom Teaching to Confession: How the Disciples Began to Understand Jesus"; "Toward Jerusalem: The New Reality, Part 2"; "The Passion Week: Controversy, Prediction of Judgment and Return, Trial, Death, and Resurrection." In *Jesus According to Scripture: Restoring the Portrait from the Gospels*, 2nd ed., 272–275, 279, 306–308, 351–352, 354–356, 422–423, 433–437. With Benjamin I. Simpson. Grand Rapids, MI: Baker Academic, 2017.

Connick, C. Milo. "Crowds and Critics." In *Jesus: The Man, the Mission, and the Message*, 2nd ed., 172–177. Englewood Cliffs, NJ: Prentice-Hall, 1974.

Foster, R. C. "Controversies in Galilee." In *Studies in the Life of Christ: Introduction, the Early Period, the Middle Period, the Final Week*, 426–439. Joplin, MO: College Press, 1995.

Guthrie, Donald. *Jesus the Messiah: An Illustrated Life of Christ*, 123–136. Grand Rapids, MI: Zondervan, 1972.

Chapter 11: Jesus and the Weak

From Adventist Writers

Davidson, Jo Ann. "John 4: Another Look at the Samaritan Woman." *Andrews University Seminary Studies* 43, no. 1 (2005): 159–168.

Liu, Rebekah. "A Dog Under the Table at the Messianic Banquet: A Study of Mark 7:24–30." *Andrews University Seminary Studies* 48, no. 2 (2010): 251–255.

White, Ellen G. "'Thou Canst Make Me Clean'" (chapter 27). *The Desire of Ages*. Mountain View, CA: Pacific Press, 1898. https://egwwritings.org/?ref=en_DA.262¶=130.1212.

______. "Blessing the Children" (chapter 56). *The Desire of Ages*. Mountain View, CA: Pacific Press, 1898. https://egwwritings.org/?ref=en_DA.511¶=130.2495.

______. "The Feast at Simon's House" (chapter 62). *The Desire of Ages.* Mountain View, CA: Pacific Press, 1898. https://egwwritings.org/?ref=en_DA.557¶=130.2715.

From Other Writers

Bock, Darrell L. "More Galilean Ministry: Miracles, Mission to the Outcasts, and Discipleship in the Face of Opposition." In *Jesus According to Scripture: Restoring the Portrait from the Gospels,* 2nd ed., 235–282. With Benjamin I. Simpson. Grand Rapids, MI: Baker Academic, 2017.

______. "The Initial Portrait of Jesus's Galilean Ministry: Teaching, Healing, and Controversy." In *Jesus According to Scripture: Restoring the Portrait from the Gospels*, 2nd ed., 172–177, 180–186. Grand Rapids, MI: Baker Academic, 2017.

Foster, R. C. "The Syro-Phoenician Woman." In *Studies in the Life of Christ: Introduction, the Early Period, the Middle Period, the Final Week,* 675–679. Joplin, MO: College Press, 1995.

Guthrie, Donald. *Jesus the Messiah: An Illustrated Life of Christ,* 106, 251. Grand Rapids, MI: Zondervan, 1972.

Hardin, Leslie T. "Care for the Oppressed." In *The Spirituality of Jesus: Nine Disciplines Christ Modeled for Us,* 118–133. Grand Rapids, MI: Kregel, 2009.

Laymon, Charles M. "The Ministry of Service." In *The Life and Teachings of Jesus,* rev. ed., 133–143. New York: Abingdon, 1962.

Chapter 12: The Shadow of the Cross

From Adventist Writers

Gane, Roy E. "The Gospel According to Moses and Elijah." *Andrews University Seminary Studies* 48, no. 1 (2010): 7–15.

Morris, Derek J. "What Jesus Taught about His Church." In *The Radical Teachings of Jesus,* 114–128. Hagerstown, MD: Autumn House, 2009.

Sadiq, Younis M. "Matthew 16:13–20: Jesus' Warning to His Disciples." *Ministry Magazine* 82, no. 12 (December 2010): 24–27.

White, Ellen G. "The Crisis in Galilee" (chapter 41). *The Desire of Ages.* Mountain View, CA: Pacific Press, 1898. https://egwwritings.org/?ref=en_DA.383¶=130.1834.

______. "The Foreshadowing of the Cross" (chapter 45). Mountain View, CA: Pacific Press, 1898. *The Desire of Ages.* https://egwwritings.org/?ref=en_DA.410¶=130.1990.

______. "He Was Transfigured" (chapter 46). *The Desire of Ages.* Mountain View, CA: Pacific Press, 1898. https://egwwritings.org/?ref=en_DA.419¶=130.2042.

From Other Writers

Bock, Darrell L. "From Kingdom Teaching to Confession: How the Disciples Began to Understand Jesus"; "Continuing toward Jerusalem: Ministry in Judea and Final Lessons"; "The Book of Signs: Before the Hour." In *Jesus According to Scripture: Restoring the Portrait from the Gospels*, 2nd ed., 302–304, 318–325, 327–328, 403–405, 561–563, 569–571. With Benjamin I. Simpson. Grand Rapids, MI: Baker Academic, 2017.

Foster, R. C. "The Feeding of the Five Thousand"; "The Good Confession"; "The Transfiguration." In *Studies in the Life of Christ: Introduction, the Early Period, the Middle Period, the Final Week*, 629–644, 699–741. Joplin, MO: College Press, 1995.

Guthrie, Donald. *Jesus the Messiah: An Illustrated Life of Christ*, 170–177. Grand Rapids, MI: Zondervan, 1972.

Chapter 13: Darkness and Light

From Adventist Writers

Papaioannou, Kim. "Creation, Salvation, and the Divinity of Christ: A Look at John 1:1–13." *Ministry Magazine* 88, no. 11 (November 2016): 11–14.

White, Ellen G. "'The Light of Life'" (chapter 51). *The Desire of Ages*. Mountain View, CA: Pacific Press, 1898. https://egwwritings.org/?ref=en_DA.463¶=130.2253.

From Other Writers

Bock, Darrell L. "The Book of Signs: Before the Hour." In *Jesus According to Scripture: Restoring the Portrait from the Gospels*, 2nd ed., 588–592. With Benjamin I. Simpson. Grand Rapids, MI: Baker Academic, 2017.

Foster, R. C. "The Sermon on the Light of the World," "The Man Born Blind." In *Studies in the Life of Christ: Introduction, the Early Period, the Middle Period, the Final Week*, 810–836. Joplin, MO: College Press, 1995.

Janzen, J. Gerald. "'I Am the Light of the World' (John 8:12): Connotation and Context." *Encounter* 67, no. 2 (2006): 115–135.

Kim, Stephen S. "The Significance of Jesus' Healing the Blind Man in John 9." *Bibliotheca Sacra* 167, no. 667 (July–September 2010): 307–318.

Leslie, Britt. *One Thing I Know: How the Blind Man of John 9 Leads an Audience Toward Belief.* Eugene, OR: Pickwick, 2015.

Muropa, Clyde. "The Johannine Writings: Symbolism and the Symbol of 'Light' in the Gospel of John." *Asbury Journal* 67, no. 2 (Fall 2012): 106–113.

Wright, N. T. "The Light of the World." In *The Challenge of Jesus: Rediscovering Who Jesus Was and Is,* 174–197. Downers Grove, IL: InterVarsity Press, 2015.

Chapter 14: A Spectacular Miracle

From Adventist Writers

Liu, Rebekah. "A Dog under the Table at the Messianic Banquet: A Study of Mark 7:24–30." *Andrews University Seminary Studies* 48, no. 2 (2010): 251–255.

Sabuin, Richard A. "Zacchaeus: A Man with Many Connections." *Ministry Magazine* 82, no. 6 (June 2010): 6–9.

White, Ellen G. "The Last Journey from Galilee" (chapter 53). *The Desire of Ages.* Mountain View, CA: Pacific Press, 1898. https://egwwritings.org/?ref=en_DA.485¶=130.2371.

______. "'Lazarus, Come Forth'" (chapter 58). *The Desire of Ages.* Mountain View, CA: Pacific Press, 1898. https://egwwritings.org/?ref=en_DA.524¶=130.2556.

______. "The Law of the New Kingdom" (chapter 60). *The Desire of Ages.* Mountain View, CA: Pacific Press, 1898. https://egwwritings.org/?ref=en_DA.547¶=130.2654.

______. "Zacchaeus" (chapter 61). *The Desire of Ages.* Mountain View, CA: Pacific Press, 1898. https://egwwritings.org/?ref=en_DA.552¶=130.2686.

From Other Writers

Bock, Darrell L. "From Kingdom Teaching to Confession: How the Disciples Began to Understand Jesus"; "Toward Jerusalem: The New Reality, Part 2"; "Continuing toward Jerusalem: Ministry in Judea and Final Lessons"; "The Book of Signs: Before the Hour." In *Jesus According to Scripture: Restoring the Portrait from the Gospels,* 2nd ed., 308–310, 353, 408–409, 598–603. With Benjamin I. Simpson. Grand Rapids, MI: Baker Academic, 2017.

Burke, Alexander J. *The Raising of Lazarus and the Passion of Jesus in John 11 and 12: A Study of John's Literary Structure and His Narrative Theology.* Lewiston, NY: Mellen, 2003.

Corbin Reuschling, Wyndy. "Zacchaeus' Conversion: To Be or Not to Be a Tax Collector (Luke 19:1–10)." *Ex Auditu* 25 (2009): 67–88.

Foster, R. C. "The Raising of Lazarus." In *Studies in the Life of Christ: Introduction, the Early Period, the Middle Period, the Final Week,* 968–985. Joplin, MO: College Press, 1995.

Kim, Stephen S. "The Significance of Jesus' Raising Lazarus from the Dead in John 11." *Bibliotheca Sacra* 168, no. 669 (January–March 2011): 53–62.

Yancey, Philip. "Miracles: Snapshots of the Supernatural." In *The Jesus I Never Knew,* 163–184. Grand Rapids, MI: Zondervan, 1995.

Chapter 15: What Jesus Taught about God

From Adventist Writers

White, Ellen G. "Teaching in Parables" (chapter 1). *Christ's Object Lessons*. N.p.: Review and Herald, 1900. https://egwwritings.org/?ref=en_COL.17¶=15.31.

———. "The True Motive in Service" (chapter 4). *Thoughts from the Mount of Blessing*. Mountain View, CA: Pacific Press, 1896. https://egwwritings.org/?ref=en_MB.79¶=150.407.

From Other Writers

Bock, Darrell L. "The Book of Glory: The Farewell Discourse and the Johannine Passion Account—the Hour Has Come." In *Jesus According to Scripture: Restoring the Portrait from the Gospels*, 2nd ed., 622–625. With Benjamin I. Simpson. Grand Rapids, MI: Baker Academic, 2017.

Harris, Murray J. *Jesus as God: The New Testament Use of Theos in Reference to Jesus*. Grand Rapids, MI: Baker Book House, 1992.

Hultgren, Arland J. "Parables of the Revelation of God." In *The Parables of Jesus: A Commentary*, 20–91. Grand Rapids, MI: Eerdmans, 2000.

McVerry, Peter. *The God of Mercy, the God of the Gospels*. Dublin: Veritas, 2016.

Sontag, Frederick E. "The God Behind the Gospels." *Encounter* 42, no. 1 (1981): 45–47.

Wright, N. T. "Jesus and God." In *The Challenge of Jesus: Rediscovering Who Jesus Was and Is*, 96–125. Downers Grove, IL: InterVarsity Press, 2015.

Chapter 16: What Jesus Taught about Himself

From Adventist Writers

Morris, Derek J. "What Jesus Taught about Himself." In *The Radical Teachings of Jesus*, 12–25. Hagerstown, MD: Autumn House, 2009.

Thiele, David. "The Parable of the Unmerciful Servant and the Problem of the (Ir)revocability of Forgiveness (Matthew 18:23–35)." In *Biblical Parables: Essays in Honor of Robert M. Johnston*, edited by Thomas R. Shepherd and Ranko Stefanovic, 94–108. Berrien Springs, MI: Andrews University, 2016.

White, Ellen G. "The Light of Life" (chapter 51). *The Desire of Ages*. Mountain View, CA: Pacific Press, 1898. https://egwwritings.org/?ref=en_DA.463¶=130.2253.

———. "The Divine Shepherd" (chapter 52). *The Desire of Ages*. Mountain View, CA: Pacific Press, 1898. https://egwwritings.org/?ref=en_DA.476¶=130.2331.

From Other Writers

Bailey, Kenneth E. *The Good Shepherd: A Thousand-Year Journey from Psalm 23 to the New Testament.* Downers Grove, IL: InterVarsity Press, 2014.

Bock, Darrell L. "The Book of Signs: Before the Hour"; "The Book of Glory: The Farewell Discourse and the Johannine Passion Account—the Hour Has Come." In *Jesus According to Scripture: Restoring the Portrait from the Gospels*, 2nd ed., 581–588, 592–598, 607–612, 629–632. With Benjamin I. Simpson. Grand Rapids, MI: Baker Academic, 2017.

Connick, C. Milo. *Jesus: The Man, the Mission, and the Message.* 2nd ed. Englewood Cliffs, NJ: Prentice-Hall, 1974.

Foster, R. C. "The Good Shepherd." In *Studies in the Life of Christ: Introduction, the Early Period, the Middle Period, the Final Week*, 837–841. Joplin, MO: College Press, 1995.

Chapter 17: What Jesus Taught about the Holy Spirit

From Adventist Writers

Dederen, Raoul. "Reflections on the Doctrine of the Trinity." *Andrews University Seminary Studies* 8, no. 1 (1970): 1–22.

Paroschi, Wilson. "'Another Paraclete': The Holy Spirit in John 14–17." *Ministry Magazine* 84, no. 4 (April 2012): 25–27.

Whidden, Woodrow W. "God the Holy Spirit: His Divine Personhood and Ministry." *Ministry Magazine* 74, no. 4 (April 2003): 21–23.

White, Ellen G. "The Gift of the Spirit" (chapter 5). *The Acts of the Apostles.* Mountain View, CA: Pacific Press, 1911. https://egwwritings.org/?ref=en_AA.47¶=127.180.

______, Ellen G. "'Let Not Your Heart be Troubled'" (chapter 73). *The Desire of Ages.* Mountain View, CA: Pacific Press, 1898. https://egwwritings.org/?ref=en_DA.662¶=130.3257.

From Other Writers

Aloisi, John. "The Paraclete's Ministry of Conviction: Another Look at John 16:8–11." *Journal of Evangelical Theological Society* 47, no. 1 (March 2004): 55–69.

Bock, Darrell L. "More Galilean Ministry: Miracles, Mission to the Outcasts, and Discipleship in the Face of Opposition"; "Toward Jerusalem: The New Reality, Part 2"; "The Book of Glory: The Farewell Discourse and the Johannine Passion Account—the Hour Has Come." In *Jesus According to Scripture: Restoring the Portrait from the Gospels*, 2nd ed., 275–276, 358–359, 625–628, 635–636, 637–639. With Benjamin I. Simpson. Grand Rapids, MI: Baker Academic, 2017.

Foster, R. C. "The Blasphemy Against the Holy Spirit." In *Studies in the Life of Christ: Introduction, the Early Period, the Middle Period, the Final Week*, 541–555. Joplin, MO: College Press, 1995.

Guthrie, Donald. *Jesus the Messiah: An Illustrated Life of Christ*, 311–314. Grand Rapids, MI: Zondervan, 1972.

Thiselton, Anthony C. "The Holy Spirit in the Synoptic Gospels." In *The Holy Spirit: In Biblical Teaching, through the Centuries, and Today*, 33–48. Grand Rapids, MI: Eerdmans, 2013.

Warringston, Keith. "The Synoptic Gospels." In *A Biblical Theology of the Holy Spirit*, edited by Trevor J. Burke and Keith Warrington, 84–103. Eugene, OR: Cascade Books, 2014.

Chapter 18: What Jesus Taught about the Kingdom of Heaven

From Adventist Writers

Kidder, S. Joseph. "'This Generation' in Matthew 24:34." *Andrews University Seminary Studies* 21, no. 3 (1983): 203–209.

Nixon, John S. "The Second Coming: Knowing and Not Knowing." *Ministry Magazine* 73, nos. 6/7 (June/July 2000): 24–27.

White, Ellen G. "The Beatitudes." *Thoughts from the Mount of Blessing*. Mountain View, CA: Pacific Press, 1896. https://egwwritings.org/?ref=en_MB.6¶=150.52.

______. "The Spirituality of the Law." *Thoughts from the Mount of Blessing*. Mountain View, CA: Pacific Press, 1896. https://egwwritings.org/?ref=en_MB.45¶=150.237.

From Other Writers

Bock, Darrell L. "Jesus's Central Message: The Kingdom of God"; "The Nature of the Kingdom: Presence, Realm, Ethics, Messiah, and the Father." In *Jesus the God-Man: The Unity and Diversity of the Gospel Portrayals*, 15–64. Grand Rapids, MI: Baker Academic, 2016.

Connick, C. Milo. *Jesus: The Man, the Mission, and the Message*, 2nd ed., 208–224, 228–236, 243–244. Englewood Cliffs, NJ: Prentice-Hall, 1974.

Currie, James S. *The Kingdom of God Is Like . . . Baseball: A Metaphor for Jesus' Kingdom Parables*. Eugene, OR: Cascade Books, 2011.

Guthrie, Donald. *Jesus the Messiah: An Illustrated Life of Christ*, 141–144. Grand Rapids, MI: Zondervan, 1972.

Laymon, Charles M. "Preaching the Kingdom of God." In *The Life and Teachings of Jesus*, rev. ed., 168–178. New York: Abingdon, 1962.

Snodgrass, Klyne. "Parables of the Present Kingdom in Matthew 13, Mark 4, and

Luke 13." In *Stories with Intent: A Comprehensive Guide to the Parables of Jesus,* 179–254. Grand Rapids, MI: Eerdmans, 2008.

Wright, N. T. "The Challenge of the Kingdom." In *The Challenge of Jesus: Rediscovering Who Jesus Was and Is,* 34–53. Downers Grove, IL: InterVarsity Press, 2015.

Chapter 19: What Jesus Taught about Grace

From Adventist Writers

Morris, Derek J. "What Jesus Taught about Salvation." In *The Radical Teachings of Jesus,* 38–51. Hagerstown, MD: Autumn House, 2009.

Mulzac, Ken. "Grace in the Synoptic Teachings of Jesus." *Journal of the Adventist Theological Society* 14, no. 2 (2003): 66–79.

White, Ellen G. "'Lost and Is Found.'" *Christ's Object Lessons.* N.p.: Review and Herald, 1900. https://egwwritings.org/?ref=en_COL.198¶=15.833.

______. "The Measure of Forgiveness." *Christ's Object Lessons.* N.p.: Review and Herald, 1900. https://egwwritings.org/?ref=en_COL.243¶=15.1027.

______. "The Reward of Grace." *Christ's Object Lessons.* N.p.: Review and Herald, 1900. https://egwwritings.org/?ref=en_COL.390¶=15.1754.

______. "Two Worshipers." *Christ's Object Lessons.* N.p.: Review and Herald, 1900. https://egwwritings.org/?ref=en_COL.150¶=15.617.

______. "Without a Wedding Garment." *Christ's Object Lessons.* N.p.: Review and Herald, 1900. https://egwwritings.org/?ref=en_COL.307¶=15.1349.

From Other Writers

Bailey, Kenneth E. *The Cross and the Prodigal: Luke 15 through the Eyes of Middle Eastern Peasants.* Rev. ed. Downers Grove, IL: InterVarsity Press, 2005.

Bock, Darrell L. "Confession and Prediction: The New Reality, Part 1"; "Toward Jerusalem: The New Reality, Part 2"; "Continuing toward Jerusalem: Ministry in Judea and Final Lessons"; "The Passion Week: Controversy, Prediction of Judgment and Return, Trial, Death, and Resurrection"; "The Book of Signs: Before the Hour." In *Jesus According to Scripture: Restoring the Portrait from the Gospels,* 2nd ed., 336–337, 376–378, 384, 391, 402–403, 427–428, 579–581. With Benjamin I. Simpson. Grand Rapids, MI: Baker Academic, 2017.

Caneday, A. B. "The Parable of the Generous Vineyard Owner (Matthew 20:1–16)." *Southern Baptist Journal of Theology* 13, no. 3 (Fall 2009): 34–50.

Foster, R. C. "The Parable of the Prodigal Son." In *Studies in the Life of Christ: Introduction, the Early Period, the Middle Period, the Final Week,* 934–945. Joplin, MO: College Press, 1995.

Guthrie, Donald. *Jesus the Messiah: An Illustrated Life of Christ*, 188–189, 210–214. Grand Rapids, MI: Zondervan, 1972.

Hultgren, Arland J. "Parables of the Revelation of God." In *The Parables of Jesus: A Commentary*, 20–91. Grand Rapids, MI: Eerdmans, 2000.

Neufeld, Edmund K. "The Gospel in the Gospels: Answering the Question 'What Must I Do to Be Saved?' from the Synoptics." *Journal of the Evangelical Theological Society* 51, no. 2 (June 2008): 267–296.

Snodgrass, Klyne. "Grace and Responsibility"; "Parables of Lostness." In *Stories with Intent: A Comprehensive Guide to the Parables of Jesus*, 61–144. Grand Rapids, MI: Eerdmans, 2008.

Chapter 20: What Jesus Taught about Discipleship

From Adventist Writers

Christian, Ed. "Hate Your Family and Carry Your Cross: A Doctrine of Discipleship." *Journal of the Adventist Theological Society* 10, nos. 1–2 (1999): 259–267.

Rice, George E. "Luke's Thematic Use of the Call to Discipleship." *Andrews University Seminary Studies* 19, no. 1 (1981): 51–58.

White, Ellen G. "The Call by the Sea" (chapter 25). *The Desire of Ages*. Mountain View, CA: Pacific Press, 1898. https://egwwritings.org/?ref=en_DA.244¶=130.1120.

______. "The First Evangelists" (chapter 37). *The Desire of Ages*. Mountain View, CA: Pacific Press, 1898. https://egwwritings.org/?ref=en_DA.349¶=130.1678.

______. "Who Is the Greatest" (chapter 48). Mountain View, CA: Pacific Press, 1898. *The Desire of Ages*. https://egwwritings.org/?ref=en_DA.432¶=130.2101.

From Other Writers

Bock, Darrell L. "Jesus' Community of the New Era: The Calling of Those Who Respond." In *Jesus the God-Man: The Unity and Diversity of the Gospel Portrayals*, 123–148. Grand Rapids, MI: Baker Academic, 2016.

England, Frank. "A Shoe, a Garment, and the Frangible Self in the Gospel of Mark: Christian Discipleship in a Postmodern World." *Neotestamentica* 47, no. 2 (2013): 263–302.

Fever, Kyle Thomas. "The Downward Mobility of Discipleship in Matthew's Gospel." *Lutheran Forum* 47, no. 4 (2013): 16–19.

Hardin, Leslie T. *The Spirituality of Jesus: Nine Disciplines Christ Modeled for Us*. Grand Rapids, MI: Kregel, 2009.

Mills, Kathleen Elizabeth. *Kinship of Jesus: Christology and Discipleship in the Gospel of Mark*. Eugene, OR: Pickwick, 2016.

Snodgrass, Klyne. "Parables about Discipleship." In *Stories with Intent: A Comprehensive Guide to the Parables of Jesus,* 327–388. Grand Rapids, MI: Eerdmans, 2008.

Stott, John R. *The Beatitudes: Developing Spiritual Character.* Downers Grove, IL: InterVarsity Press, 2008.

Chapter 21: What Jesus Taught about the Sabbath

From Adventist Writers

Bacchiocchi, Samuele. "Matthew 11:28–30: Jesus' Rest and the Sabbath." *Andrews University Seminary Studies* 22, no. 3 (1984): 289–316.

McIver, Robert K. "The Sabbath in the Gospel of Matthew: A Paradigm for Understanding the Law in Matthew?" *Andrews University Seminary Studies* 33, no. 2 (1995): 231–243.

Morris, Derek J. "What Jesus Taught about the Sabbath." In *The Radical Teachings of Jesus,* 66–83. Hagerstown, MD: Autumn House, 2009.

Shea, William H. "The Sabbath in Matthew 24:20." *Andrews University Seminary Studies* 40, no. 1 (2002): 23–35.

Tonstad, Sigve K. *The Lost Meaning of the Seventh Day.* Berrien Springs, MI: Andrews University Press, 2009.

White, Ellen G. "Bethesda and the Sanhedrin" (chapter 21). *The Desire of Ages.* Mountain View, CA: Pacific Press, 1898. https://egwwritings.org/?ref=en_DA.201¶=130.907.

______. "The Sabbath" (chapter 29). *The Desire of Ages.* Mountain View, CA: Pacific Press, 1898. https://egwwritings.org/?ref=en_DA.281¶=130.1322.

From Other Writers

Bock, Darrell L. "The Initial Portrait of Jesus's Galilean Ministry: Teaching, Healing, and Controversy"; "More Galilean Ministry: Miracles, Mission to the Outcasts, and Discipleship in the Face of Opposition"; "Toward Jerusalem: The New Reality, Part 2"; "The Book of Signs: Before the Hour." In *Jesus According to Scripture: Restoring the Portrait from the Gospels,* 2nd ed., 193–195, 266–267, 367–368, 555–561. With Benjamin I. Simpson. Grand Rapids, MI: Baker Academic, 2017.

Burer, Michael H. *Divine Sabbath Work.* Winona Lake: Eisenbrauns, 2012.

Collins, Nina L. *Jesus, the Sabbath, and the Jewish Debate: Healing on the Sabbath in the 1st and 2nd Centuries CE.* London: Bloomsbury T&T Clark, 2014.

Foster, R. C. "The Sabbath Controversy." In *Studies in the Life of Christ: Introduction, the Early Period, the Middle Period, the Final Week,* 455–461. Joplin, MO: College Press, 1995.

Hagner, Donald A. "Jesus and the Synoptic Sabbath Controversies." *Bulletin for Biblical Research* 19, no. 2 (2009): 215–248.

Chapter 22: What Jesus Taught about the End

From Adventist Writers

Gallusz, Laszlo. "Synoptic Tradition in the Apocalypse: The Influence of the Lukan Parables of the Watching Servant and the Thief (Luke 12:35–40)." In *Biblical Parables: Essays in Honor of Robert M. Johnston,* edited by Thomas R. Shepherd and Ranko Stefanovic, 140–154. Berrien Springs, MI: Andrews University, 2016.

Lennox, Abrigo. "Jesus' 'Betrothal Promise' in His Bride's Guarantee of Heaven." *Ministry Magazine* 86, no. 6 (June 2014): 24–26.

Morris, Derek J. "What Jesus Taught about the Judgment." In *The Radical Teachings of Jesus,* 84–97. Hagerstown, MD: Autumn House, 2009.

White, Ellen G. "On the Mount of Olives" (chapter 69). *The Desire of Ages.* Mountain View, CA: Pacific Press, 1898. https://egwwritings.org/?ref=en_DA.627¶=130.3081.

______. "'The Least of These My Brethren'" (chapter 70). *The Desire of Ages.* Mountain View, CA: Pacific Press, 1898. https://egwwritings.org/?ref=en_DA.637¶=130.3127.

From Other Writers

Bock, Darrell L. "The Vindication to Come: Warning to Israel, Gentile Inclusion, and the Son of Man's Return to Judge." In *Jesus the God-Man: The Unity and Diversity of the Gospel Portrayals,* 149–158. Grand Rapids, MI: Baker Academic, 2016.

______. "Toward Jerusalem: The New Reality, Part 2"; "The Passion Week: Controversy, Prediction of Judgment and Return, Trial, Death, and Resurrection." In *Jesus According to Scripture: Restoring the Portrait from the Gospels,* 2nd ed., 387–389, 438–456. With Benjamin I. Simpson. Grand Rapids, MI: Baker Academic, 2017.

Connick, C. Milo. "Sermon and Eschatology," "Eschatology and Ethics"; "Apocalyptic Interlude." In *Jesus: The Man, the Mission, and the Message,* 2nd ed., 260–264, 348–351. Englewood Cliffs, NJ: Prentice-Hall, 1974.

Foster, R. C. "Warning Concerning the Judgment Day"; "The Destruction of Jerusalem"; "The Second Coming." In *Studies in the Life of Christ: Introduction, the Early Period, the Middle Period, the Final Week,* 889–902, 1184–1210. Joplin, MO: College Press, 1995.

Guthrie, Donald. *Jesus the Messiah: An Illustrated Life of Christ,* 293–297. Grand Rapids, MI: Zondervan, 1972.

Merkle, Benjamin L. "Who Will Be Left Behind? Rethinking the Meaning of Matthew 24:40–41 and Luke 17:34–35." *Westminster Theological Journal* 72, no. 1 (2010): 169–179.

Snodgrass, Klyne. "Parables of Future Eschatology." In *Stories with Intent: A Comprehensive Guide to the Parables of Jesus,* 477–564. Grand Rapids, MI: Eerdmans, 2008.

Chapter 23: What Jesus Taught about Prayer

From Adventist Writers

Hasel, Frank M. "Prayer That Pleases God," *Perspective Digest,* www.perspectivedigest. org/article/133/archives/19–2/prayer-that-pleases-god.

Taber, Gary. *Surprised by the Lord's Prayer.* Bloomington, IN: WestBow Press, 2016.

White, Ellen G. "The Privilege of Prayer" (chapter 11). *Steps to Christ.* Mountain View, CA: Pacific Press, 1892. https://egwwritings.org/?ref=en_SC.93¶=108.367.

From Other Writers

Bock, Darrell L. "Jesus's Teaching on Relating to God and Others: The Sermon on the Mount and the Sermon on the Plain"; "Toward Jerusalem: The New Reality, Part 2"; "The Book of Glory: The Farewell Discourse and the Johannine Passion Account—the Hour has Come." In *Jesus According to Scripture: Restoring the Portrait from the Gospels,* 2nd ed., 216–218, 224–225, 349–351, 390, 641–643, 644–651. With Benjamin I. Simpson. Grand Rapids, MI: Baker Academic, 2017.

Connick, C. Milo. "Disciples' Prayer." In *Jesus: The Man, the Mission, and the Message,* 2nd ed., 250–255. Englewood Cliffs, NJ: Prentice-Hall, 1974.

Foster, R. C. "Discourse on Prayer"; "Parables on Prayer." In *Studies in the Life of Christ: Introduction, the Early Period, the Middle Period, the Final Week,* 860–867, 998–1010. Joplin, MO: College Press, 1995.

Oakman, Douglas E. *Jesus, Debt, and the Lord's Prayer.* Eugene, OR: Cascade Books, 2014.

Snodgrass, Klyne. "Parables Concerning God and Prayer." In *Stories with Intent: A Comprehensive Guide to the Parables of Jesus,* 437–476. Grand Rapids, MI: Eerdmans, 2008.

Stiller, Karen, ed. *The Lord's Prayer.* Eugene, OR: Wipf and Stock, 2017.

Chapter 24: What Jesus Taught about Power, Sex, and Money

From Adventist Writers

Christian, Ed. "The 'Hard Sayings' of Jesus and Divorce: Not Commandments but Goals." *Journal of the Adventist Theological Society* 12, no. 2 (2001): 62–75.

Mueller, Ekkehardt. "Did Jesus Permit Divorce and Remarriage?" In *Interpreting Scripture: Bible Questions and Answers*, edited by Gerhard Pfandl, 280–284. Silver Spring, MD: Biblical Research Institute, 2010.

White, Ellen G. "The Sermon on the Mount" (chapter 31). *The Desire of Ages*. Mountain View, CA: Pacific Press, 1898. https://egwwritings. org/?ref=en_DA.298¶=130.1414.

———. "'One Thing Thou Lackest'" (chapter 57). *The Desire of Ages*. Mountain View, CA: Pacific Press, 1898. https://egwwritings. org/?ref=en_DA.518¶=130.2528.

From Other Writers

Bock, Darrell L. "Confession and Prediction: The New Reality, Part 1"; "Toward Jerusalem: The New Reality, Part 2"; "Continuing toward Jerusalem: Ministry in Judea and Final Lessons"; "The Passion Week: Controversy, Prediction of Judgment and Return, Trial, Death, and Resurrection." In *Jesus According to Scripture: Restoring the Portrait from the Gospels*, 2nd ed., 329–331, 359–361, 372, 395–397, 398–402, 405–407, 466–467. With Benjamin I. Simpson. Grand Rapids, MI: Baker Academic, 2017.

Foster, R. C. "Broken Homes Versus Happy Homes"; "The Rich Young Ruler." In *Studies in the Life of Christ: Introduction, the Early Period, the Middle Period, the Final Week*, 1011–1029. Joplin, MO: College Press, 1995.

Hurtado, Larry W. *Mark: A Good News Commentary*, 144–150. Grand Rapids, MI: Baker Books, 1989.

Loader, William R. G. "Did Adultery Mandate Divorce? A Reassessment of Jesus' Divorce Logia." *New Testament Studies* 61, no. 1 (January 2015): 67–78.

McKnight, Scot. *Sermon on the Mount*. The Story of God Bible Commentary. Grand Rapids, MI: Zondervan, 2013.

Oakman, Douglas E. *Jesus, Debt, and the Lord's Prayer: First-Century Debt and Jesus' Intentions*. Eugene, OR: Cascade Books, 2014.

Snodgrass, Klyne. "Parables about Money." In *Stories with Intent: A Comprehensive Guide to the Parables of Jesus*, 389–436. Grand Rapids, MI: Eerdmans, 2008.

Chapter 25: From "Hosanna" to "Crucify Him!"

From Adventist Writers

Kay, Warren. "At Jesus' Feet," *Ministry Magazine* 80, no. 2 (February 2008): 21–22.

Rice, George E. "The Role of the Populace in the Passion Narrative of Luke in Codex Bezae." *Andrews University Seminary Studies* 19, no. 2 (1981): 147–153.

White, Ellen G. "The Feast at Simon's House" (chapter 62). *The Desire of Ages.* Mountain View, CA: Pacific Press, 1898. https://egwwritings.org/?ref=en_DA.557¶=130.2715.

______. "'Thy King Cometh'" (chapter 63). *The Desire of Ages.* Mountain View, CA: Pacific Press, 1898. https://egwwritings.org/?ref=en_DA.569¶=130.2781.

From Other Writers

Bock, Darrell L. "Continuing toward Jerusalem: Ministry in Judea and Final Lessons"; "The Passion Week: Controversy, Prediction of Judgment and Return, Trial, Death, and Resurrection"; "The Book of Signs: Before the Hour." In *Jesus According to Scripture: Restoring the Portrait from the Gospels*, 2nd ed., 411–413, 457–458, 603–607. With Benjamin I. Simpson. Grand Rapids, MI: Baker Academic, 2017.

Foster, R. C. "Simon the Pharisee"; "The Anointing of Jesus by Mary"; "The Triumphal Entry." In *Studies in the Life of Christ: Introduction, the Early Period, the Middle Period, the Final Week*, 533–539, 1075–1102. Joplin, MO: College Press, 1995.

Guthrie, Donald. *Jesus the Messiah: An Illustrated Life of Christ*, 265–272. Grand Rapids, MI: Zondervan, 1972.

Chapter 26: Messiah versus the Temple

From Adventist Writers

Brooks, Oscar S. "The Function of the Double Love Command in Matthew 22:34–40." *Andrews University Seminary Studies* 36, no. 1 (1998): 7–22.

LaRondelle, Hans K. "'This Generation Will Certainly Not Pass Away': What Did Jesus Mean?" *Ministry Magazine* 72, no. 9 (September 1999): 24–28.

White, Ellen G. "A Doomed People" (chapter 64). *The Desire of Ages.* Mountain View, CA: Pacific Press, 1898. https://egwwritings.org/?ref=en_DA.580¶=130.2836.

______. "The Temple Cleansed Again" (chapter 65). *The Desire of Ages.* Mountain View, CA: Pacific Press, 1898. https://egwwritings.org/?ref=en_DA.589¶=130.2874.

______. "Controversy" (chapter 66). *The Desire of Ages.* Mountain View, CA: Pacific Press, 1898. https://egwwritings.org/?ref=en_DA.601¶=130.2938.

From Other Writers

Bock, Darrell L. "Jesus's Final Week: A Dispute over Authority." In *Jesus the God-Man: The Unity and Diversity of the Gospel Portrayals*, 159–168. Grand Rapids, MI: Baker Academic, 2016.

______. "Toward Jerusalem: The New Reality, Part 2"; "The Passion Week: Controversy, Prediction of Judgment and Return, Trial, Death, and Resurrection"; "The Book of Signs: Before the Hour." In *Jesus According to Scripture: Restoring the Portrait from the Gospels*, 2nd ed., 346–348, 366–367, 416–421, 424–427, 429–433, 573–579. With Benjamin I. Simpson. Grand Rapids, MI: Baker Academic, 2017.

Connick, C. Milo. *Jesus: The Man, the Mission, and the Message*. 2nd ed. 328–345. Englewood Cliffs, NJ: Prentice-Hall, 1974.

Foster, R. C. "The Cursing of the Fig Tree"; "Jesus and the Pharisees"; "Jesus and the Sadducees"; "The End of the Debate." In *Studies in the Life of Christ: Introduction, the Early Period, the Middle Period, the Final Week*, 1103–1112, 1125–1155, 1174–1179. Joplin, MO: College Press, 1995.

Guthrie, Donald. *Jesus the Messiah: An Illustrated Life of Christ*, 275–287. Grand Rapids, MI: Zondervan, 1972.

Chapter 27: The Last Thursday

From Adventist Writers

Augsburger, Daniel. "John and the Institution of the Lord's Supper." *Andrews University Seminary Studies* 1, no. 1 (1963): 3–24.

Mueller, Ekkehardt. "Seventh-day Adventists and the Lord's Supper." *Ministry Magazine* 76, no. 4 (April 2004): 10–13.

White, Ellen G. "'In Remembrance of Me'" (chapter 72). *The Desire of Ages*. Mountain View, CA: Pacific Press, 1898. https://egwwritings.org/?ref=en_DA.652¶=130.3208.

______. "Gethsemane" (chapter 74). *The Desire of Ages*. Mountain View, CA: Pacific Press, 1898. https://egwwritings.org/?ref=en_DA.685¶=130.3359.

From Other Writers

Bock, Darrell L. "The Passion Week: Controversy, Prediction of Judgment and Return, Trial, Death, and Resurrection"; "The Book of Glory: The Farewell Discourse and the Johannine Passion Account—the Hour has Come." In *Jesus According to Scripture: Restoring the Portrait from the Gospels*, 2nd ed., 459–465, 467–469, 470–472, 615–621. With Benjamin I. Simpson. Grand Rapids, MI: Baker Academic, 2017.

Connick, C. Milo. *Jesus: The Man, the Mission, and the Message*, 2nd ed., 360–372.

Englewood Cliffs, NJ: Prentice-Hall, 1974.

Foster, R. C. "In the Upper Room"; "In the Garden." In *Studies in the Life of Christ: Introduction, the Early Period, the Middle Period, the Final Week*, 1211–1239. Joplin, MO: College Press, 1995.

Guthrie, Donald. *Jesus the Messiah: An Illustrated Life of Christ*, 303–310. Grand Rapids, MI: Zondervan, 1972.

Hobbs, Herschel. "The Gathering Gloom." In *The Illustrated Life of Jesus*, 226–253. Nashville: Holman Bible Publishers, 2000.

Schreiner, Thomas R., and Matthew R. Crawford. *The Lord's Supper: Remembering and Proclaiming Christ until He Comes*. NAC Studies in Bible and Theology. Nashville: B&H Academic, 2010.

Chapter 28: The Judge on Trial

From Adventist Writers

Bacchiocchi, Samuele. "Rome and Christianity until 62 AD." *Andrews University Seminary Studies*, 21, no. 1 (1983): 3–25.

White, Ellen G. "Before Annas and the Court of Caiaphas" (chapter 75). *The Desire of Ages*. https://egwwritings.org/?ref=en_DA.698¶=130.3419.

———. "Judas" (chapter 76). *The Desire of Ages*. Mountain View, CA: Pacific Press, 1898. https://egwwritings.org/?ref=en_DA.716¶=130.3509.

———. "In Pilate's Judgment Hall" (chapter 77). *The Desire of Ages*. Mountain View, CA: Pacific Press, 1898. https://egwwritings.org/?ref=en_DA.723¶=130.3548.

From Other Writers

Bock, Darrell L. "The Passion Week: Controversy, Prediction of Judgment and Return, Trial, Death, and Resurrection"; "The Book of Glory: The Farewell Discourse and the Johannine Passion Account—the Hour has Come." In *Jesus According to Scripture: Restoring the Portrait from the Gospels*, 2nd ed., 472–490, 651–663. With Benjamin I. Simpson. Grand Rapids, MI: Baker Academic, 2017.

Connick, C. Milo. "The Condemnation and Crucifixion." In *Jesus: The Man, the Mission, and the Message*, 2nd ed., 375–386. Englewood Cliffs, NJ: Prentice-Hall, 1974.

Foster, R. C. "The Good Confession Before Pontius Pilate." In *Studies in the Life of Christ: Introduction, the Early Period, the Middle Period, the Final Week*, 1255–1264. Joplin, MO: College Press, 1995.

Guthrie, Donald. *Jesus the Messiah: An Illustrated Life of Christ*, 321–340. Grand Rapids, MI: Zondervan, 1972.

Hobbs, Herschel. "The Crucifixion of Jesus." In *The Illustrated Life of Jesus*, 254–283. Nashville: Holman Bible Publishers, 2000.

Chapter 29: Calvary

From Adventist Writers

Paroschi, Wilson. "The Significance of a Comma: An Analysis of Luke 23:43." *Ministry Magazine* 85, no. 6 (June 2013): 6–9.

White, Ellen G. "Calvary" (chapter 78). *The Desire of Ages*. Mountain View, CA: Pacific Press, 1898. https://egwwritings.org/?ref=en_DA.741¶=130.3660.

______. "'It Is Finished'" (chapter 79). *The Desire of Ages*. Mountain View, CA: Pacific Press, 1898. https://egwwritings.org/?ref=en_DA.758¶=130.3742.

From Other Writers

Bock, Darrell L. "The Passion Week: Controversy, Prediction of Judgment and Return, Trial, Death, and Resurrection"; "The Book of Glory: The Farewell Discourse and the Johannine Passion Account—the Hour has Come." In *Jesus According to Scripture: Restoring the Portrait from the Gospels*, 2nd ed., 492–499, 663–666. With Benjamin I. Simpson. Grand Rapids, MI: Baker Academic, 2017.

Connick, C. Milo. "Crucifixion"; "Burial." In *Jesus: The Man, the Mission, and the Message*, 2nd ed., 386–397. Englewood Cliffs, NJ: Prentice-Hall, 1974.

Foster, R. C. "The Death of Christ." In *Studies in the Life of Christ: Introduction, the Early Period, the Middle Period, the Final Week*, 1265–1304. Joplin, MO: College Press, 1995.

Hobbs, Herschel. "The Crucifixion of Jesus." In *The Illustrated Life of Jesus*, 254–283. Nashville: Holman Bible Publishers, 2000.

Stott, John R. *The Cross of Christ*. Downers Grove, IL: InterVarsity Press, 2006.

Wright, N. T. "The Crucified Messiah." In *The Challenge of Jesus: Rediscovering Who Jesus Was and Is,* 74–95. Downers Grove, IL: InterVarsity Press, 2015.

Chapter 30: He Is Risen!

From Adventist Writers

Hasel, Gerhard Franz. "The Resurrection of Jesus Myth or Historical Reality?" *Journal of the Adventist Theological Society* 6, no. 1 (1995): 5–57.

Moore, Marvin. *The Case for the Investigative Judgment*. Nampa, ID: Pacific Press, 2010.

Paulien, Jon. "The Resurrection and the New Testament: A Fresh Look in Light of Recent Research." *Andrews University Seminary Studies* 50, no. 2 (2012): 249–269.

White, Ellen G. "In Joseph's Tomb" (chapter 80). *The Desire of Ages.* Mountain View, CA: Pacific Press, 1898. https://egwwritings.org/?ref=en_DA.769¶=130.3790.

______. "'The Lord Is Risen'" (chapter 81). *The Desire of Ages.* Mountain View, CA: Pacific Press, 1898. https://egwwritings.org/?ref=en_DA.779¶=130.3841.

______. "'Why Weepest Thou?'" (chapter 82). *The Desire of Ages.* Mountain View, CA: Pacific Press, 1898. https://egwwritings.org/?ref=en_DA.788¶=130.3880.

______. "The Walk to Emmaus" (chapter 83). *The Desire of Ages.* Mountain View, CA: Pacific Press, 1898. https://egwwritings.org/?ref=en_DA.795¶=130.3913.

______. "'Peace Be Unto You'" (chapter 84). *The Desire of Ages.* Mountain View, CA: Pacific Press, 1898. https://egwwritings.org/?ref=en_DA.802¶=130.3940.

______. "By the Sea Once More" (chapter 85). *The Desire of Ages.* Mountain View, CA: Pacific Press, 1898. https://egwwritings.org/?ref=en_DA.809¶=130.3977.

From Other Writers

Bock, Darrell L. "The Passion Week: Controversy, Prediction of Judgment and Return, Trial, Death, and Resurrection"; "The Book of Glory: The Farewell Discourse and the Johannine Passion Account—the Hour has Come." In *Jesus According to Scripture: Restoring the Portrait from the Gospels*, 2nd ed., 503–515, 671–678. With Benjamin I. Simpson. Grand Rapids, MI: Baker Academic, 2017.

Connick, C. Milo. "The Resurrection." In *Jesus: The Man, the Mission, and the Message*, 2nd ed., 398–413. Englewood Cliffs, NJ: Prentice-Hall, 1974.

Foster, R. C. "The Resurrection"; "A Geographical Study of the Final Week." In *Studies in the Life of Christ: Introduction, the Early Period, the Middle Period, the Final Week*, 1305–1336. Joplin, MO: College Press, 1995.

Guthrie, Donald. *Jesus the Messiah: An Illustrated Life of Christ*, 356–366. Grand Rapids, MI: Zondervan, 1972.

Hobbs, Herschel. "The Crucifixion of Jesus." In *The Illustrated Life of Jesus*, 254–283. Nashville: Holman Bible Publishers, 2000.

Wright, N. T. "The Challenge of Easter." In *The Challenge of Jesus: Rediscovering Who Jesus Was and Is*, 126–149. Downers Grove, IL: InterVarsity Press, 2015.

Wright, N. T. *The Resurrection of the Son of God.* 3 vols. Minneapolis: Fortress Press, 2003.

______. *Simply Jesus: A New Vision of Who He Was, What He Did, and Why He Matters.* New York: Harper One, 2011.

Yancey, Philip. "Resurrection: A Morning Beyond Belief." In *The Jesus I Never Knew*, 207–222. Grand Rapids, MI: Zondervan, 1995.

Chapter 31: Story without End

From Adventist Writers

Holbrook, Frank B. *The Atoning Priesthood of Jesus Christ.* Berrien Springs, MI: Adventist Theological Society Publications, 1996.

Moskala, Jiří. "The Intercessory Ministry of Jesus Christ." *Perspective Digest* 23, no. 2 (April–June 2018). http://www.perspectivedigest.org/article/266/archives/23–2/the-intercessory-ministry-of-jesus-christ.

Ott, Helmut. *Perfect in Christ: The Mediation of Christ in the Writings of Ellen G. White.* Hagerstown, MD: Review and Herald, 1987.

White, Ellen G. "Facing Life's Record" (chapter 28). *The Great Controversy.* Mountain View, CA: Pacific Press, 1898. https://egwwritings.org/?ref=en_GC.479¶=132.2168.

———. "Joshua and the Angel" (chapter 53). *Testimonies for the Church,* 467–476. Mountain View, CA: Pacific Press, 1889. Vol. 5. https://egwwritings.org/?ref=en_5T.467¶=113.2304.

———. "To My Father, and Your Father" (chapter 87). *The Desire of Ages.* Mountain View, CA: Pacific Press, 1898. https://egwwritings.org/?ref=en_DA.829¶=130.4080.

———. "What Is the Sanctuary?" (chapter 23). *The Great Controversy.* Mountain View, CA: Pacific Press, 1898. https://egwwritings.org/?ref=en_GC.409¶=132.1851.

From Other Writers

Berkouwer, G. C. "Christ and the Future." In *The Work of Christ.* 242–252. Grand Rapids, MI: Eerdmans, 1965.

Bruce, F. F. *Jesus Past, Present, and Future: The Work of Christ.* Downers Grove, IL: InterVarsity Press, 1979.

Letham, Robert. *The Work of Christ: Contours of Christian Theology.* Downers Grove, IL: InterVarsity Press, 1993.

Owen, John. *The Priesthood of Christ: Its Necessity and Nature.* Ross-shire, Scotland: Christian Heritage, 2010.

Toon, Peter. *The Ascension of Our Lord.* Nashville: Thomas Nelson, 1984.

Wright, N. T. "Cosmic Future: Progress or Despair?"; "What the Whole World's Waiting For"; "Jesus, Heaven, and New Creation"; "When He Appears"; "Jesus, the Coming Judge." In *Surprised by Hope: Rethinking Heaven, the Resurrection, and the Mission of the Church.* 79–92, 93–108, 109–122, 123–136, 137–146. New York: HarperCollins, 2008.

NOTES

Preface

1. Reza Aslan, *Zealot: The Life and Times of Jesus of Nazareth* (New York: Random House, 2013).

Prologue

1. Boris Pasternak, *Doctor Zhivago* (New York: Pantheon Books, 1958), 43.

2. Reynolds Price, "Jesus Second Millennium: A New Gospel," *Time*, December 6, 1999.

3. Walter Isaacson, "Einstein and Faith," *Time*, April 5, 2007.

4. Tacitus, *Annals* 15.44.

Chapter 1

1. Ellen G. White, *The Desire of Ages* (Mountain View, CA: Pacific Press, 1940), 32.

Chapter 2

1. Craig L. Blomberg, *The Historical Reliability of the Gospels* (Downers Grove, IL: InterVarsity, 2007), 324.

2. Ellen G. White, *Selected Messages*, vol. 1 (Washington, DC: Review and Herald, 1958), 21.

Chapter 5

1. Ellen G. White, *The Desire of Ages*, 109 (emphasis added).

Chapter 6

1. Ellen G. White, *Education* (Mountain View, CA: Pacific Press, 1952), 57.

Chapter 7

1. F. D. Nichol, ed., "Maps and Charts Illustrating the Life and Ministry of Jesus," *Seventh-day Adventist Bible Commentary*, 7 vols. (Washington, DC: Review and Herald, 1957), 5:229–232.

Chapter 8

1. Based on Raymond E. Brown, *The Gospel According to John, I–XII* (Garden City, NY: Doubleday, 1966), 176–177.

2. Ellen G. White, *The Desire of Ages,* 200.

Chapter 15

1. Ernest Renan, *The Life of Jesus* (London: Trübner, 1864), 221.

2. *The Seventh-day Adventist Bible Commentary*, ed. Francis D. Nichol, vol. 5 (Hagerstown, MD: Review and Herald, 1980), 204.

Chapter 16

1. Ellen G. White, *Selected Messages*, vol. 1, 296.

2. Ibid., 226.

3. Ellen G. White, *The Desire of Ages*, 463.

Chapter 17

1. Ellen G. White, *The Acts of the Apostles* (Mountain View, CA: Pacific Press, 1911), 52.

2. James Russell Lowell, "The Present Crisis" (1845) in *English Poetry III: From Tennyson to Whitman*, ed. Charles W. Eliot, Harvard Classics, vol. 42 (New York: P. F. Collier & Son, 1909–1914).

Chapter 18

1. Glenn W. Barker, William L. Lane, and Ramsey Michaels, *The New Testament Speaks* (New York: Harper and Row, 1969), 82.

Chapter 19

1. Ellen G. White, *The Desire of Ages*, 25.

2. Ellen G. White, *Christ's Object Lessons* (Washington, DC: Review and Herald, 1941), 310–311.

Chapter 20

1. William Wordsworth, "Lines Composed a Few Miles above Tintern Abbey, on Revisiting the Banks of the Wye During a Tour, July 13, 1798."

Chapter 21

1. Here we adopt the sequence set out in *The Seventh-day Adventist Bible Commentary*, ed. Francis D. Nichol, vol. 5 (Hagerstown, MD: Review and Herald, 1980), 210–213.

2. Ellen G. White, *The Desire of Ages*, 287.

3. *The Seventh-day Adventist Bible Commentary*, ed. Francis D. Nichol, vol. 5 (Hagerstown, MD: Review and Herald, 1980), 587.

Chapter 22

1. Ellen G. White, *Selected Messages*, vol. 1, 189.

Chapter 23

1. Ellen G. White, *Steps to Christ* (Mountain View, CA: Pacific Press, n.d.), 93.

Chapter 24

1. Ellen G. White, *Signs of the Times*, February 28, 1906.

2. Larry W. Hurtado, *Mark*, 146–147.

3. Ibid., 148.

Chapter 25

1. Ellen G. White, *The Desire of Ages*, 83.

2. Ibid., 571.

Chapter 26

1. Larry W. Hurtado, *Mark: A Good News Commentary* (San Francisco: Harper and Row), *Mark,* 174.

2. *Seventh-day Adventist Bible Dictionary*, s.v. "Sadducees" (Hagerstown, MD: Review and Herald, 1979), 943.

3. Ellen G. White, *Medical Ministry* (Mountain View, CA: Pacific Press, 1963), 99, 100.

Chapter 27

1. Ellen G. White, *The Desire of Ages*, 690.

2. *The Seventh-day Adventist Bible Commentary*, ed. Francis D. Nichol, vol. 5 (Hagerstown, MD: Review and Herald, 1980), 251–254.

Chapter 28

1. Ellen G. White, *The Desire of Ages*, 694.

2. George R. Knight, *Exploring Mark: A Devotional Commentary* (Hagerstown, MD: Review and Herald, 2004), 271.

3. Philo, *Embassy to Gaius,* 302.

Chapter 29

1. Ellen G. White, *The Desire of Ages*, 755–756.

2. Ibid., 752–753.

Chapter 31

1. See Kevin Williams, *The Jewish Tradition of Two Messiahs* (Grand Rapids, MI: RBC Ministries, 2004).

2. See Marvin Moore, *The Case for the Investigative Judgment* (Nampa, ID: Pacific Press, 2010).

3. Ellen G. White, *The Great Controversy* (Mountain View, CA: Pacific Press, 1950), 678.

IMAGE CREDITS

Cover	Adapted from *Codex Vaticanus*, 1,293–1,294
Page 4	Adapted from *View of Modern Nazareth* by אוסאמה דאמוני (Osama Damony). Available at https://www.pikiwiki.org.il/image/view/17818 under CC BY 2.5
Page 5	Adapted from *Tiberias and the Sea of Galilee* by Tiberias Municipality. Available at https://commons.wikimedia.org/wiki/File:Dover_tverya17.jpg under CC BY-SA 3.0
Page 11	Adapted from *Pontius Pilate Inscription* by BRBurton (public domain)
Page 12	Adapted from *Scale Model of Jerusalem in the Second Temple Period*, Israel Museum by Berthold Werner (public domain)
Page 13	Adapted from *Herod's Temple Model* by Berthold Werner (public domain)
Page 16	Adapted from *Codex Sinaiticus* (public domain)
Page 81	Adapted from *The Bronze Serpent* by Gustave Doré (public domain)
Page 118	Adapted from *The Ancient Galilee Boat*, the Yigal Allon Museum by Berthold Werner (public domain)
Page 141	Adapted from *Mature fruit of Ficus Sycomorus* by Eitan F. (public domain)
Page 142	Adapted from *Ficus Sycomorus* near Abreha and Atsbeha Church in Ethiopia by Bernard Gagnon. Available at https://commons.wikimedia.org/wiki/File:Sycomore_in_Ethiopia.jpg under CC BY-SA 3.0
Page 144	*Jesus Raising Lazarus from the Dead* by William Brassey Hole (public domain)
Page 197	*The Return of the Prodigal Son* by James Tissot (public domain)
Page 199	*The Wedding Feast* by Eugène Burnand (public domain)
Page 241	*Grace* (Minnesota State Photograph) by Eric Enstrom (public domain)
Page 275	*Denarius Serratus Quintus Antonius Balbus (c. 82–83 BC)* by Carlomorino (public domain)
Page 276	*A Silver Bar Kokhba Shekel* from Simon Bar Kokhba's Revolt against Roman Rule by Classical Numismatic Group, Inc. http://www.cngcoins.com. Available at https://www.cngcoins.com/Coin.aspx?CoinID=106925 under CC BY-SA 3.0

Page 276   *The Half-Shekel Coin Discovered in Hurvat Itri* by Classical Numismatic Group, Inc. http://www.cngcoins.com. Available at https://www.cng-coins.com/Coin.aspx?CoinID=44791 under CC BY-SA 3.0

Page 279   *Prutah of John Hyrcanus (135 BCE to 104 BCE)* by Classical Numismatic Group, Inc. http://www.cngcoins.com. Available at https://www.cng-coins.com/Coin.aspx?CoinID=56002 under CC BY-SA 3.0

Page 279   *A Bronze mite, also known as a lepton* by Randy Benzie (public domain)

Page 294   Adapted from *The Sanhedrin in Session. People's Cyclopedia of Universal Knowledge* (1883; public domain)

Page 303   Adapted from *The Church of the Holy Sepulchre* by Jorge Láscar. Available at https://www.flickr.com/photos/jlascar/10350972756/in/set-72157636698118263 under CC BY 2.0

Page 304   *Rocky Escarpment Resembling a Skull,* Located Northwest of the Church of the Holy Sepulchre by Footballkickit. Available at https://commons.wikimedia.org/wiki/File:Golgotha_photo.JPG under CC BY 3.0

Page 310   Adapted from *Centurion (Roman Army), Historical Reenactment Boulogne-sur-Mer (France)* by Luc Viatour. Available at http://www.lucnix.be under CC BY-SA 3.0

SCRIPTURE INDEX

8:5 210
8:15 245
8:23 157
8:34 324
12:4–8 178
14:23 ....55, 177
16:7 90

1 CORINTHIANS

1:18–25 308
4:6 91
4:9 91
5:7 283
9:1–2 91
10:4 121
10:16 287
11:20 286
11:21–34 286
11:23–25 23
11:23–26 287
12:1–30 178
12:3 120
12:27–30 91
12:28 90
15:3 307
15:3–7 ....23, 317
15:6 ....205, 320
15:7 321
15:9 90
15:22 54

2 CORINTHIANS

5:19 307
5:21 59
10:10 6
12:9 250
12:10 ....250, 289

GALATIANS

2:8 91
2:9 91
2:11–14 121
2:20 289
4:4 ....11, 13
4:4–7 157
4:6 245

6:14 302

EPHESIANS

1:19 85
3:16 85
3:20 85
6:12 ....54, 101

PHILIPPIANS

2:5–11 ....159, 165
2:6–7 ....27, 52
2:6–11 24
2:8 28
2:9–11 ....28, 323
2:10–11 xv
3:2 139
4:22 xx

COLOSSIANS

1:15–20 ....24, 159
3:3–4 277

1 THESSALONIANS

1:1 91
2:6 91
4 228
4:13–17 327
4:16–17 326
4:17 327

2 THESSALONIANS

2 228
2:8 327

1 TIMOTHY

3:16 ....24, 159
6:10 189
6:15 326

HEBREWS

1:1–2 35
1:1–4 159
1:2–3 163
1:3 324